T0391703

Corporate Entrepreneurship and Innovation in Tourism and Hospitality

The dynamic characteristic of the tourism and hospitality industry under the influence of micro and macro environment factors requires future professionals to be equipped with appropriate skills and competencies to deal with such factors in real-life practices. In this book, scholars and industry experts analyse case studies related to real-world scenarios to expand the body of knowledge, inspiring future research and developing the field.

The Editors have compiled a compelling set of case studies covering topics centred around corporate entrepreneurship, including innovation, marketing and digital marketing, crisis management, quality development, product development and sustainability with a particular emphasis on post-Covid-19 recovery. The case studies included cover five regions, Europe, Africa, the Americas, Australia and Asia, offering enriching and diverse perspectives.

This unique collection will be a valuable resource for scholars and upper-level students across corporate entrepreneurship and innovation, as well as those researching and studying n the tourism and hospitality fields.

Teresa Aguiar-Quintana is a Full professor at the University of Las Palmas de Gran Canaria (ULPGC) in the Economics, Business and Tourism Faculty in Gran Canaria island (Spain). She is currently the Transference and dissemination director of the Institute of Tourism and Sustainable Economic development (Tides) at the ULPGC. She has published academic case study books and several scientific articles in Journal Citation Reports (JCR) like *Tourism Management*, *International Journal of Hospitality Management*, *Journal of Business Research*, *Tourism Management Perspectives*, *Cornell Hospitality Quaterly* and *Journal of Leadership & Organizational Studies*.

Jonathon Day is Associate Professor and Graduate Program Director in Purdue's School of Hospitality and Tourism Management, Purdue University, USA. His research focuses on sustainable tourism and responsible travel. He specialises in destination stewardship, climate change and tourism, and encouraging pro-environmental consumer behaviours.

Francisca Rosa Álamo Vera is an Associate Professor in Strategic Management, specialising in tourism, cities and public administration. She has been at the University of Las Palmas de Gran Canaria for more than 30 years and has taught in different tourism MsC programmes. Currently, her research interests are focused on Tourism students' international mobility and coopetition in excellent research institutions.

Routledge Studies in Innovation, Organizations and Technology

RIOT!

For more information about this series, please visit: www.routledge.com/Routledge-Studies-in-Innovation-Organizations-and-Technology/book-series/RIOT

Corporate Entrepreneurship and Innovation in Tourism and Hospitality

Global Post COVID-19 Recovery Strategies

Edited by Teresa Aguiar-Quintana, Jonathon Day and Francisca Rosa Álamo Vera

LONDON AND NEW YORK

First published 2024
by Routledge
4 Park Square, Milton Park, Abingdon, Oxon OX14 4RN

and by Routledge
605 Third Avenue, New York, NY 10158

Routledge is an imprint of the Taylor & Francis Group, an informa business

© 2024 selection and editorial matter, Teresa Aguiar-Quintana, Jonathon Day and Francisca Rosa Álamo Vera; individual chapters, the contributors

The right of Teresa Aguiar-Quintana, Jonathon Day and Francisca Rosa Álamo Vera to be identified as the authors of the editorial material, and of the authors for their individual chapters, has been asserted in accordance with sections 77 and 78 of the Copyright, Designs and Patents Act 1988.

British Library Cataloguing-in-Publication Data
A catalogue record for this book is available from the British Library

ISBN: 978-1-032-59373-9 (hbk)
ISBN: 978-1-032-59380-7 (pbk)
ISBN: 978-1-003-45446-5 (ebk)

DOI: 10.4324/9781003454465

Typeset in Sabon
by KnowledgeWorks Global Ltd.

Contents

Introduction

The study of corporate entrepreneurship and innovation in tourism and hospitality

Teresa Aguiar-Quintana, Francisca Rosa Álamo-Vera and Jonathon Day

INTRODUCTION TO THE BOOK BY THE EDITORS

This book was conceived with a double purpose. On the one hand, to cover an important gap in the teaching materials in Economics, Business, Management and Tourism and stimulate the development of cases on corporate entrepreneurship in hospitality from different regions of the world. On the other, with a more informative purpose and the spirit of participating in the progress of the tourism and hospitality sector in Europe, America, Australia, Africa and Asia, in general, and in particular, regarding the professionals of these sectors in each region. Specifically, this book will cover **corporate entrepreneurship and innovation strategies in the tourism and hospitality industry before, during and after the COVID-19** pandemic in multiple destinations.

The tourism and hospitality sector is complex, multicultural and globalised in essence. Hence the case study, with a qualitative, human and contextual approach, provides an enriching and appropriate vision for the study of the reality of this industry. To this end, this work is offered in a special way to scholars and students of Economics, Management, Industry, Business and Tourism interested in deepening the knowledge and management of destinations worldwide, and especially their teachers, whom we believe this study will provide a useful work tool for the incursion into these sectors from the supply side.

Service companies are the true drivers of the economy in many countries. Distribution companies, transport agencies, hotels, apartments, lodges, travel agencies, restaurants, museums, rural and other tourist businesses are developed in, by and for each society and for each destination. Yet, they do not always receive the attention they deserve. This work is a tribute to all the enormous effort of the professionals of the tourism and hospitality sector, which have undertaken and have survived stages of crisis during their trajectory, have reinvented themselves, have transformed and constitute examples of corporate entrepreneurship before, during and after the COVID-19 pandemic. Hence, the tourism industry constitutes a complex system, where the territory is part of the product. Companies and institutions leave their mark

DOI: 10.4324/9781003454465-1

on each region where they operate. Well deserved, then, is to recognise the work well done and the achievements of those who have contributed to taking the destination in each continent to better levels of image and quality. After the context of the COVID-19 pandemic, many companies have adapted to new demands and have implemented new strategies to survive.

In summary, the background of corporate entrepreneurship can be associated with the external environment (sector dynamism, sector growth, technological opportunities, demand for new products, etc.) and the organisational context itself (alliances with other companies, relationships with companies, social agents, customers, etc., availability of technological, human and financial resources, organisational support in terms of training, trust in employees to detect opportunities, rewards for new ideas, procedures to manage new ideas, managerial support, time availability to search and reflect on new ideas, non-rigid intra-organisational boundaries, organisational objectives on corporate entrepreneurship, existence of standards on desirable behaviour patterns for corporate entrepreneurship, etc.). The results of these actions include growth, profitability, employment and wealth, among others. This book is based on the case study methodology. In order to achieve an homogeneous approach in the elaboration of the different case studies, we take into account the definition of corporate entrepreneurship as those activities, behaviours and intentions of behaviour within an organisation which, deviating from the usual way of doing their business, pursue the development of new products or services (innovation), the introduction of new technologies and strategies or competitive approaches after COVID-19.

Concerning the internal organisation of the case studies, the structure of each one is the following: First, an introduction section where the authors explain the context of the organisation, the people, the problems and the key elements that will be conducted in the case. In this section, issues like the background of the organisation (as an orientation according to the subject addressed in the case) and a brief description of the history of the organisation (its business activity and its organisational structure) are addressed; secondly, a section about the environment is presented with an overview of the sector in terms of competitors, markets, trends, etc., as well as of the region in which the organisation carries out its activity, with a discussion of the main political, legal, economic, technological and/or social conditions that characterise it.

Next, a section with the origin and evolution of the key elements of the business provides details and relevant information to evaluate results, in addition to tables and graphs. The development section is the part of the cases that focuses on the most outstanding corporate entrepreneurship and innovation actions carried out by the organisation, providing information on: description of the corporate entrepreneurship actions carried out and their concretion in terms of new products or services, new technologies, administrative processes, strategies and/or competitive approaches; identification of the main antecedents of such corporate entrepreneurial actions associated with the external environment (dynamism of the sector, industry growth, technological opportunities, demand for new products, the COVID-19 pandemic, etc); identification of the main antecedents of such actions associated with the organisational context (alliances with other companies, relations with companies, social agents, clients, etc., availability of technological, human and financial resources, organisational support in terms of training, trust in employees to detect opportunities, of rewards for new ideas, of procedures to manage new ideas, of managerial support, of availability of time to seek and reflect on new ideas, of non-rigid intra-organisational borders, of organisational objectives on corporate entrepreneurship, of existence of standards on patterns of desirable behaviour for corporate entrepreneurship, etc.); explanation of the process of developing corporate entrepreneurship actions, highlighting its stages (with particular attention to identifying the corporate entrepreneurship opportunity), its main support and/or difficulties, and how to overcome these difficulties; and explanation of the main achievements of corporate entrepreneurship actions; and, finally, the section with the epilogue, highlights the most relevant aspects of the corporate entrepreneurship actions described, such as the learning extracted from its development, raising possible reflection issues.

The cases that finally took part in this book have been selected and developed by each university's professor in the different regions of the five continents. These professors interviewed several managers from relevant tourist companies in their destinations. **In total, 67 authors from 24 universities from all over the world are participating in this book.** In Europe, there are 17 universities participating in this project (seven in Spain and ten from the rest of Europe). In **America**, three universities joined this project (two professors from Purdue University, USA). In Latin America, Universidad de Externado (Colombia) developed a case study about the implementation of international sustainability standards in a resort located in a famous tourist destination in Colombia (Santa Marta Beach). The University Laica Eloy Alfaro de Manabí (ULEAM) in Ecuador participated in a case study about the corporate entrepreneurship in Central America Tourism Agency. Also, professors from the two Universities in the Canary Islands (ULPGC and ULL) developed case studies about Astro-tourism in Chile, about sustainable Ecolodges in Costa Rica, Nicaragua and Panamá, and related to the promotion of multi-destinations in Belice, El Salvador, Guatemala, Honduras, Costa Rica, Nicaragua, Panamá and Dominican Republic. In **Africa,** two professors from The University of South Africa and Cape Peninsula University of Technology in South Africa developed an approach towards tourism branding and destination management in their country. In **Australia,** a professor from James Cook University worked with two professors in **Asia** (from Trisakti Institute of Tourism, Indonesia) studying entrepreneurial and innovation strategies in the hospitality business in Australia and Indonesia.

Authors from 17 universities from across **Europe** have taken part in this study. From Spain, academics from The University of Las Palmas de Gran

Canaria (ULPGC), University of La Laguna in Tenerife island, University Complutense of Madrid, University of Malaga, University of Zaragoza, University of Balearic Islands and University of Les Roches in Marbella contributed. The ULPGC in Gran Canaria island is the leader of this project with 2 editors and 23 authors in total who developed international cases focused on hotel innovation, diversification and internationalisation, new routes of airlines that grew after the COVID-19, wineries, rent-a-car, travel agencies family business and a tourism board. In Portugal, two professors from the University of Algarve made a research about the internationalisation of an important hotel group in their country; in Germany, a professor from Berlin University worked with a professor from the ULPGC to study a hospitality company that have been consolidated in Spain, Germany and Asia; in Austria, two professors from Seeburg Castle University and UMIT TIROL—Private University For Health Sciences and Health Technology—focused on a family hospitality business; in Denmark, a professor from Copenhagen Business school made her research on the case of Visit Greenland studying the Corporate Entrepreneurship within a DMO; in Sweden, a professor that studied in Warwick University and is actually a visiting professor in the ULPGC worked about the innovation strategies and Corporate entrepreneurship in Scandic hotels, a famous hospitality company in Northern Europe; in Italy, two professors from the University of Naples Federico II and FS Research centre worked with other two professors from the ULPGC about TrenItalia strategies towards a sustainable mobility in a train company; in the UK a professor from Greenwich University developed a case study about the most international association in tourism studies globally (ITSA); and finally, in France, two professors from the University of Paris-Est Créteil studied the ACCOR company and, in Switzerland, the University of Les Roches worked with professors of Les Roches in the Campus of Marbella to develop a case study focused on the innovation in the international educational experience for luxury resorts.

Considering the contents of the case studies, the intended audience includes primarily scholars (disciplines: Economics, Management, Industry, Business and Tourism), professionals (tourism and hospitality fields), or students (undergraduate and post-graduate). Also, the book would appeal most to professionals and universities in the five continents. The subject area of this research work is widely taught, but there is a need for real examples after COVID-19 (new strategies for corporations in tourism and hospitality). Finally, this book adds value to the existing literature as it not only focuses on the theoretical exploration of the corporate entrepreneurship definitions, process and implementation, but it also relates to real global case studies. Moreover, all the cases are related to the hospitality and tourism industry. In addition, this new book focuses on new corporate entrepreneurship and innovation strategies before, during and after the COVID-19 pandemic.

CONCEPTUALISATION OF CORPORATE ENTREPRENEURSHIP
IN TOURISM AND HOSPITALITY

Rosa M. Batista-Canino and M. Pino Medina-Brito

> *No calm sea made a sailor an expert*
>
> R. Vargas

Introduction

Entrepreneurship is in the DNA of human beings, strongly attached to the instinct for survival. Thus, a life full of challenges and uncertainties is undertaken, and decisions are made to shape the course of the individual's unique history.

But when we talk about entrepreneurship, our attention is inevitably focused on the world of business and enterprise. Thus, since the report "The Job Creation Process" by David Birch was presented to the US Congress in the late 1970s to highlight the important role of small businesses in job creation, compared to the contribution of large corporations, entrepreneurship has gained prominence as a management paradigm. The flexibility shown by startups and small businesses to respond to the competitive challenges of the environment has ensured they play a crucial role in the economy. Thus, their ability to generate value and results in economic terms and returns for investors, as well as generate employment, has been impressive. This agility of small companies to respond to the competitive environment became the envy of large corporations to such an extent that "Gazelles and Elephants dance without stepping on each other" (Ortega Cachón et al., 2016) recognises a kind of silent cooperation between large companies and startups that bears results.

It is the emulation by large companies of the flexibility and lightness of small companies in responding to the challenges of the environment that has given rise to and inspired the philosophy of corporate entrepreneurship. But large and long-established companies do not just want to dance WITH the gazelles; they want to dance LIKE them. Thus, corporate entrepreneurship is a sign that cooperation is possible, but it has also pointed the way for established companies to exercise their rigid muscles and make their entire structure more flexible to generate more and better competitiveness and long-term survival by practising the very thing that gave them birth: the systematics of entrepreneurship.

But before better understanding this concept, let's start at the beginning by knowing what corporate entrepreneurship is and how to distinguish it from other related concepts, what elements are key in this entrepreneurial work system, and what it is most common corporate entrepreneurial forms in the tourism sector we are dealing with.

Corporate entrepreneurship *vs* intrapreneurship

Today's company is based on the classic model of separation of ownership and control. Whereas ownership is the mere tenure of shares in a company that entitles the holder to receive the returns on the investment made in the company's capital, control is the ability to determine the company's objectives and define its strategies. Thus, corporate control is exercised to influence a company's assets and its economic future. This capacity to control and make decisions is known as corporate management.

However, the highly turbulent environment that companies have had to get used to, first with the emergence of globalisation at the end of the last century, which opened up all markets to companies determined to reach them, and recently with crises of various origins and the accelerated digitalisation of the economy, has led these business managers to rethink their objectives, refine their strategies, and broaden their management horizons.

They found that the main traits usually associated with entrepreneurship, such as the need to grow, innovate, and develop new ways of creating value for the customer but also for the shareholder, were desirable traits for large companies. Entrepreneurship has been thus associated with small businesses and startups to the extent that, for some, it is the entrepreneur's natural habitat (Bracker & Pearson, 1986). This is how what is known today as corporate entrepreneurship came about, a reality that began to be discussed in the early 1990s (Stevenson & Jarillo, 1990).

This is how large and established companies have been showing interest in the entrepreneurial spirit of small, startup, and developing businesses. Without leaving behind any of the advantages linked to their size (Burgelman, 1983), they have tried to add those of small businesses to come up with the concept of intrapreneurship. This concept emerged as an attempt to generate entrepreneurial behaviour, not to say entrepreneurs themselves, within large organisations and established companies, especially to meet their internal needs, as we shall see below.

However, from a practical point of view, the concepts of corporate entrepreneurship and intrapreneurship are often used as if they were synonyms, and there is still no clear consensus on these terms (Pirhadi & Feyzbakhsh, 2021; Urbano et al., 2022), and they are often confused with innovative behaviour in companies.

In recent decades, many scientific works have tried to investigate the phenomena to distinguish and characterise them. The conceptual version of Guth and Ginsberg (1990) has become widespread in the scientific community to define corporate entrepreneurship as applying entrepreneurial initiatives to large and complex organisations. As Miller (1983) pointed out, this implies incorporating product and technology innovation, risk-taking, and proactivity into companies' management approach.

This definition also implies that the essential ingredient of the corporate business function is that decisions are made and actions are taken in such a way that they result in a new combination of resources that create value for the customer and the company's investors.

Corporate entrepreneurship is thus constituted in two types of phenomena: (i) in the birth of new businesses within existing organisations through internal innovation; and (ii) in the transformation of organisations through the renewal of the key ideas on which they are built, referring, in this case, to strategic renewal (Guth & Ginsberg, 1990). The corporate entrepreneur, whether as an individual or in a team (Sharma & Chrisman, 1999), must, therefore, carry out these functions in the course of his or her business. In this way, the role of the corporate entrepreneur will involve not only ensuring efficiency in the use of resources to achieve the best results but also continuously reconfiguring the company's business portfolio by seeking new opportunities for the company. Senior management would then embody the role of the entrepreneur in large companies, with the figure of the strategic and business controller playing an important role in this task.

However, corporate entrepreneurship must be differentiated from intrapreneurship. Initially introduced by Pinchot in the mid-1980s, this function is seen as developing entrepreneurial activities within established organisations (Hornsby et al., 2002). In this concept, it is important to understand that the activity is carried out in a large organisation for its internal markets and the creation of relatively small and independent units, and these activities are designed to test the market internally and to develop staff able to deliver better and/or more innovative services, technologies, or working methods. For meticulous authors, in their attempt to differentiate the two concepts (Jennings & Lumpkin, 1989), the essence of intrapreneurship is the practice of the entrepreneurial function within a large organisation for its internal market, finding better solutions and ways of doing things. Thus, while the corporate entrepreneur has a strong market orientation, aiming to develop advantageous positions for the company in external markets, regardless of the organisation's size, the intra-entrepreneur focuses on the internal markets of large multi-divisional companies.

Despite this controversy, the current trend seems to distinguish the concepts by characterising corporate entrepreneurship through a broad vision that implies understanding the company as a dynamic and flexible entity capable of taking advantage of the opportunities in the market and accepting the risk and uncertainty that comes with initiative. This entrepreneurship seeks to create and add new business to the company while fostering innovation, change, and strategic renewal. In contrast, intrapreneurship is more closely linked to the organisation's internal processes that may or may not lead to new business, products and innovations aimed at their commercialisation.

Key elements of corporate entrepreneurship

The ultimate goal of corporate entrepreneurship is to keep the company competitive in the market by generating new value for the customer and the investors in the organisation. For this, the source of inspiration for entrepreneurial activity can be both internal and external to the company, i.e., it can come from the superior perception, observation, and experience of both the company's management teams and its employees in any functional area of the company, as well as from the suggestion of customers and other stakeholders in the organisation.

Just as in individual entrepreneurship, in corporate entrepreneurship, the relationship between the company and its environment is key and explains the very essence of entrepreneurship at this level. Thus, corporate entrepreneurship cannot be understood without the omnipresence of the environment that challenges its continuity and sustainability in the long term. It is the company's effort to maintain and expand its competitive position that explains the existence of this form of management, which takes all its meaning from the very essence of entrepreneurship. This implies a continuous fight to cope with uncertainty and risk, while openness to change and innovation is essential to navigating waters that are generally not calm.

Therefore, among the key elements of corporate entrepreneurship as a management philosophy is, first and foremost, the environment that acts both as a provider of challenges and opportunities and resources for the development of an initiative.

The second key element of corporate entrepreneurship is initiative. Corporate entrepreneurial initiatives reside in either the corporation's governance teams or in the corporation's employees, if not in both. However, for these initiatives to succeed, a key intangible is essential: an organisational culture that is open and permissive to change management, innovation, and cooperation among peers and between managers and employees. Therefore, organisationally, it is not only the key people but also the prevailing values in the organisation that support corporate entrepreneurship. These values include cohesion, collaboration, and communication in the company and a certain degree of shared leadership. Leadership must recognise that ideas come from anywhere in the organisation and that for them to bear fruit, they require the team's involvement.

Therefore, human capital is the second key element for corporate entrepreneurship in terms of both leadership and motivation. These flexible and proactive organisational cultures incentivise employees to get involved as entrepreneurs within the corporation. The means are also important but not essential. What is more important is an environment rich in human capital, both from inside and outside the organisation, as this allows projects to grow and develop.

However, economic and financial resources facilitate investments so that any surplus produced by normal business activity and new contributions from business owners are helpful for the progress of a new project. The third key factor is, therefore, the direction of the resources available to the venture and how these are acquired and developed.

Fourth, a strategic orientation of the company towards entrepreneurship is key. In other words, knowing what motivates this way of managing companies is important. Thus, it is not the same whether the motivation is purely aimed at strengthening the company's competitive position in the same market or at seeking new business horizons in the form of exploring new strategies—e.g., a strategic reorientation of the business, reconfiguration of the business model, exploration of new avenues for growth, etc.—or making new investments in new business models and companies that may or may not be related to the main one. It is in the latter case that new forms of business cooperation between long-established companies and startups that explore new business projects and renew the business portfolio of the former and their investors are consolidated.

For corporate entrepreneurship to succeed, Strategy, Structure, Organisational Culture and Communication practices are key. Thus, evidencing the company's strategic belief and practice and its orientation towards entrepreneurship is key to communicating inspires and motivates the company.

In another vein, demonstrating agile and flexible operating structures is crucial but surely the most difficult part of this engagement. The natural tendency to protocolise and perpetuate formulas that once worked well is natural and intrinsic to human nature and, therefore, to the nature of any organisation.

It is, therefore, important to avoid heavy, pharaonic, and bureaucratic structures and, at the same time, to install an agile culture of teamwork that keeps alive the spirit of shared leadership. This shared leadership must emulate the highly productive camaraderie of multidisciplinary entrepreneurial teams, and it is also key that it accompanies the process. This will require fluid communication and collaboration practices that prioritise agile ways of working with frequent meetings of short duration.

For all this, it is important to provide continuous training for staff at all levels, including senior management, not only technically but also in soft skills that facilitate interpersonal relations so everything runs smoothly. Therefore, human resources practices are the most powerful within the set of elements that can exert the greatest force to establish an entrepreneurial culture. Salary and promotion incentives, as also the working environment and co-responsibility in projects, are important for this business management approach. Attracting and managing talent within the organisation is a priority. However, it is not effective for intra-entrepreneurial units to be enclosed and isolated from the normal course of business activity. For this practice to be effective, it must involve the entire organisation, permeating the *company's modus operandi* in all its management facets.

The attached figure summarises the above elements. However, it is good to keep in mind that the ultimate goal of corporate entrepreneurship is not only to satisfy current and potential customers, for which the improvement of the brand image and the creation of new and reputable brands are key, but also the investors who have placed their best expectations in the projects (Figure 0.1).

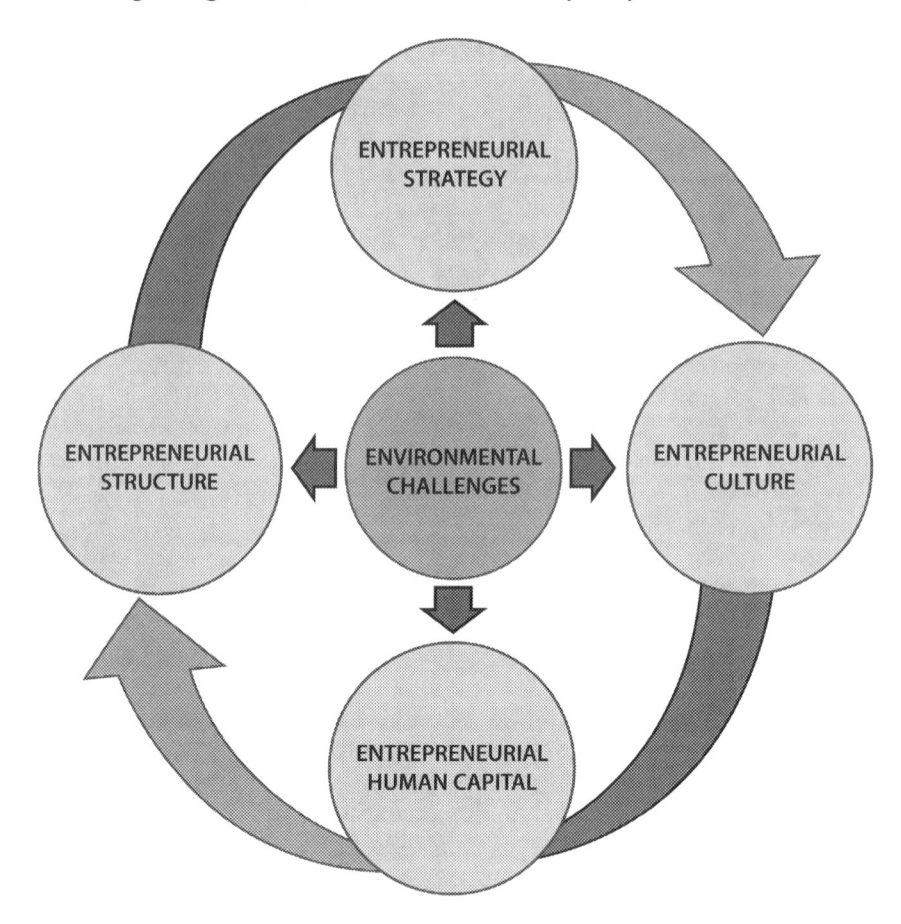

Figure 0.1 Key elements of entrepreneurship: A guide for corporate management.
Source: Prepared by authors.

Forms of corporate entrepreneurship in the tourism sector

However, all the intangible assets that support an entrepreneurial organisation have value when they are embodied in the form of new projects, products, services, and ideas for improvements to be implemented in the company. Thus, and without wishing to systematise the possible expressions of corporate entrepreneurship in the tourism sector, these may be the main forms that can be found:

- *Development and implementation of internal projects to improve the tourism organisation and its strategies:* Among these, we can highlight those aimed at creating new ways of undertaking internal processes, establishing proposals to gain efficiency and reducing time in the development of the tasks carried out in the different functional areas of the company; putting into practice plans to reduce costs without lowering quality; defining new internal organisation or organisational communication strategies; to propose new tactics for decision-making and their implementation; to create new operational management positions or figures; to develop new lines or areas of business management; to define proposals for reducing the hierarchical structure of the company; to develop the organisational and management mindset; to define new ways of capturing and processing useful information for management and for customer attraction and retention.

- *Development and implementation of projects to gain competitiveness in the tourism sector, both in its current and potential markets*: In this case, we are talking about the development of new tourism products and services that complement the original ones, as well as the development of new entrepreneurial projects within the tourism sector.
- *Development and implementation of business diversification projects outside the tourism sector*: Sometimes, diversification of the business portfolio is the best way to maintain and gain a reputation, as well as to generate a cross-subsidy between projects that allows the entrepreneurial initiative to survive in the long term. It is from this venture into new unrelated markets where strategies of forward and backward integration take shape, but also where creativity gains value by generating lines of business unrelated to the original one, and which allow the entrepreneurial spirit to be exercised to its full extent. This happens when an entity operating in the tourism sector decides to explore the development of an unrelated industry, its presence in the distribution sector of products that have nothing to do with tourism or its incursion into the primary sector whose production is not intended for self-supply.

The first category grouped those cases that academics link strongly to intrapreneurship, but they are often powerful sources of inspiration for developing new projects grouped in the second and third groups of expressions. Thus, many entrepreneurial projects that have incorporated backward integration processes in the tourism sector have come about precisely due to a deep concern to improve efficiency and reduce costs without reducing the quality of the product or service. They find such advantageous business pratices in their solutions that their promoters launch them on the market to supply others with the same benefits. We have found notable cases of backward integration in the founding of tour operator brands created by resorts themselves. But we have also observed more modest initiatives seeking excellence in food and beverage products for their establishments. Likewise, it is also not difficult to see the development of initiatives that grow by offering related products and services, such as the accommodation activities promoted by active tourism and recreation entrepreneurs to improve and complement the service to their clients.

The book you now hold in your hands pays an important tribute to corporate entrepreneurship, showing interesting cases that illustrate how it can occur in the tourism sector. The challenge is now open for the reader to analyse and study each case analysed here, placing it in one or more of the above categories of corporate entrepreneurship.

Conclusion

Although the concept of corporate entrepreneurship is still under debate in academia, companies remain dynamic and unaffected by the discussions, sometimes showing unimaginable energy and proactivity in their application of the process. The tourism sector is a good example of this. Its nature as a sector of sectors where inter-sectoral relationships flow intricately has created an ideal ground for entrepreneurship to develop to its full extent. This book highlights examples of corporate entrepreneurship that demonstrate the concept is an exciting subject for research and inspirational for businesses.

References

Birch, D. (1979). The job generation process. MIT Program of Neighborhood and Regional Change. Available at: http://ideasarchive.org/www/Job%20Generation%20Process,%20The%20-%201979%20-%20David%20Birch.pdf

Bracker, J. Y., & Pearson, J. N. (1986). Planning and financial performance of small, mature firms. *Strategic Management Journal*, 7 (6): 503–522. doi. 10.1002/smj.4250070603

Burgelman, R. A. (1983). Corporate entrepreneuship and strategic management. *Management Science*, 29(12), 1349–1364. doi. 10.1287/mnsc.29.12.1349

Guth, W. D., & Ginsberg, A. (1990). Guest editors' introduction: Corporate entrepreneurship. *Strategic Management Journal*, 11, 5–15. Available at: https://www.jstor.org/stable/2486666

Hornsby, J. S., Kuratko, D. F., & Zahra, S. A. (2002). Middle managers' perception of the internal environment for corporate entrepreneurship: Assessing a measurement scale. *Journal of Business Venturing*, 17(3), 253–273. doi. 10.1016/S0883-9026(00)00059-8

Jennings, D. F., & Lumpkin, J. R. (1989). Functioning modeling corporate entrepreneurship: An empirical integrative analysis. *Journal of Management*, 15(3), 485–502. doi. 10.1177/014920638901500310

Miller, D. (1983). The correlates of entrepreneurship in three types of firms. *Management Science*, 27(7), 770–791. doi. 10.1287/mnsc.29.7.770

Ortega Cachón, I., de Pablo López, I., & Salanueva, I. (2016). *Emprendimiento corporativo en España. Situación y claves de la colaboración entre empresas y emprendedores para innovar y ser más competitivas*. CISE.

Pirhadi, H., & Feyzbakhsh, A. (2021). Corporate entrepreneurship, its antecedents, process, and consequences: A systematic review and suggestion for future research. *Journal International Entrepreneurship*, 19, 196–222. doi. 10.1007/s10843-021-00294-8

Sharma, P., & Chrisman, J. J. (1999). Toward a reconciliation of the definitional issues in the field of corporate entrepreneurship. *Entrepreneurship Theory and Practice*, 23(3), 11–28.

Stevenson, H. H., & Jarillo, J. C. (1990). A paradigm on entrepreneurship: Entrepreneurial management. *Strategic Management Journal*, *11*, 17–27.

Urbano, D., Turró, A., Wright, M., & Zahra, S. (2022). Corporate entrepreneurship: A systematic literature review and future research agenda. *Small Business Economics*, *59*, 1541–1565. doi. 10.1007/s11187-021-00590-6

CONCEPTUALISATION OF INNOVATION IN TOURISM AND HOSPITALITY

Julia Nieves and Javier Osorio

For many years, economic theories on innovation have focused on its technological aspects, tending to ignore services or assuming that innovation in this field was mainly based on adopting innovations developed in the industrial sector. According to this traditional view, services had little capacity for change, especially from within, because they depended on externally developed technologies to provide new services or improve their production methods (Tether, 2003). However, the profound structural transformation experienced by the most developed countries in the past thirty years, evolving towards a service economy, has led to specifically addressing the innovative activity carried out in the sector. Thus, innovation research evolved towards a new and broad perspective on the nature of innovation: technological innovations are no longer the only types of innovation, and R&D is not the only source of innovations (Smedlund & Toivonen, 2008). Recognising that the concept of product and process technological innovation did not adequately reflect many of the innovation activities in the services sector, the third edition of the Oslo Manual (OECD, 2005) eliminated the identification of product and process innovation with technological change and incorporated service innovations that did not necessarily have a technological component. Hence, the scope of what was considered innovation was broadened to include organisational innovations and marketing innovations. This typology was modified in the fourth edition of the Oslo Manual, which introduces two main categories by object: product innovation and business process innovation (OECD, 2018). Product innovation involves a new or improved good or service that differs significantly from the firm's previous goods or services and has been placed on the market. Business process innovation involves a new or improved business process for one or more business functions that differs significantly from the firm's previous business processes and has been put into practice in the firm. Product innovations are divided into two main types (goods and services). In contrast, business process innovations are divided into six broad types (production of goods or services, distribution and logistics, marketing and sales, information and communication systems, administration and management, and product and business process development).

Furthermore, innovations can be considered in terms of their novelty and impact. The intensity of a change can be drastic or progressive, aspects that have been assimilated into radical or incremental innovations. However, this distinction is easier to intuit than to define or measure. This typology is frequently debated in the literature because it is difficult to interpret. On the one hand, it is not easy to establish whether a category belongs to the continuous range that represents the degree of change. On the other hand, different criteria are used to measure the magnitude of the changes. For example, a criterion for the degree of change could be the technological progress necessary to develop the product. In this scenario, the innovation incorporated into Ryanair's business model in the late 1990s would not be considered radical. However, Ryanair altered the patterns of competition in the airline industry through novel decisions such as the use of secondary airports, intensive use of aircraft, agreements with hotels and rental companies, elimination of intermediaries, charging for services such as food on board or luggage in the hold, paying lower wages than the competition, and so on. Although their proposals were initially underestimated by the established airlines due to being inferior in quality, their low-cost business model eventually prevailed and changed the dynamics of competition in the sector. Therefore, the innovation introduced by Ryanair can be categorised as radical if we consider the potential to transform the market in which it operates as a criterion for the degree of change.

The specific properties of services have important particularities compared to innovations in products. On the one hand, innovation activities in the field of services are characterised by the intangible nature of their outputs. Whereas a produced good acquires a physical appearance, many services do not meet this condition, which means their qualities are not visible, making it difficult to detect the novelties introduced in the sector. This intangible character also means that service firms find it difficult to protect their innovations from the competition because they do not have a patent system like the one in the products industry. Therefore, achieving a sustainable competitive advantage requires firms to innovate constantly and more rapidly than their competitors.

On the other hand, services usually present simultaneity between production and consumption, such that the client participates in the production of the service. This situation implies a personal interaction between the person providing the service and the person receiving it, thus highlighting the decisive role played by the human factor in innovation in the sector. Particularly in the tourism sector, the close and long-standing relationship with customers means that frontline employees are an important source of new ideas in developing new services. In this sector, employees probably know the demands, complaints, and preferences of the users better than anyone. Therefore, they can provide ideas for developing new services or relevant information about whether to maintain or phase out existing services. However, frontline employees are generally unable to formulate their ideas and perspectives because they are often not involved in companies' strategic decisions. Hence, it would be essential to establish training schemes to provide these employees with skills and capabilities that allow them to recognise the potential of the information they receive and foment their creativity. These types of policies would improve employee motivation and, consequently, increase their productivity while at the same time reducing employee turnover.

The COVID-19 pandemic was a major shock to the world's tourism industry. The economic effects on tourism-dependent economies and societies were significant. Parallel to the lockdown and the drastic reduction in tourism activity, the importance of reducing energy consumption in this sector and protecting biodiversity has been gaining momentum. The need to change the current paradigm and turn tourism into a powerful driver for sustainable development has been openly acknowledged[1]. This need was echoed by the UN Secretary-General, who stated, "There is no time to waste. Let us rethink and reinvent tourism and together deliver a more sustainable, prosperous, and resilient future for all"[2]. The tourism industry is one of the most vulnerable to climate change, but at the same time, tourism activity causes significant environmental damage. Changing our way of thinking about tourism to make it a more environmentally friendly industry has to involve developing and adopting innovations. Innovation is necessary if governments, businesses, and consumers are going to align tourism practices with the Sustainable Development Goals and a 1.5°C future and, create decent jobs and ensure profits that benefit the host country and local communities. These innovations are necessary for the survival of this industry and many tourist destinations.

Fortunately, the hospitality and tourism industry has always been a clear example of a sector that is constantly innovating to adapt to the changing needs of its customers. This continuous adoption of innovations in the sector has attracted the attention of researchers and practitioners. This interest is reflected in the large number of literature reviews that include research studies focused on a wide variety of types of innovations or their management in the field of tourism and hospitality. Thus, for example, from a management perspective, we can find research related to intellectual capital as a source of innovation (Zermeno-Flores & Cuevas-Contreras, 2015), collaborative innovation in tourism and hospitality (Marasco et al., 2018), creativity and innovation in the tourism sector (Liberato et al., 2020), leadership for innovation in hospitality and tourism (De Lacerda et al., 2021), and ethical issues in hospitality and tourism innovation (Oskam & De Visser-Amundson, 2022).

Moreover, from the point of view of the typology of innovation in the field of tourism, we find studies related to service innovation in hospitality and tourism (Shin & Perdue, 2022) and process innovation in tourism management (Damian & Suarez-Barraza, 2015). More specific studies can be found in other areas, such as those related to innovation in rural tourism (Kumar & Shekhar, 2020), green innovation for tourism (Satta et al., 2019), technological innovations in the tourism industry (Giotis & Papadionysiou, 2022), and public policies for tourism innovation (Mei et al., 2012). It should also be noted that the literature has included studies related to the COVID-19 pandemic and its implications for fostering sustainable innovation in hospitality and tourism (Elkhwesky et al., 2022).

The large number of studies related to innovation in the tourism sector reflects the fact that innovation in tourism is a complex and multidisciplinary topic. Tourism products are composite goods, which makes innovation in the industry challenging. Technology currently seems to be an important driver of innovation in the tourism sector. Thus, social media, mobile phones and smartphones, websites, multimedia, virtual and augmented reality, artificial intelligence, and several other technological advances in the tourism industry have helped to develop operations and make the process of travelling a much more pleasant and efficient experience. Virtual reality and augmented reality options when viewing rooms, destinations, or tours give guests a preview of the experience they are about to book. Virtual tours with remote-controlled guides are one of the top travel and tourism innovations implemented after the COVID-19 pandemic. Niche tourism innovations, such as female-focused home-sharing communities, have also emerged. Innovations in the tourism industry include chatbots for making reservations and mobility solutions for tourists. In addition, cloud/SaaS (Software as a Service) in hospitality, improved in-room technology, and self-service tech are recent innovations in the hospitality industry.

Innovation has accompanied activity in the tourism industry since its beginnings. It will continue to do so, given that it plays a critical role in enhancing guests' experiences, improving business operations, and making tourism more sustainable.

Notes

1 UNWTO Secretary-General Zurab Pololikashvili's message for the Official Opening of ITB Berlin 2023, first in-person event since 2019.
2 UN Secretary-General António Guterres' message for the World Tourism Day "Rethinking tourism", in September 2022.

References

Damian, I. E., & Suarez-Barraza, M. F. (2015). Process innovation in tourism management. A review of the literature. *Intangible Capital, 11*(2), 147–165.

De Lacerda, L. L., Cunha, C. J., & Biz, A. A. (2021). Leadership for innovation in hospitality and tourism: Integrative literature review. *Rosa dos Ventos-Turismo e Hospitalidade, 13*(1), 22–49.

Elkhwesky, Z., El Manzani, Y., & Salem, I. E. (2022). Driving hospitality and tourism to foster sustainable innovation: A systematic review of COVID-19-related studies and practical implications in the digital era. *Tourism and Hospitality Research.* 10.1177/14673584221126792

Giotis, G., & Papadionysiou, E. (2022). The role of managerial and technological innovations in the tourism industry: A review of the empirical literature. *Sustainability, 14*(9), 5182. doi. 10.3390/su14095182

Kumar, S., & Shekhar (2020). Technology and innovation: Changing concept of rural tourism - a systematic review. *Open Geosciences*, *12*(1), 737–752.

Liberato, M. M., Batista, N. R. A., Silva, C. C. S., Abud, A. K., & Holanda, F. S. (2020). Creativity and innovation in the tourism sector: A systematic literature review. *Revista Geintec-Gestao Inovacao e Tecnologias*, *10*(3), 5517–5526.

Marasco, A., De Martino, M., Magnotti, F., & Morvillo, A. (2018). Collaborative innovation in tourism and hospitality: A systematic review of the literature. *International Journal of Contemporary Hospitality Management*, *30*(6), 2364–2395.

Mei, X. Y., Arcodia, C., & Ruhanen, L. (2012). Towards tourism innovation: A critical review of public polices at the national level. *Tourism Management Perspectives*, *4*, 92–105.

OECD (2005). Oslo Manual. Guidelines for collecting and interpreting innovation data. Available at: https://ec.europa.eu/eurostat/web/products-manuals-and-guidelines/-/OSLO

OECD (2018). Oslo Manual. Guidelines for collecting and interpreting innovation data. Available at: https://www.oecd.org/science/oslo-manual-2018-9789264304604-en.htm

Oskam, J. A., & De Visser-Amundson, A. (2022). A systematic review of ethical issues in hospitality and tourism innovation. *Journal of Hospitality and Tourism Insights*, *5*(4), 782–803.

Satta, G., Spinelli, R., & Parola, F. (2019). Is tourism going green? A literature review on green innovation for sustainable tourism. *Tourism Analysis*, *24*(3), 265–280.

Shin, H., & Perdue, R. R. (2022). Hospitality and tourism service innovation: A bibliometric review and future research agenda. *International Journal of Hospitality Management*, *102*, 103176.

Smedlund, A., & Toivonen, M. (2008). Editorial. *International Journal Services Technology and Management*, *9*(3/4), 195–198.

Tether, B. S. (2003). The sources and aims of innovation in services: Variety between and within sectors. *Economics of Innovation and New Technology*, *12*(6), 481–505.

Zermeno-Flores, S. G., & Cuevas-Contreras, T. (2015). Systemic review of articles about intellectual capital as source innovation in health tourism. *Teoría y Praxis*, *11*(18), 9–34.

TOP 20 INNOVATIONS FOR THE INTERNATIONAL DEVELOPMENT OF THE TOURISM INDUSTRY: A LOOK AT AGENDA 2030

Antonia M. García-Cabrera, M. Gracia García-Soto, Francisco J. Gutiérrez-Pérez and M. José Miranda-Martel

The tourism industry currently finds itself in the time of the United Nation's Agenda 2030 and Sustainable Development Goals(SDGs); however, the research that links tourism with SDGs is rather recent (Ferrer-Roca, Guia & Blasco, 2022). Agenda 2030 and SDGs offer a broad scope for considering the suitability and consequences of certain decisions and innovations meant to facilitate international development within the industry, as well as move towards a better world generally (Gabay & Ilcan, 2017). With tourism being one of the world's largest industries, it definitely has a great responsibility to ensure sustainability and help reach the goals of Agenda 2030 (Ferrer-Roca et al., 2022).

Specifically, tourism is one of the fastest-growing contributors and largest sources of foreign exchange and employment (e.g., Vrontis et al., 2022); thus, the United Nations has highlighted the relevance of this sector as a force for poverty alleviation (United Nations, 2018). Accordingly, the worldwide development of tourism is considered an effective way of improving the economic well-being of people in many countries, especially in developing countries (e.g., Go & Kang, 2023). In this context, the innovative actions needed to promote the development of this industry are highly relevant, as well as being an opportunity to advance in achieving the objectives of Agenda 2030 (e.g., SDG 1 – No poverty; SDG 9 – Industry, innovation and infrastructure).

However, activity based on tourism is also linked to the overuse of natural resources and the encroachment on local customs at destinations (Go & Kang, 2023). As a consequence of such negative impacts, voices warning that tourism may jeopardise environmental and social well-being in countries have emerged (e.g., Ferrer-Roca et al., 2022; Vrontis et al., 2022). Thus, innovations designed to boost development in the tourism industry should consider the sustainability approach advocated by the World Tourism Organisation (UNWTO); in other words, innovations should contemplate that tourism must "[…] takes full account of its current and future economic, social and environmental impacts, while addressing the needs of visitors, the industry, the environment and host communities". This is in line with the definition of *sustainable tourism* proposed in the Rio + 20 outcome by the United Nations (2012), where sustainable tourism is defined as a significant contributor "to the three dimensions of sustainable development"—i.e., *economic, social* and *environmental* (Govindan et al., 2013)—if well-designed and managed (United Nations, 2012; paragraph 130).

Being aware of the impact of tourism in achieving sustainability, when the United Nations General Assembly approved the 17 SDGs in 2015, they urged the tourism industry to address priority areas in *sustainability development*. As a direct consequence, UNWTO (2017, 2023) has been working on boosting a form of tourism that is sustainable and contributes towards achieving the universal aims of Agenda 2030 for Sustainable Development and the SDGs.

Because of the potential positive effects of *tourism development* on the economic, social and environmental well-being of countries and in reaching the goals of Agenda 2030 (Ferrer-Roca et al., 2022), there is a need to eradicate the conception of tourism as a simple leisure activity that overexploits natural resources, which are, therefore, seen as expendable. In this respect, advancing the understanding of the relationship between tourism and SDGs—whose study is still limited (Ferrer-Roca, Guia & Blasco, 2022)—is highly relevant and appropriate.

Accordingly, this chapter aims to highlight the top 20 innovations that *must* be implemented if the tourism industry is to develop internationally while taking Agenda 2030 into consideration. In other words, it puts forward the changes that *must* happen in order to increase the sustainable development of tourist destinations and their associated companies.

The Top 20 innovations were identified by a panel of tourism experts, following a two-step method. We first conducted qualitative research to identify all the possible changes required in the tourism industry in February 2019. We collected 269 ideas, which were organised into 139 potential changes (García Cabrera et al., 2019). Second, we carried out (in July 2020) a quantitative study to rank the 139 potential changes according to their importance for the industry's development. Specifically, Likert scales of seven items were used for experts to assess the degree of importance they attached to each possible change, where 1 meant "strongly low" and 7 "strongly high". While 16 managers of Spanish entities affiliated to UNWTO participated in the first qualitative study, 36 managers of European entities also affiliated with the UNWTO participated in the subsequent quantitative study.

Experts in phase 2, who assessed the importance of possible changes for the industry, were from Spain (52.8%), France (11.1%), Germany (2.8%), the United Kingdom 8.3%), Italy (11.1%), Portugal (11.1%) and Austria (2.8%) - that is, from the countries with the highest competitiveness index in Europe (World Economic Forum, 2019). The gender distribution of this panel of experts is balanced (44.4% were female and 55.6% male). The mean age of the participants is 52.2 years, ranging between 50 and 55 years. All the experts have managerial positions within their respective entities and have, on average, around 28.7 years of experience. Finally, the experts work mainly for entities involved in tourism promotion (22.2%), universities/research centres (33.3%), companies (16.7%), public administration (11.1%), business cluster/ associations (5.6%), and private (non-profit) organisations (11.1%).

Table 0.1 shows the 20 innovations most valued by the panel of experts (out of 139 available), according to their perceived importance for the international development of the tourism industry. Table 0.1 also shows the contribution of these innovations to the SDGs, as each innovation is linked to one or more of the Goals.

Innovations 1 and 2, the two most relevant according to the panel of experts, are in line with the Rio + 20 outcome document *The Future We Want*, where in paragraph 131, member states encourage the promotion of investment in sustainable tourism, including cultural tourism (United Nations, 2012). What is more, according to the panel of experts, the overall analysis of the innovations identified suggests that the current priority, is not the development of resources and services to facilitate the operations of the sector (e.g., infrastructures, leisure complementary activities, etc.). However, they must also certainly be reconfigured to ensure the sustainability of the destinations. On the contrary, it is the need to generate new cultural values among the population, firms, and governments that must be prioritised; it is crucial that awareness of the sustainability of destinations and the respect for and acceptance of tourists become generalised.

Table 0.1 Ranking of top 20 innovations and SDG

Innovation	
1. Create policies that foster the development of sustainability values in companies and tourists, raising awareness of the practice of responsible tourism (e.g., conservation of the land and marine environment, respect for cultural heritage and legacy, responsible consumption, reduction of noise pollution, eradication of customs that cause damage to ecosystems, etc.)	• 6. Clean water and sanitation • 12. Responsible consumption and production • 13. Climate action • 14. Life below water • 15. Life on land
2. Create policies based on environmental, cultural and economic sustainability to improve *tourist experience* (e.g., regulate the carrying capacity of destinations, regulate access to and the use of natural spaces re. organising events).	• 6. Clean water and sanitation • 12. Responsible consumption and production • 13. Climate action • 14. Life below water • 15. Life on land
3. Foster values associated with 'interculturality' to enhance the relationship between locals and tourists (e.g., embracing diversity, showing respect and practising tolerance towards tourists, etc.).	• 16. Peace and justice strong institutions
4. Generate synergies through the collaboration of companies to facilitate destination development (e.g., exchange market intelligence, create tourism products tailored to the demand, leverage the attractions at the destination, benefit from the "country" brand, etc.).	• 8. Decent work and economic growth • 17. Partnerships to achieve the goal
5. Enhance the 'friendliness' and hospitality of the local population towards tourists in order to improve the destination's attractiveness to visitors (e.g., encourage locals to share their knowledge and exchange experiences with tourists).	• 8. Decent work and economic growth • 11. Sustainable cities and communities
6. Assumption by the tourism company of the role of the 'sustainability agent' at the destination, defining and implementing responsible and sustainable practices that are compatible with tourists' enjoyment (e.g., circular economy).	• 6. Clean water and sanitation • 11. Sustainable cities and communities • 12. Responsible consumption and production • 13. Climate action • 14. Life below water • 15. Life on land
7. Implement training plans based on sustainability at the tourism company aimed at promoting responsible tourism and raising environmental awareness at all professional levels (e.g., top management, middle management, supervisors, miscellaneous staff, etc.).	• 4. Quality education • 8. Decent work and economic growth • 12. Responsible consumption and production

(Continued)

Table 0.1 (Continued)

Innovation

8. Adoption of human resources practices that focus on the recruitment of talent to the tourism sector while also eliminating subcontracting, which results in poor working conditions for operational staff (e.g., hiring personnel who meet the required educational profile for each position, offering fair compensation, etc.).	• 1. No poverty • 2. Zero hunger • 8. Decent work and economic growth • 10. Reduced inequality • 16. Peace and justice strong institutions
9. Elevating the status of tourism studies and training as a discipline, turning it into a widely-recognised educational speciality (e.g., social recognition of a Bachelor's or Master's degree in tourism and the importance of continuous training for sector employees).	• 4. Quality education • 8. Decent work and economic growth • 10. Reduced inequality
10. Develop new products, services, and business models that replace outdated offerings and contribute towards the renewal of the sector (e.g., innovating the services offered by hotels and restaurants, complementary tourist activities, etc.).	• 8. Decent work and economic growth • 9. Industry, innovation and infrastructure
11. Carry out *digital transformation* in all sub-sectors of the tourism industry, with priority given to the implementation of this innovation by SMEs.	• 9. Industry, innovation and infrastructure
12. Train researchers and data analysts specialising in the tourism sector (e.g., big data management, application of data analytics, business intelligence, deriving implications for management practice based on big data exploitation, development of executive reports, etc.).	• 4. Quality education • 8. Decent work and economic growth • 9. Industry, innovation and infrastructure
13. Recovering the spirit of hospitality among employees in the tourism sector in order to ensure the delivery of an "emotional" service to the tourist (e.g., listening carefully to the customer's needs and providing solutions, being proactive in assisting the customer before a request is made, making personalised recommendations to enhance their experience, etc.).	• 8. Decent work and economic growth • 16. Peace and Justice Strong Institutions
14. Formulate corporate social responsibility policies aligned with the United Nations Sustainable Development Goals (SDGs).	• 8. Decent work and economic growth • 12. Responsible Consumption and Production • 17. Partnerships to achieve the Goal

(Continued)

Table 0.1 (Continued)

Innovation

15. Ground political-legal decisions to be implemented in the tourism industry on scientific and technical criteria (e.g., destination development planning, establishment of promotion and marketing policies, etc.).	• 9. Industry, innovation and infrastructure • 11. Sustainable Cities and Communities
16. Disseminate data and transfer knowledge from public and educational entities to managers of tourist destinations in areas of interest for tourism development (e.g. tourist demand forecasts, evolution of tourist profiles, etc.).	• 8. Decent work and economic growth • 9. Industry, innovation and infrastructure • 17. Partnerships to achieve the Goal
17. Implement programmes to support the tourism sector in promoting its development as a smart destination and integrative hub for the different territories or tourist areas of the country.	• 8. Decent work and economic growth • 9: Industry, Innovation and Infrastructure • 11. Sustainable Cities and Communities • 17. Partnerships to achieve the Goal
18. Implement laws that regulate and promote the reform and reconversion of mature tourist destinations (e.g., renewal of tourism infrastructure, the adoption of sustainable models, etc.).	• 9: Industry, Innovation and Infrastructure • 11. Sustainable Cities and Communities • 12. Responsible Consumption and Production
19. Promote greater social awareness about the importance of tourism to the national economy, demystifying the mistaken idea that this sector is less relevant than other local industries or services.	• 8. Decent work and economic growth
20. Develop a national statistics plan allowing for greater results disaggregation by subsectors, tourist areas, and future perspectives.	• 9. Industry, Innovation and Infrastructure

Source: Prepared by authors.

In addition, Figures 0.2 and 0.3 show the Top 20 innovations to be carried out by the actors mainly responsible for implementing them: governments and public policy makers or companies. As shown in the figures, a higher number of innovations seem to require the support of governments (12 innovations), who must pass regulations and create new policies to implement them. This finding is again in line with the Rio + 20 outcome document, where in paragraph 131, member states "underline the importance of establishing, where

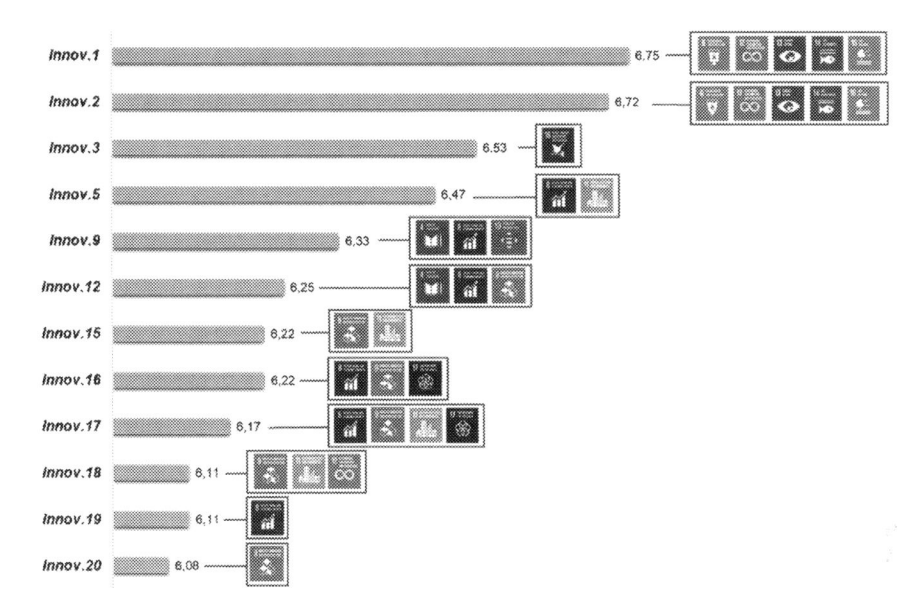

Figure 0.2 Top 12 innovations to be implemented by governments.

Source: Prepared by authors.

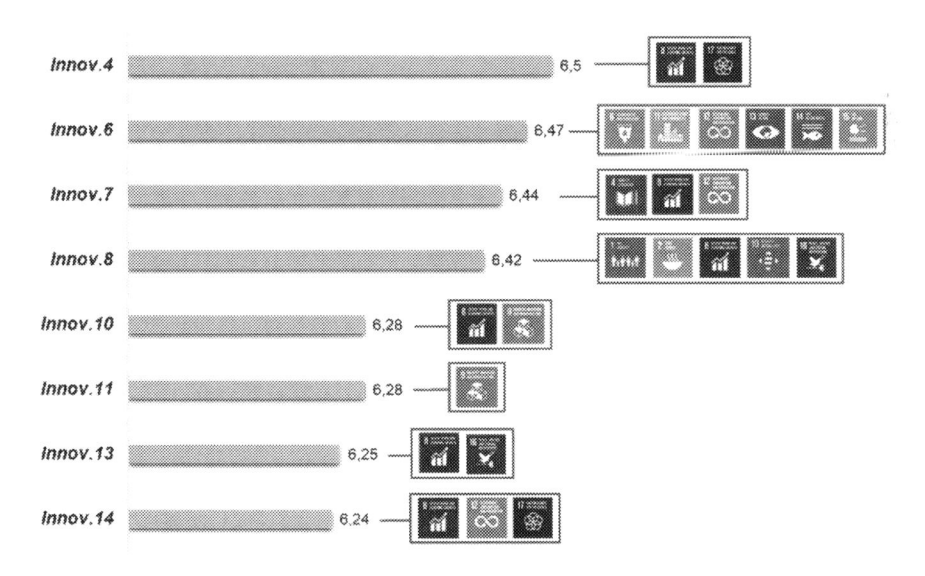

Figure 0.3 Top 8 innovations to be implemented by companies.

Source: Prepared by authors.

necessary, appropriate guidelines and regulations in accordance with national priorities and legislation for promoting and supporting sustainable tourism" (United Nations, 2018). It should be remarked that, according to the results, governments may contribute to innovations in the tourism industry that contribute towards achieving 12 out of 17 SDGs (SDGs 1, 2, 3, 5 and 7 seem to be beyond the scope of the priorities required in the government action), and play an active role in boosting the three dimensions of *sustainable tourism* (economic, social and environmental).

In addition, a set of 8 relevant innovations are mainly the responsibility of the companies in the tourism sector. Globally, they may contribute towards achieving 14 out of 17 SDGs, SDGs 3 (Good health and well-being), 5 (Gender equality), and 7 (Affordable and clean energy) not being a priority for these innovations. Thus, SDGs mainly related to the *people/social* dimension of sustainability aim to end poverty and hunger in all forms and ensure dignity and equality, which seem to be somewhat further away from the innovation priorities to be implemented by the companies in the sector. On the other hand, the economic dimension of sustainability (SDGs 8, 9, 10 and 11) and, to a lesser extent, the environmental dimension (SDGs 6, 12, 13, 14, 15) are highly relevant in such innovations.

Finally, it is worth noting that a warning has been issued regarding how tourism may have overestimated its potential to contribute to sustainability and that the reality shows that, in many cases, sustainable tourism aimed at achieving the SDGs is not being implemented (Ferrer-Roca et al., 2022). Being aware of this, the present work offers 20 innovations for the industry to be able to lead the change toward a better world. In this vein, and borrowing the thought of Hollenhorst et al. (2014, p.36), although modifying the sense of their words, we believe that the 20 innovations offer hope for building "the world we want to live in, the environments we want to inhabit, and the economy we want to participate in".

Acknowledgement

Project: PID2021-123274NB-I00

References

Ferrer-Roca, N., Guia, J., & Blasco, D. (2022). Partnerships and the SDGs in a cross-border destination: The case of the Cerdanya Valley. *Journal of Sustainable Tourism*, *30*(10), 2410–2427.

Gabay, C., & Ilcan, S. (2017). Leaving no-one behind? The politics of destination in the 2030 sustainable development goals. *Globalizations*, *14*(3), 337–342.

García Cabrera, A. M., Gutiérrez Pérez, F. J., & García Soto, M. G. (2019). Impulsando la competitividad internacional de la empresa turística en España: Una agenda de cambio institucional. *Revista de Contabilidad y Tributación – CEF*, *437–438*, 155–198.

Go, H., & Kang, M. (2023). Metaverse tourism for sustainable tourism development: Tourism agenda 2030. *Tourism Review*, 78(2), 381–394.

Govindan, K., Khodaverdi, R., & Jafarian, A. (2013). A fuzzy multi criteria approach for measuring sustainability performance of a supplier based on triple bottom line approach. *Journal of Cleaner Production*, 47, 345–354.

Hollenhorst, S. J., Houge-Mackenzie, S., & Ostergren, D. M. (2014). The trouble with tourism. *Tourism Recreation Research*, 39(3), 305–319.

United Nations (2012). A/RES/66/288 - The Future We Want – Outcome document. *Sustainable Development Goals, Knowledge Platform*. Available at: https://sustainabledevelopment.un.org/futurewewant.html [08.05.2023].

United Nations (2018). Sustainalbe tourism. *Sustainable Development Goals, Knowledge Platform*. Available at: https://sustainabledevelopment.un.org/topics/sustainabletourism [08.05.2023].

UNWTO (2017). UNWTO Tourism highlights: 2017 Edition. Available at: https://www.e-unwto.org/doi/pdf/10.18111/9789284419029 [08.05.2023].

UNWTO (2023). Tourism 4 SDGs. *Join us on the 2030 Journey platform*. Available at: https://www.unwto.org/tourism4sdgs [08.05.2023].

Vrontis, D., Christofi, M., Giacosa, E., & Serravalle, F. (2022). Sustainable development in tourism: A stakeholder analysis of the Langhe Region. *Journal of Hospitality & Tourism Research*, 46(5), 846–878.

World Economic Forum (2019). *Travel and Tourism Competitiveness Report 2019*. Available at: https://cutt.ly/imRjhA0 [16.12.2019].

THE STUDY OF CASES AS A RESEARCH AND TEACHING METHODOLOGY: ITS APPLICATION TO GLOBAL BUSINESS IN THE TOURISM SECTOR

Silvia Sosa-Cabrera

Tourism is one of the most important activities in the world economy, with a significant impact on the global economy and the social, cultural and economic development of countries. As a consequence, tourism activity has become a subject of study and discussion in various fields, including economics, sociology, anthropology, geography, psychology and education.

However, the complexity of tourism as a social and economic phenomenon means that its study requires a specific methodology that facilitates a comprehensive and holistic understanding of its various aspects. In this sense, the use of case studies has become fundamental in tourism research and teaching, as it allows a deeper and more detailed approach to the reality of tourism activity through the analysis of specific and concrete situations, the identification of problems and practical solutions adapted to each context, the understanding of different scenarios that may arise in the tourism industry, the discovery of the perspective of tourism service providers, tourists or the local community itself, etc.

Case studies in the tourism sector can address different topics, such as the impact of tourism on the local economy, sustainable tourism development, tourism destination management, tourism planning and tourism crisis management, among others, in addition to the in-depth study of the companies dedicated to the sector and their way of dealing with organisational growth and development, changes in the environment, entrepreneurship and intrapreneurship and the generation of a culture of open innovation. In this sense, through the analysis of cases, it is possible to identify the best practices and the challenges faced by key agents in the tourism sector, which can help to gain in-depth knowledge of the sector and improve decision-making and management of the tourism activity.

Case studies are not a new teaching or research methodology. Proof of this is that it is now more than 100 years since the case study method was first applied in the classroom. Since 1920, using case studies has been the fundamental teaching practice at Harvard Business School to prepare students for their role as leaders, managers and decision-makers (Harvard Business School, 2022). Its long history of teaching is underpinned by the principles of constructivist theory, as the in-depth analysis of real-world examples brings together theoretical concepts and practice in a reflective process that generates meaningful learning. This learning is made possible by the information the case shows about how practitioners, experts or managers have solved a problem or made certain decisions or about the values, techniques and resources involved in possible alternatives. De Miguel Díaz (2005) includes the case study as a suitable teaching method for the development of competencies in higher education since the need to fully understand and interpret the case, as well as the decisions and possible points of view of its actors, generates active learning that transcends the limits of the teaching-learning space itself and serves to generate solutions, contrast them and even train in possible solution procedures. In the same didactic line, Asopa and Beye (1997) define case studies as a learning method based on the participation and active and cooperative dialogue of students in a real situation, overcoming the obstacles of agendas, time, etc., of the professionals invited to the classroom to share their knowledge and experience. Thus, the case study becomes a useful tool that introduces an aspect of that reality into the classroom so that students can analyse, reflect and draw conclusions (Gómez Carrasco & Rodríguez Pérez, 2014). Therefore, a case study can be considered a dynamic and accurate description of an analytical or decision-making situation faced by a person at a given moment in a real situation, allowing students to play a leading role in the situation.

In organisational research, Yin (1994) is the most cited author on case-based research and has become a key reference for all who use this methodology. According to this author, case studies are defined as empirical research that studies a contemporary phenomenon within its real context, where the lines between the phenomenon and the context are not clearly visible, and where different sources of evidence are used for its preparation. In this sense, the case study is an in-depth analysis to investigate the context and processes involved in the phenomenon under study. It can, therefore, be considered an intensive study of selected examples.

The methodological aspects of the case study as a research strategy in tourism have been reinforced by Xiao and Smith (2006), who argue that this approach has contributed considerably to advances in tourism research and science, thus dismissing the prevailing arguments that case studies are conceptually and analytically weak. Indeed, Marujo (2016) adds that the case study method in tourism research plays an important role in the production of new knowledge and the creation of hypotheses or propositions, also allowing the researcher to test existing theories. However, Strandberg et al. (2018) show that qualitative research designs remain relatively constant in tourism research but that case studies and interviews have lost ground to content analysis manuscripts. Agapito (2020) concludes that discursively informed methods, based on interviews and focus groups, are considered the most appropriate for collecting data on lived experiences, which generally result in individual case studies, such as the one developed by Zhang et al. (2021) on tourism entrepreneurship. This has meant that, for example, Moyle et al. (2021), in their review of sustainable tourism literature, have highlighted the need for case studies to contribute more noticeably to the advancement of science and practical applications for the sector, generating critical mass that links one aspect to another.

Regardless of their use, whether for research or teaching, given the increasing complexity of organisational phenomena in any sector, studies of an exploratory and comprehensive nature based on qualitative characteristics are needed, especially when the purpose is to understand and interpret events as a whole, providing analysis documents that facilitate learning about complex situations and realities. These analyses can facilitate the development of general learning competencies (e.g., observation, identification and evaluation of situations and cases, analysis, reasoning and decision-making) linked to the subjects they are used for (e.g., theoretical approaches, applied solutions) and to the professional profile itself (e.g., aspects for employability in a sector); processes, terms and professional context; making judgments), in addition to the intellectual, communication, interpersonal and organisational skills and abilities associated with the process of analysing the cases under study (De Miguel Díaz, 2005).

The case study is therefore considered appropriate when we are interested in explaining the complex human and organisational situation that has occurred or is occurring in the organisations under study, or events that occurred in the past but whose participants can still account for them (Sosa Cabrera, 2015), especially highlighting the analysis of processes of organisational change, business development, family succession, innovation, entrepreneurship and intra-entrepreneurship. Therefore, the social sciences and humanities, to which tourism belongs, seem to be appropriate areas of knowledge for the application of case studies, both for research and teaching, given that the object of analysis is a complex social phenomenon that involves many interrelated participants in a process that is prolonged over time.

The international character of this handbook has been a major challenge in its development, as it aims to cover the key issues of tourism management considering different geographical, cultural, academic and social contexts. Following Pettigrew's (1990) recommendations, when the cases are from the same sector, the academic committee makes an initial proposal of tourism cases that have developed entrepreneurial activity, this being the key process for defining the unit of analysis and, therefore, the case under study. To do this, it was necessary to determine which companies—and, in some cases, social phenomena related to the sector—would be the object of study and why, which individuals would be considered decision-makers, participants and those involved in the sector, and the time frame of the case to be analysed. These aspects determined both the selection of the cases and the design of the data collection protocols. Once the cases had been selected, the researchers collected secondary information from the different entities based on their experience as collaborators with tourism companies. They carried out a general survey by consulting corporate websites, annual sector directories, data series, etc.

Once the case studies had been pre-selected, it was necessary to contact the chosen companies by telephone to obtain their agreement to participate in the process, asking people directly related to the founders or, failing that, the management teams of the organisations involved. Questionnaires, interviews, documentation reviews and company visits were then used by the researchers, in combination and to a greater or lesser extent, to construct the narrative of the case study. After data collection, steps were taken to write and revise the preliminary reports, establishing the same guidelines for all cases in terms of structure and wording to allow their use as elements of analysis and discussion in the classrooms. The cases were approved by the key informants, who checked the reliability of the information and the facts described. They stressed the veracity and seriousness of the treatment of the information on the entity.

On the one hand, this case manual allows interested students to play an active role in the teaching-learning process, developing their criteria and learning to evaluate situations, identify problems and make decisions. On the other hand, the case study, used as a group and collaborative work tool by Sánchez Moreno (2008), will also help students to manage in situations that involve discussion and defence of a certain vision and to make consensual decisions, encouraging intellectual exchanges and fostering students' social skills, aspects that discussion facilitates and which are basic for their professional performance.

Finally, it will also help the teacher to gain a better understanding of the business reality and even to monitor the cases dealt with to keep up to date with the evolution of the companies analysed in the classroom. Finally, it will be a reference for professionals in the sector, delving into issues that are often hidden in the decision-making and entrepreneurial processes. This is why case studies bring undeniable advantages, not only at an academic level but also at a personal and professional level.

References

Agapito, D. (2020). The senses in tourism design: A bibliometric review. *Annals of Tourism Research*, *83*, 1–15. doi. 10.1016/j.annals.2020.102934

Asopa, V. N., & Beye, G. (1997). *Management of agricultural research: A training manual*. United Nations, FAO.

De Miguel Díaz, M. (2005). *Modalities of teaching focused on the development of competences. Orientaciones para promover el cambio metodológico en el marco del EEES*. Oviedo, Asturias, Spain: Servicio de Publicaciones de la Universidad de Oviedo.

Gómez Carrasco, C. J., & Rodríguez Pérez, R. A. (2014). Learning to teach social sciences with enquiry methods. Case studies in teacher training. *REDU Revista de Docencia Universitaria*, *12(2)*, 307–325.

Harvard Business School (2022). *From inquiry to action. Harvard business school & the case method. 100 years case method*. Boston: Harvard Business School.

Marujo, N. (2016). The case study in tourism research: A methological approach. *Tourimo-Estudios e Praticas*, *5(1)*, 113–128.

Moyle, B., Moyle, C., Ruhanen, L., Weaver, D., & Hadinejad, A. (2021). Are we really progressing sustainable tourism. *Journal of Sustainable Tourism*, *29(1)*, 106–122. doi. 10.1080/09669582.2020.1817048

Pettigrew, A. (1990). Longitudinal field research on change: Theory and practice. *Organization Science*, *1*, 267–291.

Sánchez Moreno, M. (2008). *How to teach in university classrooms through case studies*. Institute of Education Sciences. University of Zaragoza. Available at: http://www.unizar.es/ice/images/stories/calidad/Casos.pdf

Strandberg, C., Nath, A., Hemmatdar, H., & Jahwash, M. (2018). Tourism Research in the new millennium: A bibliometric review of literature in Tourism and Hospitality Research. *Tourism and Hospitality Research*, *18(3)*, 269–285. doi. 10.1177/1467358416642010

Sosa Cabrera, S. (2015). The case study as a research and teaching methodology: Its application to success stories in the Canary Islands tourism sector. In A. Quintana (ed.). *Casos de Éxito Turístico en Canarias*. Sintesis Editorial (pp. 23–26).

Xiao, H., & Smith, S. L. (2006). Case studies in tourism research: A state-of-the-art analysis. *Tourism Management*, *27*, 738–749. doi. 10.1016/j.tourman.2005.11.002

Yin, R. K. (1994). *Case study research. Design and methods*. London: SAGE.

Zhang, H., Lu, L., & Sun, F. (2021). Changing role of lifestyle in tourism entrepreneurship: Case study of naked retreats Enterprise. *Tourism Management*, *84*, 104259.

Case 1 Internationalisation of the Pestana Hotel Group chain through corporate entrepreneurship

From family hotel to multinational hotel chain

Helder Brito Carrasqueira and Luis Nobre Pereira

Introduction and case selection

Tourism is one of the fastest-growing sectors of economic activity, having shown resilience in recovering from the COVID-19 crisis. In Portugal, tourism represented 2% of the GDP in 1974, and there were 259 hotels, while in 2019, it was worth 8% of the GDP and 1,407 hotels were registered, accounting for 24.6 million international tourist arrivals (INE, 2020).

The Pestana Hotel Group (PHG) began in 1974, at a time of economic crisis. After finishing his degree, a young man returned to the island of Madeira to manage the hotel his family had built as it was going through a difficult period. This experience would transform the young man into an entrepreneur, and 50 years later, he is the president and largest shareholder of PHG, the largest Portuguese hotel chain with 100 hotels, over 11,000 rooms, and 6,000 employees (PHG, 2020).

This case study on PHG aims to show how corporate entrepreneurship transformed a family hotel into an international hotel chain. Research in this field of entrepreneurship, as applied to hospitality, is currently limited, and this study thus contributes to the field (Fu et al., 2019).

The first part of this case study describes PHG, the theoretical framework, the corporate entrepreneurship process, and the consolidation of PHG's internationalisation. The second part explains the effect of COVID-19 on PHG and the strategic options taken to face this crisis. Finally, the conclusions highlight the use of corporate entrepreneurship theories in the expansion of PHG. The data was collected through document analysis and in-depth telephone interviews due to the COVID-19 pandemic, and the information was subsequently validated via email.

Business profile and framework

According to the tourism satellite account (INE, 2019), hotels and similar businesses are the most important sub-sector generating gross value added

DOI: 10.4324/9781003454465-2

in the tourism sector. The domestic market in Portugal remains very fragmented, with many independent hotels. However, of the 20 leading chains operating in the country (Deloitte, 2020), PHG holds a 22% market share in terms of the number of hotel units. At the level of the ten largest Portuguese chains with hotels abroad, PHG holds a market share of 29% (PHG, 2020). PHG is the only company that has managed to pursue the entrepreneurship and growth strategies of the main Iberian chains beyond its home market, as we can see in Figure 1.1 (the other Portuguese chain with a robust international presence chose to specialise in Brazil, where all its hotels are based).

The PHG hotel chain is present in five tourist regions across the globe (Western Europe, the Mediterranean Basin, South America, North America (USA), and Africa). It continues to be a family-based chain, however, with its assets in a strong position (net debt/total assets ratio: 47%) (PHG, 2020). PHG originated as a resort hotel and later evolved to join the corporate market in large cities. At present, PHG's offer is structured into four major brands of 4- and 5-star hotels: Pestana Hotels & Resorts (units for sun and beach tourism holidays), Pestana Pousadas (units in historic buildings, castles, and palaces), Pestana Collection Hotels (exclusive, high-level units in reference cities), and Pestana CR7 (lifestyle-type accommodation units).

For many years, PHG maintained a focus on the vertical integration of its business, having been co-owner of an airline company and owner of a tour operator, travel agencies, casinos, and golf courses. In recent years, however, it has been focusing on the hotel business, with divestment into hotel distribution

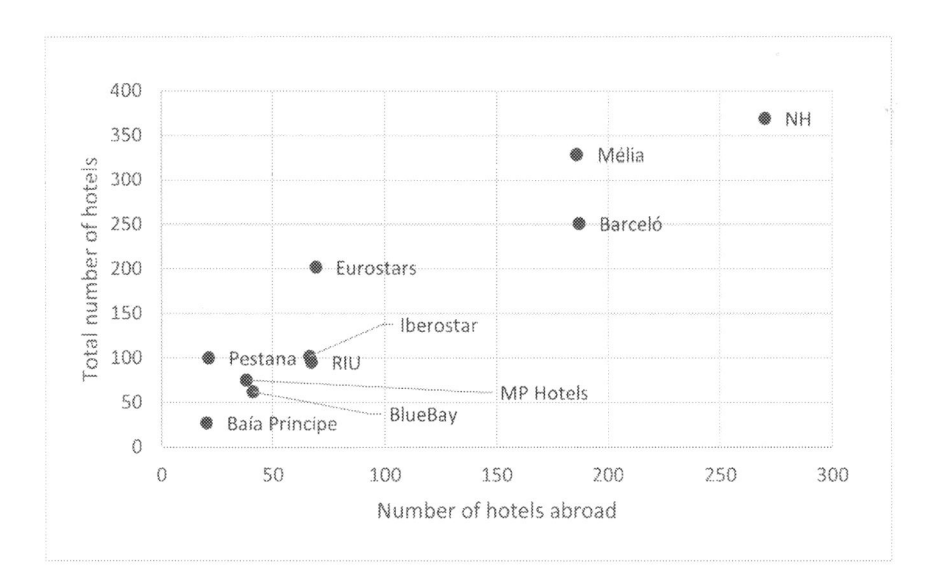

Figure 1.1 Total hotels versus hotels abroad of the leading Iberian companies.

Note: Only Iberian hotel companies with more than 20 hotels abroad were included; P = 0.9430 (Carrasqueira, 2021).

and transport. Nevertheless, the group maintains an important position in tourism real estate and significant know-how in the supply of time-share hotels.

Corporate and international entrepreneurship: Literature review

Company access to international markets can be explained via two main approaches: the economic and the behavioural models (Anderson, 2002). Economic models, such as market power, internalisation, and ecletics paradigm theories, are usually applied to large companies seeking efficiency and profit maximisation.. The market power theory is based on extending dominant positions in businesses abroad through direct investment, namely in atomised markets (Hymer, 1976). According to internalisation, a firm integrates the transactions that the market carries out in an inefficient or more costly manner within itself (Ietto-Gillies, 2015). The eclectic paradigm theory integrates the previous theories and adds the importance of location and intangible aspects such as know-how (Dunning, 1980, 2015). Risk reduction is particularly relevant in the behavioural models, which explain the options of medium and small enterprises, where the Uppsala, networks, and international entrepreneurship theories are notable. According to the Uppsala theory, a company will tend to choose nearby marketswhich can be operationalised more easily due lower physical distance (e.g., nearby countries) or cultural distance (e.g., common language and culture) (Johanson & Vahlne, 1977; Vahlne & Johanson, 2020). According to networks theory, markets should be seen as networks of firms to be integrated (Forsgren, 2016; Mattsson & Johanson, 2006). Finally, according to international entrepreneurship, internationalisation occurs when entrepreneurs recognise, analyse, and exploit opportunities in foreign countries (Oviat & McDougall, 2005; Tegersen et al., 2016).

Corporate entrepreneurship has been considered a continuous process of implementing actions aimed at innovation, openness and proactivity in business (e.g., Holt et al., 2007). International entrepreneurship has become an autonomous field of research in which the figure of the entrepreneur and the dimensions in which they are called upon to make decisions assume particular importance, and the following abilities have been identified: international opportunities, the propensity to adapt, networking, the ability to innovate, attitude to risk and the development of competitive resources (Dalbosco et al., 2017; Leite & Moraes, 2014; Schwens et al., 2018).

The research that led to this work allowed us to identify how an entrepreneur and their team conducted the internationalisation process in very diverse contexts and markets, with natural levels of adjustments but consolidating the development phases before evolving to new markets. The resilience and perseverance shown in these theories led the company to take an important position in the global market. Those who work in the tourism sector know that the business depends on the discretionary income of consumers, which allows them to be tourists. An expansionary economic cycle usually coincides with good results in the sector, while recession leads to poor results. The consumption of tourism also requires a unique attribute: security. Various factors affect the perception of safety, such as wars, terrorist attacks, and unpredictable natural events (e.g., earthquakes, tsunamis, volcanoes, and pandemics). Diseases caused by viruses have been recurrent throughout history; however, the unpredictability of when and where they might occur make it difficult to manage those types of crisis. In 2003, the SARS-CoV1 pandemic mainly affected Asia (Dombey, 2004). In 2019, SARS-CoV2 broke out, giving rise to the COVID-19 viral disease, which spread rapidly around the world via the primary means of tourist mobility, the aeroplane (Nicola et al., 2020). During the pandemic there were periods in which the population was restricted from travel, causing insecurity in the tourism sector; as both international tourist arrivals and revenues fell sharply (Davahli et al., 2020).

The hotel sub-sector was strongly affected, and it was necessary to take draconian measures and resort to the support made available by governments (Alonso et al., 2020). We present the PHG case study against this background and within the framework of the international entrepreneurship and internationalisation theories.

Evolution and consolidation of the PHG internationalisation process

The first PHG hotel opened in 1972 at the outermost point of Portugal, on the island of Madeira. Four years later, the current chairperson and largest shareholder was asked to take over its management. He was then a young man who had finished his degree in South Africa. The hotel operated under the well-known international Sheraton brand. In addition to bringing the hotel to operational profitability, the manager took advantage of the opportunity to gain a whole panoply of knowledge inherent to the relationship and demands of working with an international benchmark chain. The hotel's insertion in this network was its first contact with the internationalisation process—let us say of the soft kind. It should be recalled that network theory states that business dynamics often determine the internationalisation decisions that a company makes.

The company evolved into a hotel chain with organic growth on the island of Madeira. This growth allowed it to increase operational capacity, market size, and financial capacity. The strengths of the company, combined with the entrepreneurial spirit of its chairperson, led it to expand into mainland Portugal in 1992 with the acquisition of several hotel units. This opening to the market meant that a new operational base had to be set up from scratch; this learning process in the domestic market was the basis of the group beginning its internationalisation process. The position of the largest Portuguese hotel company was consolidated, and it grew to a dozen hotel units.

The challenge of continuing to grow involved some internal constraints. The domestic market had limited growth prospects, was highly dependent on the same markets, and was affected by seasonality in a way that limited profitability and operation on an optimal scale. Despite these issues, there were opportunities, such as the government's financial and political incentives for internationalisation.

International expansion followed opportunities in the market due to the privatisation of three hotels in Mozambique, where the official language is Portuguese. Once again, the entrepreneurial spirit of the chairperson, who was born in neighbouring South Africa and had lived in Mozambique in his youth, led him to buy the three hotels. He also made a complementary investment in South Africa (a lodgetype hotel in the Kruger Park, an important natural park close to Mozambique), which allowed him to design a tourist package better suited to international demand in terms of the products to be offered. In other words, he innovated the local supply and made the tourist package more competitive.

PHG's first internationalisation movement can be framed within the scope of behavioural theories. It fits the Uppsala model due to the psychological proximity of characteristics among those countries (common language, knowledge of culture and business practices). It fits the theory of international entrepreneurship in its recognition and exploitation of this market opportunity. As mentioned, the entrepreneur was familiar with both countries (Mozambique and South Africa), and this step of internationalisation reflects his knowledge of the reality that largely explains that investment with controlled risk.

Following the PHG's first movement, an opportunity arose to continue the process in the same line of psychological proximity through investment in two hotels in Brazil. By then, Brazil and South America generally had good growth prospects but were still not on the radar of the large international hotel companies. PHG thus came to own nine hotels in Brazil, creating an important regional operational base for Latin America and enabling them to expand into Argentina, Venezuela and Colombia, taking advantage of business opportunities. PHG's corporate entrepreneurship then led it to expand to Miami in the United States of America (USA), which is considered very close, in terms of relationships, to the Caribbean and Latin American areas. The second movement of PHG's internationalisation process ends here.

Internationalisation could be described as continuing under the Uppsala model, given the sequential way in which PHG has accumulated knowledge on the market and how it works, showing adaptability and sequentially increasing its responsibilities; however, this would be limited. Another characteristic of the internationalisation process should be pointed out: PHG generally opted to

> keep itself as a property owner; it favoured direct investment abroad and sought to own the physical property of the hotels. This positioning can be explained through economic-based theories related to the promotion of efficiency, which is typical of multinationals, in which there is a need for "internalisation", with the control of operations at an organic level as a guarantee of the quality of the service to be provided – their competitive advantage. The eclectic paradigm should be mentioned in the same sequence, highlighting the advantages of ownership in terms of intangible assets, such as business knowledge and management know-how regarding multiple aspects of the hotel unit.

In summary, the two families of models were combined, including a mix of prudence, as marked by a positioning of corporate entrepreneurship and the goal of becoming a multinational company. It is also relevant to note that the internationalisation process allowed the company to develop competitive resources such as the specialisation of teams and accumulation of experience; the ability to attract managers and qualified personnel; a stronger relationship with financial institutions and suppliers of goods and services; negotiating power as regards tourism distribution; and a reputation with decision-makers and clients (current and potential).

> Internationalisation is a demanding process in financial terms. It is not exempt from contextual risks at political, economic, social, cultural, legislative, and fiscal levels. A company will only be successful abroad if its profits are greater than the costs of "internalisation" combined with the costs of regular operation. This is the decisive factor marking the difference between the initial phase and continuing successfully abroad. PHG thus had to reassess its internationalisation process since the expected growth of South American countries towards high-performance economies, with the desired increase in the middle class, fell short of expectations. The new flows of tourism were coming from Asia and heading to the large cities of Europe and the USA, where hotels have consistently very high occupancy rates – this was an emergent opportunity.

PHG took a risk and made its footprint in the markets where the largest hotel companies were already established. This new strategy began with massive investment in London, followed by Berlin and New York. The group divested itself of some hotels in Brazil and Colombia but invested in Uruguay. PHG continued in Europe, opening hotels in Amsterdam, Madrid and Barcelona. The group innovated by becoming the first Portuguese hotel company to segment its hotel offer into three distinct brands in 2015, to which it added the CR7 brand for the lifestyle segment when it entered into a partnership with the renowned footballer Cristiano Ronaldo in 2016.

The group has defined itself as a multinational company in the hotel sector. Given the prospect of increased market power and associated profits, it was willing to accept the costs and risks of internationalisation in highly competitive markets. Because hotel costs are high, and international expansion requires many resources, it had followed the trend of other large companies, giving up some of its hotel properties in favour of a positioning, known as sale and lease back, which partly adapts the hotel chain to an asset light model. Simultaneously, PHG has hotels that are part of prestigious international consortiums, such as the Leading Hotels of the World, integrated into relationship networks that allow access to market segments composed of sophisticated clients. We consider this the third phase of PHG's internationalisation.

> The research carried out and the clarifications obtained indicate the following key procedures as crucial elements in the consolidation of the internationalisation process (see Table 1.1), which also involve attitudes and behaviours regarding the risk of undertaking such plans: careful analysis of investments; formalisation of procedures – guaranteeing replication in different contexts and geographies; experience of a robust back office, allowing decentralised management processes; internalisation of a systematic training policy; and proximity to the customer (notion of service).

In the COVID era – coping with the unforeseen

The year 2020 started well for PHG, given that January and February were the best months in year-on-year terms, and also included the opening of a new hotel in New York. In March, however, the unthinkable happened and the COVID-19 pandemic led to the closure of all hotels in Portugal. As a result, 2020 was a year that almost did not exist in terms of tourism/hotels. It was necessary to take extraordinary measures. PHG's hotels resorted to laying off staff in order to guarantee some permanent employees (although they could not avoid the departure of employees in technology who moved to other sectors that generated better opportunities during the pandemic). They renegotiated contracts with suppliers but also took the opportunity to carry out maintenance in some hotels and invested in a new electronic check-in app, positioning themselves in the digital market. 2020 was also marked by the group's first loss in forty years (a 75% drop in hotel revenues) and the recourse to state support. Even so, PHG's EBITDA was positive due to the surprising growth of the business in real estate.

Table 1.1 PHG chain internationalisation timeline

Being part of an international hotel chain	-	-	1st step: Int. to Mozambique and South Africa	2nd step (A): Int. to Brazil	2nd step (B): Expansion to South America	3rd step: Int. to Europe/ USA; integration into consortium networks
Initial learning	Local/national entrepreneurship		International entrepreneurship			
Functional internationalisation: stems from the relationship with the tourist distribution (e.g. tour operators) and tourists (international customers)						
1974	-	1992	1998	1999	2001	2010/13 (Until now)
First hotel	Expansion on Madeira's island (domestic market)	Entry and expansion in the mainland Portuguese market	-	-	-	-

The pandemic showed signs of being under control in the first half of 2022, and tourism demand returned to values close to 2019. PHG began its spring by hiring 900 employees in Portugal and plans to end the year with 5,500 employees globally, with a return to full activity.

The pandemic has resulted in three strategic options. The first is diversification with a focus on real estate, with faster capital recovery, as a new opportunity. The second is maintaining the hotel growth plan (five new hotels were opened during the pandemic: Madrid, New York, and Marrakech, and two more in Portugal). Seven more hotels are in the pipeline (including Paris, the USA and Uruguay). The third option is doubling funding for the Pestana Academy to improve workers' skills by developing competitive resources. All indicators reveal that PHG is recovering, and the opening of several hotels during the pandemic is another sign of the corporate entrepreneurship that has contributed to its resilience to disruptive events such as a pandemic or financial crisis.

Epilogue

A company that started as a single-family hotel and, after half a century, has grown to one hundred hotels and a place near the top 100 hotels internationally has followed a path worthy of a case study. This is even more interesting when it is the same young man who managed the first hotel and undertook national and international ventures as its chairperson and principal shareholder. PHG is currently a family-controlled multinational company.

This case study confirms that expansion can be explained by theories of the internationalisation of companies, namely the behavioural theory of Uppsala (due to the gradual form of the process and initial psychological proximity) and network theory (through its insertion in business networks), as well as the economic theories of internalisation, due to the need to preserve its competitive added value, which is based on service quality.

The COVID-19 pandemic greatly affected the group from a financial point of view, as it experienced its first loss in 40 years. From a human resource view, the group was affected by the loss of qualified employees to other sectors. The pandemic also opened up new business opportunities and strategic decisions, even in a scenario of disruptive events. It demonstrated the PHG's conviction in continuing to take entrepreneurial risks with the opening of new hotels.

The theory of international entrepreneurship is also well imprinted since the referred framework was confirmed: adaptability, adherence to networks, ability to identify and seize new opportunities and innovate, attitude towards risk, and the definition and maintenance of competitive advantage.

In conclusion, PHG's long-term corporate and international entrepreneurship stance can be described by the word prudence: the careful analysis of investments. The chairman notes, "It is necessary to evaluate opportunities, decide and not be dragged along by fashions". COVID-19 was a test, and the

CEO's advice is: no matter how good the management, an event can always surprise us, no matter how well prepared we are; we have to show resilience and creativity to turn things around (Lider, 2021).

References

Alonso, A., Kok, S., Bressan, A., O'Shea, M., Sakellarios, N., Koresis, A., & Santoni, L. (2020). COVID-19, aftermath, impacts, and hospitality firms: An international perspective. *International Journal of Hospitality Management*, 91, 102654.

Andersen, O. y Buvik, A. (2002). Firms' internationalization and alternative approaches to the international customer/market selection. *International business review*, 11(3), 347-363.

Carrasqueira, H. (2021). *Hotelaria internacional*. Lisboa: Actual Editora.

Dalbosco, I., Tonial, G., & Werlang, N. (2017). Empreendedorismo internacional: Um estudo de caso em um cluster internacionalizado. *Ágora: Revista de divulgação científica*, 22(1), 4–24.

Davahli, M., Karwowski, W., Sonmez, S., & Apostolopoulos, Y. (2020). The hospitality industry in the face of the COVID-19 pandemic: Current topics and research methods. *International Journal of Environmental Research and Public Health*, 17(20), 7366.

Deloitte (2020). *Atlas da hotelaria portuguesa 2020*. 15a Edição.

Dombey, O. (2004). The effects of SARS on the Chinese tourism industry. *Journal of Vacation Marketing*, 10(1), 4–10.

Dunning, J. (1980). Toward an eclectic theory of international production: Some empirical test. *Journal of International Business Studies*, 2(3), 9–31.

Dunning, J. H. (2015). The eclectic paradigm of international production: A restatement and some possible extensions. In J. Cantwell (eds.). *The eclectic paradigm*. London: Palgrave Macmillan. https://doi.org/10.1007/978-1-137-54471-1_3

Forsgren, M. (2016). A note on the revisited Uppsala internationalization process model – the implications of business networks and entrepreneurship. *Journal of International Business Studies*, 47, 1135–1144. https://doi.org/10.1057/s41267-016-0014-3

Fu, H., Okumus, F., Wu, K., & Köseoglu, M. (2019). The entrepreneurship research in hospitality and tourism. *International Journal of Hospitality Management*, 78, 1–12.

Holt, D. T., Rutherford, M. W., & Clohessy, G. R. (2007). Corporate entrepreneurship: An empirical look at individual characteristics, context, and process. *Journal of Leadership & Organizational Studies*, 13(4), 40–54.

Hymer, S. (1976). *The international operations of national firms: A study of direct foreign investment*. Cambridge, MA: The MIT Press.

Ietto-Gillies, G. (2015). Innovation, internationalization, and the transnational corporation. In D. Archibugi & A. Filippetti (eds.). *The handbook of global science, technology, and innovation*, Wiley Blackwell. https://doi.org/10.1002/9781118739044.ch6.

INE (2019). *Conta satélite do turismo*. https://www.ine.pt/scripts/ws_tur_docs/20191218_Workshop_Turismo_INE.pdf.

INE (2020). *Estatísticas do Turismo de 2019*, Ed. 2020.

Johanson, J., & Vahlne, J. (1977). The internationalization process of the firm: A model of knowledge and increasing foreign market commitment. *Journal of International Business Studies*, 8(1), 23–32.

Leite, Y. V. P., & Moraes, W. F. A. (2014). Facetas do risco no empreendedorismo internacional. *Revista de Administração Contemporânea, 18*(1), 96–117. https://doi.org/10.1590/S1415-65552014000100007

Lider (2021). A visão da Pandemia por José Theotónio, CEO do Grupo Pestana. Available at: https://lidermagazine.sapo.pt/e-sempre-possivel-haver-um-acontecimento-que-nos-pode-surpreender-por-mais-bem-preparados-que-estejamos-a-visao-da-pandemia-por-jose-theotonio-ceo-do-grupo-pestana/.

Mattsson, L., & Johanson, J. (2006). Discovering market networks. *European Journal of Marketing, 40*(3/4), 259–274. https://doi.org/10.1108/03090560610648048.

Nicola, M., Alsafi, Z., Sohrabi, C., Kerwan, A., Al-Jabir, A., Iosifidis, C. … Agha, R. (2020). The socio-economic implications of the coronavirus pandemic (COVID-19): A review. *International Journal of Surgery, 78*, 185–193.

Oviatt, M., & McDougall, P. (2005). Defining international entrepreneurship and modeling the speed of internationalization. *Entrepreneurship Theory and Practice, 29*(5), 537–553.

PHG (2019). Relatório e contas consolidado, Grupo Pestana SGPS SA. Available at: https://www.pestanagroup.com/wp-content/uploads/2017/08/GP_SGPS_Relat%C3%B3rio_e_Contas_Consolidado_2019-1.pdf.

PHG (2020). Pestanagroup website. Available at: www.pestanagroup.com/

Schwens, C., Zapkau, F., Bierwerth, M., Isidor, R., Knight, G., & Kabst, R. (2018). International entrepreneurship: A meta–analysis on the internationalization and performance relationship. *Entrepreneurship Theory and Practice, 42*(5), 734–768. https://doi.org/10.1177/1042258718795346

Terjesen, S., Hessels, J., & Li, D. (2016). Comparative international entrepreneurship: A review and research agenda. *Journal of Management, 42*(1), 299–344.

Vahlne, J., & Johanson, J. (2020). The Uppsala model: Networks and micro-foundations. *Journal of International Business Studies, 51*, 4–10. https://doi.org/10.1057/s41267-019-00277-x

Case 2   Seaside hotels

Corporate entrepreneurship strategies in Spain, Germany and Asia

Teresa Aguiar-Quintana and Sabine Haller

Introduction and case selection

This case study evaluates the corporate entrepreneurship (CE) actions of a company that started its activity in the Canary Islands. First, we examine the antecedents of this international company and its settings with a brief theoretical framing in corporate entrepreneurship.

Sharma and Chrisman (1999) describe the hierarchy of CE and explain that corporate venturing (CV) can be divided into internal and external. Internal CV relates to the creation of new businesses that reside within the corporate structure or may be located outside the firm. However, corporations may also invest in early growth-stage businesses created by external parties (external CV), which includes corporate venture capital (CVC), licensing, acquisitions and joint ventures. This case study has the objective of providing the example of a family business (SC) as a good example of corporate entrepreneurship related to 'innovation actions' and the new acquisitions added to their portfolio over the last 40 years.

We start this section by explaining the context of this organisation and the key elements that will be conducted in this case. We then go on to study the environment and present an overview of the region where the organisation carries out its activities. Lastly, we detail the origin and evolution of the key elements of SC's corporate entrepreneurship actions.

For this study, three semi-structured interviews were conducted: the first with the Sales & Marketing Director of SC in Gran Canaria, Mrs Astrid van Wijk; the second with one of the owners, Mr Gregor Gerlach; and the third with Mr Pablo González-Haba, the Financial Director. The interviews were developed using an interview guide between April 2022 and September 2022.

Business profile and framework

Seaside Collection (SC) is an international hotel company founded in 1974 by Mr Theo Gerlach on the island of Gran Canaria. Currently, it has four hotels in the Canary Islands, one in mainland Spain, six in Germany and one in the Maldives. After 40 years of management, its business model has

DOI: 10.4324/9781003454465-3

become a benchmark for quality, reaching the highest levels of customer satisfaction and loyalty, and its hotels have been awarded the most prestigious[1] international awards and tributes. The commitment of SC to offering the highest levels of quality to its customers is evident through the management of the only 5-star deluxe hotel in Gran Canaria (whose customers include members of European royalty, film celebrities and famous entrepreneurs who access the island via their private jets) (Figure 2.1).

Theo Gerlach, a German businessman in the construction industry, first visited Gran Canaria in 1970. Surprised by the climate and landscape of the island, he decided to invest in several plots in the most selected areas that attracted the majority of tourists, all of them being situated in prime locations by the sea.

At that time, Germany offered a tax incentive for foreign investments in developing countries, as was the case with Spain in the late sixties. This circumstance encouraged him to launch real estate projects to sell to German investors. At that time, he could have hardly imagined that one day he would become a hotel investor. However, a change in German laws curtailed the initial project, and, given the difficulty of attracting investors, Mr Gerlach decided to rent his facilities to a hotel management company called Hotesa. More often than not, commercial endeavours occur during adversity, not unlike the present-day situation. The oil crisis of the early 70s had paralysed

Figure 2.1 Palm Beach hotel photo.

hundreds of projects, and Mr Gerlach watched with concern how the company that operated the hotels not only did not meet the established profitability indicators but also did not reach German customers' expectations who also voiced their discontent with the service received.

At that point, he decided to personally step in, creating his own tourist brand and managing and marketing varying business initiatives, starting in 1974 with the Hotel Don Gregory. His restless nature, passion for travel, and vast entrepreneurial wisdom formed the basis for the necessary training as an hotelier, predominantly based on his own insight as a client. Accordingly, his key objective was to provide his guests with the same attention he expected to receive at the world's best hotels. Given his discerning and demanding nature, as well as his keen assessment of good taste, the company's quality, service and professionalism were established from then onwards.

By this time, Mr Gerlach had chosen the Canary Islands, with its year-round vacation climate as the focus of his hotel chain. Following the fall of the Berlin Wall he decided to diversify and bought several properties in need of renovation in the east of the reunified Germany. Later, hotels in the north of the country were added to their portfolio. Almost 40 years later, SC is an international company (see Table 2.1). SC and its brand were officially established in 1984, with a logo design that portrays a seahorse, which embodies the main feature of its tourist hotels, i.e., the seaside. Today, SC comprises 12 hotels, all of which are consistently oriented to the principle of the luxury segment. As different as the target groups of the individual hotels may be, the orientation towards the needs of the luxury traveller is printed in the corporate strategy.

In addition to managing other businesses[2], the Gerlach family oversees the company, which is comprised of a well-established business group that has become a benchmark for quality, with a highly considered philosophy, a trademark of the owner and his children. The latter is actively involved in the management of the company, upholding the unique character and the vision on which the chain was founded: to offer its customers everything that they, as expert travellers, would expect to receive in the world's best hotels. In business terms, it could be said that the family has implemented a strategy associated with its business model, reaching the standards of the world's finest hotels. The Gerlach family, father Theo, son Gregor and daughter Anouchka, make all central decisions for the group. Today, Anouchka Gerlach is mainly responsible for the hotels in Spain, and Gregor Gerlach manages the German hotels, although he is also very involved in decisions on Spanish properties.

Some of the hotels have been hand-picked as part of select and unique portfolios of renowned hotels, such as the Gewandhaus, located in an historic building in the middle of the baroque old town in Dresden, which is part of the Marriott Autograph Group, a group of independent upper-upscale to luxury hotels with a strong identity, design style and high standards. Seaside Palm Beach in Gran Canaria and SIDE Hotel in Hamburg are associated with Design Hotels, a group of privately owned and operated hotels

Table 2.1 Seaside collection chain

Hotels in Spain	*Number of beds in the Canaries: 2,390*		
Gran Canaria	*Seaside* **Grand Hotel Residencia 5*GL**		
			Member of *The Leading Hotels of the World* – 94 rooms, 188 beds
			Built in 2000
	Seaside **Palm Beach 5***		
			Member of *Design Hotels* 328 rooms, 656 beds
			Built in 1974, completely renovated in 2004 and category upgraded
	Seaside **Sandy Beach 4***		
			256 rooms, 486 beds
			Built in 1986, completely renovated in 2004 and category upgraded
Lanzarote	*Seaside* **Los Jameos Playa 4***		
			530 rooms, 1,060 beds
			Built in 1994, continually Renovating
Valencia	*Westin Valencia 5*GL*		
			135 rooms, 270 beds
			Member of Westin
Hotels in Germany	*Number of beds in Germany: 1,400*		
	SIDE Hamburg 5* (Design Hotel) – 178 rooms		
	Park Hotel Leipzig 4* - 288 rooms		
	Abito Suites in Leipzig - 18 rooms		
	Residenz Hotel Chemnitz 4* - 193 rooms **Aalernhüs Hotel & Spa en St. Peter-Ording 5*** - 62 rooms **Gewandhaus Dresden 5*** - 97 rooms back in the hands of the Gerlach Family since 2015, member of Marriott Autograph Group		

(*Continued*)

Table 2.1 (Continued)

Hotels in Maldives	*Number of beds in Maldives: 272*
	Finolhu 125 Villas, 272 beds Built in 2016, owned since 2019 Member of Design Hotels

Source: Seaside Collection (2023).

distinguished by their original design, culture and architecture, and Grand Hotel Residencia, also in Gran Canaria, is a member of The Leading Hotels of the World, a collection of authentic luxury hotels committed to delivering an extraordinary experience of comfort and quality, and passionate service (Figure 2.2).

The Gerlach family doesn't like to speak about a 'hotel chain', which is why the company name was changed from Seaside Hotels to Seaside Collection.

Figure 2.2 Hotel gewandhaus.

The new name implies a 'collection' of exceptional and distinctive items, hotels with their own unique identity and marked individuality. With many hotel chains, all the 4- and 5-star hotels look alike. However, this is not the case with SC, where each hotel is unlike any of the others. What they all do have in common, though, is that they offer the best gastronomy in each category and the highest level of service. All four hotels in the Canary Islands are also similar in terms of location, in that they are all near the sea (Seaside) and all offer large terraces where guests can sit outside to have their meals and enjoy the excellent climate of eternal spring on the Islands all year through.

Regarding the question of the business organisation, Theo Gerlach, the founder of the company, is no longer working in the day-to-day running of the company. However, he is still involved in matters concerning new investments and the expansion of the business. His two children now run the hotel arm of the company. On the one hand, Gregor Gerlach is dedicated to the operations but also to the sales strategies, and on the other hand, Anouchka Gerlach is dedicated more to the decoration of the hotels, as well as being the sole owner of the Valencia Hotel. Both of them, brother and sister, are involved in all the other SC hotels. Therefore, at the top of the scale of the organisational chart would be the children of Theo Gerlach.

The Director of Sales & Marketing, Mrs Astrid van Wijk, is often in contact with Gregor Gerlach and consults him when she needs approval for sales-related matters. Furthermore, between them and the Director of Distribution & Revenue, they decide what they will do in relation to the contracts with tour operators and the rates to be established.

In the main office, they also have a Financial Director, Mr Pablo González-Haba, who has the role of CFO. Within the organisational structure, the general managers of the hotels report to CFO, and below them are the department managers. The main divisions are: Human Resources, Technical, Sales & Marketing, Reservations & Revenue & Distribution, Purchasing, and the Administration department. The Sales & Marketing Department is in charge of signing contracts with tour operators and agencies and everything related to sales & marketing, such as advertisements in magazines or online promotions not only abroad but also in the regional and national territories. They also attend international fairs and road shows to promote the hotels. Delving deeper into the Sales department, it is organised by markets, with a sales representative in charge of each country, thereby facilitating dialogue and knowledge of the current trends in each country in order to improve business management and communication within the company. Another noteworthy feature of the sales division is that it emphasises the importance of arranged informative visits for collaborating tour operators, as well as the press, paying close attention to every detail of these professional gatherings, an endeavour that contrasts with many of its competitors. The company's philosophy regarding the importance of attention to detail also manifests in its dealings with agencies and local representatives with whom it maintains a very close relationship. Moreover, annual meetings are held, which are highly valued within the industry and ensure continuity in the relationships between its members.

Looking back to the history of this organisation can give us an overview of the region in which the organisation carries out its activities, as well as the main political, legal, economic, technological and social conditions that characterise it. The history of SC also gives us an overview of the sector in terms of competitors, markets and trends.

In relation to the environment of the organisation and the respective competitors, markets and trends, Mrs Astrid van Wijk looks at a competitive set focused on analysing those hotels that compete with each of the hotels in SC's collection. In addition, she helps facilitate the company's constant evolution since the hotels are also continually changing in terms of refurbishments and service improvements. She confesses to us that, for them, their Grand Hotel Residencia has no competition on the island since it is the only 5-star Grand Luxury resort hotel in Gran Canaria; it can only be loosely compared with a small number of hotels in Tenerife, such as the Bahía del Duque, Iberostar Grand Mirador or The Ritz-Carlton Abama. On the other hand, their 5-star hotels do compare with other hotels on the island of Gran Canaria, and, in this sense, they have a new competitor: the Lopesan Costa Meloneras hotel, which has become a 5-star hotel. Mrs van Wijk, from her point of view, still does not see it as a true competitor due to the size of the Costa Meloneras hotel, which has 1,138 rooms. However, they are trying to raise the quality (for example, they have renovated all the rooms and even added two more rooms and a VIP area with Balinese beds), and thus, they have raised their prices, so it is actually starting to be considered as a competitor of Seaside Palm Beach hotel. In the competitive set, they also include The Villa del Conde hotel and the Hotel Faro, as both can be compared in some way with the Palm Beach Hotel, and the 4-star superior Santa Monica hotel is compared, for example, to the 4-star Seaside Sandy Beach.

In describing the environment, the Sales & Marketing Director first describes it in terms of the political sphere. He goes on to explain that they are unhappy about not having quality sunbeds on the beach for the guests, as well as good facilities like "Chiringuitos" that offer quality food and service. They also include the unfavourable conditions in which Playa del Inglés finds itself, due mainly to the outdated shopping centres, some of which are even being gradually abandoned. This is a weakness of the micro-destination in the municipality of San Bartolomé de Tirajana in Gran Canaria, which is one of the most important tourist destinations in Spain in terms of employment.

At a technological level, Mrs van Wijk points out that the local Tourism Board (Cabildo de Gran Canaria) is doing a great job since they are promoting technological progress on the island in terms of the Canary Islands website— making it very interactive and cutting edge—and the Internet and Wi-Fi service. This is a very important action because when fibre optics did not reach many locations on the island, they often had to deal with customer complaints; however, this was resolved some years ago. These technological advances have been even more difficult in Lanzarote as installation takes much longer. However, in terms of technology, the company representative admits that the tourism board is doing good promotions and working well on the issue of connectivity, although they still have a lot of work to do at the council level.

In terms of the economic aspect of the environment, Mrs Van Wijk confirms that a high volume of traffic comes through the municipality of San Bartolomé de Tirajana, where all the company's hotels are located on the island. She is optimistic about the winter season, as there is a tendency for an increase in sales.

As a typical entrepreneur, Theo Gerlach acted when opportunities arose to expand his portfolio without too much risk. One must understand his position in the early seventies in order to understand his vision of the service provided by his hotels. The owner could not understand how the operator of his hotels, and most of the tourist companies on the island at that time, offered such inadequate service to their customers without considering their characteristics and customs. The first decision that marked the launch of his company was based on that observation. Thus, in 1974, Mr Gerlach changed the whole gastronomic offering, the schedules, and even the ways meals were served in the hotels to suit the tastes of his guests. He was a pioneer in introducing "German-style" brewed coffee and would allow customers to consume as much as they wanted without having to pay for each additional cup. He also introduced the full breakfast buffet, with a wide selection of foods, which other hotels would soon copy. Thus, he began his efforts to ensure the best quality in culinary offerings, which would become the most significant feature of the excellent service ratings from his hotels' guests.

The company's strategy is focused on the main objective of the company, which is to offer the luxury of the highest quality to their customers throughout all areas of their hotels. When asked how the group's hotels differ from their competitors, son Gregor Gerlach answers: the food. Early on, father Theo Gerlach recognised that, "[…] every euro invested in improving food quality impacts more on customer satisfaction than any other action carried out with the same amount of money". The value he gives to the cuisine is so high that the food vendor selection takes place through the blind tasting of the quality of each product, without making price a decisive factor in the selection criteria.

Therefore, new opportunities arose to acquire and extensively renovate hotels in the south of Gran Canaria. In 2018, the land to build a luxury hotel in Pasito Blanco was prepared, followed by the acquisition of the resort in the Maldives in 2019. This expansion was prompted by the consideration that the Canary Islands were often no longer the main holiday destination for European tourists, who instead considered a third or fourth vacation during the year. The Gerlach family searched for new attractive destinations and found what they were looking for in the Maldives. However, all of the Seaside Group's projects have one thing in common: they appeal to guests in the luxury segment. This decision forms the core of the hotel group's competitive strategy.

The relationship between the property and the staff is competent and effective, based on clearly illustrating professional objectives and offering the staff flexibility to make the appropriate decisions to achieve these objectives without neglecting the necessary supervision to transmit and safeguard the standards set forth by the family. Accordingly, if you visit one of the company's hotels, you will notice a second special feature: the well-trained, helpful and accommodating staff. This also led to a competitive advantage because the overall design and the rooms of 5-star hotels are often not significantly different from one another, but excellent staff are very difficult to emulate for the competition.

For any hospitality company, the most difficult task is perhaps staff management. Theo Gerlach laments how difficult it is to get qualified personnel to cover basic positions in hotels. He thinks that language training is clearly insufficient for the importance of the industry in the Canaries and that training efforts have focused mainly on managerial positions, forgetting the importance of staff who have daily direct relationships with clients as receptionists, waiters, pool maintenance staff, and front-office staff in general.

The management assesses the skills and behaviour of these professionals from the moment they start their internship at the hotel, underlying the importance of the hotel staff's attitude towards the customer as the most important quality dimension to consider when assessing the potential of a future employee. Meanwhile, SC offers training to all their employees and reinforces language training through exchanges with their hotels in Germany, assuming all the training costs. In addition, the company establishes wage conditions superior to the average remunerations in the sector. It justifies this distinction because they also believe that their employees are better prepared than the industry average, and consequently, a better-trained employee deserves a higher salary. The company has 778 employees in its four hotels in the Canaries.

When looking at the key elements of the business, we can see that much of its success is due to meeting and satisfying the needs of the most demanding customers, continuously developing and improving services found in the world's most exclusive hotels. But with the company's expansion, new tasks appear. Guests from different countries have a wide variety of demands that need to be recognised and anticipated. Moreover, external factors, such as the COVID-19 pandemic, with its accompanying lockdowns and travel bans, also presented new challenges that the hotel company was not initially prepared for. However, it has overcome the difficulties of the last few years through corporate entrepreneurship and innovation actions.

Corporate entrepreneurship and innovation actions

According to Phan et al. (2009), corporate entrepreneurship (CE) refers to the process of organisational renewal and, previously, Guth and Ginsberg (1990) defined CE as related to two phenomena: (1) innovation and corporate venturing activities, and (2) renewal activities related to a corporation's ability to compete and take risks. Sharma and Chrisman (1999) describe the hierarchy of CE and explain that corporate venturing (CV) can be divided into internal and external. Internal CV relates to the creation of new businesses that reside within the corporate structure or may be located outside the firm. However, corporations may also invest in early growth-stage businesses created by external parties (external CV), which includes corporate venture capital (CVC), licensing, acquisitions and joint ventures. Seaside Collection (SC) is a good example of corporate entrepreneurship related to innovation actions and the new acquisitions added to their portfolio during the last 40 years.

Regarding the most notable corporate entrepreneurship actions carried out in recent years, the Sales & Marketing Director describes the innovative actions around the implementation of a new Property Management System (PMS) called Protel, which was already installed in hotels in Germany before the pandemic, as well as in the Grand Hotel Residencia. After the Grand Hotel Residencia, it was installed in the new 5-star hotel in the Maldives, called Finolhu Maldives. After the reopening of the hotels after lockdown, it was installed in the rest of the hotels, this being one of the most important projects in recent years after the pandemic. Protel has very good "business intelligence", so getting statistics is easy, and you can build it your way, and from there, you get the data relevant for hotel managers. With this PMS, a new Point of Sale System (POS) called "SELZ" was installed. This helps to take orders from the waiters digitally without the need to use pen and paper. A new interface between this POS and the storage control program called "KOST" was also developed.

In addition, the construction of the new business offices in Gran Canaria, where the different departments are located, was another corporate entrepreneurship action after COVID-19, bringing more innovation and space for the company staff.

Thus, new processes have taken place in the hotels in Gran Canaria with renovations inside the kitchens and other departments that have led to greater customer satisfaction, as well as better working conditions for employees. The selection of name-brand products for the room amenities, fresh fruit in lounges available to customers, and a dedicated concierge service eager to meet any special (or simple) requests, such as medicine from the pharmacy, are some of the common attentions received in SC's hotels.

Furthermore, they invested around 8 million euros in the Lanzarote hotel, which included refurbishing not only the swimming pools and Pool Bar but also the "Piano bar" and the "Belingo bar" (where performances are held at night), and one of the meeting rooms was also completely changed. They changed all the railings, windows and floors of the balconies throughout the hotel and renovated the bathrooms in the junior suites. The rooms were not restored due to the pending Pasito Blanco project for which they received permission in December 2019. The construction was due to take place in June 2020, but due to the pandemic, it had to be stopped. In this case, the entire refurbishment of the Jameos Hotel in Lanzarote was not carried out and was postponed. In the future, they plan to start changing the furniture, starting with the blocks furthest from the centre of the hotel and with the bathrooms and finishing with the central part of the hotel. These corporate entrepreneurship and innovation actions are planned to be taken within 3–4 years, including another refurbishment of the pool area for families and children, where they have the tennis court that would be located on a plot of land in front of the hotel.

In the hotel in Valencia, the refurbishment of the restaurant, corridors and rooms is being carried out during 2021, 2022 and 2023, starting with the restaurant refurbishments. The person in charge of interior design works from the headquarters located in Gran Canaria and travels abroad for the various projects. Many famous soccer players stay at the Valencia Hotel since it is close to the stadium and has about 135 rooms, including the suites.

At the vacation destinations, the focus is on vacationers, whereas in the German city hotels, it is mainly business travellers who are addressed. They are expected to fill the hotels to capacity during the week, while private guests make up the bulk of bookers at the weekend.

However, the main antecedents of the company's corporate entrepreneurial actions are associated with the external environment. Tourism is a global industry, and the dynamism of the sector is evident, with more than 15 million tourists arriving in the Canary Islands in 2019 (before COVID-19). Furthermore, the internationalisation of many tourism companies is a strategy in response to the new global markets. For SC, 20 years ago, 80% of the company's target group consisted of German guests. This made it easier for management to identify and satisfy their needs. However, by the mid-2010s, new opportunities for greater diversification arose due to internationalisation. Today, the clientele comprises numerous nationalities, with guests coming from the United Kingdom, Spain, The Netherlands, Belgium, France, Scandinavia, some Eastern European countries, the United States, South America, Australia, India, and China, in addition to Germany. This brings a number of advantages since if bookings from one country collapse, they can be compensated by those from another country. In this respect, diversification has led to greater stability. Hence, the demands on hotel quality management are growing because different cultures also have different quality requirements. Here, the family business faces the great challenge of doing equal justice to all guests. While for German tourists, the food quality is the most significant factor, for the British, food and service quality are equally decisive. For South Americans, service makes up 100% of a successful vacation experience.

Other antecedents of the company's corporate entrepreneurial actions are associated with the organisational context. In this sense, SC highly values its business relationship with tour operators and agencies. Far from seeing them as a threat or as an intermediary to sidestep, they are considered as business partners. Traditional travel agencies have been instrumental in its positioning strategy. The company enjoys the highest quality recognition from German agencies that recommend SC hotels to their most demanding and discerning customers. Even nowadays, when bookings via the Internet dominate and sales via travel agencies are already frequently regarded as outdated, this travel agencies still represents the most important sales channel for SC. As such, SC avoids the price competition that is typical when bookings are made via platforms on the internet. In order to escape this price competition, travel agencies experienced in consulting offer an alternative for the sale of stays in luxury hotels. It forms the central pillar of the sales strategy. Bookings supplement this via the company's own website and sales via booking platforms. In this way, the company operates on multiple channels and is not dependent on a single form of distribution.

Another antecedent of the company's corporate entrepreneurship action is the high customer retention rate by the SC group. The company enjoys a high percentage of repeat guests, especially during the winter months. For the Gerlach family, the customers are loyal to their hotels because of the care they receive. They are especially helpful with repeat clients; for example, 60% of the guests at Palm Beach Hotel are Mr Gerlach's acquaintances and have been for over 30 years. Repeat customers feel at home, and many of them ask to stay in the same room. This is one customer request that the hotel tries to guarantee from the moment the booking is made. The staff remembers their names, their tastes and even their favourite appetiser. Likewise, a change is offered if a customer does not feel comfortable in his or her room. The staff moves and rearranges the customer's belongings without causing him or her any discomfort.

There are no special customer relationship programmes for guests, but returning customers can enjoy welcome gifts and special attention. However, the Seaside loyalty points programme is of great importance for the company, which is directed exclusively towards agencies, who can obtain points according to their sales volume so that their employees can enjoy vacations at the company's hotels. To do this, they have a website exclusively designed to cater to travel agents and to facilitate the redemption of points (http://sunshine-club.Seaside-hotels.de/).

Asked about the external triggers that initiated the previously mentioned corporate entrepreneurship actions, Mrs van Wijk conveys that changes in the times and styles and tastes are directly linked to the refurbishment projects. She remarks that SC retains a very high standard of maintenance of the hotels' facilities but concedes that although, by way of an example, the non-renovated bathrooms at the Seaside Los Jameos in Lanzarote remain in perfect condition, if the hotel were to be built today, the bathrooms would not be done in the same way—they would be done in a more modern way, using other types of materials. She also points out that, over the years, some hotels have undergone refurbishment only when the elements of the rooms or bathrooms have begun to deteriorate; thus, they decide to refurbish to improve the overall condition. The Sales & Marketing Director tells us that times change and that the hospitality industry must adapt to today's trends, adding that customers' requirements, in turn, change. An example is the Hotel Palm Beach: if this hotel had been built today, they would have chosen to make the bathrooms larger, as well as the rooms, but at that time, the style and design of the facilities met the standards of the guests and was in vogue. The refurbishment of the offices was carried out to serve new projects on the horizon and the growth of the company, which includes the Pasito Blanco hotel, along with other new projects.

Regarding the question about the main supporting infrastructure that allows corporate actions to be carried out, Mrs van Wijk mentions financing as among the most crucial supports. In part, financing is done through banking entities, but also through what revenue SC as a whole has generated over the years; this is why the pandemic, which led to several months of closure for the hotels, forced the decision to suspend Pasito Blanco development. However, the Sales & Marketing Director is assured that the earthwork will resume; the hole where the foundations of the hotel will be located has already been made. The area of one of the two hotels has also been fenced, but as of now, they are waiting for the post-COVID-19 recuperation of hotel profits, after which reinvestment will be made. She also adds that it was much more profitable for them to open the hotels as soon as possible after the pandemic rather than to keep them closed, with the exception of the Jameos Playa in Lanzarote (they decided to keep it closed in order to reform it fully).

The most recent and severe difficulty for the process of innovation and corporate entrepreneurship was the COVID-19 lockdown and the following sanitary requirements. The company had to decide based on the "break-even" and "break-open" points. The latter ratio considers the point where it costs less to open the hotel than to have it closed. Currently, all the hotels are open. In any case, the company was able to turn this a priori negative event into a productive time for developing certain actions that were planned but were difficult to organise with an open hotel full of guests. For example, in Finolhu, the hotel in Maldives, they had planned to renew the area where the seaplane arrives to drop off guests and to substitute the wooden passageways to the villas, which need to be changed every 3–4 years due to climatology; thus, they took advantage of that time to do this, along with a complete redecoration of restaurants and rooms, consequently and fortuitously avoiding the disturbances it likely would have caused to guests and their experience of such a high-level hotel. This hotel opened in November 2020 and has not closed again. The purchase of Finolhu was a very long and complex process; Astrid van Wijk tells us she received a call at the end of December 2018 commenting that the family was about to buy a hotel in the Maldives and from that moment on, she spent seven months working non-stop, gathering information and learning about the Maldives in order to implement the SC system and initiate sales through all the various distribution systems. She had to make contact with a large number of tour operators, take into account many factors regarding how tourism develops in the Maldives, establish which markets work best, and many other things. It was an intensive process of receiving all the contracts Finolhu had with different companies, tour operators and suppliers. She confirms it wasn't easy, but she learned a lot (Figure 2.3).

Figure 2.3 Finolhu hotel photo.

The installation of the PMS "Protel" was also a very long and drawn-out process. The first few years were spent just evaluating other systems since implementing such a complex program represents a huge investment in time and money and takes many years to set up. It is also very difficult to execute since you must have the necessary training for employees; the old program must be removed and the new one installed.

To overcome challenges in implementing corporate entrepreneuial actions, many decisions are centralised.—As such, they are made by the owners and communicated to the directors once the decision has been made. An example of this procedure was the purchase in the Maldives. On the other hand, other decisions are discussed in the weekly management meetings and are held by the directors of the four hotels in Gran Canaria. They normally discuss how the sales are going and whether any important decisions need to be made. In turn, they discuss details about the staff and—on a monthly basis—ideas related to hotel refurbishment and modernisation that may appeal to new and specific customer segments. Finally, the meeting with the owners is held and every two months and Gregor Gerlach also usually visits the island 4–5 times a year. During these visits where meets with the hotel managers individually and the whole board of directors.

Finally, the main barriers or difficulties for corporate entrepreneurship actions are mostly related to issues in the supply chain. The Ukrainian war and the associated distribution problems are causing suppliers to either fail to deliver, or for the materials to be delayed. These issues can also be attributed to lagging effects of the pandemic, with difficulties supplying metals and transportation problems causing significant delays.

Regarding the most significant achievements among them are the positive reviews of their customers, the high retention rates of guests and their positive evaluations of the renovations accomplished by the company. As for the PMS, decision-making is much easier since it provides better data, and everything is much faster and more agile, especially given that the guest now has to spend less time waiting. There is even a connection between the opening of doors: they changed the locks—in the past, a card had to be inserted, but now they are contactless; in the future, the doors will be opened using a smartphone app or with a smartwatch or bracelet, this being a great innovation.

Epilogue

Like all companies in the hotel industry, SC was hit hard by the pandemic and the associated lockdowns and travel restrictions. Temporarily, sales plummeted by up to two-thirds in some cases. However, the choice of locations and the decisions made years earlier to diversify helped to dampen the impact and stabilise the financial situation. The Canary Islands were less affected by the spread of the virus than Central Europe due to their climatic conditions in the winter months of 2020. Not all countries were equally severely affected by the lockdowns at the same time. If it was problematic for, for example, the Germans to travel, the British could come and vice versa. But the star of the group during the pandemic was the hotel in the Maldives, with its highly international target group and booking figures that were higher than in 2019.

In general, the leisure sector is proving to be very stable considering the fact that people want to travel, especially after long periods of restriction. At the beginning of 2022, more bookings than ever before were made for hotels, although cancellations also rose to unprecedented levels. By contrast, the situation was more problematic for German hotels, where bookings at the start of 2022 were still well below those in 2019. However, in the Canary Islands, there are signs that the leisure sector is proving stable. Before 2019, the ratio was 60% business to 40% leisure. At the beginning of 2023, the leisure segment accounted for 70% of bookings.

The main lesson learned is that a forward-looking strategy and a strong commitment to core values, as embodied by the Gerlach family, can bring a company safely through turbulent times. When we asked Mr Gerlach for his recommendations to future tourism professionals in the Canaries, his answer was: "Travel more. Travel the world and see what they do in other parts of the world. Be mindful of the fact that we compete with everyone, not only with the neighbouring hotel. Be open-minded, pay attention and choose the best references for each activity. I would also recommend this to the politicians of the Canaries. You should study how the tourist areas, beaches and public services are managed elsewhere. In these matters, the Islands are at a disadvantage with respect to other destinations, and here we rely heavily on tourism".

Even today, the ongoing analysis of the best practices of service in tourism is carried out by assessors travelling to the most innovative and luxurious establishments in the world. Lodged as customers, they evaluate every detail within each facility: the decor, hotel staff performance, special facilities, gastronomy, communal areas within the hotel premises, swimming pools, sun beds, the quality of amenities, customer fidelity and, ultimately, any infrastructure or service that can be integrated into their own hotels to ensure they maintain the same level as any state-of-the-art, luxury property in the world. In this way, new developments and trends are identified very early on and can be adapted and adopted by the company's hotels.

Theo Gerlach and his family are aware that their business consists of a few individual hotels and that they cannot compete with large chains in the context of the global hotel industry. Therefore, they set certain standards that every new property must meet. In addition to the importance of an excellent location, these include a minimum size that should be met. They assume that each hotel generates an average annual turnover of 20 million euros per year. They are very selective in their expansion plans; a small hotel chain cannot afford to make bad decisions. One basic consideration is the high level of political stability of the region, which makes it possible to plan for the long term.

One other important lesson that he highlights came via the analysis of the purchase of the hotel in the Maldives; he emphasises the hardships of those months due to the sheer amount of work. However, he also concedes that it represented seven months of valuable learning, which was also very interesting. It stands to reason that each project provides the opportunity to acquire new knowledge, which helps with the decisions on what should or should not be done in future.

Sources

The following people have been interviewed to develop this case:
   Mr Theo Gerlach (President of the Seaside Collection Hotels)
   Mr Gregor Gerlach (Owner of Seaside Collection Hotels)
   Mrs Astrid van Wijk (Director of Sales & Marketing Seaside Collection Hotels Canary Islands)

Notes

1 *Tui Holly, Condé Nast Traveler, 2022 Grand Hotel Residencia Number 2 of the best 25 hotels in Spain in Trip Advisor, Holidaycheck*. In 2022, the *Seaside Grand Hotel Residencia* was awarded 1st Price as the best hotel in the Western Mediterranean and Atlantic amongst the 100 best hotels of the *TUI* program in the world. In 2021 all four hotels in the Canaries where awarded Travelife Gold Sustainibility award.
2 The Group owns several companies in Germany dedicated to different activities, from construction (Theo Gerlach Wohnungsbau-Unternehmen GmbH & Co. or

Gerlach Wohnungsbau AG), to hotels, food companies (Bagel Bakery GmbH) and restaurants (VAP Leipzig GmbH & Co). It is a fairly complex network of companies, in which several subsidiaries are included by different Gerlach family members with varying degrees of ownership interest in each.

References

Guth, W., & Ginsberg, A. (1990). Guest editors' introduction: Corporate entrepreneurship. *Strategic Management Journal*, 11(S), 5–15.

Phan, P., Wright, M., Udrasaran, D., & Wee-Liang, T. (2009). Corporate entrepreneurship: Current research and future directions. *Journal of Business Venturing*, 24, 197–205.

Sharma, P., & Chrisman, J. J. (1999). Toward a reconciliation of the definitional issues in the field of corporate entrepreneurship. *Entrepreneurship Theory and Practice*, 23, 11–27.

Case 3 More than a crisis? Corporate entrepreneurship and COVID-19 pandemic in Austrian tourism
Case study of a family-run hospitality business

Christoph Pachucki and Ursula Scholl-Grissemann

Introduction and case selection

Tourism plays a crucial economic role in many countries around the world. With more than 46 million annual arrivals and about 153 million overnight stays, Austria is one of the most tourism-intense states globally (Federal Ministry Republic Austria, 2019). Family-run SMEs make up 67% of Austrian tourism businesses (Austrian Institute for SME Research, 2020). Although definitions of family business vary, they widely agree on constitutive core characteristics: the business is family-owned, family members are involved in management, and objectives go beyond profit maximisation. In addition to profitability, stability, autonomy, cross-generational business continuation and qualitative factors (e.g., enjoyment of work, tradition) drive family enterprises. Geographically, Austrian family-run tourism businesses are particularly located in rural regions with low population density (Andersson et al., 2002). These features guided the selection of the business for this case study. Specifically, the *Relax Resort Kothmühle* (hereafter called *Kothmühle*) was chosen because it is an Austrian family-run hospitality business.

The case study investigates corporate entrepreneurship (CE) in Austrian hospitality from two perspectives. First, triggers, settings and outcomes of CE are examined. Second, the impact of COVID-19 on CE is studied. Before the actual case study, the specific business, its environment, and a brief theoretical framing are presented. The case study collected data from a literature review, secondary data analysis (e.g., business reports) and semi-structured interviews. The interviews were conducted with the junior CEO of the company between December 10th 2021, and April 30th 2022, using an interview guide.

Business profile and environment

The case studied in this paper, the *Kothmühle*, is a family-owned hotel currently run by the fourth generation. The land, originally a mill for agriculture,

DOI: 10.4324/9781003454465-4

has been owned by the family since 1866. The farm was first used for hospitality in 1920 when an inn was opened and further expanded with rooms in 1955. Today, the *Kothmühle* operates as 4-star superior hotel and provides 92 rooms, 9 meeting rooms and an 800 m² wellness area. The business operates in two sectors. On the one hand, leisure travellers are a target group. Products and services aim to fulfil their relaxation, culinary, regional exploration, and outdoor activity needs. By contrast, the hotel also addresses the meetings industry and business travellers. Currently, these two sectors are balanced (50% leisure travellers, 50% business, meetings, and events).

Since 2004, the business has been structurally with three levels: management, middle management, and staff. The fourth generation of the family is currently responsible for management. The third generation, as former general managers, and the fifth generation, as future general managers, are also actively involved in hotel operations. The hotel management by the family with cooperation between various generations is essential for both the image of the business and service provision. Middle management consists of four department heads (reception, floor, kitchen, service). With 55 employees, the hotel is classified as a medium-sized enterprise. Due to the shortage of regional hospitality employees, the staff structure is shifting (2010: 90% regional employees, 2022: 65% regional employees and 35% national and international employees).

The *Kothmühle* is located in Lower Austria, with a geographical size of 19,179.56 m², the largest of nine states in Austria. Lower Austria is separated into six tourism destinations (Lower Austria Tourism, 2021). One of these destinations is the *Mostviertel*, which is home to the *Kothmühle* resort. Although Austria is a globally popular tourism destination, only 4.7% of total overnight stays in Austria can be attributed to Lower Austria. Thus, compared to Austria's leading destinations (e.g., Vienna, Tyrol), tourism in Lower Austria is less pronounced and the destination itself is less in demand nationally and internationally. For the business, the environment results in benefits but also drawbacks. On the one hand, the hotel business faces little regional competition. Of 16,649 accommodation establishments in Austria, only 1,375 are located in Lower Austria. Hence, Lower Austria has relatively few hospitality businesses compared to the provinces with the most (Tyrol: 5,656, Salzburg: 2,610). Of the hospitality businesses in Lower Austria, 338 of these are classified as hotels.. Only 23 of these hotels are, in turn, categorised as 4-star superior hotels like the *Kothmühle* (Austrian Economic Chamber, 2021). On the other hand, the comparatively low demand for stays in Lower Austria demonstrates the need to actively establish an image, create brand awareness, and provide attractive products to generate consumers.

Corporate entrepreneurship and COVID-19 pandemic in tourism: Literature review

Subject to many external impacts (e.g., economic, political, social, technological), high competition, and its service- and experience-based character, the tourism sector requires high levels of innovation. The need for entrepreneurial behavior arises from both constant trends in markets (e.g., consumer behavior) and disruptive changes (e.g., crises) (Backer & Ritchie, 2017; Çakar, 2018; Ritchie & Jiang, 2019). The impact of COVID-19, as such a disruptive event, on tourism businesses results from two main factors: first, authority decisions (e.g., level of state subsidies, length of lockdowns) and second, internal business characteristics (e.g., types of products, number of employees, financial reserves) (Breier et al., 2021). In the course of the COVID-19 pandemic, most national authorities alternated between phases of lockdown and phases of gradual opening alongside specific restrictions and regulations (Ketter & Avraham, 2021). This also applies to the state of Austria, which resulted in three lockdowns between March 2020 and May 2021. Austrian hotels had to close for months, and due to their service character, hospitality products cannot be stored for sale later. Thus, the Austrian hospitality industry was hit hard by the crisis (Bachtrögler et al., 2020; Pachucki et al., 2022), which in turn resulted in an increasing need for CE first to overcome the crisis and second recover and restart after the crisis (Breier et al., 2021).

Current research defines CE as business innovation, openness, and proactiveness. CE represents a process rather than a punctual implementation of discrete measures (e.g., Holt et al., 2007). Both internal and external factors drive CE processes in tourism. While external triggers refer to constant market changes (e.g., consumer behaviour, competition) and disruptive events (e.g., tourism crises), internal triggers stem from the business itself (e.g., core competencies, culture, visions) (Backer & Ritchie 2017, Kessler et al., 2015; Mumford & Hester, 2012). Once processes of CE are triggered, they need to be transferred into specific concepts and finally result in innovation as the outcome (Bascavusoglu-Moreau et al., 2013; Holt et al., 2007). Innovations vary in their focus (products and services, marketing methods, internal processes), orientation (infrastructure resource innovations vs marketing management innovations), time factor (strategic vs operative), technological involvement (technological vs nontechnological innovations), and level of novelty (business, local, regional, national, global) (Kuscer, 2013; Ottenbacher, 2007; Zach, 2012). Figure 3.1 demonstrates the process of CE.

COVID-19-evoked changes (e.g., travel restrictions, lockdowns) resulting in new market conditions, requiring CE. Similar to a non-pandemic context, CE during COVID-19 resembles incremental processes rather than distinct individual innovations (Breier et al., 2021). The question of how far a hospitality business can drive CE during a pandemic depends on its crisis

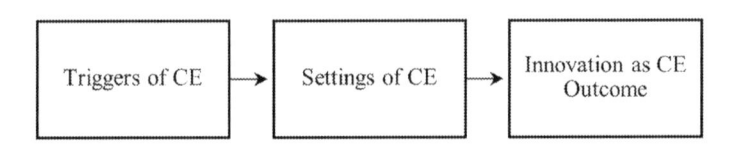

Figure 3.1 Corporate entrepreneurship process.

resilience (Provenzano & Volo, 2022; Weidmann et al., 2022). According to Ketter and Avraham (2021), crisis management can be separated into three stages: crisis preparation, crisis response, and crisis recovery. Establishing resilience and, hence, conditions that enable CE during crises is part of the preparation period. Many countries around the world, including Austria, implemented measures (e.g., subsidies) to lessen the economic impact of the pandemic. However, overcoming crises in the long run depends on the resilience of individual businesses (e.g., financial reserves) (Kuscer et al., 2021; Weidmann et al., 2022). Current research reveals both COVID-19-evoked impacts that hinder and those that facilitate CE (e.g., Breier et al., 2021; Kuscer et al., 2021). Due to its impact, the pandemic further results in the modification of tourism business models in terms of cancellation policies, product portfolio (e.g., discontinuation of services), and human resource strategies (e.g., reduction of leave, short-time working) (Breier et al., 2021; Weidmann et al., 2022).

Corporate entrepreneurship and COVID-19 in Austrian hospitality: Triggers, settings, and outcomes of corporate entrepreneurship

Studying the specific case of *Kothmühle* supports the understanding of CE as a corporate attitude and intra- and intergenerational process: "*It's a process. The process of constantly asking: what can we do and what needs to be done.*" In line with previous research (cf. Figure 3.1), such processes are triggered by internal and external drivers, further shaped by organisational settings, and finally result in innovation as an outcome.

The case study confirms the relevance of ***internal and external triggers*** for CE (cf. Table 3.1). Based on the semi-structured interviews, ***external drivers*** can, in turn, be classified into global and regional factors. Global factors refer to changes in consumer behaviour arising from socioeconomic conditions

Table 3.1 Triggers of Corporate Entrepreneurship

Triggers of corporate entrepreneurship		
external triggers	global	COVID-19, consumer behaviour, market trends, digitalisation, urbanisation
	regional	location and destination, regional cooperation
internal triggers	structural-organisational	defined areas of responsibility, clear organisational and procedural structure, advice from external experts, training and education
	personal	experiences, qualifications, competencies, needs and visions of business stakeholders

Source: Prepared by authors (2023)

(e.g., urbanisation, digitalisation) and disruptive events (e.g., the COVID-19 pandemic). The interviewee explained, for instance, that customers from the meeting industry have significantly changed. They now expect not only a high-quality meeting infrastructure but also additional products and services (e.g., wellness, culinary, regional experiences). Another example of changes in consumer behaviour is the increasing demand for outdoor and nature-based products, which the COVID-19 pandemic has further strengthened. Regional factors as external drivers refer to the specific conditions at a destination. As mentioned, the *Kothmühle* operates in a low tourism destination, the *Mostviertel*. The interviewee explains: "*We need to actively generate guests and establish a strong image because the region is not one where people just go.*" In the hospitality sector, a unique selling proposition can result from the specific location and destination (e.g., location directly at the ski lift, location at the bathing lake). In the case of the *Kothmühle*, the location is more of a competitive disadvantage (e.g., low demand, less familiar destination), which results in a need for constant CE in terms of business strategy, business model, marketing communication, and product development. Next to location, cooperation is a regional driver of CE. According to the qualitative study, regional businesses (e.g., farms, restaurants, hotels) often focus on a niche (e.g., pear mustard, cider road). These specific regional concepts lead to cooperation, resulting in CE in terms of new products or events (e.g., theme dinners).

Entrepreneurial activities further arise from *internal triggers*, which, in the case of *Kothmühle,* can be distinguished into structural-organisational and personal triggers. Structural-organisational factors refer to positions in the business. Clearly defined positions and the distinction between strategic and operative tasks foster innovation. "*Once you are involved in everyday business, you lose the strategic view*" the interviewee explained. Structural-organisational drivers further refer to the creation of framework conditions favouring CE. The business, for instance, is regularly coached by tourism consultants and conducts workshops for families and staff. Personal drivers, on the other hand, represent preferences and qualifications of individual business stakeholders (e.g., family members and employees). Typically, in family businesses, the individual family members also bring individual experiences to the business. This is either professional experience (e.g., internships, former employment) or personal experience (e.g., travel, holidays).

Once processes of CE are triggered, *settings* to establish and specify concepts are required. In the case of *Kothmühle*, the conversion of triggers into specific concepts takes place through communication and the generation of frameworks. According to the qualitative interviews, communication is key to managing CE in the conceptualisation and implementation phases. While communication with and to employees happens in formal settings (e.g., weekly meetings with team leaders, training for employees), communication within the family occurs mainly in informal situations (e.g., lunch, family events). Alongside communication, settings impact entrepreneurial development. According to the *Kothmühle*, it is essential to regularly generate settings in which relevant stakeholders actively work on CE themes. First, the family itself regularly conducts annual workshops coached by tourism consultants (e.g., takeover of the business, investments, renovations). Second, weekly meetings with the department leaders are held. Third, employees are trained in internal and external workshops.

Once CE is triggered by internal and external factors and further focused by communication and frameworks, it results in ***innovation***. In the semi-structured interviews, the *Kothmühle* was asked about specific past innovations as outcomes of CE. The examples given show that all types of innovations (product, marketing, process, organisational) are relevant to the business. Below, two innovations (marketing innovation, product innovation) are described. As mentioned earlier, the hotel operates in a low tourism region, which results in a constant need for marketing communication, image establishment, and brand positioning. The management decided on a brand-redesign since the resort was formerly more known for meetings, events, and business customers. To address leisure travellers specifically, the name was changed to *Relax Resort Kothmühle*. The innovation can be classified as new for the business and further as a non-technological promotional innovation with a marketing focus. In 2019, the last rooms from the 80s were renovated entirely (e.g., sanitary facilities, technical equipment, interior design). Since rooms represent the core products of a hotel, the renovation resulted in a higher quality of overall service provision. This innovation can be described as an infrastructure-resource investment and, further, as a technological and non-technological product innovation.

According to the case study, CE is hindered by two main factors: the specific characteristics of a family business and economic aspects. The business is currently run by the fourth generation. Generational experiences, approaches, and values interact, influencing innovation processes. On the other hand, economic aspects affect innovations. While a major innovation is implemented (e.g., conversion of rooms, expansion of wellness area), hotel operation is possible only to a limited extent or not at all. In this respect, innovations must be planned precisely and economic considerations must be integrated.

Impact of COVID-19 pandemic on corporate entrepreneurship

As discussed in Sections 3 and 4.1, internal and external factors trigger CE in tourism. The COVID-19 pandemic represents an external driver. COVID-19-evoked changes (e.g., travel restrictions, lockdowns) result in new market conditions, which require entrepreneurial thinking and actions. Studying the family-run hotel business *Kothmühle* in the context of COVID-19 reveals factors shaping CE ability as well as impacts fostering and hindering CE during crises (cf. Table 3.2).

The case study confirms previous research findings on the importance of building ***crisis resilience*** over the long term. In the *Kothmühle*, strategic forecasting and planning (e.g., market observation), establishing financial reserves

Table 3.2 Corporate Entrepreneurship in Austrian Hospitality and COVID-19 Crisis

Corporate Entrepreneurship in Austrian Hospitality and COVID-19 Crisis

factors shaping resilience and CE during crises	strategic forecasting and planning, financial reserves, avoiding investment backlog, communication with customers and employees
impacts fostering CE	increase in national and regional demand longer stays, development and strengthening of products, available time resources (e.g., for training), strategic and operational improvement (e.g., handbooks, guidelines, working from home)
impacts hindering CE	loss of bookings, financial pressure, waste of resources (e.g., food products, unused infrastructure), loss of employees, migration of workforces to other sectors

Source: Elaboration by authors (2023).

(e.g., constant analysis of saving potentials), constant investment, and thus avoiding investment backlogs, as well as communication to customers and employees, are specific measures shaping business resilience. These factors enable tourism businesses to overcome the COVID-19 pandemic, recover in the aftermath, and even use crisis periods for CE.

In line with current publications, the present case study reveals both **positive impacts fostering CE** and negative impacts hindering CE. The COVID-19 pandemic is increasing demand for rural regional and national destinations with low population density. The case examined here, the *Kothmühle*, benefits from this trend. The increased demand for domestic travel led to an increase in the length of stays, especially in the summer season. Longer stays, in turn, result not only in economic potential but also in the need to develop new products and enhance established services. "*If guests stay a week rather than a weekend, you need to provide more and new products and services, from culinary to activities*", the interviewee explained. The company investigated in the case study assumes that the higher interest in domestic travel will continue after the pandemic. Another positive impact identified in the case study is available resources. The specific circumstances of COVID-19 (e.g., lockdowns, travel restrictions) freed up time and human resources, which were actively used to support CE. In the case of *Kothmühle*, available resources have been used in two main ways. First, for strategic and operational improvement, which results in more modern and effective processes and structures (e.g., working from home, guidelines for onboarding new employees, handbooks). As supported in the qualitative interviews, usual hotel operations and scarce resources often hinder enhancements: "*A total cut can be a chance, because in daily routine, very little change is possible.*" Second, available resources have been used for employee training. For example, in the wake of the COVID-19 pandemic, the business established intra- and interdepartmental workshops to support corporate know-how and team spirit.

COVID-19 further evoked changes in fostering CE; the present case study indicates various ***negative impacts*** of the pandemic. Loss of bookings results in financial deficits and pressure. The case study indicates that in the short term, measures and subsidies from authorities support the financial situation. However, according to the case study, overcoming the crisis in the long run depends on financial reserves by individual hospitality businesses. Forecasting and communicating negative impacts is key to managing crises such as COVID-19. The interviewee stated: "*Forecasting made it possible to clearly communicate to employees, which in turn generated stability and confidence.*" The lockdowns, some of which were imposed at short notice, further led to a waste of resources, as food, for example, had to be disposed of. The tourism industry is heavily dependent on human resources for both service delivery and innovation. Even before the COVID-19 pandemic, the *Kothmühle* suffered a lack of employees. Although the business operates all year and thus provides long-term rather than seasonal employment, a lack of staff accommodation and the rural location requiring a car are employer drawbacks. Due to the low level of tourism in the region, the business mainly competes with local industries (e.g., metal industry) for applicants. The comparatively low salary level in the hospitality industry is a disadvantage compared to other sectors. The COVID-19 pandemic has further exacerbated labour shortages as workers have moved to other sectors that are also seeking employees but have been less affected by the crisis. According to *Kothmühle*, it is important to actively react to the labour market situation with new human resource strategies. First, with more diverse job positions and flexible recruiting. This is necessary to attract both skilled workers and lateral entrants. The interviews revealed that lateral entrants provide disadvantages in terms of qualifications (e.g., no skills and experience in leisure and business tourism) but also advantages in terms of competence diversity (e.g., former electrician works as a masseur in the hotel but also undertakes electronic tasks). Second, with the modernisation of structures. In the specific case, this means increasing options to work from home, part-time positions, and a number of interns.

Given these positive and negative effects, COVID-19 led to a modification of the business model of *Kothmühle*. Some of these are short-term or temporary adjustments (e.g., short-term working due to lockdown). On the other hand, the pandemic has also strengthened business strategies established pre-COVID rather than disruptively changing the business model (e.g., fostering leisure travellers, strengthening outdoor and wellness products).

Epilogue

The aim of this case study was to shed light on triggers, settings, and outcomes of CE as well as to examine the impact of the COVID-19 pandemic on CE in the Austrian hospitality industry.

The case of the Austrian hotel *Kothmühle* demonstrates that CE is key to staying sustainably competitive both in a crisis and non-crisis context.

In family-run hospitality businesses, CE resembles a corporate attitude and ongoing intra- and inter-generational process, rather than discrete measures. Such processes are driven by external (e.g., location in low tourism region) and internal factors (e.g., competencies of business stakeholders), further shaped by communication and frameworks (e.g., workshops), and finally result in specific innovations (e.g., brand redesign, new hotel rooms). Due to its disruptive character, the COVID-19 pandemic as an external trigger further increased the importance of CE for tourism organisations. On the one hand, regulatory restrictions (e.g., lockdown) are forcing the hospitality industry to adapt their business models. On the other hand, it is down to the individual companies whether and to what extent times of crisis are used for innovation.

The ability to overcome COVID-19, economically recover, and ultimately continue in business depends on business resilience, which needs to be established pre-crisis. The current pandemic makes it clear that crises can occur anytime and that constant crisis preparation is necessary (e.g., financial reserves, forecasting). Resilience enables hospitality businesses to actively drive CE during a crisis. Summing up, the case study reveals that COVID-19 is more than a crisis. The pandemic represents a crisis in terms of loss of bookings, income, and employees. On the other hand, it represents an opportunity to drive national demand while resources are freed up to enable the improvement of products and processes. In the end, it depends on corporate attitude on how crises are used for CE and, thus how challenging periods are overcome.

From a managerial point of view, the case study reveals five main implications for tourism and hospitality businesses. First, the case study emphasises the variety of internal and external triggers for CE. Strategic forecasting and constant market observation are needed to identify and react to chances and risks. Second, hospitality organisations can learn how to actively drive CE by establishing frameworks and settings (e.g., training, workshops) both in a crisis and non-crisis context. Third, the case study demonstrates the wide scope for CE action in hospitality businesses, from marketing to product innovations. Fourth, using strategic forecasting, communication, and financial reserves, hospitality businesses need to build up a resilient operational structure in the long term before any crisis. The Austrian tourism industry experienced constant growth over the years. However, COVID-19 demonstrates that crises can occur anytime. Fifth, despite negative effects, crises need to be actively used to improve processes and products (e.g., training of employees, internal handbooks, menus).

Limitations

The business chosen in this case study reflects the majority of hospitality organisations in Austria in many respects. First, it is a family-owned and family-run hotel. Second, the business is located in a rural region with a low population density. Third, given its size, the business is classified as an SME. However, the business has a distinctive environment. Unlike many other

Austrian states, tourism is not very prevalent in Lower Austria. Core aspects of competitiveness, such as an attractive location, are not sufficient to ensure profitable operation. Hence, CE plays a particularly important role.

At the time the paper was written, the COVID-19 pandemic was levelling off but was not completely over. The qualitative interviews make it clear that the final impact also depends on the further course of the pandemic. The case study collected data from literature review, desk research, and qualitative interviews. However, all interviews were conducted with the junior CEO of the hotel. These methodological limitations need to be considered in the interpretation of findings.

References

Andersson, T., Carlsen, J., & Getz, D. (2002). Family business goals in the tourism and hospitality sector: Case studies and cross-case analysis from Australia, Canada, and Sweden. *Family Business Review, 15*(2), 89–106.

Austrian Economic Chamber (2021). Tourism and leisure industry in figures. https://www.wko.at/oe/tourismus-freizeitwirtschaft/tourismus-freizeitwirtschaft-in-zahlen-2021.pdf

Austrian Institute for SME Research (2020). Family businesses in Austria. https://news.wko.at/news/oesterreich/kmu-forschung-bericht-familienunternehmen-2019.pdf

Bachtrögler, J., Firgo, M., Fritz, O., Klien, M., Mayerhofer, P., Piribauer, P., & Streicher, G. (2020). Regional differences in the economic impact of the current COVID-19 crisis in Austria. Austrian Institute of Economic Research. https://www.econstor.eu/bitstream/10419/220080/1/169470212X.pdf

Backer, E., & Ritchie, B. W. (2017). VFR travel: A viable market for tourism crisis and disaster recovery? *International Journal of Tourism Research, 19*(4), 400–411.

Bascavusoglu-Moreau, E., Kopera, S., & Wszendyby-Skulska, E. (2013). The role of creativity in development of innovation in tourism. *Journal of Entrepreneurship, Management and Innovation, 9*(1), 5–16.

Breier, M., Kallmuenzer, A., Clauss, T., Gast, J., Kraus, S., & Tiberius, V. (2021). The role of business model innovation in the hospitality industry during the COVID-19 crisis. *International Journal of Hospitality Management, 92*, 102723.

Çakar, K. (2018). Critical success factors for tourist destination governance in times of crisis: A case study of Antalya, Turkey. *Journal of Travel & Tourism Marketing, 35*(6), 786–802.

Federal Ministry Republic Austria (2019). National data.

Holt, D. T., Rutherford, M. W., & Clohessy, G. R. (2007). Corporate entrepreneurship: An empirical look at individual characteristics, context, and process. *Journal of Leadership & Organizational Studies, 13*(4), 40–54.

Kessler, A., Pachucki, C., Stummer, K., Binder, P., & Mair, M. (2015). Types of organizational innovativeness and success in Austrian hotels. *International Journal of Contemporary Hospitality Management, 27*(7), 1707–1727.

Ketter, E., & Avraham, E. (2021). *#Stayhome today so we can #traveltomorrow*: Tourism destination's marketing strategies during the COVID-19 pandemic. *Journal of Travel & Tourism Marketing, 38*(8), 819–832.

Kuscer, K. (2013). Determining factors of mountain destination innovativeness. *Journal of Vacation Marketing*, 19(1), 41–54.

Kuscer, K., Eichelberger, S., & Mike, P. (2021). Tourism organizations' responses to the COVID-19 pandemic: An investigation of the lockdown period. *Current Issues in Tourism*, 25(2), 247–60.

Lower Austria Tourism (2021). Destinations. https://tourismus.niederoesterreich.at/tourismusdestinationen

Mumford, M. D., & Hester, K. S. (2012). Creativity in organizations: Importance and approaches. In M. Mumford (ed.). *Handbook of organizational creativity*. London: Elsevier.

Ottenbacher, M. C. (2007). Innovation management in the hospitality industry: Different strategies for achieving success. *Journal of Hospitality & Tourism Research*, 31(4), 431–454.

Pachucki, C., Grohs, R., & Scholl-Grissemann, U. (2022). Is nothing like before? COVID-19-evoked changes to tourism destination social media communication. *Journal of Destination Marketing & Management*, 23, 100692.

Provenzano, D., & Volo, S. (2022). Tourism recovery amid COVID-19: The case of Lombardy, Italy. *Tourism Economics*, 28(1), 110–130.

Ritchie, B. W., & Jiang, Y. (2019). A review of research on tourism risk, crisis and disaster management: Launching the annals of tourism research curated collection on tourism risk, crisis and disaster management. *Annals of Tourism Research*, 79, 1–15.

Weidmann, S., Filep, S., & Lovelock, B. (2022). How are tourism businesses adapting to COVID-19? Perspectives from the fright tourism industry. *Tourism and Hospitality Research*, 23 (1), 121–126.

Zach, F. (2012). Partners and innovation in American destination marketing organizations. *Journal of Travel Research*, 51(4), 412–425.

Case 4 Entrepreneurial innovation in the Binter Airline Company

New routes in Europe and Africa after COVID-19

Juan Carlos Martín, Concepción Román and Teresa Aguiar-Quintana

Introduction and case selection

Binter is a referent company in the airline industry in the Canary Islands. It has a clear objective to be the wings of the Canarian residents and of those who visited the islands as tourists. After experiencing a turbulent period in the business environment when the company left to be a subsidiary airline of Iberia in 2002, multiple actions have been accelerated by the entrance of new subsidiary firms of the group in vertical and horizontal sectors such as handling, aircraft maintenance, cargo and logistics, low-cost operations, information and communication technology (ICT), and training. Binter case study reveals that the various corporate entrepreneurship (CE) initiatives taken by the airline were proactive rather than reactive. In this case study, the main objective is to study the strategies developed by the company, its learning capabilities, and related CE actions. Also, another aim is to describe how the company has been reorganised to respond to the emerging and uncertain environment.

According to Phan et al. (2009), corporate entrepreneurship (CE) refers to the process of organisational renewal. The main antecedents of this company's corporate entrepreneurship (CE) actions are associated with the external environment. The current airline industry could not have taken off without the European Union air transport deregulation in 1997, in which all the airlines that belonged to the state members could enjoy the cabotage eighth and ninth freedoms. These freedoms allow airlines to carry passengers and cargo in any country in the European Union.

Corporate Entrepreneurship is defined by Guth and Ginsberg (1990) as related to two phenomena: firstly, it refers to innovation and corporate venturing activities, and secondly, it consists of renewal activities related to a corporations' ability to compete and take risks. Later, Sharma and Chrisman (1999) explain that corporate venturing (CV) can be divided into internal and external. Internal CV relates to the creation of new businesses that reside within the corporate structure or may be located outside the firm. However, corporations may also invest in early growth-stage businesses created by external parties, which includes corporate venture capital (CVC), licensing,

DOI: 10.4324/9781003454465-5

acquisitions and joint ventures. Next, we describe the antecedents, development and the main lessons learnt by Binter through its corporate entrepreneurship actions developed by the company in the last 30 years.

Business profile and framework

It all started on the morning of March 26th 1989, when Binter—at that time BinterCanarias—a regional airline belonging to Iberia, began operations to link the islands of the Canary archipelago by air. The first flight, NT 104, took off from Tenerife North Airport at 8:00 a.m. on the route to Gran Canaria to fly over the north coast of Tenerife after passing over the Anaga mountains. Cabin crew member Katia Fernández and commanders Ricardo Génova and Alfonso García Bach were fortunate to be the first crew members to attend to the 40 passengers on this inaugural flight.

The Casa CN 235, manufactured by the Spanish company Construcciones Aeronáuticas, was the aircraft chosen for the first months of operation of Binter. At the time, it made 36 daily flights, covering routes between only four of seven islands in the archipelago: Gran Canaria, Fuerteventura, La Palma and Tenerife.

In January 1990, the first ATR 72 unit was added to the fleet, which would soon become the company's flagship. From the 36 daily operations of that spring of 1989, the traffic rocketed to the current 220 flights each day, covering all inter-island routes, with connections to the eight airports of the archipelago. Binter began a great adventure operating in the archipelago to fly between the islands to make the cohesion of a fragmented territory possible.

At a glance, the history of Binter can be described as follows: (1) In 1999, the fleet was made up of 11 aircrafts; (2) its international expansion began in 2005 in Marrakech, El Aaiún and Madeira, where it became possible to fly there directly for the first time without the inconvenience of stopping in Madrid; (3) in 2009, the company undertook a profound restructuring to be more efficient and provide better service to the passengers; (4) in 2012, the airline owned and managed one of the largest fleets of ATR aircraft in Europe, and extended the international market to Agadir, Casablanca, Cabo Verde and Lisbon; (5) in 2013, Binter inaugurated its new headquarters in Tenerife and added two new destinations in Africa: Banjul and Dakar; (6) in 2014, Binter celebrated its 25th anniversary with two new international connections: Sal and Nouakchott; (7) in 2015, it undertook a new fleet renewal with the acquisition of 18 new aircraft (ATR 72 600); (8) in 2017, three Bombardier CRJ1000 jets were added to the Binter fleet to make some international routes more comfortable, and a new West African destination was added to the airline's schedule: Dakhla; (9) in 2018, Binter took a new leap in its business model by starting to fly to two national destinations regularly: Mallorca and Vigo; in addition, the Canarian airline began to operate the inter-island routes of the Portuguese archipelago of Madeira; (10) in 2019, coinciding with its 30th anniversary, the airline added three new domestic destinations: Pamplona,

Zaragoza and Murcia; that same year, received three E195-E2 jets from the manufacturer Embraer and renewed the staff uniforms who have direct contact with customers; (11) in 2020, Binter added four new national destinations to its program: Santander, Vitoria, Jerez and Asturias, expanding further its penetration within the domestic market; and (12) in 2021, the airline began its operations with France and Italy, with regular flights to Toulouse, Marseille, Lille, Turin and Venice. The national network was also expanded with two additional connections: A Coruña and San Sebastián.

In summary, since its inaugural flight, the Spanish airline has become a benchmark for transport in the Canary Islands and has taken a leading role in Europe and has been recognised with seven awards from the European Regional Airlines Association). It offers a high-quality service to its customers, and carries out extensive activities within the society as part of its commitment to the Canary archipelago.

Environment

As said, Binter has its *raison d'etre* in the Canary Islands. The Canary Islands are a Spanish autonomous community and archipelago in Macaronesia, in the Atlantic Ocean. At its closest point to the African coast, the archipelago is 100 kilometres (62 miles) west of Morocco. They are the southernmost of the autonomous communities of Spain. The islands have a population of 2.2 million people in 2021, and the archipelago is the most populous ultra-peripheral territory of the European Union. The eight main islands are (from largest to smallest in area) Tenerife, Fuerteventura, Gran Canaria, Lanzarote, La Palma, La Gomera, El Hierro and La Graciosa. Due to its strategic location, the Canary Islands have historically been considered a link between the three continents: Africa, America and Europe.

The population is mostly concentrated in the two capital islands: around 43% on the island of Tenerife and 39% on the island of Gran Canaria. The Canary Islands, especially Tenerife, Gran Canaria, Fuerteventura, and Lanzarote, are major tourist destinations in the European Union, with about 15.6 million tourists in 2019. This is due to their beaches, subtropical climate, and important natural attractions, such as Maspalomas in Gran Canaria, Teide National Park and Mount Teide (a World Heritage Site) in Tenerife. Mount Teide is the highest peak in Spain, with an altitude of 3,715 metres, and it is the third tallest volcano in the world. Tourism boosted a very large increase in inter-insular mobility as well as with the rest of Spain and Europe over the last two decades.

The distribution of the population and tourism accommodation within the archipelago varies considerably. There are a number of parameters that affect this observation, from historical reasons to the possibility of investing in the development of tourist products, which are associated with the existence of natural attractions such as beaches and the development of airport infrastructures. For this reason, the demand for air transport services varies also considerably from almost negligible needs, such as in La Gomera or El Hierro, to intermediate needs in La Palma, Fuerteventura and Lanzarote, and maximum needs in Tenerife and Gran Canaria.

Hernández-Luis (2004) contended that scheduled air transport plays a crucial role for the Canary Islands. Its efficiency is vital not only for residents in the archipelago but also for an economy highly dependent on tourism. There is an important segment of tourists who use inter-island transport, either by air or sea, to visit more than one island during their vacations.

In 2002, the air transport traffic reached over 2.4 million inter-island passengers, 2.6 million with the rest of Spain, and 9.8 million with the rest of the countries. The increase in travel demand is confirmed, reaching up to a total of 4.6 million for inter-island passengers, 4.5 million for the rest of Spain, and 13.2 million for the rest of the countries in 2019. Regarding the importance of the airports, it can be said that Gran Canaria and Tenerife North are the two most important airports for the inter-island and with the rest of Spain markets and that the role of the island of Tenerife is taken by Tenerife South in the case of the rest of the country market.

An analysis of the previous figures for the period 2002–2019 in the inter-island passenger market concludes that the market has grown by 75% and that the airports of Fuerteventura, Tenerife North and La Palma have experienced the largest increases with 182%, 153% and 102%, respectively.

Organisational structure

Binter has gone from being a subsidiary airline of Iberia to a group of 15 companies offering comprehensive services to their customers and providing the highest possible quality in each branch of the air transport sector. The evolution of Binter company is represented in its corporate entrepreneurship (CE) actions that constitute the Binter System compelling 15 companies: (1) Binter Vende; (2) Atlántica Handling; (3) Binter Technic; (4) Atlantis Cargo; (5) Gestión Aenonáutica; (6) Sfyra; (7) Binter Sistemas; (8) Atlantis Technology; (9) Sati; (10) Atavis; (11) Binter Airlines; (12) Canair; (13) Binter Formación; (14) ADM Tech; and (15) Isa.

Atlántica Handling began its activity on October 1st 2005, and was created to improve the ground service provided by Binter to its customers at all airports in the Canary Islands. Until now, Atlántica Handling is the baby company with the largest number of employees, reaching 400. Binter Technic has been the aircraft maintenance company for the group since 2008. It was also the repair shop for other airlines: in Spain, Iberia or Air Nostrum; in Europe, TUI, Danube Wings or Swiftair; in South America, BQB in Uruguay or DAE in the Netherlands Antilles; in Africa, TACV in Cabo Verde; or in Asia, KBZ in Myanmar. BT is considered a world leader in excellence in the maintenance of ATR manufacturer aircraft, which has led it to be shortlisted as MRO (Maintenance Repair and Overhaul) to be an official "dealer" of the ATR company.

Atlantis Cargo was a company created in June 2009, intending to sell the cargo space in the bellies of aircraft. It is already transporting approximately 2,000 tonnes in inter-island freight traffic and has established itself as the main air cargo operator in the Canary Islands. The objective of Atlantis Cargo is to unite the islands with each other and the Canary Islands with national and international air transport networks, contributing to its consolidation as an intercontinental air cargo hub and logistics platform with the African continent. Atlantis Technology is a young company, created in 2013 under the umbrella of Binter Sistemas. Its vision is to be a benchmark company within the information and communications technology (ICT) sector at a national and international level. The company offers clients consulting services—designing plans for new technological projects or correcting deficiencies, training in ICT, and installing and maintaining technological solutions and software development, among others.

Atavis is a young company that began its activity in 2013 and is dedicated to aeronautical logistics services. It currently has more than 40 employees, most of them professionals with extensive experience in the sector. Atavis's activities include purchasing, selling, storing and distributing aviation products, parts and equipment, and offering various aeronautical material management services, such as rental, exchange and rotatable repair management. Canair was born in September 2011 with the mission of being an efficient and flexible operator with high productivity and adjusted costs to offer competitive prices with the same quality of service. It carries out its fundamental activity as a franchise for Binter.

Binter Formación was created to respond to the training needs adjusted to the demand of the aeronautical sector, for which it develops training programs to obtain a suitable curriculum for each student and company. The company was certified as an EASA (European Aviation Safety Agency) Training Centre and as a Private Professional Training Centre for a Higher Degree Cycle in Aeromechanics and Avionics by the Ministry of Education of the Government of the Canary Islands for the training of Turbine Aircraft Maintenance Technicians, as well as for the Transport of Dangerous Goods by Air (CAT 1 to 12) (9284/AN905) by ICAO (International Civil Aviation Organization). ADM Tech was created to design and manufacture aeronautical parts for use and sale to third parties. The firm specialises in producing small components, with a unique offer in Spain. It has the EASA.21J.457 certifications for design for aeronautical components and minor aircraft modifications and ES.21G.003 for the manufacturing of aeronautical components.

Corporate entrepreneurship actions

The main antecedents of this company's corporate entrepreneurship (CE) actions are associated with the external environment. The current airline industry could not have taken off without the European Union air transport deregulation that changed the level playing field of the single market on April

1st 1997, in which all the airlines that belonged to the state members could enjoy the cabotage eighth and ninth freedoms. These freedoms allow airlines to carry passengers and cargo in any country in the European Union. Martín and Román (2008) noted air transport deregulation in the EU was based on the demonstrative effect caused by the US 1978 air transport liberalisation. Since then, the air transport market has become more competitive, and airlines are subject to significant challenges to their operational performance.

The gradual EU air transport deregulation ignited Iberia (the former full legacy airline in Spain) privatisation in 1999. It was after the privatisation of Iberia when the baby company Binter Canarias was sold to Hesperia Inversiones Aéreas, S.A. (a group of Canarian investors) in July 2002. The corporate entrepreneurship actions carried out by Binter are focused on the development of new strategies, new technologies and new products and services. In terms of new strategies, in 2007, the new company envisioned consolidating the traffic in the inter-island air transport market in the archipelago. To support this vision it bought the Spanish airline Naysawhich operated inter-island flights in the Canary Islands and some connections between the archipelago and the African continent.

In terms of new products, the current fleet of Binter is made up of 25 ATR 72 and 5 Embraer 195-E2. The ATR 72 aircraft is considered an ideal model for regional aviation due to the possibility of taking off and landing on shorter runways using turboprops. It is much more ecological than other jets, polluting less, saving fuel and reducing CO_2 emissions. Also, the new ATR 72 600 model incorporates the latest technologies in assisted navigation tools and the highest standards of comfort. They have five LCD digitised screens in the cockpit that facilitate piloting, positively impacting safety during the flight. They also have thinner seats, which leave more passenger space, and larger luggage compartments.

Thus, Binter acquired five new E195-E2 (Figure 4.1) aircraft from Embraer manufacturer, thus becoming the first European company to operate this model. It is the largest and most modern aircraft in the E-Jet E2 family of medium-range, twin-engine commercial jets. Its interior is a benchmark in the aeronautical industry thanks to its 2+2 seating configuration and upper compartment, doubling the capacity of regional reactors. The E-Jets E2 are the quietest, cleanest and most efficient single-aisle jets in the world, and the Canarian company has ordered them with a special configuration of 132 seats in a single class and a comfortable distance between them of 79 cm. The seat pitch configuration is one of the most important attributes that passengers consider when they evaluate the airlines' service quality (Espino et al., 2008; Martín et al., 2008).

The main support to carry out these CE actions is the company's vision of maintaining a constant renewal of the fleet and the availability of technological, human and financial resources. Also, the organisational support in terms of training, the trust in employees to detect opportunities and the company's vision focused on the renewal of the fleet have recently been externally

Figure 4.1 Binter embraer E195-E2.

recognised by Ch-Aviation by its annual award in which Binter got the third position in the ranking of the youngest aircraft fleets in Europe (with an average of 4.8 years of its 30 aircrafts). Thus, the search for excellence in customer service is pursued by all the employees of the airline, especially those who have direct contact with the passengers. For instance, Binter combats the flying fear by offering a practical free session with therapists, pilots and other specialised personnel.

The dynamic of the sector constitutes another antecedent of the company's entrepreneurial actions. The airline's growth has been constant since the inaugural flight in 1989. The airline transported 4 million passengers in 2019, operating 200 daily flights with eight inter-island destinations, 13 national and 17 international destinations. However, some difficulties in this CE process came in 2020 when, on March 11th, the World Health Organization declared the outbreak of the COVID-19 pandemic. On the 20th of April, all the countries in the world introduced travel restrictions. On the 1st of November, 27% of the countries still kept their borders completely closed to international tourists. Even during the worst times of the pandemic crisis in 2020, the airline transported 2.2 million passengers, being vital in maintaining air transport connectivity in the archipelago.

Most countries have taken various travel restrictive measures since the beginning of 2020 to prevent the spread of the COVID-19 pandemic. The consequence of the measures was that the air transport industry was severely hit worldwide. In 2020, the total number of passengers travelling by air in the EU was only 277 million, a substantial decrease of 73.3% compared with 2019. All Member States registered large drops in 2020 compared with 2019. In Spain, the decline was higher than the EU average by 1.3 points (−74.6%).

A simple comparison of these figures concludes that Binter was not so severely affected as the company's drop was less than 50% (45%). This figure is lower than the declines observed in Ryanair and IAG (the airlines' group that owns Iberia), which were 81% and 74%, respectively. Hollinger (2020) contended that airlines were in shock in 2020 as more than 60% of the total commercial aircraft were halted.

The COVID-19 pandemic dramatically changed the playing field of European aviation. Albers and Rundshagen (2020) analysed airline reactions to overcome the COVID-19 crisis in the spring months of 2020 based on the four general crisis response strategies suggested by Wenzel et al. (2020), such as retrenchment, persevering, innovating, and exit-oriented. Due to the pandemic, in 2020, with all the travel restrictions imposed by the national health systems, most airlines were obliged to apply massive retrenchment measures. Binter was not an exception to these extraordinary measures, but perseverance measures were also the norm during this difficult year, especially in the inter-island market, and these measures allowed the company to overcome the difficulties experienced in the period.

In 2021, Binter is recovering part of the demand (3.1 million passengers) as the travel restrictions in the EU were partly lifted, and air transport began to be re-opened. The EU provides information on travel and health measures in the EU during the COVID-19 pandemic, with the aim that passengers could exercise their right to free movement while staying safe and healthy. National health authorities of each member state are in charge of issuing the EU Digital COVID Certificate which partially alleviates some of the reminiscence measures regarding the necessity of showing a negative test.

Nevertheless, in Morocco, Mauritania and Cabo Verde, some travel restrictions still persist, and it represents difficulties in the company's entrepreneurship actions. For example, passengers who travel to Mauritania must have a negative COVID-19 PCR test taken at most 72 hours before departure from the first embarkation point. The test result must be in Arabic, French, English or Spanish; or a COVID-19 vaccination certificate showing that passengers were fully vaccinated at least 14 days before arrival with AstraZeneca (SK Bioscience), AstraZeneca (Vaxzevria), Covishield, Covovax, Moderna (Spikevax), Nuvaxovid (Novavax), Pfizer-BioNTech (Comirnaty), Sinopharm (BIBP) and Sinovac, or they were vaccinated at least 28 days before arrival in the case of Janssen, they were fully vaccinated and received a booster dose at least seven days before departure, or they have a COVID-19 recovery certificate at least 11 days and at most six months before departure. In addition, passengers could be subject to a COVID-19 RT-PCR test upon arrival, and if the test is positive, quarantine for ten days is mandatory. In Cabo Verde and Morocco, the travel restrictions are less severe and consist of presenting a vaccination certificate or a negative PCR test up to 72 hours or antigens test up to 48 hours before the trip or a valid recovery certificate.

Ryanair and Iberia led air traffic in Spain in the first quarter of 2021, with 6.9 million passengers, 80% of pre-COVID volume, and 4.8 million, 77%, respectively, according to AENA dataset. Both airline groups are, therefore, getting closer to their pre-pandemic levels. Nevertheless, Binter obtained a higher recovery percentage of 99%, with 831,337 passengers. If we compare the overall figures for the whole year 2021, it can be concluded that Binter is getting closer to its normal pre-pandemic activity with a decline of 22%, compared with the declines of Ryanair and IAG which were 35% and 67%, respectively.

Binter needed to organise adequate anti-COVID measures to guarantee the health and safety of the passengers and employees (Nathan, 2000; Wenzel et al., 2020) and to overcome the difficulties during the pandemic period. It is strange that Albers and Rundshagen (2020) could only find as innovative airline responses to covid the conversion of passenger aircraft into cargo transporters and the preparations for joint ventures as Bintner undertook a range of activities to maintain regular operations.

The anti-COVID-19 measures instrument is based on a three-dimensional scale containing several items on individual responsibility, airlines and airport measures. Thus, the items used to evaluate the anti-COVID airlines' measures are related to the specific measures implemented by the airlines, mainly inside the aircraft. The following six items were included in the instrument: (1) special prevention protocols during boarding and disembarking processes; (2) implementation of safety distance in the aircraft, specifically from seat to seat; (3) distribution of free disposable sanitary wipes to the passenger when entering or exiting the aircraft; (4) distribution of individual bags for waste or garbage when entering or leaving the aircraft and during the flight; (5) cleanliness and hygienic conditions of the aircraft, which includes the seat you were seated in, adjacent seats, and the lavatory of the aircraft; and (6) explanation of COVID-19 hygiene measures prior to your flight either by email, in writing on paper or over the aircraft loudspeaker.

Escolà-Gascón (2022) analysed the perception of compliance with anti-COVID measures for three different segments: passengers, cabin crew members and ground crew members. They found finds that the perception of compliance was lower on aeroplanes than at airport facilities and concludes that a priority reinforcement of anti-COVID-19 mitigation measures needs to be applied inside aeroplanes. It was quite common during the year 2020 that passengers were worried about the scarce distance that exists between seats on several domestic flights. Nevertheless, pilots and air hostesses explain that the probability of being contagious during the flight was very low because of the existing high-efficiency particulate air (HEPA) filters of the aircraft.

In addition, to overcome the difficulties during the pandemic period, Binter strengthened all the protocols and procedures to ensure the safety of both passengers and employees, implementing more than forty specific anti-COVID measures. Preventive health and hygiene measures were applied throughout the process, making safety the highest priority at each stage of the journey to guarantee the best possible travel experience.

Thus, Binter decided to reinforce the cleaning and disinfection of the passenger cabin before the first-morning flight and several times a day. This can be considered overcompliance with the EASA directive that only requires aircraft to be disinfected every 24 hours. Upon entering the plane, individual hydro-alcoholic wipes that are effective against COVID-19 are distributed to all passengers. These are also available to passengers in the lavatory and at any time needed throughout the flight. All crew members received information on how to deal with cases of respiratory infection or coronavirus symptoms on board. Other changes introduced include limiting access to the aircraft to strictly necessary ground crew and scheduling staff groups in steady teams to prevent cross-infection. COVID-19 immunity test and contagion monitoring system were implemented for all company staff members and, especially, those in direct contact with customers, both on aircraft and at airports. During access to the aircraft, boarding was staggered and carried out by rows to avoid crowding and maintain a safe distance between passengers. Similarly, disembarking takes place in order, starting with the rows closest to the aircraft door, preventing crowding in the aisle and ensuring the social distance between passengers.

As a result, Binter complied with a high mark on the whole set of indicators included in the scale developed by Escolà-Gascón (2022).

Epilogue

The most relevant aspects of Binter's CE actions described in this case study relate to developing a customer-oriented culture. The learning extracted from its development is that the company has jumped from being a referent in the inter-island market to being a relevant actor in all the air connections in the archipelago by developing new international and national routes.

Related to that, the innovation in products and services allows the company to offer its customers daily connections to all the islands of the Canary archipelago, with a wide variety of schedules, thanks to the 200 flights that operate each day on average. Thus, since 2005, the airline has also offered international routes that connect the Canary Islands abroad with direct flights, thus strengthening the position of the archipelago as a hub. There are currently 17 international destinations served: ten in Africa (Agadir, Banjul, Dakar, Dakhla, El Aaiún, Fez, Guelmin, Marrakech, Nouakchott and Sal Island) and eight in Europe (Madeira and Ponta Delgada in Portugal; Toulouse, Marseille and Lille in France; Florence, Turin and Venice in Italy). In addition, in 2018, it began to fly to national destinations outside the Canary Islands, currently offering weekly links with 13 destinations (Mallorca, Vigo, Pamplona, Zaragoza, Murcia, Santander, Vitoria, Asturias, Jerez de la Frontera, A Coruña, Menorca, San Sebastián and Valladolid).

One of the key elements of the Binter company is represented in its corporate entrepreneurship actions that constitute the Binter System, compelling 15 companies that provide services in different economic sectors. The main difficulties in their growth strategy were due to COVID-19 issues and related to that, recently, Cabrera-López and Suárez-Ortega (2022) analysed how Binter was the only Spanish airline ranked as one of the best airlines in the world in times of COVID-19, where the level of flexibility for changes and cancellations, average reimbursement time or hygienic measures to avoid contagion were the main key variables.

The lessons learned from the corporate entrepreneurship actions taken by Binter have permitted the company to be a referent in the airline industry in the Canary Islands, to dream about being the wings of the Canarian residents, and why not, of those who visited the islands as tourists. The actions commenced after experiencing a turbulent period in the business environment when the company left to be a subsidiary airline of Iberia in 2002. Since then, multiple actions have been accelerated by the entrance of new subsidiary firms of the group in vertical and horizontal sectors such as handling, aircraft maintenance, cargo and logistics, low-cost operations, information and communication technology (ICT), and training. Binter case reveals that the various CE initiatives taken by the airline were primarily proactive rather than reactive. Binter could develop strategies, learning capabilities, and related CE actions to anticipate a future full of success. The company is reorganised to respond to the emerging and uncertain environment.

Finally, in the context of Europe, the pandemic crisis has produced a major policy turn regarding the financial aid that airlines could receive from the governments (Sinha, 2019). Martín-Domingo and Martín (2022) analysed the role of state aid that some EU airlines have received during the COVID-19 pandemic using 27 cases for a total amount of €31 billion. The results indicate that the largest economies in the EU (Germany and France) and some countries in northern Europe support national airlines more decisively than the rest of Member States. It is not yet clear how state intervention will evolve in the future, but it seems that some airlines now resemble the former public flag carriers of the past. Nevertheless, the decisions taken in periods of crisis will affect the future post-COVID-19 air transport, raising possible reflection issues for the different companies in this sector.

Sources

For the elaboration of this case study, the following persons were interviewed:
Jonay Lobo (Chief Network, Revenue Management & Alliances).
Miguel Ángel Suárez (Sales and Marketing manager).

References

Albers, S., & Rundshagen, V. (2020). European airlines' strategic responses to the COVID-19 pandemic (January-May, 2020). *Journal of Air Transport Management*, 87, 101863.

Cabrera-López, M., & Suárez-Ortega, S. M. (2022). CASO EMPRESARIAL BUSINESS CASE. Binter Canarias: Un caso de éxito de las estrategias de respuesta a la COVID-19. *Emprendimiento y Negocios Internacionales*, 7(1), 30–36.

Escolà-Gascón, Á. (2022). Statistical indicators of compliance with anti-COVID-19 public health measures at European airports. *International Journal of Disaster Risk Reduction*, *68*, 102720.

Espino, R., Martín, J. C., & Román, C. (2008). Analyzing the effect of preference heterogeneity on willingness to pay for improving service quality in an airline choice context. *Transportation Research Part E: Logistics and Transportation Review*, *44*(4), 593–606.

Guth, W., & Ginsberg, A. (1990). Guest editors' introduction: Corporate entrepreneurship. *Strategic Management Journal*, *11*(S), 5–15.

Hernández-Luis, J. A. (2004). The role of inter-island air transport in the Canary Islands. *Journal of Transport Geography*, *12*(3), 235–244.

Hollinger, P. (2020). How coronavirus brought aerospace down to earth. FT.com. Retrieved from https://www.ft.com/content/3fe8a876-7d7c-11ea-8fdb-7ec06edeef84. Accessed on 10 June 2022.

Martín, J. C., & Román, C. (2008). Airlines and their focus on cost control and productivity. *European Journal of Transport and Infrastructure Research*, *8*(2), 117–136.

Martín, J. C., Román, C., & Espino, R. (2008). Willingness to pay for airline service quality. *Transport Reviews*, *28*(2), 199–217.

Martín-Domingo, L., & Martín, J. C. (2022). The effect of COVID-related EU state aid on the level playing field for airlines. *Sustainability*, *14*(4), 2368.

Nathan, M. (2000). The paradoxical nature of crisis. *Review of Business*, *21*(3/4), 12.

Phan, P., Wright, M., Udrasaran, D., & Wee-Liang, T. (2009). Corporate entrepreneurship: Current research and future directions. *Journal of Business Venturing*, *24*, 197–205.

Sharma, P., & Chrisman, J. J. (1999). Toward a reconciliation of the definitional issues in the field of corporate entrepreneurship. *Entrepreneurship Theory and Practice*, *23*, 11–27.

Sinha, D. (2019). *Deregulation and liberalisation of the airline industry: Asia, Europe, North America and Oceania*. London: Routledge.

Wenzel, M., Stanske, S., & Lieberman, M. B. (2021). Strategic responses to crisis. *Strategic Management Journal*, *42*(2), O16–O27. https://doi.org/10.1002/smj.3161

Case 5 Innovation strategies and corporate entrepreneurship in Northern Europe, Scandic Hotels

A case study of the pandemic effect on the Swedish revenue management

Staffan Hedén

Introduction

This article concentrates on recovery strategies for COVID-19, from early 2020 to December 2022, regarding entrepreneurship and innovation on five continents in tourism and the hospitality industry. To highlight the consequences further, it may also be important to see the changes from 2019, as represented in Graph 5.1.

The total number of hotels amounted to 1270 (Hotelstatistics.com), and in 2020, a total of 43.3 million guest nights were registered in Sweden, 24 million fewer than in 2019, which corresponds to a decrease of 36% (Swedish Agency for Economic and Regional Growth, facts about Swedish Tourism 2020). As with many other countries, demand disappeared completely in the market when COVID-19 created a Force Majeure in early March 2020. Most bookings disappeared immediately, and hotels were forced into drastic cuts and furloughs. Slowly, hotels could open with the business mix also changing as few or no international trips are allowed, meaning most overnight stays became domestic.

Many smaller players became completely dependent on various temporary government subsidies, and the larger ones are trying to redirect their business gradually because the entire market is uncertain. Many believed in a quick return, but the summer of 2020 was about 40% of 2019 in hotel night occupancy and the summer after was better than 2019 for a few weeks. Through stricter rules for COVID-19 abroad, Swedes chose to holiday in Sweden to a greater extent than before 2020 and 2021, which affected the market positively. At the same time, it meant a reversal of segments for several hotels, especially those that had been focused on the business market with meetings and conferences. The foreign holidaymakers usually arrived later and, since they could not come, the graph also fell.

The entire market was negatively affected by large variations in the local market that depended mainly on where the hotel was located, what direction the hotel had towards business travellers/leisure, Swedish guests/foreign

DOI: 10.4324/9781003454465-6

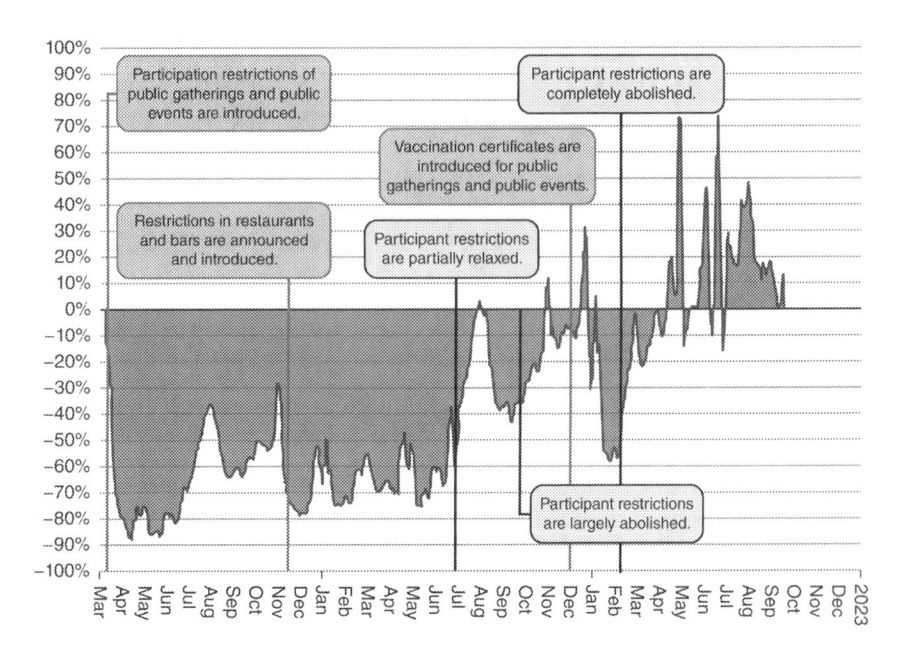

Graph 5.1 Sweden – Change in % accommodation revenue per day. March 1st 2020 to September 20th 2022. As well as the corresponding days of the week 2019–2020. Seven-day intervals. Benchmarking Alliance.

guests, seasonal orientation, possible transport options and how the opening hours were affected by the whole situation; see booking situation below (Jakobsson, 2022) in Graph 5.2.

The average price was also negatively affected by the restrictions and fell sharply during these periods, which means that the nights spent had the customers paying significantly less. The effect was greater than just the lost revenue from rented hotel rooms; reduced restaurant operations also often affected revenue. The price reflects the total revenue divided by the number of rooms rented, and the change is about the guest mix where the leisure traveller usually pays less than the business traveller (Jakobsson, 2022), as indicated in Graph 5.3.

The overall impact of COVID has been large during the period for the entire hotel market, but a recovery gradually began in 2022. The recovery in the international market has already started, and companies have returned to more regular operations and, in general, more people have wanted to meet as they did before, although restrictions have also affected everyone's behaviour even into the future.

Business settings: Environment and selected case

Business environment

There are about 1270 hotels in Sweden with a very varied selection; of these, there are about 210 in the three largest cities (Stockholm 120, Gothenburg

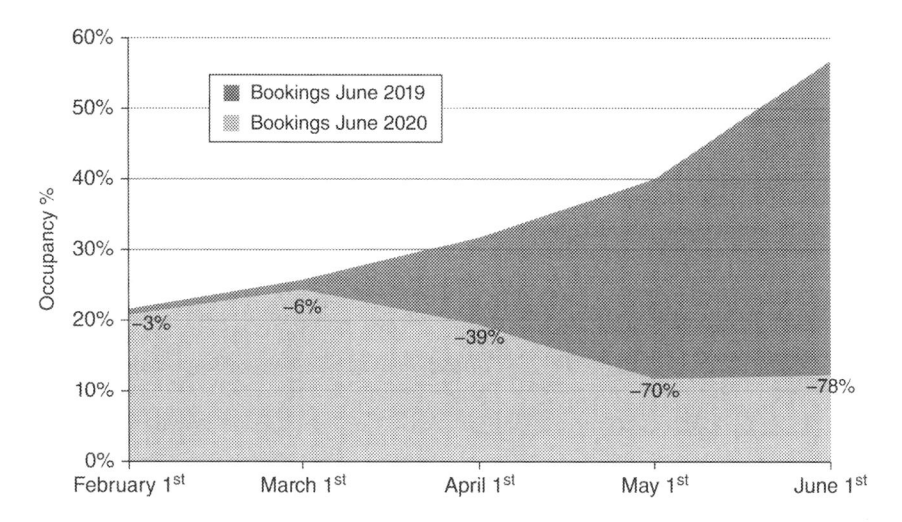

Graph 5.2 Booking situation for the month of June at different month-end 2020 compared to 2019 Percentage change one year in per cent compared to one year earlier in figures. (Base 307 hotels in Sweden). Benchmarking Alliance.

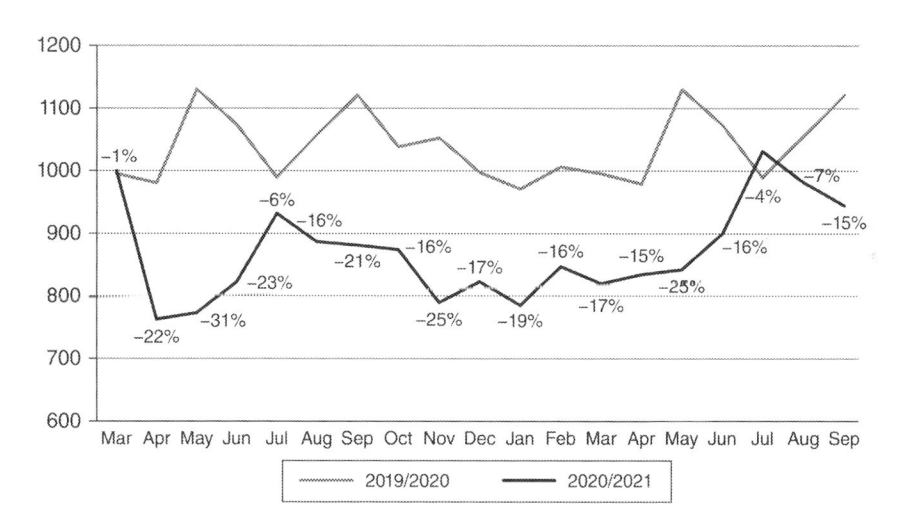

Graph 5.3 Average accommodation revenue per hotel stays per month 2019–2021. Crowns, percentage difference. SCB/the growth agency.

60 and Malmö 30). If we instead include the ten cities with the most hotels, we end up with about 340 hotels. There is a big difference in the size of the hotels, where the smallest are very small, and the largest hotel in Gothenburg, Gothia Tower, has 1131 rooms (Hotelstatistics.com).

The market is dominated by some major chains where Scandic Hotels is the largest with 89 hotels, Nordic Choice has 85 hotels, Best Western has

69 hotels, First Hotels has 39 hotels and Elite Hotels of Sweden has 35 hotels. The chains are also different in strength geographically. The large chains cover both business travellers and leisure travellers (Hotelstatistics.com).

In recent years, with the pandemic, competition has been affected by external conditions where lockdowns, restrictions and other prohibitions have changed customer behaviour patterns. It also led to changes in the company's internal conditions, with the number of employees and capital being subjected to rocking throughout closures, shared closures or certain prohibitions that meant a certain amount of handling in a hotel. The initial broadly sweeping national decision affected everyone, but after that, the decisions could also look different in regions or locally. The government actively contributed to offering support in various forms, but for the large companies, there were no customers at all, which under no circumstances would cover running a profitable business.

The trends today point towards an advantage for international hotel guests, the return of companies and more selective solutions for the private market. Broadly speaking, all bookings disappeared at the beginning of COVID-19 and later contributed to more private guests rather than companies.

COVID-19 has shown that it is central to have some elasticity even for what is thought to be impossible should it happen. The questions were centralised around how corporate processes could develop new entrepreneurial solutions without data support and instead with admissions. This happened at the same time as the companies were close to financial collapse and had to renegotiate rents and lay off staff to make ends meet in the long run. In Sweden, just as in most countries, actual measures were implemented in how many people were infected and passed away. For companies, it was rather about crisis preparation, response and later recovery. In the most acute crisis, many new modifications were created in tourism with policies, products and strategies for how key resources are used.

Business case

Scandic Hotels was founded in the early 1960s (1963) and has driven market development in the Nordic region for several decades. Today, they are a market-leading hotel listed on the Stockholm Stock Exchange through Scandic Hotels Group AB. Operations are located in the Nordic countries of Sweden, Norway, Finland and Denmark, as well as in Poland and Germany. The company has the largest and widest hotel network in the Nordic market with the idea of delivering a great hotel experience for many people—it should be an attractive hotel and location with a local touch. The vision for the group is to be a world-class Nordic hotel company. The business is focused on the mid-range segment and offers different types of hotels. But it is important that customers recognise the hotels themselves regardless of where they are located in Sweden or in other countries. The business is divided into country organisations with overall CEO and support functions and the head office in Stockholm.

Scandic is present in almost 130 locations, and the number of rooms in operation and under development amounts to 58,000 rooms distributed in 280 hotels. Revenues are divided into several segments but mainly come from two areas: business travellers and conferences as well as private individuals, although the segments are more numerous.

Before the pandemic, revenue distribution had a stronger focus on business travellers and meetings—about 70% versus 30%. During the pandemic, this distribution has been affected and created a different mix of revenue, a mix that, over the past year, also affected the overall strategies of the company. Initially, it was a reverse situation with 80% private market and 20% corporate business. At the same time, the current flow of revenue reflects a return to a stronger business life, but with interesting new questions and customer needs. The case focuses on understanding how the pandemic affected the Swedish organisation's revenue streams in the approximately 89 hotels. Informed by Eisenhardt (1989), this will be done through a within-case analysis that focuses on understanding and making sense of both the initial situation and the development of each case firm.

Corporate entrepreneurship in Scandic Hotel: Revenue management (Sweden)

Overview

Corporate entrepreneurship comes from both external market conditions and disruptive changes that affect the tourism industry with authoritarian decisions and companies' internal conditions. The need for change and changed behaviours comes from both constant trends in markets and disruptive changes (Backer & Ritchie, 2017; Ritchie & Jiang, 2019).

Research in the two overall areas usually distinguishes between external and internal driving forces: 1) external – fast and slow market changes, increased competition and disruption with a crisis, and 2) internal – vision, business focus, systems, skills, finance and more. When the changes are then put into context, it is also about conditions that are national, regional or local. They can also include structural issues before they are jointly transferred to concepts and later implemented as innovations. In this, it is easy for leaders to underestimate the importance of understanding the business model and in their work with business model innovation, this comes into conflict with the model (Markides, 2013). The innovations can have many different focuses from market, external and internal processes, among others.

The challenge for technical managers is to link the physical to economic domains (Chesbrough & Rosenbloom, 2002). It is therefore important to understand the underlying drivers of a change for managers,, whether external or internal, and how these will affect the structure and the organisation going forward. Changing the business model faster and providing corrected strategies can commercialise hidden values faster and with economic competitive advantages.

External and internal drivers, settings and innovations

The company was directly affected by external drivers at the end of February 2020, when the first signs were that international group bookings began to be cancelled. After that, the course of events passed quickly, and a force majeure situation was evident to the entire industry within a week. In the long run, overcoming crises really depends on the resilience of individual businesses (Kuscer et al., 2021).

The internal drivers were about ensuring finances, communication with the stock exchange, making quick action plans and targeting short-term crisis groups from the overall management and its support functions. As the course of events progressed rapidly, central control tools also became an important issue for short-term decision-making—where the systems no longer received the necessary data to function fully either for management or to be able to support diversified customer management. Teece (2010) argues that to be successful (contribute to competitive advantage), business models must evolve over time in anticipation of, or in response to, changes in markets, technology or legal structures.

The extremely rapid changes contributed to the company's bookings of customers in all parts being cancelled outright or rescheduled. It affected the market, processes and, of course, the organisation across the company. A focus on creating new things was immediately initiated in a very difficult situation. Leaders were facing two questions for resource functions and use. In the literature for business model research, there is a fundamental need for business model innovation (Chesbrough & Rosenbloom, 2002; Teece, 2010) to create new opportunities (Zott & Amit, 2010).

Impact of COVID-19 on the department and company as a whole

The external drivers were travel restrictions, lockdowns and other local restrictions. The new market conditions created new behaviours immediately and at the same time with very different rules throughout Sweden and the world. The company quickly negotiated with the hotel's landlords about changing rental conditions, 80% redundancies, including layoffs, occurred and the remaining group was furloughed at various levels, including with working from home. The management had to deal with the crisis primarily with new short-term and long-term plans, financial holdbacks, ensuring more capital/investments and working personnel issues. Since the external changes were rapid, the internal changes also needed to go fast. The ambition was to use the time to ensure that those allowed to travel would also have a good, world-class experience. It was not easy.

For the department within revenue management, the abrupt forced halt meant completely changed working conditions for those who remained. Since the various computer systems that calculate prices and forecasts received no input, the new conversation with the hotel managers became to talk about assumptions instead. The effects were mainly two-part: 1) strategic – more focus on mentoring and creating good conditions, having more focus on assumptions (when the data disappeared), managing information more overall and at the same time focus on streamlining data, and 2) operational – it will be a tighter organisation with closer contacts both in the department and with the hotel managers, and the previous weekly calls now instead became communication via email along with phone calls because they were also not allowed to meet face to face initially.

There were many positive effects that can be described as innovations: more private customers, more flexible bookings, fluctuations in segmentation, consolidations in the offer by closing certain hotels completely, testing more and contributing to changed conditions for developing corporate entrepreneurship.

The turnaround to private customers during the coming summer contributed directly to the company switching to a more flexible pricing with three different options: fully flexible (cancelable), fixed price with the possibility of rebooking or a mix of both. For the hotels, it also meant changes in the view of the rooms, and while bookings in the summer of 2020 corresponded to 40% of the summer before, customers also demanded a cheaper price. The opportunity to test more with campaigns later became central, partly because the mix of customers demanded it and that there was more time. However, there were limitations on what was possible financially, and some old system support has now turned out to require completely different and more flexible solutions than before. The company reasoned that the testing was also important to still be an active market leader and not lose previous competitive advantages that have been developed over many years.

The negative effects were many both for the company as a whole as well as for the department. Initially, the concern was all of the lost bookings that came quickly and later also other types of bookings, which required more of the hotels as they were mainly focused on business travellers. Now, it was instead families who previously travelled abroad who booked, families who travelled to Sweden to visit their families or couples who wanted to travel after feeling trapped. The reasons were many and vastly different for every individual traveller. All redundancies and layoffs posed a major challenge for the company, as many employees had to leave, and those who remained had to take increased responsibility. In addition, wage levels were lower, which increased the risk that those made redundant would find other jobs with higher wages. The financial issues also had an impact in the fact that the company had to change virtually all its plans and how/what investments should be made.

The single biggest impact was communication. For the department, which helps to be an engine in forecasting, pricing and strategic issues for the hotels' budgeting and organising how the rooms should be filled, the relationships instead became focused on making assumptions. In the short term, it meant returning to the time before data but, at the same time, also trying to estimate when the market would open and be brought back to life.

The most dramatic events went on for a number of months in the spring of 2020, then the summer was operating at about 40% of the year before and the situation continued with restrictions in the autumn. In 2021, things gradually turned around, but it was still mostly business clients rather than leisure travellers. The summer of 2021 was even better than the year before, partly due to the fact that some companies that operated simply as tourist attractions were allowed to reopen. This year, 2022, things have turned around more as restrictions were removed and during the autumn the corporate business has also recovered despite new issues with inflation and war in Europe.

Achievement of entrepreneurship and innovations

It is possible to gather a number of new insights that show what COVID-19 has affected: 1) understand that it can happen, so there is also a need for awareness and crisis preparation in the future for a total lockdown because it can happen again, 2) the company and the department work more closely together with fewer employees, 3) the company now also focuses more on the soft aspects and more directly on the customer, 4) more flexible solutions have been required, and now the company needs more flexible data to be able to adjust faster than before (modern API), and 5) a specific change in the business model as a result.

The new conditions will require more from the company going forward, both in Customer Relationship management (CRM) and other business systems. A big part of the business is to work for the people, and in line with previous growth, it has perhaps been more about actual systems and recognition in branding and the hotels. The new conditions will also require more of the employees' knowledge of the products and improved possible service. The department reasons that knowledge needs to be developed on several levels due to the need for increased communication.

Epilogue

The overall goal was to highlight corporate entrepreneurship and innovations in the tourism industry by highlighting a case, Scandic Hotel's Revenue Management in Sweden and how these were affected by COVID-19.

The case study clearly shows that corporate entrepreneurship is central long-term both in crisis and when there is no crisis. For the chosen company, it was essential to quickly make changes and react to the external drivers in the short term. In the short term, an orientation towards the existing market was needed, and it was to be done without data but with assumptions based on insights from the hotel managers. Their knowledge also became analytically important for the entire company because they built their decisions on assumptions before, even if they had data to help, which the larger company also used to manage the effects and create changes on internal driving forces.

The external drivers quickly drove internal issues of terminations/layoffs and overall changed conditions.

The first year was split into two parts—the spring, when there was nothing in bookings and revenue and the autumn, which was better, but everyone was waiting for it to come off properly. The mix of revenue changed drastically to a reverse distribution of business travellers and individuals, which was reinforced by the complete disappearance of international sales. There was a certain customer need left with the guests involved in the construction of roads, infrastructure and construction, but most of businessess were closed, and many customers were not allowed to go out but encouraged to work from home.

The pandemic has meant an increased focus on the effects of the overall delivery of customer value. The company has had to adapt its existing business model and fundamentally change its product offering. This crisis was both negative and positive. A sharp reversal of the market to those who were allowed to travel initially—private individuals with holidays—and, of course, those people wanted to travel again, especially domestically. This was reinforced by the complete absence of international guests in 2020 and partly in 2021 due to tighter lockdowns and restrictions. However, a positive effect is that the company and the department have also gained better control over who actually books. It also provided a better understanding of when the business traveller returned.

The company has a centralised function for revenue management where everyone is gathered in Stockholm and Gothenburg, though more in Stockholm. During the pandemic, the company has also centralised its group bookings to the head office. The tasks shifted from data and forecasting to assumptions with email instead of physical meetings and to accommodate more hotels where several individuals had to quit. In total, the department was 40 people at the onset of COVID-19, was reduced to 20 people, but is now back to 27 people, on their way to 30 people.

Revenue Management belongs to a commercial group along with strategic pricing, rate loading and channel support, commercial and CRM included. Much of the work is the same as before—work with the hotel managers and have about 4–6 hotels per person. The differences are, above all, that it is more personal today and that the changed mix also requires new knowledge about customer behaviour.

The greatest needs are in improving business systems due to digitalisation, changing and improving the data platform (they have developed 139 improvement points for 2023), not laying all the eggs in the same basket, instead spreading the risks and knowledge better and running faster in the department as here lies a great opportunity in developing terms and conditions even better.

The external driving force was great, but the company managed a quick internal adaptation, and the department went from data to mentoring with assumptions and has changed communication interpersonally.

References

Backer, E., & Ritchie, B. W. (2017). VFR travel: A viable market for tourism crisis and disaster recovery? *International Journal of Tourism Research*, 19(4), 400–411.

Benchmarking Alliance (2022)

Chesbrough, H., & Rosenbloom, R. S. (2002). The role of the business model in capturing value from innovation: Evidence from xerox Corporation's technology spin-off companies. *Industrial and Corporate Change*, 11(3), 529–555.

Eisenhardt, K. M. (1989). Building theories from case study research. *Academy of Management Review*, 14(4), 532–550.

Hotelstastatistics.com (2022), *Hotel statistics for Sweden.*

Jakobsson, T. (2022) Visita hospitality industry 2022: *The effect of the restrictions on the Swedish hotel market, an update after the pandemic.*

Kuscer, K., Eichelberger, S., & Mike, P. (2021). Tourism organizations' responses to the COVID-19 pandemic: An investigation of the lockdown period. *Current Issues in Tourism*, 25(2), 247–260.

Markides, C. (2006). Disruptive innovation: In need of better theory. *Journal of Product Innovation Management*, 23(1), 19–25.

Markides, C. (2013). Business Model Innovation: What Can the Ambidexterity Literature Teach US? *Academy of Management Perspectives*, 27(4).

Ritchie, B. W., & Jiang, Y. (2019). A review of research on tourism risk, crisis and disaster management: Launching the annals of tourism research curated collection on tourism risk, crisis and disaster management. *Annals of Tourism Research*, 79, 1–15.

SCB Central Bureau Statistics (2022) the Swedish government agency operating under the Ministry of Finance and responsible for producing official statistics for decision-making, debate and research.

Swedish Agency for economic and regional growth, about Swedish Tourism, 2020

Sweden Agency for economic and regional growth (2022)

Teece, D. J. (2010). Business models, business strategy and innovation. *Long Range Planning*, 43(2–3), 172–194.

Zott, C., & Amit, R. (2010). Business model design: An activity system perspective. *Long Range Planning*, 43(2–3), 216–226.

Case 6 Alfa Aldea

Astrotourism innovation in Chile[1]

*Carlos Fernández Hernández
and Carmelo J. León*

Introduction

Antecedents of Alfa Aldea astronomic centre

Astrotourism began to be implemented in the Coquimbo region (Chile) in the second half of the 90s. The presence of astronomical scientific observatories and high-quality dark skies for observation generated an incipient demand that was channelled with the creation of astronomical observatories for tourist use, promoted and managed by public bodies. In the mid-2000s, the region adopted the name "La Región Estrella" as a tourist brand. Thus, the National Tourism Service (SERNATUR) has designed a product plan that aims to position astrotourism as one of the differentiating products of regional tourism. In this way, a set of astrotourism programs for the entire country began to be activated with travel agencies. The consolidation of the Route of the Stars in the region as an emblematic route of the Bicentennial of the country constitutes a milestone that gives way to the internationalisation of astrotourism promotion.

In this context, the Alfa Aldea project was born, located between reference scientific facilities and public astronomical observatories that try to contribute to scientific dissemination and satisfy a growing demand for observation linked to tourism (Fernández Hernández et al., 2017).

The origin of entrepreneurship is spontaneous. Marco Antonio Rudolffi Iglesias, who owns an 8-hectare farm dedicated to vineyards in the municipality of Vicuña, in the Elqui Valley, and is unemployed, together with his wife María Elena Espejo Sirvent, and with a son who stayed for four years in a wheelchair, received a telescope from a friend to look at the stars and the moon.

> "We were feeling kind of sad and while we were watching we were entertained and forgot our problems for a moment. Later, we talked, and an uncle gave us a telescope and that's how we learned with friends from the Mamalluca [Observatory] and we were seduced by the subject of galaxies and the universe."[2]

DOI: 10.4324/9781003454465-7

The chapter presents the strategic blueprint actions carried out from an innovation-based approach that leads to the creation of new products and services. The impact is demonstrated in the growth in the number of clients, in the consolidation of the project and a clearly differentiated position in the national astrotourism market (Soleimani et al., 2019).

The centre: Beginnings, key issues, problems and activities

In the beginning, the centre had a cabin to accommodate tourists interested in astronomy located on the farm. It was surrounded by mountains and the Gemini, SOAR and Vera Rubin scientific observatories are visible from the site.. Thus, it resembled a natural planetarium, where observations could be made in the open air. The promoter and his wife were the founding nucleus of the entity Alfa Aldea Astronomical Observatory, Natural Planetarium.

> "In the beginning, we started alone, with the help of friends, we did the tours in the grass, we had a small project and then we began to grow. But we made our slightly bigger leap through a project called Capital Semilla Emprende. And there they gave us, SERCOTEC, six million pesos; that was what part of the construction cost us."[3]

The public grant allowed for constructing an open-air amphitheatre with a capacity for one hundred people and acquiring the telescope equipment involved, turning the place into a natural planetarium (Image 6.1). Subsequently, the project incorporates a radio telescope. Two astronomers in training have join the entrepreneurs who manage two telescopes—solar and night—and guided groups, and two other people support logistics activities. For 2016, the astronomical centre is consolidated in an environment of notable growth of astrotourism initiatives and ventures that continue to the present day. The total material investment reaches 35 million Chilean pesos.

Image 6.1 (a, b) Installations of Alfa Aldea Natural planetary.

Source: Images from Carlos Fernández.

Tours run every day. They begin in the dome with an experiment that makes it easier to listen to the sounds of the radio telescope. A local wine accompanies the welcome and leads to the viewing of a three-dimensional film about the birth and evolution of planet Earth with the help of special lenses. Later, in the amphitheatre, an observation is made, solar or nocturnal as the case may be, supported by the telescopes. Finally, a photograph of the participants is taken, or astrophotography in the case of night tours.

The consolidation of entrepreneurship constitutes a continuous challenge for the promoters, resulting in the most outstanding problems:

a The capital needs to undertake the improvements and expansion of the facilities depend on the possibilities of self-financing.
b Optimising the use of the facility's capacities depends on attracting a greater number of astrotourists and new tourist segments based on the diversification of activities and the differentiation of the centre.
c Consolidating the growth of the observatory in a sustainable way implies a collaborative strategy that involves destination, regional and local perspectives.

History of Alfa Aldea, entrepreneurial activity and organisational structure

Alfa Aldea[4] operates with a flexible design of varied programs, whose recipients may be children, the elderly, students, companies or people with special needs, combining astronomical outreach programs with catering and accommodation services. The manager inspires all the proposals with a personal stamp: "*Under the starry dome of the world we bring the universe closer to your eyes*", operating with criteria of flexibility in design, service culture and customer focus. Alfa Aldea's service proposal addresses the following axes:

• Astrotourism experiences: solar observation, night observation, space sounds with a radio telescope and 3D talks.
• Accommodation with places of recreation.
• Learning astrophotography.
• Virtual tour "StarHome".
• Program for disseminating astronomy "*A Universe for All*", bringing astronomy closer to the whole society.
• "*Vida Planeta*" astronomy programs for children.
• Exchange programs with university students.
• Private events with scientific dissemination activities.
• Parking for caravans and location of tents with access to services.
• Cafeteria and catering service in the astronomical centre.

The organisational structure is made up of six people as the base team. Having trained and motivated professionals who respond to the flexible requirements that an activity requires is a challenge. For this, an alternative is presented in recruiting university astrophysics students who wish to combine studies and work as astroguides. Although with a certain degree of versatility in its functions, the team is made up of the following positions:

- CEO and executive director.
- Logistics, accommodation and catering services.
- Commercial and marketing manager and astroguide.
- In charge of social networks and commercial attention. Astroguide and astronomical dissemination.
- Logistics operations manager, astronomical presentations and astrophotographer.
- Logistics, guide and various services.

The promoters of Alfa Aldea develop the product "A Universe for All" as the star program of the observatory from the beginning, which transmits the values of a disinterested vocation of scientific dissemination, with which to share appreciation for the skies of the Valley and the astronomy. Thus, they start to visit with the company's staff and telescopes, the communities in rural populations, prisons and educational centres in relatively depressed or marginal areas. This program is conceived for the main mission of Alfa Aldea: to reach beyond where the telescopes can observe and where the firm is present by making the sky understood with its unique and special-ised observations and interpretations. In other words, the mission intends to boost the so-called "culture of the skies" with extension and dissemination programs or advanced tourist products for day and night observation based on a narrative created ad hoc (Image 6.2).

Image 6.2 (a) Logo of Alfa Aldea and (b) day tour.

Source: Images from Alfa Aldea astronomic centre.

The Coquimbo region: Vision and determining factors

The Coquimbo region is one of the 16 regions into which Chile is divided, located in the southern part of the Atacama desert, 250 km north of the capital, Santiago. Three provinces make up the region: Elqui, Limarí and Choapa, which have 15 municipalities. La Serena, in the province of Elqui, is the regional capital and the administrative headquarters of government agencies.

Chile has a central structure of the State and a regional structure[5]. At the regional level, the executive body is the Regional Government. Various state agencies such as the National Tourism Service (SERNATUR) aimed at fostering and promoting tourism. the Production Development Corporation (CORFO), a promoter of production and regional economic growth, or the Technical Cooperation Service (SERCOTEC), dedicated to the support of micro and small businesses and entrepreneurs, coexist as regional organisations and setting regional priorities. In addition, communal administration is autonomous and governed by democratically elected mayors.

The low rainfall in the region is a determinant of the arid nature of the landscape. This also determines in part its productive structure, dependent on mining and agriculture, fishing and manufacturing, and the growing role of tourism and trade. Its strength as a tourist destination is based on its unique attractions, magnificent beaches, and ancient forests and marine species protected in the area of the Humboldt Penguin National Reserve.

The region is home to a wide network of telescopes for astronomical observation since the 1960s, promoted by international consortia, which found ideal conditions and quality of the night skies for their location in the northern Chilean regions. There are also exceptional and stable atmospheric conditions for quality sky observation, with more than 300 clear nights a year.

Among the scientific astronomical infrastructure in the region, five international scientific observatories stand out. The attraction of these facilities and the interest in astronomy stimulated a demand that found a response in the creation of astronomical observatories for tourism purposes (Fernández Hernández et al., 2019). The first was the Mamalluca Observatory, in the municipality of Vicuña. It was the result of public-private cooperation and public ownership and began operating in 1997. This offer is currently complemented and completed with fifteen private initiative tourist observatories, including Alpha Village.

The solar eclipse of July 2nd 2019, was a powerful lever for the growth and promotion of astrotourism for Coquimbo and Chile. Today, the region is known as one of the most relevant astrotourism destinations in the world.

Origin and evolution of the key elements of the business model

The analysis of the evolution of the project allows us to observe a progressive consolidation in its ten years of existence. The number of visitors in the Centre, in its different activities, goes from 3,900 in 2014 to 8,700 in 2017; 12,500 in 2019, to reach 14,200 in 2022 after the pandemic. Alfa Aldea began its very first implementation in 2012. In 2013–2014, the essential elements of the astronomical centre with the amphitheatre were built; the portable telescopes and the interpretation and viewing room were considered essential investments for the provision of astronomical services. At this time, it started the interpretative programs in the so-called Natural Planetarium and launched the scientific dissemination program "*A Universe for All*", with a clear vocation of bringing knowledge of the sky to marginal communities and schools.

In 2015, a radio telescope was installed, which became a differentiating resource by converting radiation captured from space into sound. In addition, communication efforts in the media and social networks are intensified. In 2016, the first dome was built as an interpretation space. In parallel, innovations are made in tours and experiential programs aimed at audiences of all ages.

In 2017, an activity adapted for people with visual disabilities was launched, as well as the "*Vida Planeta*" program aimed at schools and children in general. That year, the firm received various recognitions and awards, being recognised by TripAdvisor as the number one place to visit in the municipality of Vicuña.

In February 2018, the municipality of Vicuña awarded it recognition on the anniversary of the city's founding. This year, it completed the installation of a second dome for astronomical observation, transforming the first into a "biosphere dome" dedicated to the children's program "Vida Planeta". It also consolidated its position as the most recommended observatory to visit in the Region by the TripAdvisor platform. The intense activity with schoolchildren extends to international exchanges carried out at the facilities.

In 2019, the July 2 total solar eclipse was fully visible in the Coquimbo region. It became "*that very important moment*" and "*one of the most unforgettable experiences of our lives*"[6], shared in Alfa Aldea with more than 270 students from leading universities and astronomical research centres in the United States.

Regarding its social projection, the project continued with its strong commitment to bringing astronomy closer to disadvantaged and remote communities and rural schools, this time inspired by the figure of the local writer, the Nobel Prize winner Gabriela Mistral. In addition, specific tours were offered for groups of cruise passengers arriving at La Serena.

The declaration of a "catastrophe zone" throughout the country due to the COVID-19 pandemic at the beginning of 2020 led to the complete closure of the activity for months, followed by a long period of activity with sanitary protection measures. Adapting to these circumstances led to the development of a new product, such as the virtual tour that can be enjoyed from homes called "StarHome", promoted with the slogan "*We bring the universe closer to your eyes*", launched at the beginning of 2021. In addition, it promoted the product "StarHome" box (Image 6.3) to be delivered at home with featured agri-food and artisan products from the region. As an additional innovation, renting spaces for the tourist location of caravans and tents is offered.

In 2021, Alfa Aldea continued to lead the preferences of TripAdvisor in the municipality. Online activities are permanent with participation in public

Image 6.3 (a) Product "StarHome". (b) Bringing the Universe to your eyes.
Source: Images from Alfa Aldea astronomic centre.

debates and training programs that include those produced and broadcasted from the Observatory, such as the series of chapters "*Universe for All*". In June 2022, the post-pandemic new normal activity finally becomes operational, reactivating the programs to bring astronomy closer to the educational world, the proposal for night and daytime astronomical tour programs, and presenting a new corporate image (Image 6.2). As a new line of products, the firm launches a program of private à la cart events (aimed at organisations, companies and institutions) with the collaboration of local invited companies (agro-food, pisco and artisan companies). Further, the sale of packages through consolidated travel operators is expanding nationwide.

Development

Corporate entrepreneurship as an answer to the Enterprise consolidation challenge

The key conditions for the emergence of the Alfa Aldea venture can be summed as: (a) its foundation based on family values, with personal enthusiasm and passion for the activity to be carried out; (b) the limitation of self-financed capital for investing on the full initial development of the project; and (c) the vocational innovative skills with a social service philosophy which is transmitted to all the staff.

The radio Telescope, a new tourist resource (2015)

The emergence of Alfa Aldea occurred when an offer of public astronomical observatories for tourism already existed in the region. In this offer, the

Mamalluca Observatory—located in the same municipality as Alfa Aldea—leads in reputation and the ability to meet demand. Thus, there is a need to differentiate under a double action. First, presenting sky observational narratives as an attraction enhances the value proposition. Second, by avoiding competing with the attributes offered by these observatories (dimensions of the domes and characteristics of the telescopes, capacity and resources of the interpretation rooms, location in the mountains with altitude, etc.).

Following this strategy, in 2015, a corporate venture was launched based on a new technological resource, which gives rise to new services and opens up the possibility of creating new tourism products. This was based on capturing information from the sky through a radio telescope, which was a novel development that had not been implemented in other tourist observatories in the region. The radio telescope captures the signal of objects located in the Universe coming from outer space to Earth. That signal is conducted by cable to the control room, where electronic equipment converts the electromagnetic wave inaudible to the human ear into a perceptible sound. The radio telescope has a configuration of four antennas that allow it to build up alternative narratives of the sky, i.e., special attention to people with visual disabilities.

In the organisational context, those responsible for Alfa Aldea still had basic amateur training in astronomy at that time. However, they conceived the idea of a radio telescope as an opportunity, finding support from the advice and inspiration of a local astronomer-scientist. When thinking about investing in this resource, they consider the following factors: a) the easy implantation of the antennas due to the characteristics of the terrain, b) the relative simplicity of the installation and equipment, c) the moderate scale of the investment, d) the technical advice available for installation, and e) the objective of having this differential resource.

In the context of the new investment, the relationships with professionals and scientists were key to the full functionality of the equipment. After a first installation with partial results, the interest and perseverance of the entrepreneurs led them to find a specialist who, by varying the direction of the antennas, began to record unusual sounds. The interest in deciphering the signals led to seeking help and advice from the researcher-developer of the equipment, located in a North American university, who, very interested in the findings, shares information and technical knowledge that helps to refine the sound capture to interpret their source of origin, and to treat it as interesting material for research and knowledge. In this way, the signals and sounds received by the radio telescope become a reliable source of wave emission from stellar activity, particularly from the sun. Thus, due to the novelty of the proposal, it is incorporated as an essential and differentiating resource for the interpretation proposal from the Alfa Aldea observatory. This is the only radio telescope in the region, thereby becoming the differentiating component of Alfa Aldea's offer and a key asset for the promotion of the entire project.

New tourist products for visual (2017) and motor (2018) disabled people

The radio telescope represented the possibility of rephrasing the scope of astronomical interpretation, enabling to focus on alternative segments. Thus, the new incoming sounds became the resource for designing a specific product for people with visual disabilities. The promoters favoured the innovation because of their empathy with the disabled and handicapped people due to their family circumstances.

The investment also raised opportunities to develop scope economies involving simultaneous activities. In 2017, it is developed a specific tour for disabled people. The director of the observatory and the astroguides receive support from external psycho-pedagogical experts to design the different phases of the tour. Special attention was put on defining the learning and entertainment components and giving a strong sensory base to the product. The market already offered some three-piece celestial model kits that combined with audio made it possible to provide experiences for "putting the sky in your hands". Therefore, the company acquired printed scale models of different celestial elements written in braille. The textures in these models allowed the person to perceive the profiles of the planets, constellations and some space structures. The offer of the new adapted activity required a special script that also implied the need to improve the qualifications of all the personnel in contact with the public, and in particular the astroguides[7].

In 2018, there started a second phase of this innovation by extending service to other people with special disabilities. This proposal was facilitated by personalised systems and services, developed with external advice and the family experience in the treatment of motor disability. Thus, a new product called "Inclusive Astronomical Talks and Experiences" was designed and tailored to people who also have motor disability. To this aim, the radio telescope is used to hear the sounds of space, and with 3D printed models a tactile and non-visual sensation of space is achieved. Adapted telescopes are also made available, and the astronomical centre is equipped with special access facilities such as ramps. Wheelchair facilities are implemented, and staff are trained for this type of service. This innovation generates comprehensive learning and entertainment opportunities for all visitors, where empathy between people is encouraged, and the senses of hearing, touch, and vision are used.

The external factors that have sprung entrepreneurship can be found in (1) the popularisation of astrotourism; (2) the existence of an unsatisfied demand in people with special abilities; (3) the presence of public policies that encourage the development of inclusive tourism products; and (4) the generalisation of new materials to support astronomical interpretation. From the corporate strategy of the Alfa Aldea project since its creation, these products have always been part of the objectives of the venture.

The pioneering character in the development of these products is also an opportunity to show superior performance in a competitive environment. The main handicap for this type of product is the provision of soft skills and competencies (ability to listen, service attitude, team culture, etc.). However, in the case of Alfa Aldea the staff is adequately trained. The materialisation of these products is clearly aligned with the social vocation of the enterprise, by encouraging self-esteem and the feeling of inclusion and belonging to the Universe in this segment of visitors. Thus, the mission accomplished is shown when one of the visually impaired users writes to the centre after the experience: "*Everything I touch is what I observe, and you brought the Universe into my hands*"[6].

As a public distinction of the efforts put the inclusive innovation, The Alfa Aldea Centre has been one of the three winners of the "More Tourist Value 2022" contest, awarded by the central service of SERNATUR, in recognition of its commitment to develop innovative, sustainable and inclusive tourism products. The actual fact is that Alfa Aldea is highly distinguished as an observatory where astronomy is made accessible to people with various types of disabilities.

Corporate entrepreneurship based on a competitive approach to create new products. Astrotourism in a pandemic, bringing the Universe closer to home: "StarHome" (2021)

The outbreak of the COVID-19 pandemic led to a total production stoppage in the first few months, which lasted for months with the development of activities with restrictions and sanitary protocols. It was a period of great difficulty. Overcoming the challenges raised by the pandemic required a large capacity for resistance, adaptation and innovation. Thus, it represented a time for reflection and search for new alternatives. Therefore, after various ideas and designs, it was decided to develop a new product called "Star-Home", promoting a new approach to service.

"StarHome" was conceived as an online astronomical tour product launched to the national market that could be enjoyed from home, avoiding travel and being available every day broadcasted live (Image 6.3). The product allowed the skies of Elqui Valley to be shown from the Alfa Aldea facilities. Under the name "We bring the universe closer to your eyes" Image 6.3), this new online way of making observations was carried out through the Zoom platform, allowing interaction between clients and guides. The telescopes were equipped with special cameras to enlarge the elements so they could be viewed up to a thousand times, thus providing acceptable image resolutions on the clients' devices. Based on the pre-existing products, four differentiated programs for the presentation of the Universe were designed to meet the demands of diverse audiences, from families to the most specialised in astronomy.

Epilogue

Family entrepreneurship

Family-based enterprising involves an arduous and complex path in which the entire patrimonial system is employed, as well as the work and emotional skills of the family members. The Alfa Aldea project emerged from a need for self-employment of its main promoter but encountered a useful resource in observing the sky in a country accustomed to looking deep into the ground through mining. The opportunities raised worked their magic and gained momentum by connecting with the regional and local strategies for the development of astrotourism. The key ingredients for the success of the project are found in the natural capacity to raise the value from astrotourism, the social sensitivity of the promoters, and their empowerment towards achieving innovative and impacting outcomes.

> "I remember when this was launched, I was in Santiago and I still didn't have enough resources to go. And I arrived, and I was hallucinated with what they were talking about and like I saw the future there"[8].

The challenge of entrepreneurship: Differentiation to guarantee finance

Alfa Aldea started its innovative project in a developing astrotourism market, with some iconic astromical observatory facilities for tourist use in the region, few private competitors and limited resources. The rigorous work of assessing the market potential, the availability of a network of contacts and relationships based on solvency and trust, together with the advice of friends and experts and collaboration with public entities, have been useful tools to define a successful differentiation strategy.

Innovation and creativity as a source of adaptation

The common denominator of the corporate innovations reported in this chapter has been the use of both family and endogenous resources in their different stages of development. The value proposition for creating products and services has been based on constantly exploring ideas and prototypes that connect fully with final demand. Thus, it has been possible to offer a differentiated sky story focusing on a special target audience, approaching the market with a pioneering strategy. This results from an "attitude of observation and listening" to the market and of attending to the needs of the social reality. The innovation does not only aim to guarantee profitability but also to focus on sustainability in responding to social needs. In sum, Alfa Aldea's values are central to the essence of its innovations: honesty, humility, hospitality, humanity and enthusiasm for socially oriented creativity.

Sources consulted

For the development of this case, the following have been interviewed:
Don Marco Rudolffi Iglesias, owner and promoter of the Alfa Aldea Astronomical Centre.

Notes

1 We thank Marco Rudolffi Iglesias and Pamela Duarte Ponce for their support and the information provided for this work.
2 Taken from "Vicuña: Los ojos del universo en el Valle del Elqui", article by Rebeca Luengo in Diario El Día (07/11/2016). https://www.diarioeldia.cl/region/2016/11/7/vicuna-los-ojos-del-universo-en-el-valle-del-elqui-34701.html
3 Interview with Marco Rudolffi. SERCOTEC, Chile.
4 In its constitution and consolidation, Alfa Aldea has had the support and institutional services provided by the Corporation for the Promotion of Production (CORFO), SERNATUR, the aforementioned SERCOTEC, the Municipal Tourism Corporation of Vicuña and the Department of Tourism of the Municipality of La Serena.
5 Law no. 20,990 of the Republic of Chile (publication January 5, 2017) provides for the popular election of the executive body of the Regional Government.
6 Interview with Marco Rudolffi.
7 "Talks and inclusive astronomical experiences in Alfa Aldea, winner of the contest Más Valor Turístico 2022". In: https://www.youtube.com/watch?v=WKqZSUn7N-Q. Video uploaded: January, 4th 2023.
8 Interview with Marco Rudolffi.

References

Fernández Hernández, C., Araña Padilla, J., & León González, C. J. (2017). *Estudio del producto de astroturismo en La isla de La Palma.* Santa Cruz de Tenerife: Ecointur.

Fernández Hernández, C., León González, C. J., & Duarte Ponce, P. (2019): Astroturismo en la Región de Coquimbo: Innovación de producto a partir del aprovechamiento del recurso cielo. *En 100 soluciones a 50 problemas para la gestión turística de empresas e Iberoamérica* (pp. 115–237). Madrid: Editorial Síntesis.

Soleimani, S., Bruwer, J., Gross, M. J., & Lee, R. (2019). Astro-tourism conceptualization as special-interest tourism (SIT) field: A phenomenological approach. *Current Issues in Tourism*, 22(18), 2299–2314.

Case 7 Exploring new market opportunities through entrepreneurial innovation at "El Grifo" Winery in The Canary Islands, Spain

Teresa Aguiar-Quintana,
José Luis Ballesteros and
Ma del Carmen Domínguez

Introduction and case selection

El Grifo, S.A. is the company that owns Las Bodegas El Grifo (El Grifo wineries), located on the island of Lanzarote in the Canary Islands archipelago. It is one of the oldest wineries in Spain, since its origins date back to 1775. Throughout its history, it has passed through the hands of three different families. The winery belongs to the "Denomination of Origin" (DO) *Vinos de Lanzarote* (created in 1993) and is also one of the most celebrated within the DO and from the Canary Islands.

The cultivation of wine in Lanzarote is linked to volcanic eruptions that occurred in the past. The eruption of the Timanfaya volcano from 1730 to 1736 produced a significant economic and social collapse on the island. It poured ash on much of the land that had been dedicated to growing cereals. However, the farmers who did not emigrate in the face of these adverse circumstances knew how to adapt, and they discovered ways in which to take advantage of the extreme conditions. They learned to benefit not only from the terrain generated by the eruption, but in the face the scarce (not exceeding 150 mm per year) and irregular rainfall.

In these circumstances, viticulturists cultivate the vines by digging over the *lapilli mantle* generated by *pyroclastic* rain. Thus, they dig deep until they reach fertile land, where they plant the vines either in holes or trenches. Due to its porous nature, this layer of lapilli can conserve moisture from the night and from the little rainfall that occurs on the island and channel it towards the fertile soil. Thus, the lapilli generates an insulating effect on the ground that protects the vines from heat. However, the winegrower must deal with another condition of the territory: the wind, which is almost constant throughout the year and can cause the upper layers of lapilli to damage the plants. For this reason, winegrowers have built small walls of volcanic stone (60 or 70 cm high) to protect the vines. Moreover, this wind, in many cases of Saharan origin, can quickly dry out the plants. That is why the plants used are "creeping" (stuck to the ground), spending less energy transporting the sap.

DOI: 10.4324/9781003454465-8

All these circumstances have given rise to the characteristic area in which the El Grifo winery is located, called 'La Geria', a protected landscape of enormous scenic, cultural and ethnographic value—see Image 7.1. It is also an important tourist attraction, which projects a unique and differentiating image used to promote island tourism. However, all of this has created a working environment for the vine characterised by a density of plants per hectare lower than that which can be observed in other unprotected areas of the island and which takes far less advantage of the land than is typical in other Spanish D.O.s (the density is around 950 plants per hectare). In addition, the presence of these holes and walls, as well as the unevenness of the land, prevent the use of agricultural machinery such as tractors, making the manual work of the viticulturist essential for the care of the plant and the collection of its fruits. Thus, for example, the harvest is done manually in 20 k boxes. It should also be noted that it is a crop characterised by the absence of irrigation since most of the water used on the island of Lanzarote comes from desalination, whose use in agriculture would harm the land due to boron levels. All this generates productivity levels—in kilograms of grapes per hectare worked—much lower than what can be found in other wine-growing regions in Spain. Thus, in Lanzarote, between 1,000 and 1,500 kilos of grapes are collected per hectare—significantly lower figures than those of other Spanish DOs such as *Ribera del Duero* or *Rioja*.

Finally, it should be noted that climate change is affecting the vines. Thus, the milder winters and the higher daytime temperatures affect the plants,

Image 7.1 El Grifo Winery.

Table 7.1 Evolution of annual production, 2018–2022

	2018	2019	2020	2021	2022
Total gathered	1.016.602 kg	712.362 kg	247.826 kg	424.690 kg	420.053 kg

Source: Prepared by authors.

especially their sprouting. This fact, together with the extreme conditions described above, causes great ups and downs in the winery's production, creating difficulties when it comes to marketing. In Table 7.1, the evolution of the annual production of the winery in the last five years is presented.

Business profile and framework

El Grifo is a medium-small winery with an annual production of between 300,000 and 400,000 bottles annually. The main vineyard is 50 hectares. It also employs 150 small viticulturists with old and stable relationships (an average of 15 years), which often date back to the last century. Viticulturists are a significant concern for the company since, in the past, it collaborated with more than 300 of them. The vast majority have a low professional profile. There is a problem of generational change since many young people do not want to continue working the crops of their elders. El Grifo considers the solution to inevitably involve improving grape prices (in the 2022 harvest, an average of €3 per kilo was paid) to make the activity more attractive. This will necessitate positioning the wine in the high-end range of Spanish wines. Table 7.2 presents the number of employees in the last five years.

Currently, the winery sells less than 20 products that it classifies into four large groups: 1) *Malvasía Volcánica grape* Whites – this unique variety in the world has been produced by the winery since the last quarter of the 18th century (almost 400 years ago); 2) Reds and Rosés made from the *Listán Negro grape* – this variety, originally from Andalusia, where it disappeared due to *phylloxera*, is today exclusive to the Canary Islands (which is rare in the wine world); 3) "Especially Rare" wines – among them are products such as 'Vijariego', whose grape (not being characteristic of the Canary Islands) was imported from Andalusia where today it is residual, although it persists in Las Alpujarras (and some other regions where its cultivation is now very marginal), and 'the Orange wine', which stands out for its traditional method of production; and 4) old sweet wines, with high-end category products such as 'Malvasia Canari'.

Table 7.2 Evolution of number of employees, 2018–2022

Year	2018	2019	2020	2021	2022
Number of employees	36,5	38	24	30	36

Source: Prepared by authors.

Table 7.3 Evolution of turnover, 2018–2022

	2018	2019	2020	2021	2022
Turnover (€)	3.310.876	3.989.694	2.645.283	5.141.695	5.400.000

Source: Prepared by authors.

Due to the circumstances described above, the price range of these wines is high when compared with other products made in the Iberian peninsula. This fact conditions its commercialisation, although the price differential is generally better understood in international markets than in the peninsular market itself. The latter may be due to the fact that Spain is a wine-growing country that offers excellent value for money. For this reason, it is a challenge for the company to communicate the special circumstances under which wine is produced in Lanzarote in such a way that leads to the adequate evaluation of the product by consumers in foreign markets. We present the evolution of turnover of the company from 2018 to 2022 in Table 7.3.

El Grifo considers its competition not to be other wines from Lanzarote or the Canary Islands, but rather medium-high range wines from mainland Spain (it is not limited to the other wineries represented in the D.O. Vinos de Lanzarote) since it is a company with a strong export intention that competes with large producers in the national market and in many international markets. However, when observed only within the D.O. into which it is integrated, it can be seen that the number of wineries has gone up from 14 in 2018 to 33 in 2022. In general, these are new wineries with low capacity and low production, but they reflect the growing interest in this productive activity among the island's business community, which is trying to respond to the global trend that exists for the consumption of quality wine.

Furthermore, for a long time, the company has taken advantage of its status as an old and traditional winery to promote activities related to wine tourism. El Grifo created a museum inspired by a famous Canarian artist, César Manrique, who suggested maintaining the original winery without any alterations (he helped preserve the old winery). Thus, the old facilities were used to exhibit some of the 500 pieces of equipment and machinery showing the history of wine in Lanzarote and the Canary Islands. The museum has a library focused on the world of wine, with more than 5,000 works. In addition, the museum organises painting exhibitions and concerts and collaborates with the Saramago Foundation and the Council of Lanzarote, which makes it one of the most important in the Canary Islands on this subject. The company considers the increasing number of tourists who come to Lanzarote interested in wine and visiting the winery an important source of brand loyalty.

Before the COVID-19 pandemic, the wineries received more than 80,000 people annually, some of whom took guided tours of the vineyard and the facilities and visited the Museum. It must be taken into account that, for the

Table 7.4 Evolution of percentage of sales made in the local, national and international markets

	2018	2019	2020	2021	2022
Local sales	74%	71%	70%	68%	63%
Sales in the mainland of Spain	16%	18%	16%	18%	22%
Export sales	10%	11%	14%	14%	15%

Source: Prepared by authors.

tourist who loves wine and vineyards, there is nothing comparable to the landscape of La Geria. It is a different type of cultivation than those that can be found in La Rioja, Bordeaux or Tuscany, which makes it a unique experience. For this reason, the company tries to promote these visits through different collaborations and packages for tourists. Next, in Table 7.4, the evolution of sales in the local, national and international markets is shown.

Corporate entrepreneurship actions developed

Like many other small companies, El Grifo pursues a business model that is based on the fundamental elements of sustainability, showing concern for the economy, society and, of course, the environment. The company's activity has recently responded to the impacts of the COVID-19 pandemic since its demand comes mainly from the Canary Islands and tourist visits. Sales fell considerably since a large part of them are made through the hotel and restaurant channel (HORECA), which is highly dependent on the tourist activity that entered into crisis. The company continued with its wine production, although the number of viticulturists with whom it worked was reduced, and part of the staff was laid off, given the sharp decrease in sales. However, the pandemic has motivated greater attention to online sales and exports, which has been consolidated with significant increases in export markets such as Germany and France.

Additionally, environmental sustainability has become an important axis of the corporate entrepreneurship actions carried out by the company, both in the related activity of winemaking and in that more linked to wine tourism and focused on the Museum and guided tours. Thus, initiatives have been undertaken aimed at optimising electricity consumption and water purification. At the same time, much effort has been devoted to certifying the environmental quality of work processes in the winery and the vineyards.

Regarding optimising electricity consumption, a small photovoltaic plant has been installed that provides clean and ecological energy. Thus, the company has contracted a power of 140 kW and has an energy consumption of approximately 18,000 kWh per month. The installation of this plant allows a theoretical power of 50 kW, so the energy generated, depending on the date and weather conditions, is an average of 8,000 kWh per month. This action enables energy savings of 44.4% in the months of maximum demand and the emission of tons of CO_2 into the atmosphere, which meant a saving of 41 tonnes in 2020.

The installation of an efficient system for heating water (80°C), necessary for washing machinery, facilities, bottling equipment, tanks and barrels, etc., has also been carried out. The system is based on a solar collector that captures the sun's rays, thus absorbing its energy in the form of heat. Therefore, the water is passed through solar panels, so that part of the heat absorbed by the panel is transferred to the water, raising its temperature to 80°C and then storing it in a storage tank. This system reduces the cost of heating water by 90%. In addition, the system gradually heats the water. It maintains it at no additional cost and even generates a reserve as a result of the increase in the volume of hot water. At the same time, using hot water to clean the facilities reduces the volume of water consumed and makes the use of cleaning products unnecessary.

Moreover, the winery has implemented a certified environmental quality system. The winery's quality management system is certified according to the requirements of UNE-EN-ISO 9001 for Quality Management and UNE-EN-ISO 22000 for Food Safety Management Systems, which ensures the safety and security of the grapes from the harvest to the final consumption of the wines in the winery. In addition, the winery has been certified in accordance with the UNE-EN-ISO 14001 Standard. With this combination of processes, the aim is to reduce environmental and operational impacts and costs. By relying on external control of the winery's environmental management system through an independent certifier, it is intended to achieve several objectives: 1) to increase selective waste collection, 2) to reduce the environmental impact of the waste generated by the winery, and 3) to increase energy savings through the use of renewable energy.

The increasing concern of El Grifo for the environment led the company to embark in 2018 on the ecological certification of those hectares of vineyards that they own (32 hectares) on the El Grifo estate, leaving for later the reconversion of their remaining land. The intention is to grow crops that are more respectful of the environment, which is why it is intended that the entire vineyard itself, which is cared for by permanent company personnel, be certified organic. Thus, in 2018, they began procedures to certify three plots with different types of grapes as organic (*Syrah*, 1.3 ha; *Malvasía Volcánica*, 3.5 ha; *Moscatel de Alejandría*, 0.5 ha.). The entire process is expected to be completed by the year 2024. This initiative will make it possible to obtain an organic grape with which to make an organic wine.

The close relationship with the viticulturalists and the conditions established by the DO have led the company to generate wine varieties marked by the type of grape harvested in specific plots of very high oenological potential. For this reason, the company has generated a line of work in which it promotes and helps, mainly through technical assistance, the main viticulturists with whom it collaborates to transform their plots into organic ones.

This transformation can generate benefits for both parties by expanding, on the one hand, the possibilities of making greater productions of organic wine and, on the other, by charging a higher price for organic grapes. But, in addition, from the point of view of sustainability, it must be taken into account that the carbon footprint of organic wine production is significantly lower than that of traditionally produced wines. The company's growing concern for sustainability can also be seen in other initiatives that the R&D area has launched more recently.

First of all, they have been collaborating with a Spanish company that has patented a system that allows the capture, storage and technical use of CO_2 derived from fermentation. Heat and CO_2 are produced during fermentation, and this system, from an ecological perspective and linked to the circular economy, allows the use of this CO_2 in various parts of the production process, such as: 1) the *inertisation* of the tanks with their own CO_2; 2) eliminating certain mechanical systems in the production processes of the winery (for example, in the homogenisation of oenological products without the need to use pumps, or 'batonage' with CO_2 for the removal of *lees* without energy consumption); 3) improving the management of warehouse refrigeration; and 4) in the combination of CO_2 with oxygen, favouring greater precision in macro- and micro-oxygenation.

All these processes are essential for producing quality wines, so the introduction of this technology has had a significant impact on the production process and the quality of the final product. Thus, for example, in the elaboration of white wines, less precipitate from the fermentation process itself, which, in addition to giving the wine intensity, contributes to i ageing when making aged white wines. However, for these *precipitates* or "lees" (dead yeast cells) to infuse aromas into the wine and give it smoothness and density, they must come in contact with the wine by being kept in suspension, which requires the "batonage" technique. This is the French term for the process of stirring the wine and the lees so that the latter, being in suspension, will release its compounds. That is why it is important for El Grifo wineries to use this "batonage" technique through a programmable and automated stirring method aided by inertisation (much more controlled by means of CO_2). Along the same lines, inerting with CO_2 allows the tanks to be kept sheltered from oxygen that oxidises the wine (cold without oxygen so it can oxidise the wine). Although the wine tanks are kept at a controlled temperature, a slight temperature variation modifies the volume of the liquid, which makes it necessary to make them inert if they are to be protected from atmospheric air (in these tanks, a brief temperature variation changes the wine and with the inerting systems, their temperature and maturation are controlled automatically, making the wines fresher for longer). In addition, this technology reduces the environmental impact by partially recovering those inert gases (CO_2) derived from the production process, reducing the carbon footprint of the winery while generating energy savings. Lastly, it makes it possible to reduce the risk of exposure to CO_2 in wineries, a danger that, although it produces fewer accidents and deaths, is still present as an occupational hazard in the wine sector.

These numerous improvements in the production process have been complemented by others, such as investment in pneumatic presses: the old presses had an analogue system for pressing times but are now digitalised and self-regulating, allowing time levels and pressure to be adjusted. Therefore, the main antecedents of such actions are associated with the organisation's context in terms of its availability of technological, human and financial resources.

Also, there is managerial support in developing new ideas, and two chambers have been built to cool up to 40,000 kg of grapes in their vintage boxes before pressing. In addition, there is a chamber for 25,000 bottles of natural sparkling wine to rest at 14°C before disgorging. A refrigerating room and 500-bottle crates have also been purchased, allowing the company to use the harvest peaks to make sparkling wines that will start selling in the following 4–5 years. In this way, it is possible to deal with the ups and downs of the harvest, responding to viticulturists through a product that makes it possible to make use of surplus grapes.

Secondly, the company is trying to improve the purification system for the water used in the winery. It must be taken into account that the use of water just for cleaning the tanks during the harvest is very high since the 'grape must' passes from one tank to another, creating the need for continuous cleaning. To address this issue an innovation has been introduced. The company started with a complex biological water purification system that favours the biological activity of certain bacteria and microorganisms that eliminate all those biodegradable substances. However, the water resulting from this purification process cannot be used again for cleaning or irrigation, so there is room for improvement in managing this resource. For this reason, the company is investing in a tertiary system through which previously treated water is improved with the current biological system for later use. In this way, a better use of the water consumed by the winery will be achieved.

It should be noted that some of these investments have been made with aid from European agricultural funds (Europe for machinery). However, there are other investments in infrastructure and equipment that were planned that cannot be made because of the winery's location in the protected area of La Geria. For example, the warehouses have tanks outside that do not currently have roofs above them. The fact of not being able to build a warehouse for these tanks limits their use and increases energy consumption. In fact, the wineries have been waiting for more than 20 years for the island authorities to design a special plan for La Geria, which would provide a regulatory framework for the uses and conditions of use in a protected area. This regulatory framework would make it possible to undertake certain currently paralysed investments, the delay of which harms both viticulturists and wineries.

Some other antecedents of the company's corporate entrepreneurship and innovation actions are associated with the relationship with viticulturists. It has been a fundamental axis of action since 2010, thanks to which the quality of the wine has increased due to improvements in the treatment of samples and support for viticulturists with an 'alert' system. The viticulturists take the grape samples to the winery after 'veraison' (when the grapes change colour because they begin to ripen). If they cannot do so, the winery sends its technicians to collect the samples by area. Samples of bags of 100 grapes are taken in order to examine each plot, and the oenologist determines when they should be harvested (the grapes are ready to be picked). In the past, only a single parameter was observed/analysed: the density of the *grape must*, indicative of the amount of sugar per litre, but since 2010, other parameters such as total acidity, probable alcohol levels, colour, berry volume, pH, malic acid, sugar, and nitrogen concentration. Through the analyses carried out, the optimal moment of harvest can be determined according to the variety of the grape and the location of the plot, and the viticulturist can be notified as to when to make the collection at the most opportune moment.

This close relationship with viticulturists resulted in one of the main R&D projects, related to the search for sustainability and environmental adaptation. The plot of one of the viticulturists (Las Parras), located near the coast (Playa Quemada), had ripening problems—they did not adapt to the traditional dates of the harvest on the island (July and August), perhaps because it is a warmer area. This plot is at an altitude of 140 metres above sea level and is located a kilometre and a half from the coast (relatively close to the sea). For this reason, a research group was organised, managed and coordinated by an expert oenologist (an external adviser to the winery for more than 15 years), which also included the two oenologists from El Grifo, the viticulturist owning the plot, a researcher specialising in plant physiology and, finally, the company with which the grape ripening analyses are carried out. The objective of the research was the protection of the vineyards against climate change: the increase in temperature that different wine-growing areas of Lanzarote are experiencing, increasing water stress on the vines, which harms the acidity levels of the grapes.

Thus, they began to collect data and carry out tests with the vines, which led to the first winter harvest being carried out in the Playa Quemada area in 2022. This harvest, which began at the end of March, is a milestone in Europe since it is the first to be done in the northern hemisphere during this season. It must be taken into account that this plot is located in an area that shows a worrying abandonment of the land and its crops, so this initiative opens up a viable solution for many of these plots that could give rise to new vineyards, among other potential uses, since the plants have lower consumption of water resources. In addition, this new crop cycle leads to a lower use of phytosanitary products since there is a lower incidence of pests and

diseases. However, this initiative also provokes misgivings due to the repercussions these new cultivation areas could have for wine-growing activity
in the La Geria protected area, which could lose prominence in the island's
wine production. In 2023 five plots located in various parts of the island were
established, and a harvest took place in March.

Another of the winery's great lines of action focuses on its internationalisation. In this sense, in 2019, 90% (of the half million bottles produced) of
the production was consumed within the Canary Islands' local market. In
those years, the owners of the winery set themselves the goal of selling 20%
of their production abroad. To this end, a couple of years earlier, an internationalisation plan had already been designed that opened up new markets
through collaboration with liquor importing companies and with participation in online sales through collaboration with a network of dealer partners
specialised in this type of marketing. The agreements established with partners based in Germany, Switzerland and Spain opened the possibility for the
winery's products to reach all of Europe. In addition, the company entered
the US market through collaboration with a major wine distribution firm. In
2020, the export markets of France, Scotland and Belgium grew, increasing
180% in the number of exports.

The COVID-19 pandemic led the company to strengthen its internationalisation further. Thus, the turnover in export markets increased, and online
sales intensified through a more robust platform. In this way, a wine club
was created called "Club El Grifo" (https://www.clubelgrifo.com/). This online store sends orders free of charge to all its members in Spain when they
exceed a certain purchase threshold. Thus, belonging to the club generates
an initial discount for the consumer of between 5% and 10% (depending
on whether it is done individually or as a group), but in the case of monthly
subscriptions, it can generate savings of up to 25%. In addition, the winery
is characterised by making exclusive wines, with very few units for sale.
They are wines that come from specific plots on the island with very limited
production volumes or wines that are unique in the world of wine due to
their characteristics and varieties. An example of this is the sweet red wine
'George Glas', made with the *Listán Negro* grape, which disappeared from
Andalusia after *phylloxera* and is now endemic and exclusive to the Canary
Islands. This is a reduced production wine of around 6,000 bottles made ten
years ago. These types of products often have a preference for commercial
launch through Club El Grifo. The creation of this club/online store caused
online sales to grow by 500% in 2020.

Finally, the corporate entrepreneurship of El Grifo winery is palpable in
its product line. In this way, several initiatives carried out in recent years can
be highlighted:

1 Investing in aged white wine stocks. As previously mentioned, a good
   part of El Grifo's traditional winery business has been based on white
   wines of the year (without 'crianza'). However, the company has spent

some years investing in long-lasting white wines for ageing (5–10 years), some of them made with the volcanic *Malvasía Volcánica* grape, which is the most exclusive on the island. This line of business makes it possible to generate stocks to compensate for short vintages, thus responding to problems related to the ups and downs in the production of the various vintages. White wine for ageing is a differentiation factor that distinguishes it from many of the existing wineries in Lanzarote that make young wines (they do not have vintages). It is enabling the winery to penetrate more demanding markets.

2　Delving into the 'typicity' and identity character of the wines produced. This line is pursued through various actions: 1) in 2018, the a research project has isolated, selected and preserved autochthonous yeasts from suitable environments in Lanzarote and collected from El Grifo's vineyards in order to replace commercial dry yeasts, which come from other regions such as Burgundy, Bordeaux, etc., and with which many (if not most) wines are made around the world. El Grifo's use of their own yeasts makes the wine more representative of the region and strengthens its identity. The project aims for the winery to be capable of producing autochthonous yeast on its own, which enhances the typicity of the wines. The first time that their own yeasts were used was in a 2019 'Colección Volcánica Seco Malvasía' that won the prestigious 'Baco de Oro' national award. Thus, in 2020, the entire production of the vintage was made with their own native yeasts. This project will also make it possible to deal with the growing use in the industry of genetically modified yeasts, which make it difficult to create truly organic wines; 2) the commitment to *monovarietal* wines, made with their own yeasts in such a way that gives a unique character to the wines produced. For example, these self-produced yeasts were used in 2019 with the monovarietal white wine 'Vijariego Blanco'. This wine is made with a grape native to Andalusia, where it now barely exists and which has become almost endemic to the Canary Islands; and 3) the continuation of the research into and generation of new products through a line of work known as "Vintage Experiences". Here, experiments are carried out with new products from which new knowledge applicable to the rest of the production is obtained. This initiative has resulted in products such as 'Malvasia Orange Wine', which emerged in 2017. Its intense orange colour also does not incorporate sulphites in its production (the grape ferments with its skins and seeds for three months following an ancestral method). The production of this wine in 2017 did not reach 700 bottles and is currently around 1,100. Other products from "Vintage Experiences" include: 'Ancestral', a sparkling wine made from the *Malvasía Volcánica* grape using the *Ancestral Method* in a single fermentation. This wine is of very limited production - just 1,000 bottles since it comes from only 300 vines located in just one hectare of vineyard; 'Listán Negro Grano a Grano', which was/has been produced in 2021 and 2022; 'Malvasía Vendimia de Invierno' from the Playa Quemada plot, to which we referred before, of slightly less than 4,000 bottles; 'Malvasía Natural 2020', a wine from which 326 bottles were produced from a plot where the vine is grown in perimeter trenches, in which legumes and cereals are also grown. These 'Experience' wines are sold mainly through the museum shop.

Many of these initiatives take the form of products that are being highly valued in the international wine competitions recognised by the OIV (International Organisation of Vines and Wine), in which the winery participates, receiving multiple awards in recent years.

Finally, another major line of action, which today already accounts for 25% of the winery's total sales, is that which is based on 'Wine Tourism'. Currently, investments of close to 400,000 euros have been made to create a tasting room, improve the old winery, create audio guides, install Wi-Fi systems and create new "wine spaces" where the winery's products can be tasted. In this sense, this line is also connected with the efforts towards sustainability since initiatives have been undertaken to reduce the energy consumption of the museum (about 2,000 square meters). Thus far, all the lighting has been replaced by high-performance LED lighting. In addition, the electrical installation began to be managed by a remote automation system that offered better control of the installation. In this way, the lights in certain rooms turn on only when there are visitors, remaining off the rest of the time, while the outdoor lights turn on and off via a twilight sensor. All of this is expected to generate savings of more than 40% in the museum's energy consumption.

Epilogue

Despite empirical evidence that family firms are less entrepreneurial, many family firms compete by repeatedly engaging in corporate entrepreneurship actions, often across multiple generations (Miller & Le Breton-Miller, 2005; Nordqvist & Melin, 2010). For instance, El Grifo is a magnificent example of a company in which corporate entrepreneurship has been embedded into the organisational culture. The company has had to adapt to much tougher conditions than most wineries in the world usually encounter. The lack of essential resources such as water, the harsh weather conditions, the greater difficulty for marketing due to the island's remoteness and relative isolation, and climate change, among other things, have meant that the company has had to generate innovative responses. To this end, the company has made a strong commitment to R&D, and valuable knowledge has been generated through various projects that have created new lines of action, both in work processes and in products.

At the same time, the company is adapting to a consumer who is increasingly demanding 'quality' products and who is interested to know about—and who values—the different types of manufacturing processes, as well as the qualities of the raw materials used in the wines.

In short, it can be seen that very important values for corporate entrepreneurship stand out in this winery, such as courage and resilience.

References

Miller, D., & Le Breton-Miller, I. (2005). *Managing for the long run: Lessons in competitive advantage from great family businesses.* Harvard Business Press.

Nordqvist, M., & Melin, L. (2010). Entrepreneurial families and family firms. *Entrepreneurship & Regional Development*, 22(3-4), 211–239. doi. 10.1080/08985621003726119.

Case 8 Corporate entrepreneurship based on growth strategies of an island hotel chain

The case of beCordial hotels & resorts in Europe

Francisca Rosa Álamo-Vera,
Francisco Javier Gutiérrez-Pérez,
Teresa Aguiar-Quintana and
Yazmina Araujo-Cabrera

Introduction and case selection

Based on the concept of cordiality and to offer its guests accommodation services that represent the best value for money and allow them to enjoy memorable tourist experiences, beCordial Hotels & Resorts has been progressively expanding and diversifying its strategic business units. In this way, this case study aims to present a clear example of corporate entrepreneurship (CE) in an SME in the European tourism sector, mainly due to its continuous search for new alternatives to make its customers feel as if they are at home.

Current research defines CE as business innovation and a process rather than the punctual implementation of specific measures (e.g., Holt et al., 2007). In tourism, CE processes are driven by internal and external factors. While external triggers refer to constant market changes that result in changes in consumer behaviours or new competitors, internal triggers stem from the business itself through its core competencies, culture and visions (Kessler et al., 2015). Once CE processes are triggered, they result in innovation as the outcome (Holt et al. 2007). The main objective of this case study is to analyse the corporate entrepreneurship processes developed by beCordial and the innovations that took place as a result of these processes.

Against the backdrop of the COVID-19 pandemic, as well as administrative issues in one of the expansion areas of the company and the socio-economic trends in the Canary Islands and on the mainland, beCordial has been able to design a corporate strategy mainly based on diversification within the accommodation industry and to implement it by making use of CE actions under the guidance of the top management team and its CEO, Nicolás Villalobos.

DOI: 10.4324/9781003454465-9

beCordial: Business profile and framework

The Cordial chain first entered the tourist accommodation market in the Canary Islands, Spain, at the end of the 1980s. At that time, various renowned business people in the region agreed to jointly invest in two bungalow complexes that were well-positioned in the market: Green Golf and Sandy Golf. Both establishments, which are still in operation today and belong to Cordial, are located in the surroundings of the Maspalomas International Golf Course, south of the island of Gran Canaria. This golf course is one of the main tourist destinations in the Canary Islands due to its proximity to the Dunes of Maspalomas. The natural enclave is unmatched for its beauty and biodiversity.

The founding investors of the project were all prominent figures and companies in the Canary Islands' industrial sector (Araujo, 2015, p.214), including Antonio Vega (from the Tropical brewery), Domingo González (from the Agua de Firgas bottling company), Lizardo Martell (responsible for Vidrieras Canarias and the marketing of the Pepsi and Schweppes brands in the Canary Islands) and José Sánchez (from the food distribution company JSP). All of them were authentic drivers of an industrial activity that, at the time, was mainly focused on the local market. The Villalobos de Paiz family subsequently joined the project and incorporated the Bungalows Biarritz complex under shared management. These bungalows are located in Playa del Inglés, another area of intense tourist activity in the south of Gran Canaria island.

In order to attempt to successfully launch a new brand and try to raise the group's profile in the main issuing markets of the Canary Islands (Germany, the United Kingdom and the Nordic countries), at the end of the 1990s, Cordial formed an economic interest group with other independent hoteliers under the commercial brand Amigos HBA. However, this economic interest group dissolved in 2003, which led to the birth of the current Cordial brand. In the subsequent years, new partners joined the project, such as Sergio Alonso, who was involved in promoting the development of the Cordial Mogán Playa Hotel and the Cordial Mogán Valle apartment complex in the coastal area of the municipality of Mogán, also in the south of Gran Canaria. These decisions led to the creation of a hotel chain structure at the beginning of 2004 named Cordial Canarias Hotels & Resorts. The successful results achieved by this Group through the beCordial brand have enabled it to continue to attract renowned investors, such as the famous international footballer from Gran Canaria, David Silva, who acquired a significant shareholding at the end of 2013.

The activity of the Cordial Group can be summed up as offering both foreign and local consumers solutions to their different accommodation needs, whether in hotels or other forms of accommodation and whether in urban or holiday settings. A shared philosophy exists throughout its various establishments, which is focused on offering quality and an experience oriented towards guest satisfaction. The different innovations vary in their focus (products and services, marketing methods, internal processes), orientation (infrastructure resource innovations vs marketing management innovations), time factor (strategic vs operative), technological involvement (technological vs non-technological innovations), and level of novelty (business, local, regional, national, global) (Kuscer, 2013).

In terms of the accommodation structure of the Cordial Group, it is made up of establishments located in Gran Canaria, Lanzarote, and Málaga. They are distinguished by their degree of management intensity, including some that are fully managed under the Cordial brand (18 establishments) and some that are commercially managed under the Bright Side of Life brand (2 establishments), namely the Hotel Aldea Suites, located in La Aldea, and the Montemayor Apartments, in Playa del Inglés, both in Gran Canaria. With this new business unit, Cordial manages establishments with high customer satisfaction rates that, due to their small size, do not have the specialisation and professionalisation required by the marketing channels of the 21st-century vacation tourism product.

The Cordial brand hotels comprise 1,783 accommodation units distributed as follows: 16 establishments on the island of Gran Canaria, a 4-star hotel in Lanzarote and a 4-star aparthotel on the Costa del Sol (Málaga). The star product in this portfolio is the Hotel Cordial Mogán Playa, a 4-star hotel with 487 rooms that has received numerous awards throughout its history. Table 8.1 shows the main characteristics of the accommodation establishments of the Cordial Group.

Table 8.1 shows that the growth strategy followed in the city of Las Palmas de Gran Canaria, the capital of the province of Las Palmas, focuses on the acquisition and remodelling of iconic buildings in the city's historic centre formed by the neighbourhoods of Triana and Vegueta in the southern cone of the capital (see the facade of the Hotel Cordial Malteses in Image 8.1). The group converted buildings that are part of the Canary Islands' historical heritage and that, after their restoration, preserve their historical essence in combination with modern and functional decoration.

In the words of Mr Villalobos, "After establishing ourselves as one of the leading hotel chains in the south of the island, with establishments in Puerto de Mogán, Taurito, Arguineguín, Maspalomas and Playa del Inglés, we also had to be present in our capital" (Canarias7, 2021). Of the 20 managed establishments, one is considered rural (La Aldea Suites), four urban (boutique hotels), and the remaining 15 are accommodation for sun and beach tourism, a segment in which the Cordial chain concentrates its offer.

The recent inauguration of the Perchel Beach Club (see Image 8.2), the largest beach club in the Canary Islands with more than 6,000 square metres dedicated to leisure, relaxation, and family fun, represents an innovative complement to the Cordial chain's historical activities. The aim was to open a new line of beach club business aimed at family tourism while continuing to achieve the highest customer satisfaction levels at all times. The Perchel Beach Club, together with the neighbouring Cordial Santa Águeda holiday

Table 8.1 Characteristics of the accommodation establishments of the Cordial Group. https://www.becordial.com

Establishment	Official category	Segment	Location
Cordial Mogán Playa	4-star hotel	Sun and beach	Gran Canaria - South (Canary Islands)
Cordial Mogán Valle	3-star apartments	Sun and beach	Gran Canaria - South (Canary Islands)
Cordial Muelle Viejo	Holiday home	Sun and beach	Gran Canaria - South (Canary Islands)
Cordial Mogán Solaz	Holiday home	Sun and beach	Gran Canaria - South (Canary Islands)
Cordial Mogán Paraíso	5-star apartments	Sun and beach	Gran Canaria - South (Canary Islands)
Cordial Magec Taurito	3-star apartments	Sun and beach	Gran Canaria - South (Canary Islands)
Cordial Santa Águeda	Holiday home	Sun and beach	Gran Canaria - South (Canary Islands)
Cordial Green Golf	Apartments 2 keys	Sun and beach	Gran Canaria - South (Canary Islands)
Friendly Sandy Golf	Apartments 1 key	Sun and beach	Gran Canaria - South (Canary Islands)
Cordial Biarritz	3-star apartments	Sun and beach	Gran Canaria - South (Canary Islands)
Cordial Judoka Beach	Apartments 2 keys	Sun and beach	Gran Canaria - South (Canary Islands)
Cordial Macaro Beach	3-star apartments	Sun and beach	Gran Canaria - South (Canary Islands)
Cordial La Niña de Vegueta	Emblematic hotel	Urban	Las Palmas de Gran Canaria (Gran Canaria)
Cordial Plaza Mayor de Santa Ana	Emblematic hotel	Urban	Las Palmas de Gran Canaria (Gran Canaria)
Cordial La Peregrina	Emblematic hotel	Urban	Las Palmas de Gran Canaria (Gran Canaria)
Cordial Malteses	Emblematic hotel	Urban	Las Palmas de Gran Canaria (Gran Canaria)
Cordial Marina Blanca	4-star hotel	Sun and beach	Lanzarote (Canary Islands)
Cordial Mijas Golf	Aparthotel 4 stars	Sun and beach	Costa del Sol (Málaga province)

home complex, have been built by the Cordial Group in an area with significant tourist potential on the island of Gran Canaria, the mouth of the Barranco de Arguineguín. The island's cement company is located in this enclave next to the Santa Águeda wharf. The Gran Canaria Insular Land Planning document initially stated in March 2020 that the Santa Águeda pier would be used for sports/recreational purposes. However, Puertos Canarios (reporting

Image 8.1 Facade of the Hotel Cordial Malteses. Chris Taylor, in Martín Rodríguez (2021, p.16).

Image 8.2 Perchel Beach Club.

to the Government of the Canary Islands) has since announced its intention to grant a concession for the dock to be used for industrial purposes for a further ten years to facilitate the company's relocation. This matter is yet to be fully resolved and may even go to court.

Although each establishment has its own human resources department for administrative tasks, beCordial Hotels & Resorts manages the central corporate services provided to all establishments, from purchases and investments to human resources, including commercial management, reservations, finance, data processing, communication and expansion, through a managerial team that is experienced in the sector. The chain's human resources team is made up of more than 600 people.

Environment

The Canary Islands archipelago is located to the northeast of the African continent, between latitudes 27°37' and 29°5' N, and longitudes 13°20' and 18°10' W. Its geographical fragmentation, given that it is made up of eight islands, and its distance from the mainland make it a unique and distinctive territory for the development of the economic activity. The warm climate and natural resources are major assets for the Canary Islands' tourism sector, which represents around 40% of its economy and help it compete internationally with other issuing markets, mainly in the sun and beach tourism segment. However, since the 1960s, when the Canaries began their journey in this industry, up to the present day, many other segments have also been developed (including golf, rural, nature, adventures, MICE, LGTBI, etc.), which together make up a truly comprehensive offer for tourists visiting the Canary Islands.

International events and trends that have unfolded in the last few years, such as Brexit, the vacation rental boom, the closure of traditional tour operators or, more recently, the effects of the COVID-19 pandemic, have had a major impact on the hotel industry. The tourism sector was, in fact, one of the industries that was most affected by the global crisis that began in 2020 as a consequence of the pandemic, leading to reduced growth projections for 2020 and 2021 and even threatening the very survival of companies and tourist destinations (Gössling et al., 2020).

Some periods saw almost complete paralysis in the tourism industry, generating unprecedented statistics in terms of job losses and companies in the sector going out of business. The drop in tourist arrival rates reached 87% internationally in 2021 (UNWTO, 2021). In Spain, the arrival of foreign tourists by air during the first quarter of 2021 fell by 87.5% compared to the previous year, reaching 90.3% in the case of the Canary Islands (Turespaña, 2021). The number of arrivals to the region barely reached 266,000 compared to around 15 million tourists visiting in previous years.

Given this external context, there is still uncertainty regarding the actual effects of the pandemic on the tourism sector (Rodríguez-Castellanos & San-Martín-Albizuri, 2020). However, tourism companies have started to glimpse the beginning of their recovery as the pandemic and its multiple variants have gradually reduced their drastic initial impact. Thus, in 2022, there was unexpected growth in Spain's and the Canary Islands' tourism, with tourists starting to arrive in summer and continuing to arrive beyond November. In fact, at the World Travel Market tourism fair in London, the President of the Canary Islands government announced a forecast of 14.5 million tourists arriving in the archipelago by the end of the year, a figure that represents 96% of that reached in 2019, before the pandemic (Canarias7, 7/11/2022).

The Cordial chain has also been greatly affected by this entire crisis. It was forced to postpone many strategic decisions regarding the expansion of its business portfolio and its penetration into new tourist destinations. Fortunately, the new recovery scenario will allow the company to resume the postponed plans.

Corporate entrepreneurship and innovation actions

To produce this case study, we interviewed the CEO of Cordial Group, Nicolás Villalobos. He is an effective manager who has led the growth process of the chain, which is why he can be considered a genuine intrapreneur and innovative person. In addition to the interview, Mr Villalobos kindly revised the manuscript before the final version.

Concerning CE actions, it is worth highlighting those carried out in recent years in this organisation, which have materialised in new products or services, new technologies, administrative processes, strategies, and competitive approaches. From a holistic perspective, Cordial has developed a process of both territorial and conceptual expansion. Regarding the first type, this chain extends over a large part of the periphery of Gran Canaria island, from La Aldea to Puerto de Mogán, passing through the city of Las Palmas de Gran Canaria, Playa del Inglés, Maspalomas, Arguineguín and Taurito. Added to this insular expansion are the opening in Lanzarote and the first step into the mainland market, with a 4-star aparthotel in Mijas, Costa del Sol (Málaga province). Conceptually, the Cordial chain has expanded to include various accommodation spaces that have helped to ensure its future business success. Thus, the original sun and beach offer now sits alongside emblematic city hotels, holiday homes with the highest quality standards and the splendid Perchel Beach Club. This diversified range of options puts Cordial in a peerless position in the tourist environment in both the short and medium term.

The great effort the entire organisation has made to digitise its processes deserves significant mention, especially after the outbreak of COVID-19, making the most of existing technological and managerial resources. They have incorporated a new and complete ERP that supports the entire vision of the chain regarding the total digitisation of its processes, in parallel with the environmental awareness in which the Group is immersed, which helped them to win several Travelife awards, the last in December 2022.

Nicolás Villalobos, as CEO of the chain, highlights how the external triggers for such CE actions have included the dynamism and growth of the sector, technological opportunities, and the demand for new products and services. He comments that, "It is obvious that we operate in a sector that is by nature dynamic, a driver of the general economy, very mature and, therefore, with a very high degree of competitiveness. Technology is a capital aid; it has transformed our processes and the quality of our services for the better, but there is a quality only humans can provide, and that is passion. Passion for doing and not just for growing, passion for meeting challenges and goals, passion for making happiness a profitable business".

The following elements contribute to supporting these CE actions: alliances with other companies, relationships with other social agents, the availability of technological, human and financial resources, organisational support in terms of training, trusting employees to identify opportunities, and rewards for new ideas. Likewise, the many stakeholders that make up the Cordial universe have greatly supported the company's CE. All this added to a management style characterised by extensive relationships with both external and internal clients (the employees), with civil society and with the environment that surrounds them, along with the immersion of all staff in the chain's philosophy and the conviction that "cordiality is the smile of the heart", has led them to create a brand image of solidity, seriousness, honesty and sincere passion in what they do. Here is where everything that Cordial evokes comes from when talking about the brand in any social or economic context.

The opportunity to develop CE actions stemmed from experience. Years of experience in the sector gave them a humble but broad knowledge of the tourism industry and its business opportunities. Secondly, all the group members take part in the continuous training provided and share in the internal transmission of knowledge. For these reasons, the "Cordial philosophy" has permeated all individuals professionally or commercially involved in the chain. Contributions from staff members are always welcomed and are considered potentially valuable. Employees are, after all, the eyes and hands of the company, as well as the visible face of what Cordial represents, and therefore, become the engine of its CE.

The main milestones for implementing these CE actions affected many of Cordial's units and departments. Once an opportunity is identified, CE is the core focus of the entire organisation. These complex tasks require the whole team to participate by contributing their work and knowledge. Related to that, Nieves and Haller (2014) suggested that organisational knowledge is related to changes in the business in two ways. First, declarative organisational knowledge provides new options and encourages the development of capabilities for the business to renew, extend or create resources to adapt to changing contexts. Also, the routine processes which refer to the procedural knowledge act as a reference for building learning processes that allow the changes to be implemented in different contexts. Both (declarative and procedural) organisational knowledge positively affect the development of the dynamic characteristics of learning, integrating and coordinating.

However, the main barriers or difficulties for implementing their CE actions were the resources (whether financial, technical, time or human capacities) since these are limited. These scarce resources have been cautiously managed in order to develop CE. Therefore, actions have been taken with caution to be manageable within the organisation's human, technical and financial resources. That is why the management team carefully considered which opportunities to pursue from those identified. The limitation of their resources gives rise to an opportunity cost for not pursuing another venture that could also have helped the business to grow. However, these barriers were overcome through effective management, work, effort, resilience, and passion.

Regarding the main achievements and results obtained from the CE actions carried out, everything the company's employees learned and contributed was successfully channelled into implementing the actions, which quickly led the company to exponential growth. They have been able to take advantage of those results, and the achievement of scale economies has resulted in the diversification of their products in a scenario of scope economies that has made the company a more competitive and profitable Group, which has, in turn led to growth. According to Nicolás Villalobos, "The greatest satisfaction of our chain is to create sustained employment and to contribute, as we have always done, to the development of people, companies and environments where we carry out our activity".

Likewise, in Cordial Group, we identify corporate social responsibility (CSR) actions not only in the company's environmental commitment, as recognised by the Travelife awards but also through its collaboration in different academic events organised by the University of Las Palmas de Gran Canaria and other institutions in the tourism sector, such as the Maspalomas Tourism Forum (held annually in Gran Canaria).

Epilogue

The main lesson learned from the development of CE is, according to Mr Villalobos, the commitment to growth is a necessity for the entire chain. Moreover, as a result of learning from the expansion experienced by the Cordial chain, Nicolás Villalobos states that growth is necessary for every organisation to improve competitiveness through economies of scope and scale. However, he emphasises that it must be done with care to be manageable with regard to the organisation's human, technical and financial resources. He says, "We must avoid putting more than we can chew into our mouths". That is why the firm must consider which opportunities to pursue from those identified. Finally, limiting resources means accepting an opportunity cost when choosing a venture and giving up other business opportunities that cannot be pursued simultaneously.

In summary, the Cordial Hotel chain is an organisation which knows how to find and take advantage of opportunities and employ corporate entrepreneurship actions accordingly. As the CEO of the chain rightly says in the interview, this hotel group has achieved territorial expansion both at the island and national level using several corporate entrepreneurship initiatives. In addition to its expansion in its island of birth, the company has made the leap from Gran Canaria to Lanzarote, but only with one establishment up to now. In Gran Canaria Island, it has launched numerous establishments of different types in several areas of the island. With the territorial expansion towards the mainland, it has taken its first steps on the Costa del Sol (Málaga), which has been an innovation for this chain.

Also, Cordial has added to its original sun and beach establishments, emblematic city hotels, vacation homes and a beach club through another CE action, in addition to digitising its processes, making the most of its resources, and projecting an image of environmental awareness. All of this has helped it to achieve better results and successfully position itself against its competitors, in addition to the learning opportunities that this business diversification process offers them to manage businesses of a different nature but related to the tourism sector.

Finally, after carrying out this case study on the Cordial chain, we can confirm that this is an organisation that can identify and exploit new opportunities, adapt to new technologies, and innovate and use the CE actions that are most suitable for its business.

Sources consulted

The interviewee for this case was:

Mr Nicolás Villalobos Mestres (Managing Director of beCordial Hotels and Resorts).

References

Araujo, Y. (2015). Cordial canarias: Amabilidad y sostenibilidad, claves de la cultura organizativa. In J. T. Aguiar, R. M. Batista, P. Medina, L. Melián & E. Parra-López (eds.). *Casos de Éxito Turístico en Canarias* (pp. 212–219). Edit. Síntesis.

Canarias 7 (2021). Entrevista a Nicolás Villalobos . Canarias 7 local press. Septiembre 2021

Canarias7 (1/11/2022). *El Gobierno se ha plegado al interés de los cementeros y retuerce la realidad.* Retrieved from: https://www.canarias7.es/canarias/gran-canaria/gobierno-plegado-interes-20221101213755-nt.html

Canarias7 (7/11/2022). *Canarias cerrará 2022 con 14,5 millones de turistas, solo un 4% por debajo de 2019.*

Gössling, S., Scott, D., & Hall, M. (2020). Pandemics, tourism and global change: A rapid assessment of COVID-19. *Journal of Sustainable Tourism*, 22(3), 577–598. DOI:10.1080/09669582.2020.1758708

Kessler. A., Pachucki, C., Stummer, K. Mair, M., & Binder, P. (2015). Types of organizational innovativeness and success in Austrian hotels. International Journal of Contemporary Hospitality Management, 27 (7), 1707–1727.

Martín Rodríguez, Y. (2021). *Estudio del caso de cadena hotelera Cordial: Intraemprendimiento y situación actual en el año 2019-2020 en Canarias.* Trabajo Fin de Grado de la Facultad de Economía, Empresa y Turismo de la Universidad de Las Palmas de Gran Canaria.

Nieves, J., & Haller, S. (2014). Building dynamic capabilities through knowledge resources. *Tourism Management, 40,* 224–232.

OMT (2021). *UNWTO World Tourism Barometer,* 19(2). https://doi.org/10.18111/wtobarometereng.

Rodríguez-Castellanos, A., & San-Martin-Albizuri, N. (2020). Covid-19, globalización, complejidad e incertidumbre: Algunas reflexiones sobre gestión empresarial en tiempos de crisis y más allá. *Revista GEON* (Gestión, Organizaciones y Negocios), 7, 1–17.

Turespaña (2021). *Pasajeros aéreos internacionales, marzo 2021.*

UNWTO (2021). World Tourism Organization, Statistics Database. Year 2021.

Case 9 Corporate entrepreneurship within sustainable business models

The Cayuga Ecolodge Collection in Costa Rica, Nicaragua and Panamá

Eugenio Diaz-Farina, Ivelina Mirkova and Noemi Padrón-Fumero

Introduction

Background

The Cayuga Collection is a unique sustainable management company, currently integrating eight accommodation establishments in Costa Rica, Nicaragua, and Panama. The company, founded in 1999, is a pioneer in creating an eco-luxury product and affirms its dedication to enriching the lives of curious travellers, employees, and investors. It employs 450 people, 100% nationals and 90-95% of them of local origin. The average occupancy rate of its hotels is 65% per year. Cayuga's flagship is the Lapa Rios Lodge, voted one of the best resorts in Latin America by Conde Nast Traveler, Travel & Leisure Magazine, and the Andrew Harper Hideaway Report.

The company aims to provide professionalised management to owners of small tourism establishments traditionally dedicated to eco-tourism and conserving Costa Rica's biodiversity. These properties often have to face complex challenges in preserving the environmental and social values on which they were founded by their owners.

The Cayuga Collection is a partnership created by Hans Pfister, of German origin, and Andrea Bonilla, Costa Rican, friends and former classmates at the Cornell School of Hotel Administration. The goal behind this innovative hotel management company is to merge the concept of luxury with the most advanced sustainability needs in Central America. "Disruptive innovation" as a tool towards sustainability driven by Cayuga has earned it numerous international awards, including the National Geographic World Legacy Award in the category of Earth Changers at the International Tourism Fair in Berlin in 2017.

Innovation in the Cayuga business model is based on two main strategies: re-scaling its sustainability strategy and redefining the eco-luxury product. First, Cayuga has been able to overcome the limitations of small-scale, local, family-run establishments, targeting customers with strong preferences for sustainability more precisely. The company brings together small owners (and investors) traditionally committed to sustainability, internalises services

DOI: 10.4324/9781003454465-10

and processes—unlike the rest of the lodging industry—and adapts its R+D+I. The company has successfully tackled the limitations to its value creation potential and improved access to technologies and channels that dominate tourism marketing by extending its business model to eight small establishments (Padrón-Fumero et al., 2019). Therefore, by implementing profitable innovations in developing sustainable management strategies, the company has increased the scale on which it develops its marketing and direct commercialisation strategies, boosting access to new source markets (Europe) and new segments (family and luxury).

The second strategy has been to redefine the eco-luxury product. Its sites are certainly of great ecological value, each of them associated with a protected natural area or a product related to relaxation, active tourism activities, or geotourism. All the establishments are linked to the experience of healthy eating promoted by the consumption of local produce and to a professional service linked to personal growth. Food, wellness, and professional local services enhance the experience of tourist staying with local communities and their values. Therefore, linking sustainability to the concept of luxury helps define an experiential tourism product, creating a symbiosis between the establishments and the environment, as well as the social resources of the surroundings. Target segments are couples and families, all travellers with high purchasing power who seek unique experiences without sacrificing professional service or comfort (Padrón-Fumero et al., 2019).

The Cayuga business model is a clear illustration of an "integrated" model where the focal point is on the prosperity of small and medium-sized local establishments and a thriving regional community and environment (Cordero, 2006), thus helping to overcome the "segregated" model popular in the late 90s in Costa Rica. The "segregated" model is characterised by high dependency on multinational hotel companies, in which mass tourism becomes a threat to the local society and environment. Therefore, instead of generating wealth and employment for the local population, the poor governance of Costa Rican projects combined with corruption, among other factors, proved to be utterly unsustainable. The outcomes of this model were labour inequalities, natural resource contamination, deforestation and lack of access to potable water as negative externalities from massive tourism and uncontrolled building. Thus, in order to foster sustainable development, a public-private partnership, involving multi-stakeholders was created. The association between a public, private and academic partner aimed to align objectives towards a more sustainable business model (Amo & De Stefano, 2019).

Environment

Costa Rica is a leading country in the development of sustainable tourism practices (Heyne et al., 2018). Indeed, while its Central American neighbours are still threatened by the deforestation of their tropical forests, Costa Rica has managed to go from having the highest rate of deforestation (8% per

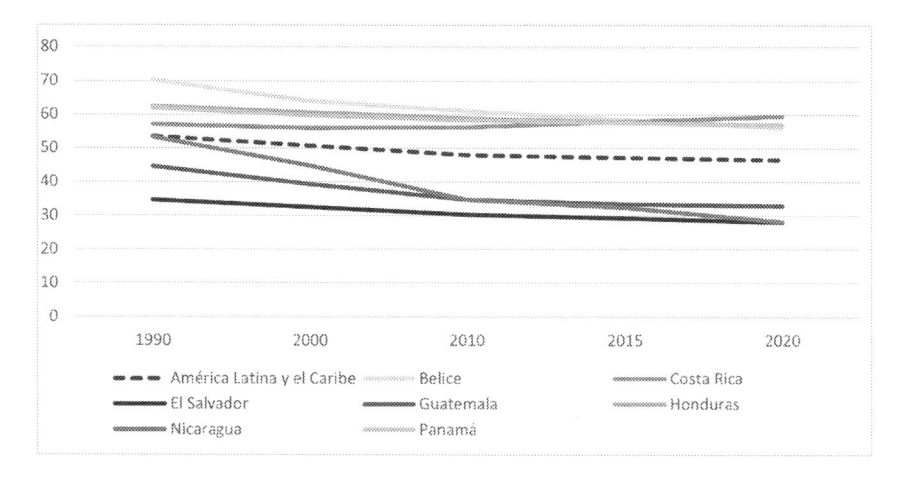

Figure 9.1 Proportion of area covered by forest in Central America, 1990–2020.
Source: (CEPAL, 2022), prepared by authors.

year in the 1980s) to having the highest proportion of area covered by forest in Central America. This coverage reached over 60% in 2020 as shown in Figure 9.1, with 25.5% being declared protected tropical forest in June 2022 (SINAC, 2022). To achieve this goal, the country has established a regulatory and financial framework that guarantees conservation income to thousands of landowners and users of land of high environmental value, while reducing the pressure exerted by illegal logging, farming and hunting on its territory and biodiversity. It is also the first country to create a carbon fund through the UN-REDD program[1] (World Bank, 2022) that recognises its global contribution to carbon sequestration, increasing the conservation value of its tropical forests.

Indeed, the concern of the Costa Rican population to adopt development policies that protect its natural resources, especially but not only its rainforest, has turned this small Central American country (5,210,196 inhabitants as of January 1, 2022) into a paradigm of sustainable development worldwide. Its economic development has historically been linked to sustainability, especially in reducing inequalities through social policies guaranteeing education, health, and access to basic resources such as water and electricity. In fact, Costa Rica is the Central American country with the highest rate of ISO 14001 companies certified per billion dollars of Gross Domestic Product (GDP), see Figure 9.2.

Few countries have managed to develop a tourism sector that contributes significantly to their growth while improving the quality of life of their citizens and preserving their natural heritage. Costa Rica's image is linked to its rich natural heritage and biodiversity, while its tourism brand has been associated for decades with wellness, adventure tourism, and the quality of life of its communities. The crisis caused by the COVID suggests that this type of

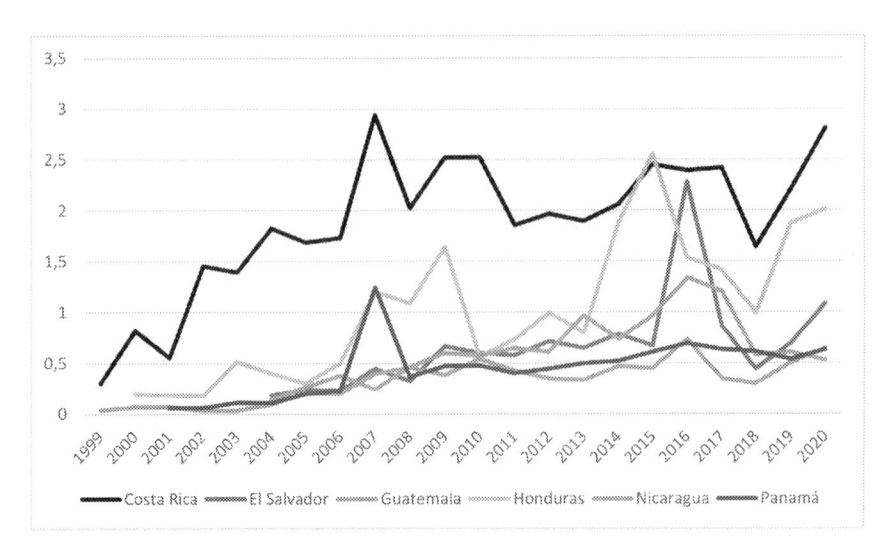

Figure 9.2 ISO 14001 certified companies per billion dollars of GDP (2010 constant prices) in Central America, 1999–2020.

Source: (CEPAL, 2022), prepared by authors.

tourism is more in demand and generates higher tourist expenditure. Tourism data show a 10 percentage point increase in non-resident tourists who visited protected wilderness areas in 2021 and an increase of 26% in the average expenditure per person in 2021 compared to 2019 (reaching US$1,497.40 in 2021), as Table 9.1 shows.

However, these features can also weaken tourism competitiveness. On the one hand, its lodging and commercial supply has traditionally been

Table 9.1 Tourism indicators of Costa Rica, 2018–2021

Tourism indicators	2018	2019	2020	2021
Average expenditure per person in US$ of non-resident tourists	1,100.80	1,190.30	1,318.60	1,497.40
Annual Average Occupancy Percentage	67.40%	66.90%	23.60%	43.30%
International Arrivals to Costa Rica	3,016,667	3,139,008	1,011,912	1,347,055
Percentage of international arrivals from Europe	15.91%	15.94%	16.79%	17.06%
Non-resident visitors to protected wilderness areas	1,156,620	1,266,801	480,154	674,126
Percentage of non-resident visitors to protected wilderness areas	38.34%	40.36%	47.45%	50.04%

Source: ICT (2002), prepared by authors.

aimed at the adventure tourism and ecotourism segment, based on a unique identity and with strong conservationist convictions. Nevertheless, strong competition from emerging destinations in the Central American region—with large-scale marketing and distribution of the ecotourism product, as well as large investments in infrastructure—could affect Costa Rica's green tourism competitiveness. On the other hand, excessive dependence on the North American market and its weakness in promoting higher value-added segments could also negatively impact the destination. In this context, according to statistical data from the Costa Rican Institute of Tourism, despite an overall decrease in total international arrivals in 2020, the percentage of arrivals from Europe has been steadily increasing in the period between 2018 and 2021, indicating successful marketing strategies.

This is where the Cayuga Collection business model has been able to circumvent the destination's weaknesses, by focusing on a very small but very profitable niche market while opening the market to European tourists. Sustainability and luxury seem incompatible; however, Cayuga has been able to specialise in offering a tourism product that combines both dimensions, without any direct competitor in Costa Rica.

Development

Current literature identifies diverse forms of corporate entrepreneurship; however, the essential common point is the power of innovation in an already established organisation. One of the most common forms of corporate entrepreneurship is corporate venturing by creating a new business inside the existing one (Narayanan et al., 2009). One way of achieving this is by entering new markets with existing products, like in the case of Cayuga, which is working on increasing its share of clients from the European market. Launching new products in existing markets represents another way of practising corporate venturing (Adim & Poi, 2022).

Corporate entrepreneurship is conditioned by external factors to the company and by organisational factors. In addition, achieving entrepreneurship actions requires opportunities to be identified and executed. For this reason, this section is structured around the corporate entrepreneurship actions developed by Cayuga, the external and organisational context, the processes that favour the detection of corporate entrepreneurship opportunities, and the main achievements arising from these actions.

Interestingly, corporate entrepreneurship actions accelerated during the crisis caused by COVID-19. Indeed, it has been detected over the course of human history that crisis represents one of the main innovation drivers (Li-Ying & Nell, 2020). Cayuga states that the months leading up to the onset of the pandemic, from November 2019 to February 2020, were the company's best until the zero-tourism occurred.

However, the lockdown provided a unique opportunity to rethink the business model and detect new opportunities to emerge stronger from this pandemic. To reaffirm the fact that crises stimulate innovation, (Filippetti et al., 2009) argue that the 2008 financial crisis has served as a market opportunity especially for small and start-up firms to invest in innovation. Schumpeter's creative destruction proves to be even more effective in an external shock like the COVID-19 pandemic (Li-Ying & Nell, 2020).

The information source for the case study development is a primary source obtained from a semi-structured interview with one of the company's CEO, Hans Pfister. The interview took place in April 2022 via video call, which has been recorded. It was decided to conduct a semi-structured interview to provide flexibility to the respondent and to ask additional questions based on the corporate entrepreneurship actions he was reporting. Furthermore, Hans was contacted later via email to clarify specific doubts about some of the corporate entrepreneurship actions and to provide more information for the proper development of the case study.

Corporate entrepreneurship actions

The corporate entrepreneurship actions developed by Cayuga can be classified into 1) a review of production processes, 2) competitive strategies, and 3) the development of new products.

Review of production processes: Promote digitalisation even if you are a small company

Digitalisation of product processes and the interconnection of different systems, such as connecting Customer Relationship Management (CRM) with accounting and between accounting and banking platforms, are ways to restructure and connect internal services in order to reduce manual labour (Agostini et al., 2020). Note also that digitalisation facilitates the monitoring of all organisational activities and their control.

An example of a corporate entrepreneurship action associated with this proposal, undertaken by Cayuga, has been the digitisation of customer satisfaction questionnaires and the automated exploitation of data with business intelligence tools for the creation of dashboards. Another example has been the simplification of sales reports, the elimination of reports that were not consulted by anyone, and an increase in the frequency of other reports. Such automatisation has allowed the company to reduce the frequency of management reports, moving from every two weeks to a monthly frequency.

Competitive strategies: How sustainability may contribute to tourism resilience

Sustainability is in the company's DNA, and this translates not only into the products offered and the production processes but also in the choice of suppliers and employees. Note that one of the most important commitments arising from applying the sustainability criterion is to seek local suppliers and employees (Font et al., 2006). This commitment has become, considering the latest shocks in the world's economy, one of Cayuga's most important competitive advantages of the company.

Indeed, the COVID-19 pandemic interrupted both the supply chain of inputs and employees' mobility between working places and home. A lower exposure to global external shocks has allowed the company to absorb the initial shock and recover losses. As a result, Cayuga is now constantly on the lookout for new companies in its environment that can become local suppliers and replace current suppliers outside the country.

The following examples may better illustrate ways sustainable practices foster Cayuga's entrepreneurship actions and how these actions lead to more sustainable practices. Due to the disruption of international trade, the company faced a shortage of French wines and Puerto Rican coconut milk to make the piña-colada cocktail. In the case of coconut milk, they found a recently created company in Costa Rica that immediately became a supplier, additionally increasing the quality of the coconut milk, since this new company uses a homemade process and does not add any artificial additives. On the other hand, they decided to eliminate wines from the menu, as they were not a differentiating element, and there is no local wine production in the region.

Another competitive strategy that has emerged from corporate entrepreneurship has been to further balance luxury and sustainability. Even though sustainability has been at fairly high levels since the company's establishment, its commitment to using contributions from local natural resources has increased due to demand requirements, especially after the pandemic. The decoration of rooms with elements of the environment, such as teak wood doors from Costa Rican sustainable forests and furniture made by a local cabinetmaker, or paintings of natural elements of the country produced by a local photographer are examples of intelligent luxury, which does not compromise sustainability. Finally, the increase in luxury has also been extended to culinary offerings. International culinary consultants were hired to design new menus and train local Cayuga chefs to prepare such new haute cuisine menus.

Hiring local employees also contributed to strengthening Cayuga's sustainable business model during the pandemic. In fact, since some of their staff were forced to stay at the establishment during the lockdown, this facilitated the provision of services to the community while providing time for training and brainstorming to reflect on future strategies.

New product development: Be alert to changing consumer preferences

In its pursuit to improve the quality of its products and offer high levels of customer satisfaction, Cayuga has developed new products to satisfy the demand for unique experiences regardless of the price to be paid. This is especially true after the COVID-19 pandemic, where price seems not to be a barrier for Cayuga's customers. This is why the company has developed new products such as private dinners in unique locations and private tours in unique and protected areas.

With the arrival of the pandemic and the fear of contagion, many customers demanded other types of tourist accommodation, such as holiday homes where they could stay with their families in a more isolated place. Also, the growing demand for medium-sized group travel, which could not be met due to the low accommodation capacity of the hotels managed by Cayuga, led the company to expand its business model to other types of tourist accommodation. Specifically, it looked for owners of large properties, around 10 rooms, of high quality to develop the eco-luxury product in vacation homes. An example of this business arrangement is the Pasha Beachfront Estate[2].

External environment

An essential external factor for corporate entrepreneurship at Cayuga has been technology. Although they have introduced new technologies, the most important aspect has been the use of existing technology in greater depth. The company has immersed itself in a process of digitalisation of the administration in which they have automated many production processes, especially focusing on reporting. In this sense, it is worth highlighting the actions focused on interconnecting the CSR system and banking information with the accounting system.

Demand for new products has also been key. In particular, customers have asked for highly personalised and unique experiences. This has led to the development of new products such as private dinners and tours. In addition, the company was receiving many calls to reserve several rooms for family events, and from those who wanted to maintain close contact only with their bubble group to avoid COVID-19 contagions. However, due to the low accommodation capacity of the hotels it manages, Cayuga was forced to turn down such group requests. However, these demands led to the search for large private homes and the expansion of its business model to luxury sustainable vacation homes.

Organisational context and process of developing corporate entrepreneurship

One of the main organisational factors of corporate entrepreneurship in Cayuga has been active listening to employees and a clear commitment to staff training and the prospect of career building. Customers are also actively listened to through a customer satisfaction form.

Before the COVID-19 crisis lockdown, the company gathered staff from different departments once a month to give feedback on their specific jobs. However, with the closure of the hotels during COVID-19, the company took the opportunity to create working groups among all the staff that remained in the company to analyse production processes and identify bottlenecks, barriers, and value-added by each action. Once opportunities for improvement had been detected, solutions were sought by consensus between employees and management.

In addition, Cayuga has recently contracted an external human resources company to conduct an anonymous survey of each employee called the "emotional pulse survey" to measure the level of employee satisfaction and detect possible areas for improvement. The results will directly impact the quality of work and, therefore, the service offered to the customer.

Achievements of corporate entrepreneurship

The main achievements of corporate entrepreneurship can be summarised in three actions. The first major achievement is related to improving the efficiency of production processes, which has a direct impact on economic profitability. Investment in technology has led to the automation of some processes that were previously carried out manually, thereby freeing up employee time for other more labour-intensive activities rather than capital-intensive ones. Efficiency has also increased thanks to investment in employee training, which has led to greater specialisation in certain areas of the production process. Some processes that did not add value to the company were eliminated, thus gaining efficiency by avoiding the need for personnel to do them.

The second major achievement has to do with the quality of the service offered while reducing the carbon footprint of the company. Investment in employee training plays a fundamental role here, not only in specific training to perform their jobs to high standards but also in the welfare of the workforce. This has led to employees demonstrating high levels of commitment to the company's objectives. In this regard, it is worth noting that Cayuga provided free room and board to employees who were unable to pay their rent during the COVID-19 pandemic. These employees have shown their full trust in the company and have repaid this great business gesture with their absolute dedication to the company. Moreover, the search for local suppliers to replace international suppliers, and thus reduce vulnerability to shocks in international trade, has had a direct impact on the reduction of its carbon footprint, opting for 0 km products with the same, or even higher levels of quality.

Finally, the third major achievement refers to the expansion of its business model to other types of tourist accommodation. In this case, Cayuga has ventured into vacation homes to serve new green market segments, such as small groups with high purchasing power.

Epilogue

External sustainable management may provide lodges with sufficient economies of scale to guarantee survival by helping them adapt managerial practices to the new tourism market environment and competition. However, major future environmental and social challenges have only begun to shape the tourism markets. In this chapter, it has been shown how sustainable practices can increase corporate resilience to natural and non-natural hazards and risks. In addition, corporate entrepreneurship plays a key role in boosting firms' economic performance.

A major finding from Cayuga's case study is not only the existence of compatibility but also synergies between luxury tourism and sustainability. The company's innovative business model should be considered a *sine qua non* for tourist destinations around the globe. From a practical standpoint, the company managed to convert a major drawback for tourism like the COVID lockdown into a competitive advantage through corporate venturing. Finally, the investment in local employees, suppliers and products not only provides employment and social well-being but also helps improve the quality of the service offered to high-end tourists.

The corporate entrepreneurship outcomes in Cayuga have been the improvement in the efficiency of production processes, a reduction in carbon footprint yet maintaining high-quality service and the expansion of the business model to vacation homes. These results have been achieved through support for human capital which, despite cutbacks has been improved with additional and specialised training. Although not so innovative, the investment in technology has also helped automate routine tasks and create more added value. Finally, reviewing relationships with suppliers and being alert in the search for high-quality local suppliers has led to great opportunities.

Notes

1 In September 2013, the Costa Rican government signed an Emission Reduction Credit Purchase Agreement with the Forest Carbon Partnership Facility (FCPF).
2 Website: https://www.cayugacollection.com/pasha-costa-rica/.

References

Adim, C. V., & Poi, G. (2022). Dynamics of corporate entrepreneurial initiatives: A literature review. *International Journal of Entrepreneurship*, 6(1), 1–13. doi. 10. 47672/ije.888

Agostini, L., Galati, F., & Gastaldi, L. (2020). The digitalization of the innovation process: Challenges and opportunities from a management perspective. *European Journal of Innovation Management*, 23(1), 1–12. doi. 10.1108/EJIM-11-2019-0330

Amo, M. D. H., & De Stefano, M. C. (2019). Public–private partnership as an innovative approach for sustainable tourism in Guanacaste, Costa Rica. *Worldwide Hospitality and Tourism Themes*, 11(2), 130–139.

Comisión Económica para América Latina y el Caribe, CEPAL (2022). Statistical Databases and Publications. Available at: https://statistics.cepal.org/portal/cepalstat/dashboard.html.

Cordero, A. (2006). *Nuevos Ejes de Acumulación y Naturaleza: El Caso del Turismo*. Buenos Aires: Consejo Latinoamericano de Ciencias Sociales.

Filippetti, A., Frenz, M., & Archibugi, D. (2009). The Effects of the Economic Downturn on Innovation: Creative Destruction versus Creative Accumulation. Paper presented at the 4th Annual Conference of the GARNET Network, Rome.

Font, X., Tapper, R., Schwartz, K., & Kornilaki, M. (2006). Sustainable supply chain management in tourism. *Business Strategy and the Environment, 17*(4), 260–271. doi. 10.1002/bse.527

Heyne, L., Vargas, J. R., & Matamoros Mendoza, S. (2018). Sustainable tourism in Costa Rica: Supporting rural communities through study abroad. In *Innovative approaches to tourism and leisure* (pp. 301–302). Cham: Springer.

Instituto Costarricense de Turismo, ICT (2022). *Cifras Turísticas*. Available at: https://www.ict.go.cr/es/estadisticas/cifras-turisticas.html.

Li-Ying, J., & Nell, P. (2020). Navigating opportunities for innovation and entrepreneurship under COVID-19. *California Management Review Insights*. Available at: https://cmr.berkeley.edu/2020/06/innovation-entrepreneurship/.

Narayanan, V. K., Yang, Y., & Zahra, S. A. (2009). Corporate venturing and value creation: A review and proposed framework. *Research Policy, 38*(1), 58–76. doi. 10.1016/j.respol.2008.08.015

Padrón-Fumero, N., Martínez-González, J. A., & Diaz-Farina, E. (2019). Caso 15. Cayuga collection: Un modelo de innovación en la gestión hotelera sostenible en Costa Rica. In *100 Soluciones a 50 Problemas para la Gestión Turística de Empresas en Iberoamérica: Manual de Casos Reales* (pp. 239–257). Síntesis.

Sistema Nacional de Áreas de Conservación de Costa Rica, SINAC (2022). *Áreas Silvestres Protegidas*. Available at: https://www.sinac.go.cr/ES/asp/Paginas/default.aspx.

World Bank (November 16, 2022). Costa Rica's Forest Conservation Pays Off. https://www.worldbank.org/en/news/feature/2022/11/16/costa-rica-s-forest-conservation-pays-off

Case 10 The creation of a fleet management model as a result of corporate entrepreneurship in a car rental company in the South of Europe

José Sanabria-Díaz,
Teresa Aguiar-Quintana,
Silvia Sosa-Cabrera and
Ana Isabel Lemes-Hernández

Introduction

Tourism is, without a doubt, one of the economic activities that contributes to the worldwide development of all tourist destinations. Last year, the industry accounted for 40% of employment in Spain and 12.1% of total employment. In 2021, the total contribution of the tourism sector to the GDP of Spain was around €88 billion, representing a contribution to the national GDP of close to 7.4%, compared to 12.4% in 2019 (INE, 2022). Within Spain, the Canary Islands have taken a strong leadership position, becoming a reference area in the tourism sector in terms of the number of tourists, accommodation, destinations, and other factors.

Throughout the world, family businesses are defined as businesses that are owned and managed by members of one or more families who have adequate participation in the capital stock and control decision-making (Belausteguigoitia, 2010), and have an average employee turnover rate of around 90% (González & Olivié, 2018), make an essential contribution to the economy and job creation (Acosta de Mavárez et al., 2019).

These companies, which have capital stock and a family workforce (Valencia, 2017), face the same challenges and threats as other companies of different sizes and natures, but must adopt different business practices depending on the resources available. For this reason, CICAR, a family car rental company (which relies on the tourism sector for the main core of its activity and has a presence throughout the Canary Islands) was chosen as a case study—see Image 10.1.

We specifically examine the case from two different perspectives in addition to the theoretical framework. On the one hand, elements that triggered a turning point in the company's management were generated by their growth. On the other hand, the measures implemented forced the revitalisation of their corporate entrepreneurship activities through innovative actions. In this specific case, the information and data were collected through a review of the

DOI: 10.4324/9781003454465-11

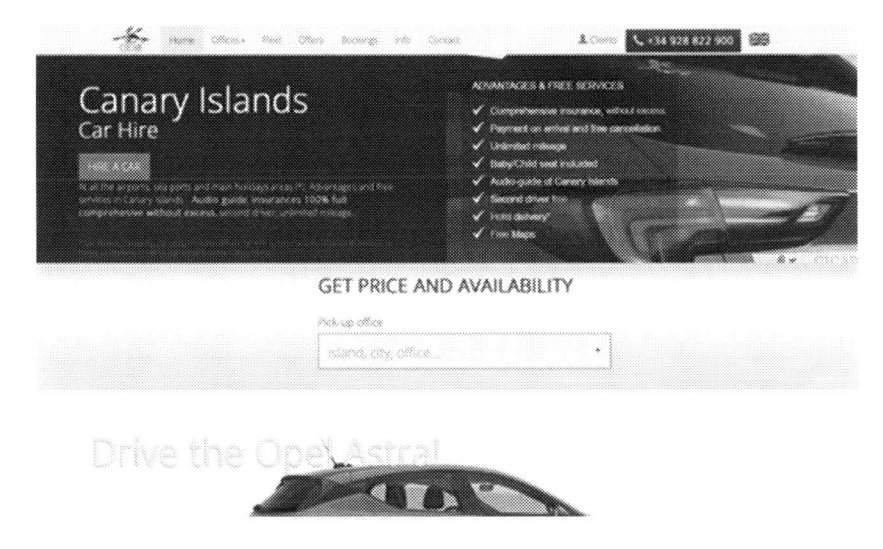

Image 10.1 CICAR website (2023). www.cicar.es.

literature and a semi-structured interview with the company's owners. The interview was conducted with one of the CEOs of the company through a formalised questionnaire.

Nature of the company and economic environment

Autos Cabrera Medina Car Rental was founded in 1967 in a modest garage in Arrecife (Lanzarote) with an initial fleet of six vehicles that came to offer a mobility alternative for the first tourists arriving on the island of Lanzarote, at a time when the precariousness of the economy, dominated by the primary sector, called into question the quality standards that could be offered in the main tourist issuing markets. Company Group currently has a fleet of more than 14,000 vehicles, which has led to the creation of approximately 1,100 jobs and an extensive network of 46 offices located in the airports, ports and main tourist destinations in seven of the eight Canary Islands.

CICAR group (Canary Islands Car, S.L.) has incorporated electric and hybrid vehicles into its fleet in recent years, which, together with its environmental responsibility policy, has led it to establish a Quality, Environment and Safety System based on the requirements of the UNE-EN-ISO 9001 (2015); UNE-EN-ISO 14001 (2015), and ISO 45001:2018 Standards. This, alongside the protection of workers' rights, has allowed them to establish a management system based on the following set of priority objectives: (1) compliance with legal requirements and applicable regulations; (2) quality assurance in all services provided; (3) continuous improvement of the procedures used, the services offered and the environmental and safety performance, adapted to the demand requirements and market requirements; (4) effective management and control of all processes; (5) effective assignment of functions and responsibilities so that the concept of quality, environment and safety is present at all levels and activities of the company; (6) protection of the environment, prevention of pollution and reduction of the environmental impacts of the company's own activities that may contribute to the deterioration of the safety and health of workers, such as the production of waste or noise, as an integral part of the daily work, by optimising the consumption of natural resources; (7) protection of workers, providing safe and healthy working conditions in favour of injury prevention and deterioration of health; (8) extension of the principles applied to the company, to suppliers and subcontractors, involving them in the quality, environment and safety policy; and finally; and (9) staff awareness and motivation with regards to the importance of implementing and developing a Quality, Environment and Safety System, guaranteeing their training to ensure the correct performance of their activities within the organisation.

As a result, the CICAR group has received numerous awards, recognitions and distinctions. In September 2007, it received the Island of Lanzarote 2007 Award from the Cabildo de Lanzarote, following the unanimous agreement of the seven municipalities of the Island of Lanzarote, the business sector and members of the journalism sector. In addition, CICAR was awarded the 2008 Tourism Excellence Medal for Business Activity by the Government of the Canary Islands. In 2009, it received the first prize for the Best Expansion Network, awarded by the Government of the Canary Islands and the regional Chambers of Commerce. In 2014, it received the Gold Medal of the Canary Islands, the highest distinction of the Government of the Canary Islands, in recognition of its work for the benefit of Canarian society. Finally, it was named the best family business in the Canary Islands in 2018 by the Association of the Family Business of the Canary Islands.

An important external factor that influenced this family business was the global COVID-19 pandemic. On March 11, 2020, the World Health Organization (WHO) declared a global pandemic, which led to an unprecedented situation across the planet that not even the two World Wars created. This global pandemic has affected all sectors and countries and the lives of all citizens. Previously, Osterholm (2017) warned that in a pandemic, the global economy would grind to a halt and, since appropriate vaccines would not be available for a long time and given the limited stocks of antiviral drugs, the scenario would be like that of 1918 (Spanish Flu), that would lead to the closure of borders to prevent the spread and even restrictions on foreign travel and commercial activity.

By the end of March 2020, almost three billion people were in some form of lockdown. From April 2020, all the world's destinations (217) had imposed different forms of travel restrictions and 107 destinations had closed their borders or suspended flights (UNWTO, 2020). In this context, the tourism industry is perhaps the sector that has been most affected by the globally accepted measures to combat the virus, including confinement and border closures, which have directly impacted two key elements of tourism: mobility and socialisation

(Sanabria-Díaz et al., 2021). This situation affected the car rental sector, given that tourism and mobility were key factors in the spread of the pandemic and also justified the need for car rental companies in tourist destinations.

The COVID-19 crisis caused the closure of small car rental businesses and, at the same time, the appearance of new providers such as flexible leasing companies offering both long-term care hire for 90 days up to 1 year as well as vehicles that can be booked by the hour or even by the minute. The situation also led to the creation of new business models, such as contactless car rentals, which involve specialised software and smartphone apps that enable the use of an electronic key, reducing the need for physical offices.

The car rental environment was affected by the semiconductor shortage since these are necessary for the manufacture of vehicles. This has caused some deficiencies in the supply of cars, which has meant a slowdown in the sale of cars to car rental companies.

After the pandemic and the gradual reopening of factories and as a consequence of the reactivation of the economy, demand for electronic devices increased exponentially. This also led to a global chip and semiconductor shortage, which adversely impacted the automotive sector given that it accounts for between 10% and 15% of global demand since they are essential for vehicle electrification, equipment or security and infotainment systems, and various other basic functionalities. This caused an increase in the price of raw materials and caused the maritime transport industry to reach saturation. This situation made renewing car rental businesses' fleets an impossible task.

Corporate entrepreneurship and SMEs in the COVID-19 crisis

In a context of high competitiveness, businesses generally establish a daily dynamic to resolve their crises. However, on some occasions, the unexpected appearance of an uncontrollable crisis causes a situation of uncertainty and vulnerability, which endangers the proper existence of companies and entrepreneurs (IDB, 2020) in the tourism industry (Li et al., 2021). The COVID-19 pandemic led to the closure of markets and tourist destinations and the disappearance of customer demand due to its impact on mobility and social interaction (Sanabria-Díaz et al., 2021), causing an unprecedented situation with significant economic effects (Verma & Gustafsson, 2020). Fearn-Banks (2016) refers to a crisis as an important event with a potentially negative outcome that affects an organisation, company or industry, as well as its audiences, products, services or reputation, which in tourism tends to jeopardise their long-term profitability (Stafford et al., 2006) and such economic risk jeopardises SMEs' chances to prosper (Mekinc & Cvikl, 2013).

However, the resilience of entrepreneurs and their ability to adapt to changes while causing minimum disruption can make them well-positioned to face crises such as the one caused by the COVID-19 pandemic (Bhaskara & Filimonau, 2021) and even to emerge stronger out of the crisis with new elements that can make them more competitive.

Focusing on smaller firms, Zahra and Pearce (1994) studied the role of environment, strategy and the organisation itself in the company's corporate entrepreneurship (CE). They supported the idea that a company is actively engaged in CE if new products are introduced or new ventures are undertaken to stimulate its growth. Similarly, Guth and Ginsberg (1990) defined CE according to two phenomena: (1) innovation and corporate venturing activities; and (2) renewal activities related to a corporation's ability to compete and take risks.

In the tourism and hospitality sector, different studies show it is possible to measure actions and behaviour within a company that creates an innovative culture (Meyer & de Jongh, 2018). Related to that, the COVID-19 pandemic has led to the need for alternative business models based on new values to help tourism emerge from the pandemic crisis, and CE through innovation is a clear example of these new types of tourism jobs.

We attempt to address in this case study the operational adjustments made by a medium-sized tourism company in the car rental sector in a mature coastal tourism destination through CE after a global crisis such as COVID-19. This analysis shows that a tactical innovative culture and experienced risk-taking (Antoncic & Hisrich, 2004) can, by itself, resolve a crisis of the business operations aggravated by other exogenous circumstances of little control (Doern et al., 2019).

The trigger that motivated the entrepreneurial activity was the growth and dynamism of the sector, and despite having a fleet of approximately 14,000 vehicles and the high demand for car rental services, the actual availability was uncertain due to the gap in knowledge among available and unavailable cars. The COVID-19 pandemic and the shortage of semiconductors, which impacted the production of vehicles and led to the impossibility of renewing the fleet, definitively motivated this CE action.

An informal working group of experienced middle managers from different departments of the company was formed in order to guide and manage the CE activities. The group included staff from the IT and development departments, the head of the reservation department, the assistant director and the area managers of each island, as well as support from the finance department, and together they helped oversee the design of the new fleet availability management model.

In addition, to create the fleet management model, the CEO of the company decided that people from the GRAFICAME business unit, the group's printing company, as well as four to five people from the services and logistics area, two people from the reservations department in the car rental offices and employees from workshops and the after-sales department, were actively included in the process. All of them contributed to creating the fleet application model, including designing procedures that feed the availability system.

Other innovations were related to digitalisation. During the pandemic, CICAR began to transform its audio guide into an app allowing customers to access in-depth knowledge about each of the tourist destinations and micro-destinations in the Canary Islands. Although the company has always considered the fleet management system to be an important asset of its business, at that time, it was still too traditional, and the processes had never been designed, which is why a process to digitalise the system was also initiated.

Another CE action was related to the implementation of an application that would allow the service staff (who manage the maintenance, preparation and tuning of the fleet) to resolve the absence of information that generated numerous errors (because of the lack of coordination) and therefore facilitating the car location and their collection processes. Using a QR code in each vehicle, the staff could check if there is any process pending to be carried out in the vehicle, if it is under repair, where it is parked, and all the information related to kilometres and fuel consumption. Once the vehicle is collected, its geolocation is established, and staff can check if the vehicle is clean and available to rent or, alternatively, if it requires some repair or cleaning.

The same application allowed CICAR to develop a more advanced fleet availability calculation model and verify with sufficient precision how many available vehicles required the mandatory ITV (car technical inspection) or any kind of maintenance, how many had been damaged in an accident, and how many had been reserved for sale as a used vehicle. In this way, they could know the exact number of vehicles available for rent at any time and consequently improve customer service processes.

In this context, external triggers, including global triggers (related to the impact of COVID-19 and its effects on consumers, markets and competitiveness) and regional triggers (linked to the importance of vehicle location in a mature coastal tourist destination in an island territory) as well as internal triggers, relating to the organisational structure (specifically the company's sound business practices and the specific nature of a multidisciplinary group) and human resources (which included experienced, competent staff who worked effectively as a team), led to the generation of a structured and complementary innovation process.

However, several obstacles also arose during the CE processes, such as the impossibility of connecting the vehicles that were available at that time, which entailed high costs, and the issue of geolocation systems being intrusive for customers, all of which were overcome by the design of a model that did not involve the geolocation of the vehicles.

The CE process benefitted from the teamwork of the intermediate-level directors and the multidisciplinary nature of the staff who contributed to the achievement of the innovative actions that led to the creation of a fleet management model and a vehicle availability and geolocation control model, and consequently to cost savings by increasing the level of efficiency and promoting teamwork. Furthermore, in the customer management department, an audio guide app was developed, customer service quality was improved, a guaranteed service was put in place, and ways to establish more competitive prices were developed despite the supply chain crisis and the increase in fuel prices (Table 10.1).

Table 10.1 CE and innovation results and barriers

Corporate entrepreneurship results		Barriers
Internal Management	Fleet of vehicles system Vehicle geolocation system Promote teamwork Cost savings	Lack of technical innovation and mature technology
Customer Management	Audio guide app Improved customer service Guaranteed service Competitive prices	Intrusive method for the customer

Source: Prepared by authors.

Epilogue

This case study analyses the innovation generation process within a company based on the triggering factors, which are directly linked to the COVID-19 pandemic crisis and the effects that occurred throughout the world, specifically in a mature coastal tourist destination such as the Canary Islands, where there is a clear need for a car rental business and which directly suffered the consequences of that crisis.

The CE process set out above, in a context of crisis and driven by a variety of internal and external, global and regional, structural and human resources triggers, led to the generation of innovation solutions that exceeded those initially proposed and which supported the adaptation processes that appeared to be necessary for the post-pandemic situation. In this way, the resilience demonstrated by the company helped it to overcome the obstacles created by the pandemic. It enabled it to maintain a situation of stability even when faced with the semiconductor shortage and the increase in fuel prices, two factors that directly impacted the automotive industry.

Thus, in a mature coastal tourist destination like the Canary Islands, the potential vulnerability to market crises gives rise to the need for constant monitoring of all relevant factors in order to make it possible to adopt tailor-made solutions at the right time to prevent more serious consequences.

The creation and makeup of the task force put in place to oversee the generation of the innovation process is key to ensuring the success of the CE. The group's knowledge of the company, its activity, its training and experience, and moral commitment to the company are relevant and essential factors that must be considered at the time of its design and creation.

The main lesson learnt was that innovative actions can even contribute to adopting solutions for social, economic and sustainability change (Zhang et al., 2022) in addition to contributing positively, through business innovation, economic digitisation and the use of technology, to business stability (Surya et al., 2022).

However, one of the main limitations of this study is that the structured interview was conducted with one of the relevant interlocutors of the company. Contrasting this data with those offered by other members of the company not involved in the innovation process, as well as internal and external clients, could definitively consolidate the contributions made.

Finally, at the time of concluding this paper, the war in Ukraine continues to impact the world economy. Various international political tensions appear to be having an impact on the movement of all people and goods and, consequently, on the tourist industry, which should highlight the value of the innovations carried out in CICAR.

References

Acosta de Mavárez, A., Molina Quiroz, C. A., Andino Chancay, T. S., & Rodríguez López, V. E. (2019). Sistema familiar y continuidad de las empresas familiares. *Revista de Ciencias Sociales*, 268.

Antoncic, B., & Hisrich, R. D. (2004). Corporate entrepreneurship contingencies and organizational wealth creation. *Journal of Management Development*, 23(6), 518–550.

Belausteguigoitia, I. (2010). El campo de las empresas familiares en Latinoamérica: Nuevas perspectivas. *Gestión y Sociedad*, 3 (1), 13–25.

Bhaskara, G. I., & Filimonau, V. (2021). The COVID-19 pandemic and organizational learning for disaster planning and management: A perspective of tourism businesses from a destination prone to consecutive disasters. *Journal of Hospitality and Tourism Management*, 46, 364–375.

Doern, R., Williams, N., & Vorley, T. (2019). Special issue on entrepreneurship and crises: Business as usual? An introduction and review of the literature. *Entrepreneurship & Regional Development*, 31(5–6), 400–412.

Fearn-Banks, K. (2016). *Crisis communications: A casebook approach*. Routledge.

González, E., & Olivié, C. (2018). Empresa familiar, emprendimiento e intraemprendimiento. *EAE business school*. España: Strategic Research Center.

Guth, W.D., & Ginsberg, A. (1990). Guest editors' introduction: Corporate entrepreneurship. Strategic management journal, 5–15.

IDB (2020), "Coronavirus: ¿cómo apoyar desde el sector de fomento a la innovación y las pymes?", available at: https://blogs.iadb.org/innovacion/es/innovacion-coronavirus-pymes-emprendimientos/ (accessed 20 september 2022).

INE (2022). Contabilidad nacional anual de España: agregados por rama de actividad. Últimos datos https://www.ine.es/dyngs/INEbase/es/operacion.htm?c=Estadistica_C&cid=1254736177056&menu=ultiDatos&idp=1254735576581

Li, Z., Zhang, X., Yang, K., Singer, R., & Cui, R. (2021). Urban and rural tourism under COVID-19 in China: Research on the recovery measures and tourism development. *Tourism Review*.

Mekinc, J., & Cvikl, H. (2013). The structure of security and safety crises in tourism. *Journal of Tourism & Services*, 4.

Meyer, N., & de Jongh, J. (2018). The importance of entrepreneurship as a contributing factor to economic growth and development: The case of selected European countries. *Journal of Economics and Behavioral Studies*, 10(4 (J)), 287–299.

Osterholm, M. T. (2017). Preparing for the next pandemic. In *Global health* (pp. 225–238). Routledge.

Sanabria-Díaz, J. M., Aguiar-Quintana, T., & Araujo-Cabrera, Y. (2021). Public strategies to rescue the hospitality industry following the impact of COVID-19: A case study of the European Union. *International Journal of Hospitality Management*, *97*, 102988.

Stafford, G., Yu, L., & Armoo, A. K. (2006). Crisis management and recovery: How Washington, DC hotels responded to terrorism. *Tourism, Security and Safety*, 291–311.

Surya, B., Hernita, H., Salim, A., Suriani, S., Perwira, I., Yulia, Y., & Yunus, K. (2022). Travel-business stagnation and SME business turbulence in the tourism sector in the era of the COVID-19 pandemic. *Sustainability*, *14*(4), 2380.

UNWTO. (2020). COVID-19: UNWTO calls on tourism to be part of recovery plans ⟨https://www.unwto.org/news/covid-19-unwto-calls-on-tourism-to-be-part-of-recovery-plans. [visited, Sep. 18th 2022].

Valencia, M. (2017). Posicionamiento de Marca y su influencia en la gestión administrativa. Bogotá: UDM.

Verma, S., & Gustafsson, A. (2020). Investigating the emerging COVID-19 research trends in the field of business and management: A bibliometric analysis approach. *Journal of Business Research*, *118*, 253–261.

Zahra, S. A., & Pearce, J. A. (1994). Corporate entrepreneurship in smaller firms: The role of environment, strategy, and organization. *Entrepreneurship, Innovation, and Change*, *3*(1), 31–44.

Zhang, W., Williams, A. M., Li, G., & Liu, A. (2022). Entrepreneurial responses to uncertainties during the COVID-19 recovery: A longitudinal study of B&Bs in Zhangjiajie, China. *Tourism Management*, *91*, 104525.

Case 11 Digital services strategy based on market expansion and management software in Spain

The case of Bamen corporation

Alfonso Cerezo Medina,
Antonio Guevara Plaza, and
Marta Lozano Domínguez

Introduction

Given increasingly dynamic external business environments, a lack of entrepreneurship in the current global economy can be a factor that triggers businesses' failure (Johnson, 2012). In this constantly changing context, the coronavirus disease-19 (COVID-19) introduced additional unprecedented levels of risk and uncertainty. Jalonen (2012) reports that entrepreneurial decisions are consistently made under these conditions, which have become part of everyday life in the tourism sector because of the recent pandemic. However, few prior studies have covered how tourism entrepreneurs in small and medium-sized enterprises (SMEs) engage with the fluid relationships fostered by uncertainty, capital scarcity, and innovation during major crises such as COVID-19 (Zhang et al., 2022).

The tourism sector is an important component of the global economy strongly affected by health crises. Intraprencurship has thus become particularly significant in this industry (World Tourism Organization, 2020, 2022). Researchers such as Díaz and Hernández (2018) in Colombia have emphasised the special relationship between intrapreneurship and SME initiatives' positive impacts (i.e., economic growth).

This chapter presents a case study based on an in-depth interview conducted with a founder of Bamen S. Coop.—a tourism company in Andalusia, Spain, that has implemented different intrapreneurship initiatives before, during and after the COVID-19 crisis. An especially important aspect of this case is that tourism is one of the most critical segments of the Andalusian economy and, simultaneously, one of the most affected by the pandemic (Regional Government of Andalusia, 2021).

The concept of corporate entrepreneurship (CE) has evolved over several decades, so its definition has varied considerably over time (Kuratko et al., 2015). In this chapter, CE is understood to be activities and behaviours—and the intention to conduct these within organisations—that deviate from

DOI: 10.4324/9781003454465-12

their usual way of doing business and pursue the development of new products and/or services (i.e., innovation). Entrepreneurship involves introducing new technologies, administrative processes, strategies and/or competitive approaches. Kuratko et al. (2015) argue that corporate entrepreneurial strategy is a vital driver of sustainable advantages. Researchers must, therefore, continue to conduct case studies worldwide to develop a fuller understanding of CE and innovation in the tourism and hospitality industry from the perspective of its main actors.

Strategic entrepreneurship approaches refer to a broad array of significant entrepreneurial activities or innovations adopted to pursue competitive advantage. They usually do not result in new businesses for the corporation. With strategic entrepreneurship, innovation can be found within any of five areas—the firm's strategy, product offerings, served markets, internal organisation (i.e., structure, processes and capabilities) and business model (Kuratko & Audretsch, 2013).

Organisational background

Bamen is a worker cooperative founded in 2014. This specific legal format was selected because the Regional Government of Andalusia's Andalusian Entrepreneurship Centres convinced the founders that this type of organisation would suit the business they wanted to develop. According to the Government of Spain (n.d.), a worker cooperative is an organisation whose primary purpose is to provide jobs to its members. Worker cooperatives organise themselves and directly invest personal time and effort to provide goods and/or services to third parties.

Bamen's trade name is Sextaplanta, which was taken from Javier Ortiz's personal blog 'Habitación 61' created two years before the cooperative started. The founding partners decided to continue the blog as part of their content strategy and commercial branding of their digital services.

Business activity

Bamen's initial business activity was offering digital services to small independent hotels seeking to strengthen their commercialisation. However, adopting technological upgrades proved to be a significant challenge for these SMEs for several reasons including accommodation managers lack of technology training. This issue confirmed that applying technologies in tourism is a primary reason for more managerial training (Cerezo, 2016). Lillo et al. (2007) suggest that technology can become a tangible competitive advantage for tourism companies, given a well-trained workforce capable of making full, effective use of this resource to adapt to new tourism demands.

After this initial setback, Bamen realised that its clients mainly needed a property management system (PMS), so the cooperative decided to develop its own programme to provide essential functions using Excel. This first platform allowed hotels to carry out primary accommodation tasks, for example, creating bookings or issuing invoices. Despite progressively introduced improvements, the programme continually presented speed problems, so Bamen decided to create the cloud-based software Six. From then on, the company attracted more customers and currently has around 100 users. Six is connected to the main distribution channels, such as Booking.com, and this software has additional modules, including data analytics.

Organisational structure

The legal format of this public limited company is a worker cooperative, whose main characteristic is a horizontal organisational structure. That is, all members are equal, and they have one vote in assemblies – a feature shared with associations. Bamen thus has a democratic structure that facilitates the participation of virtually all staff members because employees or temporary associates who cannot vote can still join in activities.

In 2019, the cooperative had ten members and 12 employees and so were required by law to form a Governing Council with a chairman, vice chairman and secretary. Like other organisations, Bamen holds general assemblies to review the annual accounts and ordinary general assemblies to make strategic business decisions.

One peculiarity of this organisation's structure is how the members' salary ranges are set. By law, each cooperative specifies salaries according to each member's working hours, but the cooperative decided to establish salary bands to match each job, responsibility and task. Overall, Bamen has general statutes and internal rules and regulations that define, among other things, different jobs and their duties and salaries. Due to these statutes' complexity, worker cooperatives have difficulty arbitrating between partners when discrepancies are found and coming to an agreement. This underscores the importance of fostering teamwork to manage these conflicts.

Business environment: Competitors, customers, markets and trends

Spain's National Statistics Institute (2021a) reports that most companies in 2020 were limited liability companies (33.5%) and self-employed workers (55.8%), so running as a cooperative (0.62%) is already a departure from normal business practices. The two main reasons for launching this firm in Malaga were the city's importance in the tourism sector and its status as a reference point in terms of technology and innovation. Malaga has essential advantages for tourism companies, including, among others, related organisations, initiatives and infrastructure, as well as a university that offers higher education programmes in tourism and computer science. This city also boasts a technological ecosystem with large information technology firms and many digital startups.

However, Bamen has developed practically all its business online, so its activities are focused on both local and global markets. The company's competitors are many well-established local firms in the same sector. Other high-profile international companies have established suitable approaches to

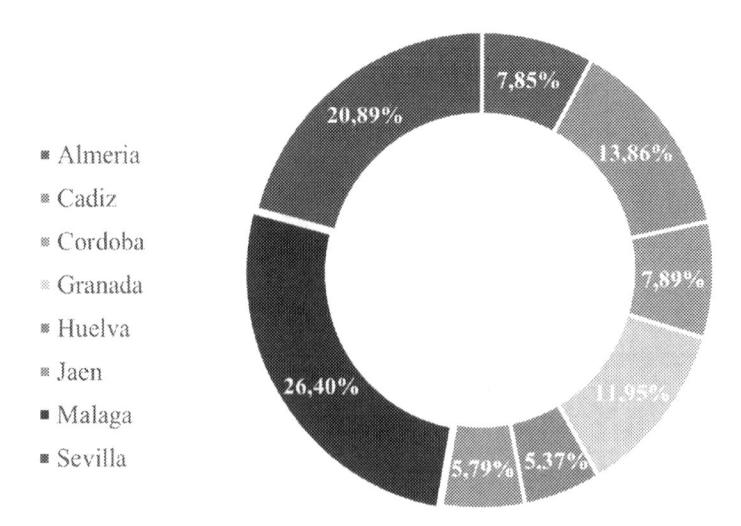

* Almeria
* Cadiz
* Cordoba
* Granada
* Huelva
* Jaen
* Malaga
* Sevilla

Figure 11.1 Distribution of Andalusian tourism companies by province.

Source: Adapted from Andalusian Institute of Statistics and Cartography (2020).

similar business endeavours, which Bamen has adapted to fit its particular circumstances. The same pattern has been established in terms of competing for clients as the firm has attracted both local and national clients.

The tourism market and its trends have been extremely changeable over the last five to ten years in the area of technology. Another advantage of Malaga is that, when any critical alteration occurs in the tourism environment, the prominence of the local tourism sector makes this city one of the first to respond to the circumstances. This tendency has helped Bamen respond quickly to substantial variations in tourism businesses.

More specifically, the Andalusian Institute of Statistics and Cartography (2020) states that Malaga has the largest number of tourism companies in the region: 16,507 firms or 26% of all firms. Figure 11.1 shows that only Seville has a similarly high percentage of tourism organisations at 20%.

Aside from the recent health crisis, tourism's overall trend has recently been expansion. This cooperative has grown by 30% each year. This figure can be considered normal for a small business in its infancy, but Bamen has registered an especially notable overall expansion. For example, in 2018 and 2019, it grew by 30–40% compared to the previous year, and the number of members increased by around two annually. The expected trend in 2020 was to continue growing significantly, but COVID-19 made this impossible.

Bamen's region

From a legal perspective, Andalusia's cooperative legislation can be considered among the most advanced in Europe because the regulations build on previous experience, especially in agriculture. For instance, this region offers tax and legal benefits to facilitate cooperative development, given this legal format's challenges and specificities. The legislation also highlights the Andalusian Federation of Worker Cooperative Enterprises' role as a promoter of these organisations' creation and synergies between them.

However, two legal aspects need to be improved for Andalusia's cooperatives. The first is the selection of business activity in the National Classification of Economic Activities list. Bamen is exclusively focused on tourism, but this company's activities officially belong to the advertising and marketing category. This feature presents no obstacles in routine situations, but during the pandemic, the company was unable to apply for official aid or join the tourism sector's specific recovery plans as the cooperative is not registered as a tourism firm.

Second, Andalusia should implement its numerous tourism policies on all levels rather than only in highly developed tourism areas or non-local, large companies. The region's tourism sector is mainly composed of SMEs that benefit from measures such as creating clusters, promoting public-private collaboration and designing large-scale synergies. According to the National Statistics Institute (2021b), nearly 99% of Andalusian tourism companies (i.e., passenger transport and hospitality) are SMEs.

Evolution of key business indicators

The present study analysed three variables to assess Bamen's key indicators: number of partners (i.e., members), services offered and customers (see Table 11.1). Figure 11.2 depicts the evolution of these variables more clearly. The firm reached its maximum level of business activities in 2019, especially regarding members and clients. COVID-19's impact was felt the most strongly in the reduced number of customers and partners, although a slight recovery occurred in 2021.

The most positive trend over Bamen's eight years has been the number of clients, which has grown overall by 47.5% at an average annual rate of 47%, except for the year of the pandemic. This positive evolution can also be

Table 11.1 Key business indicators

Year	Partners	Services	Customers
2014	3	3	2
2015	4	3	6
2016	5	4	12
2017	7	5	25
2018	8	5	32
2019	10	7	60
2020	6	7	40
2021	5	6	45

Source: Prepared by authors.

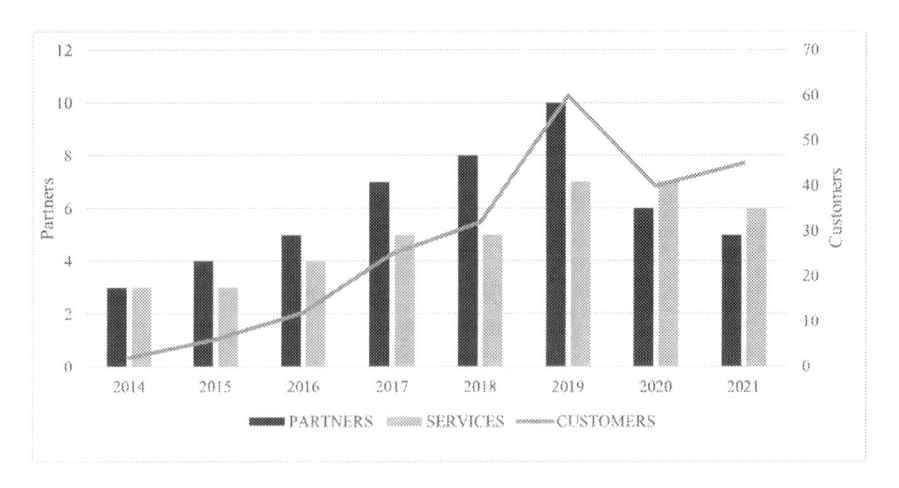

Figure 11.2 Evolution of key business indicators 2014–2019.
Source: Prepared by authors.

seen in the members and services indicators. However, the latter numbers remained relatively constant during the recent health crisis compared to 2019, despite the pandemic's severe impact on the tourism sector.

Intrapreneurship initiatives

The cooperative's internal and external environments have marked specificities, which are accentuated by Bamen's focus on tourism and digitalisation. The company has thus developed numerous intrapreneurship initiatives in different areas and tourism contexts before, during and after the COVID-19 crisis. The most important initiatives are discussed in detail in the following subsection.

Major intrapreneurship projects

Habitación 61

One of the firm's founders started a tourism blog called "Habitación 61" in 2012, two years before creating the cooperative. This blog began as a personal channel of communication through which the founding member interviewed for the present research shared his opinions and insights on tourism. After the blog was merged with the company, this project became a separate initiative that involved more cooperative partners and focused on developing the Sextaplanta brand identity.

The blog's primary function is informative as it seeks to define the brand and its values according to Bamen's business activities. The firm has adapted its operations to match the tourism sector's needs, so the blog has also adjusted its message. This intra-company project is based on sharing interesting, attractive tourism-related content (i.e., non-academic articles) in a conversational tone, which has helped shape the business image and identity of each partner participating in the blog.

Six: PMS tool

This intrapreneurship action is essential to the company because it involves all members and is constantly being improved. Over time, the cooperative's partners and customers have detected flaws in the Six platform. Members report errors through a standard application, while clients are asked to give their opinion about and suggest improvements to this tool. However, some customers are more involved in this process than others.

As a result, Six software's improvements are made on demand to ensure this flexible tool helps clients manage accommodation transactions in small, independent establishments such as hotels, guesthouses and hostels. The platform has also had to adapt to market trends, for example, the appearance of holiday and short-term rental homes, so specific improvements have been incorporated to reach these target customers. Holiday home companies typically manage these accommodations, which means two types of potential clients are involved: owners who rent their properties through intermediaries or end customers who directly manage their homes with the company's assistance. Thus, a transparency portal was created within the Six platform to allow property owners to consult how their property is being used. The latter initiative has provided a competitive advantage, given that Bamen's competitors do not share these details.

Caarta

The company's most recent intrapreneurial initiative is an expansion of its focus on accommodation providers to include hospitality, which was a response to the COVID-19 crisis. Many customers have a restaurant in addition to their accommodations, which is an opportunity to expand Bamen's market. Initially, a consultancy service was launched to assist restaurants with environmental or quality certifications and process improvement. The cooperative subsequently decided to offer help with marketing improvement. To address the ban on physical restaurant menus due to COVID-19, the firm also created Caarta, a digital menu service. Each restaurant has its own quick response code linked to a menu posted on the Internet, which customers can consult by scanning the code with their mobile phone.

Many other companies already offer this service, but Bamen's competitive advantage is that, usually, other applications connect restaurant customers to a non-editable portable document format or hypertext markup language format menu. The cooperative instead allows its clients to modify their menu as many times as needed, which is quite important to restaurants with daily menus. With this new system, restaurant customers can also highlight dishes or incorporate their own ideas.

Skills swap

The firm has additionally targeted the hospitality sector through the Skills Swap project: an Erasmus+ Key Action strategic partnership for vocational training, innovation cooperation and good practices exchange with associated companies in five countries. The goal is to create SME networks in the hospitality and tourism industry in order to trade employees in internship programmes so that they can acquire new skills.

Finally, Bamen implemented another initiative in response to the pandemic. Namely, the cooperative's physical headquarters have been replaced by telework for all partners and workers.

Triggers of intrapreneurship initiatives

The Habitación 61 blog was changed to attract customers in an extremely fragmented, competitive market. This marketing channel is the best way to reach new clients, besides word of mouth or participating in trade conferences. Getting new customers through this initiative takes a long time, but the blog has been the most effective strategy.

The Six PMS's development was promoted by Malaga's technological and tourism opportunities and clients' participation in the process. The cooperative saw the need for this type of tool as an opportunity to expand their business. In contrast, Caarta's creation and Bamen's participation in Skills Swap have mainly been propelled by the new tourism environment generated by the pandemic crisis, namely, a strategy of adapting through a more diversified business model.

Support for activities' implementation

Overall, the initiatives' main sources of support have been cooperative members and employees and their contributions to the business. However, Habitación 61 was supported by alliances with other companies and organisations, such as Andalusia Lab or the Malaga Chamber of Commerce. The Six platform, in turn, has three main kinds of support: human resources, customer support (i.e., providing feedback about the tool or testing the beta version) and student internships. The latter have been organised through the University of Malaga's Faculty of Computer Science and Faculty of Tourism or through technology vocational training centres for developing Web applications.

Development of intrapreneurship initiatives

The motivations to implement these initiatives have been quite diverse. First, Habitación 61 was created to reach out to target clients more effectively. A notable milestone was a campaign supporting the tourism sector called "Do not cancel, postpone", which was launched during the COVID-19 crisis's beginning and which ended up having significant repercussions at a national level. Notable figures in tourism and other sectors echoed the campaign, so it gave the blog and, thus, the company greater visibility.

Second, the Six platform was a response to a business opportunity to satisfy customers' needs. In this initiative, several notable milestones were reached, including the migration from Excel to a cloud web application with its own uniform resource locator and restricted access with a username and password. Other significant achievements were the connections made to a channel manager and leading online travel agencies and the platform's modification to comply with new online payment regulations (i.e., Payment Services Directive 2) by introducing novel secure payment methods and gateways. Another significant milestone was facilitating payment by mobile phone in the accommodation sector—a procedure that until then had usually involved credit card or dataphone services.

Last, Caarta's creation and Skills Swap participation were necessary to adapt Bamen's business model to changes in the tourism sector's environment due to the COVID-19 pandemic. These initiatives thus ensured the diversification needed to lower risk levels.

Main barriers to these initiatives

Market access was the main challenge, as micro-actions were required to reach individual targets. The customers' profile was quite specific because they were the clients who needed Bamen's support and services the most. One of the cooperative's social objectives is for these small tourism service providers to be able to compete within the digital marketing paradigm.

Bamen is a technology-based firm that faces challenges when seeking suitable professionals in the labour market. The member interviewed for this research considers this a major obstacle because most recent graduates aspire to work in large corporations with rigid, traditional structures rather than to engage in intrapreneurship with all its freedom and flexibility.

Initiatives' achievements

The main results have been continuously expanding business activities, maintaining economic viability through growth, and thus ensuring the company's success. On the one hand, the cooperative has improved its services constantly. For instance, the first business model was to offer consultancy services, but then the members realised that offering added value would only be possible if the technologies needed were part of these services.

Conversely, Bamen has grown by targeting other customer profiles and offering more digital services. Initially, the firm mainly focused on small businesses, but it has expanded to medium-sized companies. The cooperative has also extended its clientele's profile to include other destinations while providing complementary services such as graphic design or digital strategies.

This company's business activities are thus following the transition pathway foreseen by the European agenda for future tourism.

Main findings related to intrapreneurship initiatives

The Bamen founder interviewed for this study asserted that human resources is the most fundamental component of a tourism organisations' success. Managers must design projects that attract and retain new talent and develop employees' skills (e.g., emotional intelligence) to ensure a deeper connection with customers and co-workers. This cooperative partner said that motivating staff members is essential, including involving them in business activities and paying attention to any existing personal problems. The main aim is to build a cohesive team with the same business goals.

This case study thus revealed how Bamen has remained reliable and resilient thanks to different intrapreneurship initiatives. Major factors in this success are the firm's legal format, targeting of new customer profiles, creating digital tools in demand among customers and expanding the range of services offered in line with the tourism sector's changing characteristics.

This company's CE was analysed in terms of Sextaplanta's initiatives before, during and after the COVID-19 pandemic, which shows how the cooperative was required to expand its innovation capabilities to meet demand-related changes (Gomezelj & Smolčić, 2016). In addition, the present case study confirmed Zhang et al.'s (2022) results, finding that Bamen has generated new products and services to broaden the scope of the business services made available to customers. Therefore, the findings discussed in this chapter have practical implications for those seeking to respond to tourism crises and are potentially applicable to other regions and countries.

References

Cerezo, A. (2016). Analysis of perceptions and training needs in information and communication technologies in tourism. The case of Andalusia. Publications and Scientific Dissemination. The University of Málaga. Doctoral Thesis.

Díaz, J., & Hernández, J. W. (2018). Impact of intrapreneurship on the business growth of SMEs in the tourism sector in Villavicencio. *Estudios Avanzados Journal*. Available at: https://dialnet.unirioja.es/servlet/articulo?codigo=6703322

Gomezelj, D., & Smolčić, D. (2016). The influence of intellectual capital on innovativeness and growth in tourism SMEs: Empirical evidence from Slovenia and Croatia. *Economic Research-Ekonomska Istraživanja*, 29(1), 1075–1090.

Government of Spain (n.d.). 7.2. *Worker Cooperatives*. Available at: https://www.mites.gob.es/es/guia/texto/guia_2/contenidos/guia_2_7_2.htm

Institute of Statistics and Cartography of Andalusia (2020). *Companies by Sector of Activity and Municipality*. Available at: https://www.juntadeandalucia.es/institutodeestadisticaycartografia/badea/operaciones/consulta/anual/210?CodOper=b3_131&codConsulta=210

Jalonen, H. (2012). The uncertainty of innovation: A systematic review of the litera-ture. *Journal of Management Research*, 4(1), 1–53.

Johnson, D. (2012). *Why Kodak Failed - and How to Avoid the Same Fate*. CBS *Money Watch*. Available at: https://www.cbsnews.com/news/why-kodak-failed-and-how-to-avoid-the-same-fate/

Kuratko, D. F., & Audretsch, D. B. (2013). Clarifying the domains of corporate entrepreneurship. *International Entrepreneurship and Management Journal*, 9, 323–335.

Kuratko, D., Morris, M., & Covin, J. (2015). Corporate entrepreneurship. *Entrepre-neurship*, *3*. doi. 10.1002/9781118785317.weom030017

Lillo, A., Ramón, A. B., & Sevilla, M. (2007). Human capital as a strategic factor for the competitiveness of the tourism sector. *Cuadernos de Turismo*, 19, 47–69.

National Statistics Institute (2021a). *Companies by Province and Legal Status*. Avail-able at: https://www.ine.es/jaxiT3/Datos.htm?t=302

National Statistics Institute (2021b). *Firms by Autonomous Community, Main Activity and Employee Stratum*. Available at: https://www.ine.es/jaxiT3/Datos.htm?t=39372

Regional Government of Andalusia (2021). *Employment in the Tourism Sector in An-dalusia. Latest Data Accumulated Jan-Sep 2021*. Available at: https://multimedia.andalucia.org/saeta/coy_empleo_ene-sep_21.pdf

World Tourism Organization (2020). *COVID-19 and Tourism: 2020 Year in Review*. Available at: https://webunwto.s3.eu-west-1.amazonaws.com/s3fs-public/2021-01/2020_analisis_anual_0.pdf

World Tourism Organization (2022). *World Tourism Barometer, Volume 20, Issue 2, March 2022*. https://www.e-unwto.org/doi/epdf/10.18111/wtobarometeresp.2022.20.1.2

Zhang, W., Williams, A., Li, G., & Liu, A. (2022). Entrepreneurial responses to uncertainties during the COVID-19 recovery: A longitudinal study of B&Bs in Zhangjiajie, China. *Tourism Management*. doi. 10.1016/j.tourman.2022.104525

Case 12 Myths, legends and stories

A South African approach to tourism branding and destination development

*Matthys Andries de Beer
and Cinà van Zyl*

Introduction and background

It is difficult to be an entrepreneur in South Africa (SA), but it is a nation known for resilience. The Global Entrepreneurship Monitor (GEM) National Entrepreneurial Context Index (2023) ranked South Africa 45th out of 50 countries. Entrepreneurship in this chapter is applied from the context of small to medium tourism enterprises (SMTEs) in South Africa. Whilst entrepreneurship is seen as an engine of job creation, South Africans are not optimistic. There is still a lot to be done, as SA is known for the high failure rate of start-ups (Bowmaker-Falconer & Herrington, 2020). Some practical advice on starting your own tourism business in South Africa is summarised in Botha et al. (2006) research: "So if you want to start your own business? Where do you begin?" The answer is open to interpretation, but consider this practical, uniquely South African historical case study introduced through the story pot model as an application for SMTEs in a multicultural context.

The African model is anchored on a local symbol, namely a tripod pot, which is a black cast iron pot that stands on three legs (Figure 12.1). Although the three-legged pot has European origins, the pot has a right to be a symbol in sub-Saharan Africa, credited to nomadic farmers, missionaries, and transport drivers. The three-legged pot represents food, togetherness, and abundance. It is precisely because of the symbolism of the three-legged pot and what it means in the multicultural context of South Africa that the story pot destination marketing model is based on it. The three legs of the pot are conceptualised to represent the community, the economy, and the environment. Arguably, the community forms the backbone of most destinations. Without the insight and participation of the community in a story motif approach to the marketing of a destination, such an initiative cannot be successful. The second leg of the tripod pot model is represented by the environment—natural and cultural-historical—which are impacted by tourism and within which tourism development takes place. In our case, the emergence of guest houses as a tourist accommodation is evident (Henning & Willemse, 1998).

DOI: 10.4324/9781003454465-13

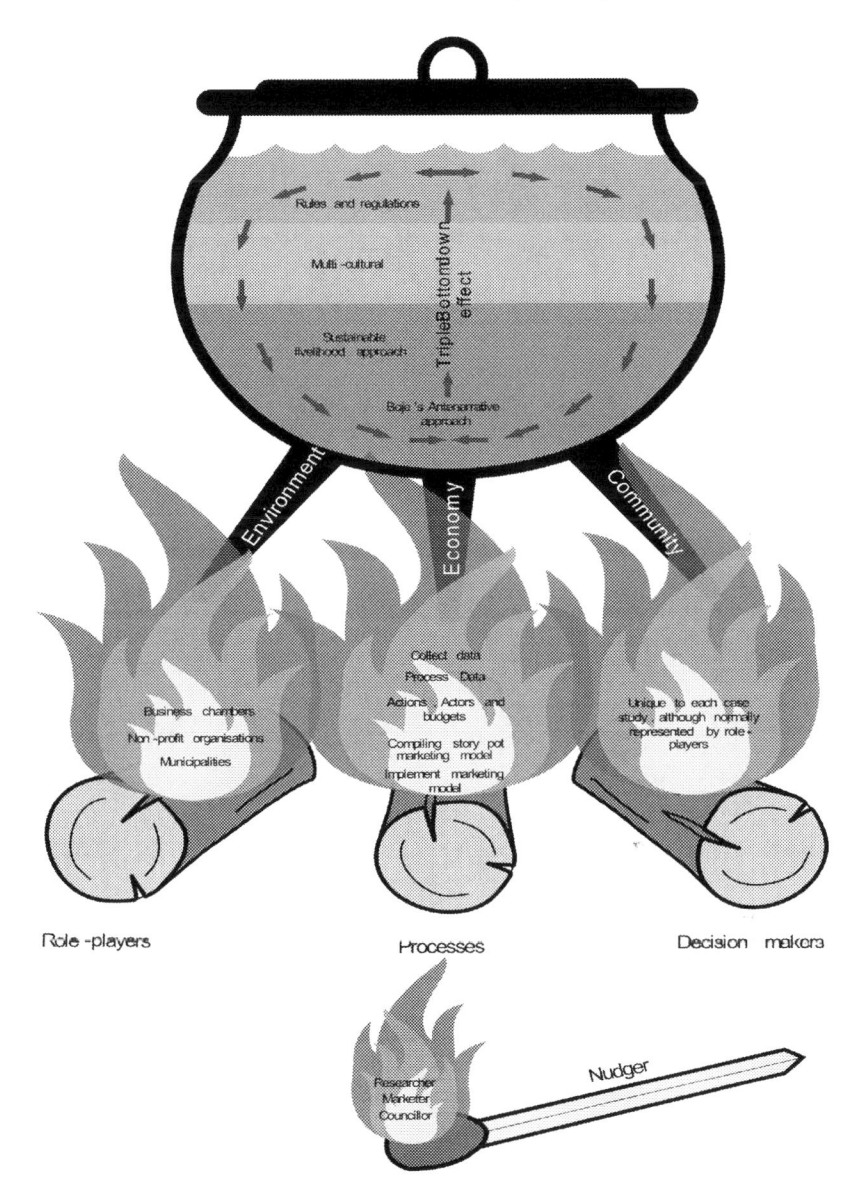

Figure 12.1 An African story-pot marketing model.
Source: De Beer (2020).

Besides the community, the environment is crucial for a place to be called a destination. Both the community and the environment contribute to formulating an appropriate storyline, a story that will fit the intended marketing model. In the case of the environment, it is the task of destination managers and marketers to conduct thorough research regarding the environment in and around the particular destination. This would include not only the geographical context patterns but also myths and legends told through tradition about the specific place.

The economy is the pivot around which tourism revolves and is the critical third leg of the tripod pot. Arguably, in small towns in general—and small-town South Africa in particular—the local tourism economy is made up of small, medium, and micro-enterprises. It is precisely the small and micro-businesses that need to be active participants in developing and applying the story-marketing model and processes because they would be its prime beneficiaries. In the context of the research on which this study is based, the businesses are referred to as accommodation establishments in ter alia guest-houses. Therefore, it is crucial that destination managers involve the small businesses from the outset and become part of the story motif approach, which potentially can be done through the vehicle of local business forums or business chambers. In this regard, the opportunity for entrepreneurial intent and activity originates.

Implementation of the story model

With the implementation of the story model, it is essential to use the implementation process framework as a guideline for SMTEs. In addition to the fact that the process takes place around a specific destination, it is essential that there should be an instigator or, in this case, a Nudger, that is, a person, whether a researcher, marketer or councilor, who, as it were, does not just plant the seed, but also manages the process of bringing together all the necessary elements for the execution and implementation of a successful storytelling approach and potential entrepreneurial action.

It will be the task of the Nudger to identify and bring together the necessary role players and decision-makers, thus setting the proverbial ball rolling in the small town. The role players include, but are not limited to, the local community, businesses, non-profit organisations, and local authorities. The decision-makers will most likely also come from the above group.

It may appear to the Nudger that certain themes, stories, and places already have a right to exist in a story pot model. However, to be successful and provide an opportunity for all to be heard and made part of the process, information gathering is a crucial starting point of the process. The assumption may be valid and well-founded, but the needs and views of the community and also the potential tourists are in a constant form of change and for the story pot model to be successful, it is crucial not to have ideas, concepts, or themes forced into an unsustainable story. However, it must also be remembered that stories are not necessarily breath-taking and self-changing. Thus, the validity of existing themes, stories, and places must be tested by gathering information through questionnaires, interviews and focus groups and adapted as needed. It is important how the questions are asked is important because neutral formulations may help to maintain objectivity. The case study is introduced as a fictitious story linking entrepreneurship activity and tourism business and demonstrates its theoretical, practical and social implications.

Case study

After his second heart attack, at age 42, Mr Xolani Ndita decided that he had enough of the hustle and bustle of Johannesburg—the economic hub of South Africa. He resigned from his corporate job, sold his property, and relocated to the Western Cape, where, over a long weekend, he happened to visit the Winelands district. After exploring the region and visiting all the towns and many of the wine farms, he fell in love with the small town named Wellington. Situated at the foot of the Hawequa mountain range, within easy reach of Cape Town, Wellington offers a quaint village lifestyle surrounded by vineyards and a majestic mountain. All this, along with the hospitality of the community, appealed to Mr Ndita's desires. After a second and third visit to the town, he moved there and opened a guesthouse. The purchasing of the property was the easy part, and even the renovation and rezoning of the property went relatively well. As an entrepreneur, the biggest problem that Mr Ndita faced was breaking into an already saturated guesthouse market in the surrounding small towns. Although Mr Ndita had been a successful businessman in his corporate life in Johannesburg, the tourism industry was unknown to him. In addition, at the time, the various risks of the post-Covid-19 recovery period were still evident in the hospitality sector in South Africa. After completing all the necessary paperwork and the renovations, Mr Ndita named his guesthouse *Lala Kamnandi*—'sleep well' in Xhosa—to celebrate his heritage and opened his doors to guests. He intended to branch the idea into other guesthouses in the vicinity.

Mr Ndita anticipated that business might be slow for the first six months, but after a year of struggling to attain full occupancy in what is a popular weekend destination, he started to question his business strategies and marketing approaches. During one of his strategic sessions, he stumbled upon an inspiring image of a marketing model in the form of a "potjie". The model not only appealed to him as a South African but made sense as a possible approach that he could adopt in order to save his business in a competitive environment.

Environment

The marketing model that Mr Ndita found on the internet (Google Scholar) was an article published in 2022, titled: *Storytelling for Destination Development: Towards an African Model* by De Beer, Van Zyl and Rogerson. At its core, the 'story-pot marketing model' is based on themes, destinations, people, and their local stories within an African context. Although the article emphasised the marketing and development of small towns in the region, the model was easy to understand, and Mr Ndita decided to apply the holistic approach taken by the model to his own tourism business. Since his business was in a small town, he thought he was already halfway there. In addition to adopting the marketing model, Mr Ndita also educated himself with additional information about the town of Wellington and its demographics— as well as learning more about his competitors.

He discovered that, within the Municipality of the small Drakenstein, of which Wellington is part, there are more than 2,000 registered businesses. Of these, 240 fall within the tourism sector. With this new information, Mr Ndita started to dissect the marketing model (see Figure 12.1) to tailor it to his business and to cater for possible future extensions. A picture—in this case, the image of a potjie—is worth a thousand words. It tells a story. The ingredients used in the African story-pot marketing model are applied practically in the next two sections as the development and method followed are described.

Development

The authors of the article (De Beer et al., 2022) used symbols and words that Mr Ndita understood and could relate to. The three-legged pot represents food, community, and abundance. The story destination marketing model is specifically based on the symbolism of the three-legged pot and what it represents in the multicultural context of South Africa. However, the three legs of the pot also represent the community, the economy, and the environment, respectively. The story-pot-based marketing model depicts tourism as a cooking pot used over a fire, as is traditional in Africa. All the story elements are added and stirred together in this pot to make a stew of stories. Coming from a culture of storytellers, Mr Ndita was very excited to test and implement his traditional heritage and knowledge. In the beginning, Mr Ndita was a bit unsure about the 'Nudger' that the model spoke of until he realised that, for his tourism business, he needed to be his own 'Nudger'—the person who ignites and drives the whole process. To succeed, he would have to look into a decentralised, flat management structure and take a hands-on approach.

Mr Ndita, now at ease with his new title as "Nudger" of his own tourism business, worked methodically and creatively to understand and implement the story-pot model approach to branding and marketing his guesthouse and, possibly, future guesthouses in surrounding areas. He also came to realise the need for clear differentiation of his tourism business in the small town guesthouse market.

After attending a few local business chamber meetings and engaging in lively discussions with other business owners, he realised that he was not only the Nudger for his own business entity but also the entire town. This left him in a predicament as his original plan was to only take care of his business. Would this have been the best approach, though? The more he thought about it, the more he realised that better business for the town would mean better business for him, and this would be even more true if the themes and stories were related to one another.

Method followed

The realisation of the situation made him consult the African story-pot marketing model again, confirming his suspicion that he was indeed the "Nudger" that the model spoke of. In his quest to understand and implement the model, Mr Ndita was forced to make contact with all the relevant stakeholders and decision-makers in the municipal district of the small town. The conversations were spontaneous and his enthusiasm contagious. Before long, he had acquired a wealth of knowledge pertaining to the heartbeat of the town of Wellington, its people, and, more importantly, the stories that go with it.

During the course of the year, more and more stories seemed to find their way to Mr Ndita's ear, and he began writing them down and sorting them according to themes. At the next business chamber meeting, Mr Ndita presented the authentic stories that he had heard. He spoke of the possibility that these stories and themes may bring potential business to the region of Wellington.

Mr Ndita's presentation was well received, and the chamber decided that a committee needed to be formed to investigate the findings of the presentation further and to incorporate other stakeholders into this storytelling initiative. The outcomes pleased Mr Ndita; he decided that he needed to move forward for the survival of his own business. Amongst the many stories that he had collected and heard of during the year, there were three in particular that captured his imagination and that he felt compelled to incorporate into his guesthouse branding and marketing strategy. The three stories were: "the man in the mountain", "the black duchess" and "the father of Pinotage".

The man in the mountain

"Hawequa" is the name given by the Khoisan or First Nation people of South Africa to the mountain range overlooking the Klein-Drakenstein Valley, including the small towns of Wellington and Paarl. In the late afternoon, during the Equinox, a shadowy figure of a man emerges from the rocky outcrops carved into the mountainside, overlooking the valley of Wellington.

The black duchess

Lady Martha Gray (née Solomons) was a British noblewoman. She was the daughter of the infamous freed slave Rebecca, who was also a woman of the night, according to legend. Martha married Harry Gray, the 7th Earl of Stamford. Even though the British Crown never recognised Martha, she was eventually made a duchess. After Harry's death, the financial benefits from England ceased, but Martha and her children had more than enough to live on. Besides establishing Martha's Stairwell (a school in Wynberg), she continued with her and Harry's other passion, which was winemaking on their family vineyard and farm. In honour of this remarkable lady, Doolhof, a vineyard (according to legend, the farm that belonged to her) on the outskirts of town, has dedicated a whole range of its wines to her.

The father of Pinotage

Despite being a genuine South African wine, Pinotage requires no introduction to the modern world. It was developed almost a hundred years ago, circa 1925. According to family legend, the father of Pinotage studied abroad and was once the Dean of Stellenbosch University. Another accolade bestowed upon him was that he was a founding member of the KWV (Ko-operatiewe Wijnbouwers Vereniging van Zuid-Afrika) (Co-operative Wine Growers Association of South Africa). Despite being a viniculture pioneer, he funded the majority of his own research. Despite the fact that the finished product received international acclaim years after his death, the mute man died bankrupt. The financial disaster was caused by a black fungus disease that infected the vineyard and destroyed almost everything. However, the story does not end there. Years later, one of his grandchildren would discover an antidote or treatment for the very black fungus that had destroyed his grandpa's finances.

The three stories mentioned above inspired Mr Ndita in such a way that he changed his perception of the small town and its heritage. He began to understand the power of place marketing and stories and how they are interlinked and crucial to the tourism and hospitality industry. This contributed to promoting and selling his accommodation establishment, luring visitors to the small town area.

The week after the business chamber's meeting, Mr Ndita changed the name of his guesthouse to 'Hawequa Guesthouse'. Within a month of the name change, his occupancy rate started to climb. The positive effect inspired Mr Ndita to explore other avenues of capitalising on the stories. Since he was already in the Winelands, he started building relationships with neighbouring wine farmers. As the relationships grew stronger, different avenues and business opportunities became available. The stories of the 'black duchess' and 'the father of Pinotage', along with the new relationships he formed with wine farmers, inspired him to start hosting wine pairings once a month at his establishment. Although most of the wines of the region receive respect at these events, as well as the opportunity to be paired with some decadent cuisine, there will always be a bottle of 'black duchess' on the table. The visual of the 'black duchess' evokes emotion, communicates instantly to all, and creates the differentiator needed in a market.

Epilogue

Mr Ndita is still an active member of the business chamber. He has become part of the committee still investigating the possibilities of using the story-pot model approach in the region. Mr Ndita is still the Nudger, for himself and the committee. The bureaucracy remains frustrating for him, but he eagerly shares the valuable lessons that he has learned and uses them to guide the group. A couple of local businesses that are not tourism-related have noted the positive changes in Mr Ndita's accommodation establishment, and a few have even consulted him and tried similar approaches with varying degrees of success. This entrepreneur demonstrated that you can turn your good idea into a great business. One lesson from the case is that guest houses remain a lucrative market opportunity for potential entrepreneurs in small towns and unique settlements in the African context.

References

Botha, M., Lubbe, B., & Fairer-Wessels, F. (2006). *Tourism entrepreneurs*. Cape Town: Juta & Co, Ltd.

Bowmaker-Falconer, A., & Herrington, M. 2020. Igniting startups for economic growth and social change. In Global entrepreneurship monitor South Africa (GEM SA) 2019/2020 report. Also available at: https://www.gemconsortium.org/news/igniting-startups-for-economic-growth-and-social-change-in-south-africa (accessed March 3, 2021).

De Beer, M. A. (2020). *'n Driepootpotverhaalbemarkingsmodel vir Kleindorpse Toerismebestemmings*. PhD Tourism Management (UNISA) 2020.

De Beer, M. A., van Zyl, C., & Rogerson, C. M. (2022). *Storytelling for destination development: Towards an African model. African Journal of Hospitality, Tourism and Leisure, 11*(4), 1491–1501.

Development: Towards an African model. *African Journal of Hospitality, Tourism and Leisure, 11*(4), 1491–1501. doi. 10.46222/ajhtl.19770720.304

Donaldson, R. (2018). *Small town tourism in South Africa*. Cham: Springer.

Donaldson, R. (2021). Small town tourism in South Africa revisited. In C. M. Rogerson & J. M. Rogerson (eds.). *Urban tourism in the global South: South African perspectives* (pp. 193–211). Cham: Springer.

Harris, K., & Botha, C. (2022). Insourcing the indigenous without outsourcing the storyteller: A sustainable African solution. In J. Saarinen, B. Lubbe & N. Moswete (eds.). *Southern African perspectives on sustainable tourism management: tourism and changing localities* (pp. 79–89). Cham: Springer.

Henning, R., & Willemse, C. (1998). *Effective guest house management* Cape Town: Juta & Co, Ltd.

The Global Entrepreneurship Monitor (GEM) National Entrepreneurial Context Index, 2023. *New GEM South Africa National Report: Early stage entrepreneurs are growing into established businesses.* Accessed 19 April 2023 https://www.gemconsortium.org

Case 13 Entrepreneurial strategies and innovation in hospitality business
Stories from Australia and Indonesia

Hera Oktadiana, Tingzhen Chen and Joko Haryono

Introduction

Scholars have been conducting various research on corporate entrepreneurship. However, there is a call for more research emphasising corporate entrepreneurship in family businesses (Minola et al., 2021). Minola et al. (2021) suggested three realms of research agenda – ontology (domain redefinition), epiphany (components and mechanism), and heterogeneity (family business variety and contingencies). It should also be noted that the roles of managers in the corporate entrepreneurship of companies should not be overlooked (cf. Wu et al., 2018). This chapter addresses those gaps by presenting the experiences of family-business owners and a hospitality manager in implementing corporate entrepreneurial practices, as reflected in the following aims. Related to epiphany, the first aim is to examine the engagement of a family restaurant business owner in corporate entrepreneurship to foster the firm's growth. To support the main purpose, the second aim is to provide insights into managerial roles in promoting corporate entrepreneurship. The second purpose is presented by an Indonesian hotelier who has worked in various international hospitality enterprises.

Autoethnography, the emerging method from the postmodern philosophy, was employed to illustrate the cases in this study. Such an approach "offers a way of giving voice to personal experience to advance sociological understanding" (Wall, 2008, p. 39). Data were gathered based on personal notes, a diary and memories. Memories of the authors' lived experiences have been well acknowledged in autoethnography as they cannot be separated from the fieldwork (Coffey, 1999; Wall, 2008). It can be argued that in this challenging time of the COVID-19 pandemic, researchers could investigate society using their own experiences as the source of data (Roy & Uekusa, 2020). Roy and Uekusa further stated that the pandemic offers opportunities for researchers to study various facets of people's experiences, socioeconomic, political and health of the crisis. Learning from other people's experiences helps us gain knowledge and understanding about how people solve problems, make decisions, and deal with complex issues and crises (Tanner, 2016).

DOI: 10.4324/9781003454465-14

The contributions of this chapter are twofold. The theoretical contribution lies in enriching hospitality literature by addressing corporate entrepreneurial practices in a family-owned hospitality business using an autoethnography account (emic perspective). As for the practical contribution, this chapter postulates useful information for individuals who are interested in operating a small business and how corporate entrepreneurship is exercised.

Environment

The first focus of this chapter is a family-owned business of sushi shop, Sushi Paradise. The shop is located at the food court of Willows Shopping Centre in Townsville, Queensland, Australia. Townsville is a coastal city in Northern Queensland with a population of about 193,601 people. The city is also known as the second capital of Queensland. The area is home to Australia's iconic landscapes – the outback, the reef, and the rainforest (City of Townsville, 2022; Townsville North Queensland, 2020).

The owners of Sushi Paradise believe that the food court is in style. They are also convinced that such a concept facilitates the local residents' lifestyle. Food courts are becoming exciting dining destinations that offer quality restaurants/shops with plenty of menu choices and fashionable interiors. For example, the Kitchens food court in Gold Coast, Australia, features 40 dining outlets, open kitchens, workshops and masterclasses. Food courts are viewed as the places where people spend their time (Mayor, 2019). People nowadays go to the food courts not just for fast service and cheap meals, but also for good quality food.

Sushi Paradise Willows was opened in 2021 by the second author and her husband. They took the shop over from the previous owner who had run the business for three years. This independent restaurant offers a takeaway scheme (Figure 13.1). The restriction of dining out during the pandemic led to the changing pattern of getting meals from food and beverage outlets. Takeaway and delivery were more favoured to minimise or avoid contact with other people.

The shop has four staff, two full-time and two part-time employees. The main owner (the second author's husband) who is also the manager, is responsible for managing the shop. The duties include planning, budgeting, ordering supplies, recruiting and managing staff, selling, and marketing. Based on the average monthly sales, it is expected that the annual sales are between A$360,000 to A$400,000.

The main competitors of Sushi Paradise comprise two groups. The first group is the other sushi shops located in the shopping centre, and the second group is the Asian food shops/restaurants. The first group of competitors is a takeaway sushi food stall near a supermarket and a dine-in sushi train restaurant. The sushi food stall has a similar business concept and trading hours as Sushi Paradise. However, they do not sell hot meals. The dine-in restaurant has a different business model, targeting customers who want to spend time to enjoy

Figure 13.1 Sushi Paradise shop.
Source: Authors' photo.

the meals in the restaurant. The Asian food shops are the Chinese and Korean takeaway that are also situated at the food court. These two shops sell hot food. The Chinese shop serves a good variety of food on hot bain-marie, and the Korean shop offers grab-and-go food in bowls but with limited choices.

Three market clusters of Sushi Paradise consist of the shopping centre staff, the shoppers, and the high school students. The shopping centre employees are the most regular customers, but they generally only buy small portions of food for lunch. The shoppers or visitors are high-spenders and likely to buy meals in large quantities. Although many of them are one-time buyers, the number of these customers is high, especially at the weekend. The high school students normally come in the afternoon after school hours, or just a couple of hours before the shop closes, between 3 PM to 5 PM. Such time is usually the quiet time at the food court. These customers always come in groups and do not spend much.

Indubitably, leadership and managerial skills are imperative in a business operation and to support corporate entrepreneurship (cf. Srivastava & Agrawal, 2010). Moreover, (middle) managers play significant roles in corporate entrepreneurship of establishments as the implementor of change and initiator of change (Wu et al., 2018). To complement the first case, the third author's 35 years of managerial experience in the hotel and restaurant industry is presented. The author has worked in several hospitality organisations globally, including Four Seasons Hotel Jakarta – Indonesia; Four Seasons Hotel Riyadh – the Kingdom of Saudi Arabia; Outback Steakhouse Jakarta – Indonesia; Wyndham Sundancer Resort Lombok and Wyndham Opi Palembang Indonesia; and Wyndham Grand Maldives. He held various managerial positions such as restaurant manager, food and beverage manager, and hotel general manager.

The author was also involved in several pre-opening teams. The most recent was as the operational director of the pre-opening of Wyndham Grand Maldives in 2019. Unfortunately, his assignment as a hotel manager for Wyndham Melbourne, Australia, was cancelled due to the long lockdown in Melbourne. Instead, he was assigned to manage the Wyndham Opi Palembang in South Sumatra Indonesia. His first experience opening a hotel was the Four Seasons Jakarta (known as Regent Four Seasons Jakarta) in November 1994. The hotel was officially opened in 1995 and became one of the 5-star luxury hotels in Jakarta.

The first establishment where the author had worked is the Canadian company of the Four Seasons Hotels and Resorts. This business launched its first hotel in 1961. It was followed by the opening of a hotel in London in the 1970s, which later became the pioneer of many Four Seasons services delivered worldwide. The company stretched its portfolio by developing resorts throughout the 1990s to respond to the new demand for leisure experience. It launched the Four Seasons experience to European and Asian destinations. Four Seasons remained growing around the world with its property on all continents except Antarctica (Four Seasons, n.d.). The second premise is Wyndham Hotels and Resorts which own 22 iconic brands and manages more than 8,900 hotels in 95 countries (Wyndham Hotels & Resorts, 2022). The company is based in Parsippany, New Jersey, and is considered as one of the world's largest hotel chains. The firm continues its business expansion in the overseas market, particularly in Southeast Asia. It also targets South America and Europe (Ganaishlal, 2019). The third enterprise is Outback Steakhouse, an Australian-themed restaurant that was founded in 1988 in Tampa, Florida, USA. With a tagline "no rules, just right", the company emphasises good quality food and service at a moderate price and casual atmosphere. Outback Steakhouse can be found in 19 countries, including Southeast Asia, Latin America, and the Middle East (Blomin' Brands, 2020).

Working in a diverse global environment has enriched the third author's perspectives, skills, and knowledge in engaging corporate entrepreneurial behaviour to manage hospitality operations. The next session depicts his corporate entrepreneurial behaviour practices when overseeing hospitality operations as well as the practices carried out by the owner of Sushi Paradise.

Development: Corporate entrepreneurship practices

This section conveyed corporate entrepreneurship exercises of the two accounts.

A family-owned business of sushi shop in Australia

Managing and operating the shop during the pandemic was challenging. The closure of the Australian border made it hard to hire competent staff. Although Townsville was not badly affected by the COVID-19 pandemic and lock down did not take place, people were cautious and reluctant to go out for indoor leisure activities such as shopping and dining in. This situation significantly impacted the sales of the business. To overcome the issues, the owners posted job vacancy advertisements in various social media, and asked for recommendations from friends and existing staff. The condition started improving in December 2021 as people went Christmas shopping and caught up with family and friends.

After several months, the owners recognised that food, business hours and suppliers were the important factors for the business. The hot food sold in a cup, such as rice and chicken teriyaki bowl, made Sushi Paradise distinct from its competitors. These hot foods were favoured by customers for their taste and value for money. At the Sushi Paradise, the foods are cooked according to an order (à la minute cooking) and served immediately. Therefore, the foods are still hot and fresh. To maintain food quality at a reasonable price, the owners actively sought cost-efficient suppliers due to the rising price of food ingredients. The owners also carried out a weekly evaluation to monitor the most popular products and the non-popular products. This helped the owners to determine the necessities. The conflict between Russia and Ukraine has disrupted supply chains and impacted the economy with increased food and energy prices (Ellyatt, 2022). The owners experienced some issues concerning communication with the key suppliers. Some suppliers tend to respond better through email, and some prefer phone calls and text messages. The owners need to accommodate the suppliers' preferences to gain effective communication. Alliances with suppliers are deemed necessary to understand the key changes and trends in customers' needs. To meet the customers' demands and lifestyle changes, the owners extended the business hours during the weekdays and weekends.

Undoubtedly, staff support is critical to carry out those practices. Staff needs to be empowered to be able to identify any opportunities arising in the market and to take appropriate actions accordingly. In developing the corporate entrepreneurship actions, the manager/owner initially identifies any problems arising from the daily sales and business activities. Secondly, the manager discusses the issues with the staff. Next, the manager, together with the staff, develops some strategies to solve the issues, and finally implements the strategy. Any adjustments will be made to improve the strategic actions based on evaluation. The manager identifies the corporate entrepreneurship opportunity through daily, weekly and monthly sales reviews, observation, customer feedback, discussion with the employees, and information from the key suppliers. Engaging the employees and having good communication with them as well as with the stakeholders is important to maintain enthusiasm for corporate entrepreneurship. Such spirit can fade away if not properly sustained as standardisation occurs and the work becomes routine (Kim & Park, 2021).

Based on Shepherd and Patzelt (2021), the corporate entrepreneurship strategies and actions carried out by Sushi Paradise management are chartered based on five key building blocks:

"(1) identifying and evaluating market opportunities in startups, (2) designing business models, (3) engaging in validated learning (including customer development), (4) building minimum viable products, and (5) learning whether to persevere with or pivot from the current course of action"

(Shepherd & Patzelt, 2021, p. 54).

The first block addresses the identification and evaluation of multiple opportunities, followed by selecting the most promising feature to start the new venture. The second block concerns a business model that underpins the business operations. Innovation in the business model will improve the performance of a new enterprise by associating business activities with the customers, partners, and vendors. The next block conveys a hypothesis that needs to be tested and validated using a scientific method. This involved learning about the new venture's market segment as well as channels to reach them and value proposition. The fourth block depicts the initial product development for the sales. Finally, the fifth block outlines pivotal or persevering decisions for the business. Following the framework, the strategies defined by the owners of Sushi Paradise are depicted in Table 13.1.

Moreover, the owners of Sushi Paradise proposed some key points to perform corporate entrepreneurship:

1 Develop a good plan and evaluate the business goals and operation from time to time.
2 Be resilient, innovative and adventurous to explore new opportunities. Do not be afraid to make changes.
3 Do not get confined within the business. Be open-minded to listen to other people's perspectives (i.e., your employees, suppliers, customers, competitors).
4 Empower your staff to take initiative, share ideas and resolve problems.
5 Expand your business network and accessibility to suppliers.
6 Use Social Media or other technological means to increase the market reach for your business, develop the business brand, attract customers and build customer loyalty.

Managerial roles and corporate entrepreneurship in hospitality businesses in Indonesia

The third author started his career as a Room Service Supervisor in Four Seasons Jakarta, until appointed as Seasons Café Manager to oversee the main dining restaurant, pool and veranda restaurant outlets. The restaurants offered breakfast, lunch, dinner, Barbeque Night, Sunday Brunch and other

Table 13.1 Sushi Paradise's corporate entrepreneurship strategies and action

Five building blocks	Corporate entrepreneurship strategies and action
Identify and evaluate market opportunities	Meeting the local residents' lifestyle and demand for takeaway food due to the COVID-19 pandemic. Target market: the shopping mall staff, visitors and students.
Design the business models	Takeaway restaurant at the shopping mall's food court (Food court is in style as the place for leisure activities).
Engage in validated learning	Focus on the foods, business hours, and suppliers as the primary success factors for the business: • Increase the quantity of high-demand food. • Reduce low-demand food. • Extend the business hours to embrace the variety of market segments. • Alliance with suppliers to understand the key changes and trends in customers' needs. • Empower the staff. • Reduce the waste for cost efficiency.
Build minimum viable products	Sushi and Japanese hot food in a bowl.
Learn whether to persevere with or pivot from the current course of action	Persevere the business: • Regular review and evaluation of the sales and services. • Recruit more staff. • Develop effective communication with different suppliers.

meals for special occasions. He was also assigned as in-room dining manager and the food and beverage manager in one the best steakhouses in town at that time, "The Regent Steakhouse, Jakarta". The author was given an opportunity to become the executive assistant manager and look after the day to day operations of the property His passion for food and beverage led him to work as a room dining manager at Four Seasons Riyadh, the Kingdom of Saudi Arabia. In leading the food and beverage division, the third author created a room service training video, assisted by his friend who worked at the production house. His video was displayed at the Annual Meeting of the Food and Beverage Division at the Four Seasons Shanghai, China.

During the Asian financial crisis in 1998, many hotel businesses suffered. Four Seasons Jakarta implemented a strategy of not reducing the room rates. Instead, the management team decided to offer extra facilities and benefits to the customers. They viewed that the continuation and growth of the business depended on the excellent quality of the products and services offered to the guests, not simply reducing the room rates. The hotel also actively promoted social corporate responsibility programs such as sports activities for different charities including the "Terry Fox Run" and "Thalassemia Donor" with Indonesia Red Cross (PMI), as well as religious events.

In 2001, the author departed to California, USA, for the MIT (Management Internship Training) Program as a General Manager for the Outback Steakhouse and the franchisee of the restaurant in Southeast Asia. The author took part in the opening team of Outback Steakhouse San Diego. After one year, he returned to Jakarta, Indonesia and opened the first store of Outback Steakhouse International at Ratu Plaza Mall Jakarta in 2001. The author successfully established the store as a training centre for the Outback Steakhouse in Southeast Asia. The author was appointed as an official instructor to train new general managers and chefs of Outback Steakhouse restaurants in Southeast Asian countries, including Indonesia, Malaysia and Thailand. One of the Outback Steakhouse outlets in Jakarta is shown in Figure 13.2.

Just one month after the opening, the author successfully generated revenue of IDR 1.1 billion (approximately USD 110,000) for the store. The key success in the sales lay in the strong branding, high product quality, strong advocate from the US Embassy in Jakarta, and the ability to attract the market. The author, as the store proprietor or managing partner, is actively involved in various US Embassy events, including social events, to gain their support. With the motto "serious food and serious service", the restaurant maintained its product quality by bringing in the primary ingredients (i.e., meats) from the US. At the same time, the company supported the local businesses by purchasing other ingredients (e.g., vegetables, seafood, poultry) according to the approved product list (APL). The restaurant's primary customers were expatriates who worked in Jakarta. As indicated in the

Figure 13.2 One of the Outback Steakhouse Outlets in Jakarta.
Source: Authors' photo.

Jakarta Post, more than 3.2 million expatriates lived and worked in Jakarta and other parts of Indonesia in 2000 (Living in Indonesia, 2019).

Managing an independent restaurant is different from managing a food and beverage outlet in a hotel. Attention to detail in all aspects is critical. This includes product and service quality, budgeting, defining food prices, revenue management, human resources management, and marketing management. If the restaurant fails to attract customers, the business may close due to the loss of revenue. The staff will lose their jobs. On the other hand, hotel restaurant outlets are part of a hotel's operations. Although income from food and beverage contributes to the hotel's revenue, the hotel can still maintain its operation by selling its rooms if the restaurant sales are unsatisfactory (cf. Sumit, 2015). As the managing partner, the author routinely participated in Outback Steakhouse's annual conference in the USA, as well as attending the regional conference every six months.

Developing a network and collaboration with the local stakeholders (e.g., local community, government officials) are essential in a business operation. Clear information and a well-defined action plan will simplify and expedite the business opening. Moreover, the opening team must be able to anticipate and address any issues that arise during the planning and implementation. The importance of learning and development or training programs also needs to be considered.

The author's working experiences in Four Seasons hotels have shaped his values as a manager in other hospitality enterprises. The credo of "Treat Others as You Wish to Be Treated" strongly influenced how he thinks and acts in managing hospitality businesses. He views the staff as the brand ambassador of the company. Thus, looking after the employees' health and well-being is important to create a positive work environment. Some of the practices include providing the staff with a dual menu arrangement for breakfast, lunch and dinner buffet, spacious locker, and gym and sports facilities. He encouraged staff to generate new ideas and share their thoughts to enhance the business operations. He also appraised the significance of open communication by considering the local customs and culture.

During his tenure at the various hospitality establishments, he allowed his staff to "take the ownership of the business". Hence, when they had to deal with problems such as guests' complaints, they could take action immediately without having to ask for his approval. During the regular briefings, the staff would provide a glitch report to inform the other staff and departments what happened, what had been done to solve the issues, which guest was impacted, and how to avoid similar problems reoccurring. Such an approach led to job efficiency and guest satisfaction. He also believes in the idea of "let's celebrate the mistake". Staff can learn more from their mistakes. The experience they have from making mistakes can strengthen innovation and creativity and open new and exciting opportunities (Alexander, 2010).

The author noted that managing the hotel operation during the pandemic was challenging (note: Wyndham Palembang, South Sumatera, Indonesia).

Many people were reluctant to stay in a hotel. Nevertheless, the business operation needs to endure. As the general manager, the author and his team earned a CHSE (Cleanliness Health, Safety, Environment) certificate from the Indonesian government to gain their customers' trust. A rigorous health protocol was strongly implemented in the hotel. The hotel targeted staycation customers from the locals and collaborated with an online travel platform, Traveloka, to attract customers. Other strategies comprised upgrading the in-room amenities for the guests, the development of a no-touch service experience, and the delivery of a full-service buffet where the foods were served by the staff wearing a special uniform to ensure the cleanliness, hygiene and safety. Due to the business low point, the author had to restructure the staff's working schedule. Their working hours were reduced from 30–31 days to 14 days in a month. However, the usage of facilities, health insurance and service charge systems remained the same. All employees were also given the COVID-19 vaccination.

Epilogue

Literature implies that corporate entrepreneurship is advanced by two key factors: environmental factors and individual characteristics. The former involves leadership, rewards and motivation, organisational systems, and organisational culture. The latter includes but is not limited to achievement motivation, locus of control, risk-taking proclivity, energy level, persistence and the need to create something on one's own (Srivastava & Agrawal, 2010). Adapting from Srivastava and Agrawal (2010), Table 13.2 summarises the two broad features that support corporate entrepreneurship based on the two cases.

It can be noted from the two narratives that innovation and corporate entrepreneurship cannot be separated. In other words, innovation occurs when corporate entrepreneurship takes place (Han & Park, 2017). Innovation is the heart of a business. Innovation adds value to the business's growth. It helps the business lead the competition in a fast-changing market and gain competitive advantage from the new technology (MasterClass, 2021; Tseng & Tseng, 2019). Yet innovation is not only associated with technology. Technological innovation is about products, services, and processes. Non-technological innovation or soft innovation includes management, marketing, and business model (Martin-Rios, n.d.). In his study, Martin-Rios asserted that although innovation in technology was widely applied in the hospitality industry, such advancement did not significantly affect customer retention and occupancy rate. Technology needs to be strengthened with other forms of innovation, service and process innovation. The combination of unique and superior services with contemporary processes in the operations will bring strong competitive advantages.

Another important attribute in the hospitality arena is adaptability (Hcareers, 2021). Adaptability is the ability to adjust to any changes in any situation and be flexible. This skill can be enhanced by becoming aware of environmental changes, developing a growth mindset, seeking feedback, and

Table 13.2 Key factors supporting corporate entrepreneurship

Environmental factors	*Leadership*
	• Foster teamwork. • Assess new market opportunities. • Create positive work environment.
	Organisational system
	• Flexible job design to suit the changing business environment. • Encourage staff to manage their work and solve problems if required. • Allow staff to do different tasks and explore. • Alliance with suppliers to understand the trends in customers' needs/accessibility of suppliers. • Promote efficiency.
	Organisational culture
	• Promote innovation as a critical factor for the business's success and its future. • Encourage staff to look at things in a new way. • Motivate staff to share ideas and provide feedback. • Develop effective communication with suppliers and staff. • Treat the staff well – consider their health and well-being.
	Rewards and motivation
	• Empower staff. • Allow staff to learn from mistakes. • Communicate business' goals with the staff. • Evaluate the goals regularly (involve the staff).
Individual characteristics	Innovative, adaptability, responsive, open-minded, resilience, eager to learn and explore, good communication skills.

being willing to step out of the comfort zone. To have good adaptability skills, individuals must possess good listening and communication skills, strategic thinking, resilience, and responsiveness (Hcareers, 2021).

Based on the cases portrayed in this chapter, several pivotal entrepreneurial strategies were noted. They include making careful planning related to the working capital, staffing, marketing and day-to-day operations; accepting and organising new ideas; meeting good contacts or networking; having good communication, willingness to learn, and having strong determination (Samantaray, n.d.; Tseng & Tseng, 2019). Implementing corporate entrepreneurship can further advance the organisations' financial performance and competitive advantage by encouraging and nurturing new ideas and knowledge, creation, and innovation (Han & Park, 2017).

Future research directions may explore how family-related factors and family relationships influence corporate entrepreneurship initiatives and how differences between family businesses and non-family establishments deal with disruptive innovation and uncertainty (McKelvie et al., 2014; Minola et al., 2021). Another agenda may involve examining and comparing various tourism and hospitality establishments, including local and international firms, and small-, medium- and large-sized enterprises in utilising corporate entrepreneurship. Thus, a distinction between various forms of hospitality operations can be drawn.

References

Alexander (2010, June 3). Top 5 reasons to celebrate mistakes at work. Available at: https://positivesharing.com/2010/06/top-5-reasons-to-celebrate-mistakes-at-work/

Bloomin' Brands. (2020). No rules. Just right. *Bloomin' Brands*. Available at: https://franchise.bloominbrands.com/global/brands/outback-steakhouse/brand-background

City of Townsville. (2022). *Living in Townsville*. Available at: https://www.townsville.qld.gov.au/about-townsville/living-in-townsville

Coffey, A. (1999). *The ethnographic self*. Sage.

Ellyatt, H. (2022, April 21). From soaring food prices to social unrest, the fallout from the Russia-Ukraine war could be immense. *CNBC*. Available at: https://www.cnbc.com/2022/04/21/from-food-to-inflation-the-russia-ukraine-war-has-aglobal-impact.html

Four Seasons. (n.d.). Four Seasons history. Available at: https://www.fourseasons.com/about_four_seasons/four_seasons_history/

Ganaishlal, J. (2019, December 18). Wyndham Hotels & Resorts explained. *Skift*. Available at: https://skift.com/2019/12/18/wyndham-hotels-resorts-explained/

Han, J., & Park, C. (2017). Case study on adoption of new technology for innovation: Perspective of institutional and corporate entrepreneurship. *Asia Pacific Journal of Innovation and Entrepreneurship*, 11(2), 144–158.

Hcareers (2021, December 7). Improving your adaptability: The most important hospitality skill. Available at: https://www.hcareers.com/article/career-advice/improving-your-adaptability-the-most-important-hospitality-skill

Kim, J. Y., & Park, M. J. (2021). Investigation of critical factors on corporate entrepreneurship: Rethinking the organization culture. *Journal of Entrepreneurship in Emerging Economies*, 13(1), 1–25.

Living in Indonesia (2019). How many expats live in Indonesia? Available at: https://www.expat.or.id/info/howmanyexpatsinindonesia.html

Martin-Rios, C. (n.d.). Industry report: Hospitality innovation strategy in practice. Available at: https://hospitalityinsights.ehl.edu/hospitality-innovation-strategy-in-practice

MasterClass (2021, September 2). Why innovation is essential for business success. Available at: https://www.masterclass.com/articles/why-innovation-is-essential-for-business-success#3-models-of-business-innovation

Mayor, A. (2019, 6 February). Six food experience trends to watch. *Dalziel&Pow*. Available at: https://www.dalziel-pow.com/news/food-experience-trends-to-watch

McKelvie, A., McKenny, A. F., Lumpkin, G. T., & Short, J. C. (2014). Corporate entrepreneurship in family businesses: Past contributions and future opportunities.

In L. Melin, M. Nordqvist & P. Sharma (eds.). *The SAGE handbook of family business* (pp. 340–363). SAGE Publication.

Minola, T., Kammerlander, N., Kellermanns, F. W., & Hoy, F. (2021). Corporate entrepreneurship and family business: Learning across domains. *Journal of Management Studies*, 58(1), 1–26. doi. 10.1111/joms.12672

Roy, R., & Uekusa, S. (2020). Collaborative autoethnography: "self-reflection" as a timely alternative research approach during the global pandemic. *Qualitative Research Journal*, 20(4), 383–392.

Samantaray, N. (n.d.). Five strategies for success for first-time entrepreneurs. *Apac Entrepreneur*. Available at: https://apacentrepreneur.com/five-strategies-for-success-for-first-time-entrepreneurs/

Shepherd, D. A., & Patzelt, H. (2021). A lean framework for starting a new venture. InD. A. Shepherd &H. Patzelt (eds.). *Entrepreneurial strategy: Starting, managing, and scaling new ventures* (pp. 51–71). Palgrave Macmillan Cham. doi: 10.1007/978-3-030-78935-0

Srivastava, N., & Agrawal, A. (2010). Factors supporting corporate entrepreneurship: An exploratory study. *The Journal of Business Perspective*, 14(3), 163–171.

Sumit, R. (2015, November 29). Hotel outlets vs standalone restaurants. Available at: https://www.linkedin.com/pulse/hotel-outlets-vs-standalone-restaurants-sumit-rana

Tanner, N. (2016, September 28). Why you should read biographies (and 10 to add to your reading list). Available at: https://nathantanner.net/2016/09/28/why-you-should-read-biographies-and-the-10-to-add-to-your-reading-list/

Townsville North Queensland. (2020). Available at: https://www.townsvillenorthqueensland.com.au/

Tseng, C., & Tseng, C. (2019). Corporate entrepreneurship as a strategic approach for internal innovation performance. *Asia Pacific Journal of Innovation and Entrepreneurship*, 13(1), 108–120. doi. 10.1108/APJIE-08-2018-0047

Wall, S. (2008). Easier said than done: Writing an autoethnography. *International Journal of Qualitative Methods*, 7(1), 38–53.

Wu, Y., Ma, Z., & Wang, M. S. (2018). Developing new capability: Middle managers' role in corporate entrepreneurship. *European Business Review*, 30(4), 470–493. doi. 10.1108/EBR-08-2016-0104

Wyndham Hotels & Resorts (2022). We are Wyndham Hotels & Resorts. Available at: https://corporate.wyndhamhotels.com/about-us/

Case 14 Corporate entrepreneurship actions toward a more sustainable tourism mobility

The case of the Ferrovie dello Stato Italiane

*Mario Tartaglia, Francesca Pagliara
and Juan Carlos Martín*

Introduction

The Ferrovie dello Stato Italiane (FS) is the holding company of the major Italian industrial Group acting in the transportation sector. The company invests in and manages railway and road infrastructure and operates rail and bus services. FS provides mobility opportunities for people at different territorial scales, from regional, national or international, and for any reason, e.g. work, education, leisure and even tourism. Although tourism is a minor cause generating people trips compared to the more systematic purposes such as work and school, it is gaining more importance within the general mobility system of a country like Italy, which traditionally attracts an important number of travellers and visitors. This chapter aims to illustrate the FS corporate entrepreneurship (CE) actions, mainly focusing on tourist and leisure transportation demand.

The tourism industry is crucial in economic value, employment, and social and cultural integration (ISTAT and Banca d'Italia, 2020). In Italy, tourism contributed to the national GDP in 2019 slightly greater than 13% compared to a world average of 10.4% (WTTC, 2021a), and the contribution of tourism to national employment was around 15% against a global average of 10% (WTTC, 2021b). Transport and tourism are very close sectors (Lumsdon & Page, 2004). Although rail transport mode accounts for a minor market share, it takes relevance concerning environmental and accessibility issues (Page, 2003). The role of railway transport in the tourism industry will be more relevant in the future in the EU after the aim of having more competitive railways (EC, 2022).

The CE analysis will be based on a case study (Yin, 1989). The case study method is mainly based on a detailed investigation of one or more organisations, or groups within organisations, to provide an analysis of the CE actions taken by the FS to develop the "railway sustainable transport support to tourism in Italy".

DOI: 10.4324/9781003454465-15

Context

FS, 100% owned by the Italian Ministry of Economy and Finance since 1992 (FS, 2021a), is one of the largest industrial companies in Italy and a vital mobility stakeholder through its subsidiaries that operate in the four Business Hubs of infrastructure, passenger transport, logistics, and urban systems (FS, 2022a). FS subsidiaries manage infrastructure facilities, such as rail tracks, railway passenger stations and road networks, and operate passenger rail and bus services. The FS Group currently has about 83 thousand employees, over 10 thousand trains running every day (circa 8 thousand in Italy and more than 2 thousand abroad), around 750 million rail passengers (600 in Italy and 150 abroad), 300 million passengers on the road per year along with 50 million tonnes of goods. The railway network managed by Rete Ferroviaria Italiana (RFI) is over 16,700 km long, of which more than 700 km is dedicated to high-speed services, while about 32.000 km of national roads are maintained by the Group's Italian road network manager, i.e. ANAS company (FS, 2022b).

The FS Group can be considered a system company with significant economic value. In the pre-pandemic situation, the 2019 annual report registered €12,4 billion in operating revenues, with €9.8 billion in operating costs, a €2,6 billion Earnings before interest, taxes, depreciation, and amortisation (EBITDA) with a margin of 21,0%, €584 million net profit and €8,1 billion technical investments, making FS the leading Italian industrial Group in terms of investments (FS, 2020). The spread of COVID-19 caused, in 2020 and partially in 2021, a considerable drawback for FS as well as for most transport companies across the globe. However, in 2021, the annual report showed a recovery of €12,2 billion in operating revenues, a €1,9 billion EBITDA with a margin of 21,0%, €193 million net profit and a record of €12,5 billion in technology investments.

Within the FS Group, transport services supporting tourism mobility are operated in Italy by Trenitalia (the passenger train company of FS), Fondazione FS (the historic passenger train company of FS), and Busitalia (the bus company of FS). Other FS companies involved abroad in passenger services are Trainose (trains and buses, Greece), Trenitalia UK (trains, UK), Ilsa (HS trains, Spain), QBuzz (buses, the Netherlands), and Netinera (trains and buses, Germany). Recently, some FS CE actions focused their support on sustainable tourism, redistributing tourist flows and improving accessibility to Italian art cities and holiday destinations. Thus, FS is increasingly advancing its role as a point of reference for the national tourism ecosystem (FS, 2022c). The innovation and digitalisation potentialities for supporting tourism are also under the focus of the FS CE actions. Several initiatives were launched to inspire train travel through digital tools, such as the foundation of acceleration pathways of innovative start-up companies for enhancing the digital tourism experience by train (FS, 2022d).

Business environment

It is challenging to approach the tourism phenomenon without linking it to the development of transport investments and accessibility gains (Campa et al., 2016; Guirao & Campa, 2016). Tourism activities are very complex and have a multidimensional component, as many service providers are involved. Tourism supply components vary from natural resources, such as good climate and beaches; cultural and historical sites, such as iconic monuments, museums, theatres, and architectural hallmarks; to more intangible issues, such as food, music, folklore, exhibitions, and festivals.

Railways are one crucial component for many tourist destinations, and rail tourism was also coined for particular iconic trains like the Orient Express that are characterised by special train operators that use rail tracks owned and managed by other infrastructure companies. Pagliara et al. (2022) analysed the relationship between High-Speed Railways (HSR) and tourism growth, finding that the relationship depends on several factors, such as the surveyed countries and the intrinsic characteristics of the existing tourism products. The authors found an important gap concerning introducing tour packages that consider different levels of integration between the main stakeholders involved, namely railways, hotels and attractions. For that, we contend here that there is a tremendous potential to develop new combined tourist products that incorporate the railway system to visit emblematic cities in Italy to impulse the recovery for both sectors, tourism and railways.

As tourism is a human activity firmly based on mobility, the COVID-19 crisis severely reduced travel and long-distance journeys, and this has also mainly led to a considerable impact on the tourism sector (Abbas et al., 2021; UNWTO, 2022a). Almost two years after the outbreak of the COVID-19 coronavirus in Wuhan, China, and about 20 months after the spread of the virus to most countries in the world, the availability of vaccines has made the global pandemic more manageable in some countries, but the crisis is far from being over (Gössling, & Schweiggart, 2022). Struggling with fifth and sixth waves, new highly infectious virus variants such as Omicron, the unavailability of vaccines in poor economies, and the protests of the "anti-vaxxers" in significant parts of the industrialised world, COVID-19 continues to affect national economies, businesses, health services and social life. While tourism advocacy organisations (WTTC, 2021a) and academics have been swiftly discussing global recovery pathways, it is currently unclear when to expect a lasting recovery.

Depending on the situation, travel restrictions, lockdowns, quarantines, and mandatory testing have affected national tourism systems, creating volatile and unpredictable business and travel environments. Notable developments included, on the demand side, the turn of business travellers to videoconferencing and the willingness—in an acknowledged absence of alternatives—of significant parts of the population in industrialised countries to embark on domestic holidays. All the while, travel restrictions, test requirements, and quarantines made international travel complicated and demanding. For example, this fact affected the 2020 and 2021 summer seasons in Europe and North America, with significant implications for shifts in spending, from which export markets profited as money was retained within national economies while destinations suffered.

These developments are mirrored in GDP changes, specifically in more substantial GDP losses. Global tourism experienced a 73% decrease in international tourist arrivals (overnight visitors), with a reduction in the economic contribution of tourism (measured in tourism direct gross domestic product) from US$3.5 trillion estimated in 2019 to US$1.6 trillion in 2020, slightly increased to US$1.9 trillion in 2021 (UNWTO, 2022b). A similar effect occurred in Italy, with a 60% drop in foreign visitors in 2020 (Banca d'Italia, 2021a, b). On the supply side, impacts on tourism have included bankruptcies and new debt, specifically among airlines and cruise operators. Tourism businesses responded to the crisis with product diversification, rebates, workforce reductions, and new marketing strategies. However, it seems clear that the effects of income losses and new debt will be felt for a considerable time.

The current world scenario, with the declared COVID-19 pandemic, is characterised by an unprecedented crisis with widespread repercussions on the entire economic system. Seeing one of the main outbreaks, Italy was hit very strongly by the virus both as regards the health system and the high number of infections, as well as the economic impact due to the lockdown of many businesses (FS, 2022e). Among these, the pandemic highly affected tourism due to the imposed restrictions on the entire travel and transport chains (FS, 2021a). The current recession, especially in tourism, leads to re-thinking and implementing new development models based on safety devices aimed at guaranteeing safety for travellers and all people, with consistency on sustainability and by reducing impacts on environmental and cultural resources, as provided by the 2030 Agenda goals of the United Nations (Ceschin & Bizzarri, 2021).

European countries gradually restored free movement within the Schengen area from June 15th 2020, but every EU member state imposed its own travel conditions to enter the country (e.g., in terms of tests and self-isolation) and updated them according to contagion trends. No particular conditions were imposed on German and Austrian tourists during the summer. As a result, travelling to Italy was possible for European Union (EU) citizens from June 15th, while non-essential travelling from third countries was not possible, except for selected countries where the epidemiological situation was considered under control. Notably, tourists from the UK, the US and China could not enter the EU during the summer of 2020 (Scuttari et al., 2021). Nevertheless, neither general mobility flows nor railway mobility levels in Italy were restored at the end of 2021 (FS, 2022f; MIMS, 2022).

In January 2022, when COVID-19 was not over, another global critical event affected travel and tourism: Russia's invasion of Ukraine. Just one week after the outbreak of the war, flight bookings within Europe fell by 23%

(Lane, 2022), whereas UNWTO estimated a possible loss of US$14 billion for the tourism economy due to the war (UNWTO, 2022b, c). Apart from the general reduction of travel due to restrictions, fuel price increases, and security issues, a not negligible impact of such conflict is certainly expected on Italy since Russia is the third extra-European country contributing to tourism in Italy according to both arrivals and expense (Banca d'Italia, 2021a).

Although travel and tourism are among the most affected sectors by both COVID-19 and the Ukrainian war scenario, tourism remains one of the most important economic sectors, with solid resilience to recover from the crisis (UNWTO, 2022d). Moreover, Peira et al. (2022, p.75) state that "railways can play a significant role in developing the attractiveness of a tourist destination and could act as a catalyst for territorial branding". As stated by the International Union of Railways (UIC), tourism by railway can offer several opportunities to develop and enjoy leisure (UIC, 2022). It can attract several types of customers, such as young people, adults, active, retired people, families, railway enthusiasts, and domestic and international tourists, who can support sustainable tourism as the railway is the most sustainable mode of transport (UIC, 2017).

Moreover, tourism may enhance the development of entrepreneurial actions in the railways that can improve the traveller experience, mixing landscape uniqueness, train carts' beauty and the onboard experience (EC, 2021). UIC analysed some opportunities for developing tourism by rail by considering the main trends in travel and tourism (UIC, 2020). For instance, the demand for more personal time and wellness created by technology evolution and hyper-connected lifestyles, the blending between work and leisure, the demographic and urbanisation trends, and the environmental and ethical concerns reshaping consumption. All these elements can contribute to the chance for railways to enhance their role in tourism by increasing demand numbers and quality.

The FS corporate entrepreneurship vision: Key elements to support a more sustainable tourism mobility

The FS Group is still undergoing a general economic crisis lasting more than two years, including a never-seen worldwide pandemic followed by a conflict at the gates of Europe. Both events caused significant impacts on mobility and tourism. In any case, FS has demonstrated a high resilience capacity so far, guaranteeing a suitable level of transport services during the crisis, recovering its financial account in just one year and holding the role of one of the leading Italian and European investors in infrastructure and technology. As FS Group is at the core of the Italian economic system, its strength has guaranteed a precise reference point for the country's stability and crucial support for mobility and tourism recovery. Nevertheless, the CE actions in FS are not exempt from facing barriers acknowledged by academics when analysing the gigantic public firms which develop antibodies to entrepreneurship (Thornberry, 2003).

As a signal of reaction, in May 2022, the FS holding company developed a new industrial plan focusing on innovation and digitalisation, increasing international presence, energy and ecological transition (FS, 2022g). The Group's organisation is based on four business hubs: infrastructure, passenger mobility, freight mobility and urban solutions. The first hub, the infrastructure, constitutes the backbone of economic and social development throughout the territory. Based on this framework, the passenger hub aims to set up and supply integrated solutions for sustainable mobility, supporting the evolution of travel and tourism. With an ancillary role, the hub aims to realise a sustainable regeneration of cities, with an expected positive effect on territory life quality and tourism attractiveness (FS, 2022h).

The approach of a transportation company to tourism can take several paths. In organising a tourism experience, a tourist may address directly to the elementary service providers (e.g., hotels and transport companies), or they can go to a travel agency (traditional or even an Online Travel Agency, OTA) or furthermore to a tour operator, with increasing levels of delegation to them regarding the organisational decision to be taken. Likewise, the attitude of a tourist to these different planning styles is strongly related to the perception of the use of intelligent tourism technologies, which can both enhance the trip experience due to the novelty-seeking satisfaction or can cause tourist worries due to trip planning difficulties (Goo et al., 2022). A holiday package is based on different tourist approaches, containing elements such as travel documents, accommodation and leisure facilities reservations, and other services.

The approach of a rail or transportation company for entering this decisional chain and providing its supplied services can be oriented in two main directions: setting up additional partnership agreements with tourism business subjects (i.e. single service providers, travel agencies or tour operators) or including an in-house tour operator able to supply complete packages.

Examples of transportation companies that developed an in-house tour operator are British Airlines, Iberia, Lufthansa, and easyJet. For instance, the British Airways website allows passengers to book flights with a hotel or rental car, hire a car or even book complete tourism experiences like holidays or breaks (British Airways, 2022). A similar configuration can be found on the Iberia website, where booking flights, rental cars, and hotels is possible by customising the chosen packages (Iberia, 2022). Lufthansa offers an in-house tour operator on the web, Lufthansa Holidays, for directly booking complete tourism experiences (Lufthansa, 2022), similar to the easyJet Holidays website (easyJet, 2022).

Among the railway companies that developed an in-house tour operator, one can find Eurostar and SBB, the Swiss incumbent rail company. Eurostar was a former partner of the Expedia Group up to 2018, but it set up its tour operator integrated with its website, supplying train and hotel bookings and offering a whole holiday or tourism experience (Eurostar, 2022). SBB website contains a special section called Leisure and Holidays, where it is possible to book whole tourism experiences chosen among hundreds of proposals browsable by a dedicated research engine (SBB, 2002).

Instead of having an in-house tour operator, some other transportation companies have established partnerships with other businesses, often maintaining a website look and feel based on the company's corporate identity. One example of the approach is the case of the Spanish incumbent rail company, Renfe, which sells tourism packages through a specific company (Renfe Viajes Ocio) operated by the travel agency Viajes Reina (Renfe Viajes Ocio, 2002) or by connections to other experience providers (Renfe, 2022). Another example of a transportation company that operates in partnership with tourism services providers is the airline company Air France, which offers additional services such as car rental with a driver, parking, accommodation (with Booking.com), car rental (with Hertz), leisure experiences (with Viator), and many other alternatives (Air France, 2022).

The two approaches described, developing an in-house operator or establishing partnerships, have both some pros and cons. The first one allows offering a one-stop-shop to the customers and better control of the business costs and revenues but needs to internalise the necessary know-how and sustain the in-house company risks and start-up times and costs. The second solution requires a more straightforward organisation, possibly allowing to quickly generate revenues and leading the transportation company into the know-how learning process for further in-house internalisation. Conversely, it permits common control of supply and customer loyalty management and requires sharing the economic margins with the partner companies.

In this competitive business context, as mentioned above, the FS approach to tourism demand is mainly based on the incumbent passenger train company Trenitalia and partially on the historic passenger train company Fondazione FS. Trenitalia's strategy is founded on partnerships. As it is displayed on the Trenitalia website, several services additional to travel are offered (Trenitalia, 2022). Among these, one can find transport supply extensions (car rental, scooter sharing, bike-sharing, and coupled trips such as train+ship, train+taxi and train+flight), hotel booking, and some partnerships with special leisure events like music concerts and museum visits, among others. Some partnerships are agreed upon with companies belonging to the same FS Group (e.g. parking supplied by the Metropark company), some with joint-venture companies (e.g. the rental car company, Enjoy), others with independent partners (e.g. the scooter sharing service provided by Cooltra and Zig Zag, the push scooter and e-bike-sharing provided by Helbiz, taxi services offered by Wetaxi and Free Now, car rental provided by Avis and other companies). Regarding the accommodation sector, the service is directly linked to the Booking.com website, although using a webpage partially customised with Trenitalia's logo.

In addition, the Fondazione FS supply is dedicated explicitly to historical tourism experiences, trips by historical trains, railway museum visits, historical railway libraries and archives availability (Fondazione FS, 2022a).

The heritage train journeys are organised on iconic railway routes, where historical trains with steam or diesel locomotives connect valuable heritage locations. Moreover, the heritage train "Pietrarsa Express" connects Naples directly to the National Railway Museum of Pietrarsa, which gathers more than 55 historical rolling stocks in the ancient pavilions of the bourbon workshop. The visit allows for a suggestive journey back in 1839, the year of the inauguration of the first Italian railway line, until more recently (Fondazione FS, 2022b). Finally, "rail-fan" tourists interested in railways can visit the historical railway library in Rome, which houses over 40,000 railway-themed volumes, including monographs, collections and magazines.

Regarding the FS CE actions for the future, the industrial plan for the decade 2022-2031 clearly states the goal of developing Italy's tourism by addressing a considerable effort toward infrastructure investments and services design dedicated to this business sector. Regarding the planned investments in the network and stations, the task is assigned to the national infrastructure managers for railways (RFI) and roads (ANAS). Meanwhile, the Group passenger business hub, which includes the Italian national incumbent rail passenger company (Trenitalia) with its subsidiaries in the UK (C2C), Greece (Trainose), France (Trenitalia France), and Spain (Ilsa), the passenger rail and bus company for South West Italy (FSE), and the Italian bus company Busitalia and its subsidiaries such as Qbuzz in the Netherlands, will design new tourist services (FS, 2022i). As reported in the FS's industrial plan, the passenger hub of FS Group aims to develop tourism in the country, offering frequent and extensive connections for those who also opt for green transport for their travels. The plan envisions an ambitious offer dedicated to tourist travel and greater integration between the various modes of transport by linking the country's three gateways: railway stations, airports and ports. Additionally, a further increase in slow tourism aboard historic trains along railway lines that are in operation or no longer used for commercial traffic is also in mind. Thus, Italians and visitors could discover Italy's cultural, scenic and culinary beauties on trains that have catalysed the history of Italy.

Epilogue

In summary, the FS Group is at the core of the Italian economic system, and its engagement in supporting sustainable tourism mobility belongs to its DNA. The most relevant features of FS CE actions described in the case study are those from the industrial plan that aims to foster more sustainable tourism mobility in Italy using the railways as the primary transport mode within the country. Different strategies and actions were compared with other CE actions developed by competitors worldwide. The lessons learned from two different approaches, in-house or partner operators, were discussed in the chapter. FS CE actions could be described as a mixture of both, with the development of the heritage trains and the partnership plans developed with other tourism agents.

Moreover, FS Group is fully aware of the challenges to be taken on in the following years, also considering the post-COVID recovery managerial perspectives, the geopolitical instability, the new passengers' and tourists' perceptions and behaviour, and other significant current and prospective research themes for the tourism sector (Menon et al., 2022; Zopiatis et al., 2021). Schwab and Malleret (2020) suggested that the COVID-19 pandemic should be a chance to enhance the whole social, environmental and economic system. Similarly, the crisis has given us an opportunity to rethink the tourism sector and its contribution to the people and the planet. The tourism industry can bounce back better towards a more sustainable, inclusive and resilient industry that guarantees the benefits are enjoyed widely and fairly (UNWTO, 2021). FS understands the challenge and is ready to assume its role in making this happen.

Third-party materials: We have not used any third-party copyrighted material that needs permission to be published.

References

Abbas, J., Mubeen, R., Iorember, P. T., Raza, S., & Mamirkulova, G. (2021). Exploring the impact of Covid-19 on tourism: Transformational potential and implications for a sustainable recovery of the travel and leisure industry. *Current Research in Behavioral Sciences*, 2, 100033. doi. 10.1016/j.crbeha.2021.100033

Air France (2022). The Air France Website. Retrieved on June 4th, 2022 from https://wwws.airfrance.fr/en

Banca d'Italia (2020). Survey on International Tourism 2019. Retrieved on April 16th, 2022 from https://www.bancaditalia.it/pubblicazioni/indagine-turismo-internazionale/index.html?com.dotmarketing.htmlpage.language=1

Banca d'Italia (2021a). Survey on International Tourism 2020 (in Italian). Retrieved on April 16th, 2022 from https://www.bancaditalia.it/pubblicazioni/indagine-turismo-internazionale/index.html?com.dotmarketing.htmlpage.language=1

Banca d'Italia (2021b). The impact of Covid-19 on international tourism flows to Italy: evidence from mobile phone data. Retrieved on April 16th, 2022 from https://www.bancaditalia.it/pubblicazioni/qef/2021-0647/QEF_647_21.pdf?language_id=1

British Airways (2022). The British Airways Website. Retrieved on June 4th, 2022 from https://www.britishairways.com/travel/home/public/en_gb/

Campa, J. L., López-Lambas, M. E., & Guirao, B. (2016). High speed rail effects on tourism: Spanish empirical evidence derived from China's modelling experience. *Journal of Transport Geography*, 57, 44–54.

Caselli, M., Fracasso, A., & Scicchitano, S. (2020). From the lockdown to the new normal: An analysis of the limitations to individual mobility in Italy following the Covid-19 crisis, GLO Discussion Paper, N. 683, Global Labor Organization (GLO), Essen.

Ceschin, F. M., & Bizzarri, C. (2021). The role of sustainability for the tourism recovery in Italy. In F. Grasso & B. S. Sergi (eds.). *Tourism in the mediterranean sea* (pp. 25–33). Bingley (UK): Emerald Publishing Limited. https://doi.org/10.1108/978-1-80043-900-920211004

easyJet (2022). The easyJet Holidays Tab within the easyJet Website. Retrieved on June 4th, 2022 from https://www.easyjet.com/en/holidays/

EC, European Commission (2021). Railway and Tourism: A Cultural Perspective. 3rd TopRail Forum. Retrieved on June 4th, 2022 from https://europa.eu/year-of-rail/events/railway-and-tourism-cultural-perspective-2021-10-26_en

EC, European Commission (2022). Mobility and Transport. Railway packages. Retrieved on June 4th, 2022 from https://transport.ec.europa.eu/transport-modes/rail/railway-packages_en

Eurostar (2022). The Eurostar Railway Website. Retrieved on June 4th, 2022 from https://www.eurostar.com/rw-en

Fondazione FS (2022a). The Fondazione FS Website. Retrieved on March 25th, 2022 from https://www.fondazionefs.it/

Fondazione FS (2022b). The National Railway Museum of Pietrarsa. Retrieved on March 25th, 2022 from https://www.fondazionefs.it/content/fondazionefs/en/explore-museum/visit-pietrarsa.html

FS, Ferrovie dello Stato Italiane (2020). FS Italiane: 2019 Annual Report. Retrieved on May 29th, 2022 from https://www.fsitaliane.it/content/dam/fsitaliane/en/Documents/investor-relations/financial-statements/FS_Italiane_2019_Annual_Report.pdf

FS, Ferrovie dello Stato Italiane (2021a). Investor Presentation, Retrieved on May 29th, 2022 from https://www.fsitaliane.it/content/fsitaliane/en/investor-relations/investor-presentations.html

FS, Ferrovie dello Stato Italiane (2021b). Reference market trends 2020, Retrieved on May 29th, 2022 from https://www.fsitaliane.it/content/fsitaliane/en/investor-relations/reference-market-trends.html

FS, Ferrovie dello Stato Italiane (2022a). FS Group, 2022-2031 industrial plan 190 billion for sustainable development of infrastructure and mobility at the service of the country. Retrieved on May 29th, 2022 from https://www.fsitaliane.it/content/fsitaliane/en/media/press-releases/2022/5/16/fs-group–2022-2031-industrial-plan-190-billion-for-sustainable-.html

FS, Ferrovie dello Stato Italiane (2022b). FS Italiane Holding. Retrieved on May 29th, 2022 from https://www.fsitaliane.it/content/fsitaliane/en/fs-group/fsitaliane-holding.html

FS, Ferrovie dello Stato Italiane (2022c). Sustainable Tourism, Retrieved on May 29th, 2022 from https://www.fsitaliane.it/content/fsitaliane/en/sustainability/environmental-commitment/sustainable-tourism.html

FS, Ferrovie dello Stato Italiane (2022d). Train Digital Tourism Experience. Retrieved on May 29th, 2022 from https://www.fsitaliane.it/content/fsitaliane/en/media/news/2021/12/20/train-digital-tourism-experience.html

FS, Ferrovie dello Stato Italiane (2022e). Annual Report 2020, Retrieved on May 29th, 2022 from https://www.fsitaliane.it/content/fsitaliane/en/investor-relations/financial-statements.html

FS, Ferrovie dello Stato Italiane (2022f). Interim Report Highlights 2021, Retrieved on May 29th, 2022 from https://www.fsitaliane.it/content/fsitaliane/en/investor-relations/financial-statements.html

FS, Ferrovie dello Stato Italiane (2022g). The Industrial Plan and the four business Hubs. Retrieved on May 29th, 2022 from https://www.fsitaliane.it/content/fsitaliane/en/fs-group/the-industrial-plan-and-the-four-business-hubs.html

FS, Ferrovie dello Stato Italiane (2022h). The Passenger Hub. Retrieved on May 29th, 2022 from https://www.fsitaliane.it/content/fsitaliane/en/fs-group/the-industrial-plan-and-the-four-business-hubs/the-passenger-hub.html

FS, Ferrovie dello Stato Italiane (2022i). Group Companies. Retrieved on May 29th, 2022 from https://www.fsitaliane.it/content/fsitaliane/en/fs-group/group-companies.html

Gössling, S., & Schweiggart, N. (2022). Two years of COVID-19 and tourism: What we learned, and what we should have learned. *Journal of Sustainable Tourism*, *30*(4), 915–931.

Guirao, B., & Campa, J. L. (2016). Should implications for tourism influence the planning stage of a new hsr network? The experience of Spain. *The Open Transportation Journal*, *10*, 22–34.

Goo, J., Huang, C. D., Yoo, C. W., & Koo, C. (2022). Smart tourism technologies' ambidexterity: Balancing tourist's worries and novelty seeking for travel satisfaction. *Information Systems Frontiers*, *24*, 2139–2158.

Iberia (2022). The Iberia Website. Retrieved on June 4th, 2022 from https://www.iberia.com/en

ISTAT (2020). Domestic and Outbound Travel and Tourism 2019 (in Italian). Retrieved on January 27th, 2022 from https://www.istat.it/it/archivio/238416

ISTAT (2021a). Domestic and Outbound Travel and Tourism 2020 (in Italian). Retrieved on January 27th, 2022 from https://www.istat.it/it/archivio/256376

ISTAT (2021b). Tourism Perspectives in Italy during the Covid era (in Italian). Retrieved on January 27th, 2022 from https://www.istat.it/it/archivio/258529

ISTAT (2022). The Italian Tourism Satellite Account 2019 (in Italian). Retrieved on January 27th, 2022 from https://www.istat.it/it/archivio/265443

ISTAT and Banca d'Italia (2020). A short guide to tourism statistics (in Italian). Retrieved on January 27th, 2022 from https://www.istat.it/it/archivio/243826

Lane, M. (2022). ForwardKeys reveals early impact of Russia's Ukraine invasion on flight bookings, The Moodie Davitt Report. Retrieved on June 10th, 2022 from https://www.moodiedavittreport.com/forwardkeys-reveals-early-impact-of-russias-ukraine-invasion-on-flight-bookings/

Lufthansa (2022). The Lufthansa Holyday Website. Retrieved on June 10th, 2022 from https://www.lufthansaholidays.com/de-de

Lumsdon, L., & Page, S. J. (2004). *Tourism and transport: Issues and agenda for the new millennium*. San Diego, CA: Elsevier.

Menon, D., Gunasekar, S., Dixit, S. K., Das, P., & Mandal, S. (2022). Present and prospective research themes for tourism and hospitality education post-COVID19: A bibliometric analysis. *Journal of Hospitality, Leisure, Sport & Tourism Education*, *30*, 100360. doi. 10.1016/j.jhlste.2021.100360

MIMS, Italian Ministry of Sustainable Infrastructures and Mobility (2022). Mobility Trend during Covid-19 Emergency, Fourth Quarter 2021 (in Italian), Retrieved on June 10th, 2022 from https://www.mit.gov.it/comunicazione/news/covid-19-pubblicato-report-osservatorio-tendenze-mobilita-quarto-trimestre-2021

Page, S. J. (2003). *Tourism management: Managing for change*. Oxford: Butterworth Heinemann.

Pagliara, F., Martín, J. C., Román, C., & Bursa, B. (2022). Supply-side trends – Transport: High-speed rail growth. In A. M. Morrison & D. Buhalis (eds.). *Handbook of trends and issues in global tourism*. Abingdon, UK: Routledge. (forthcoming).

Peira, G., Lo Giudice, A., & Miraglia, S. (2022). Railway and tourism: A systematic literature review. *Tourism and Hospitality*, *3*(1).69–79. doi. 10.3390/tourhosp 3010005

Renfe (2022). The 'Experiencias' Webpage within the Renfe Website. Retrieved on June 10th, 2022 from https://www.renfe.com/es/es/experiencias

Renfe Viajes Ocio (2002). The Rende Viajes Ocio Website. Retrieved on June 10th, 2022 from https://renfeviajes.renfe.com/es/quienes-somos-renfe

SBB (2002). The SBB Leisure and Holidays Website. Retrieved on June 10th, 2022 from https://www.sbb.ch/en/leisure-holidays.html

Schwab, K., & Malleret, T. (2020). *Covid-19: The great reset.* Switzerland: World Economic Forum.

Scuttari, A., Ferraretto, V., Stawinoga, A. E., & Walder, M. (2021). Tourist and viral mobilities intertwined: Clustering Covid-19-driven travel behaviour of rural tourists in South Tyrol, Italy. *Sustainability, 13,* 11190.

Thornberry, N. E. (2003). Corporate entrepreneurship: Teaching managers to be entrepreneurs. *Journal of Management Development, 22*(4), 329–344.

Trenitalia (2022). The Trenitalia Website. Retrieved on June 10th, 2022 from https://www.trenitalia.com/it.html

UIC (2017). Guidelines on sustainable tourism. Paris, France.

UIC (2020). Guidelines on how to increase attractiveness for rail tourism. Paris, France.

UIC (2022). Rail Tourism. Retrieved on June 4th, 2022 from https://uic.org/passenger/tourism-opportunities-for-railways/

UNWTO. (2021). This crisis is an opportunity to rethink the tourism sector. https://www.unwto.org/un-tourism-news-21

UNWTO (2022a). The UNWTO Tourism Data Dashboard, Retrieved on June 4th, 2022 from https://www.unwto.org/unwto-tourism-dashboard

UNWTO (2022b). Tourism grows 4% in 2021 but remains far below pre-pandemic levels. Retrieved on April 7th, 2022 from https://www.unwto.org/news/tourism-grows-4-in-2021-but-remains-far-below-pre-pandemic-levels

UNWTO (2022c). Impact of the Russian offensive in Ukraine on international tourism. Retrieved on June 8th, 2022 from https://www.unwto.org/impact-russian-offensive-in-ukraine-on-tourism#:~:text=A%20prolonged%20conflict%20could%20translate,US%24%204.7%20billion%2C%20respectively

UNWTO (2022d). International tourism and Covid-19. Retrieved on June 8th, 2022 from https://www.unwto.org/tourism-data/international-tourism-and-covid-19

WTTC (2021a). Travel & Tourism Economic Impact 2021. Retrieved on April 16th, 2022 from https://wttc.org/Portals/0/Documents/Reports/2021/Global Economic Impact and Trends 2021.pdf?ver=2021-07-01-114957-177

WTTC (2021b). Italy 2021 Annual Research Key Highlights. Retrieved on April 16th, 2022 from https://wttc.org/Research/Economic-Impact/moduleId/704/itemId/136/controller/DownloadRequest/action/QuickDownload

Yin, R. K. (1989). *Case study research: Design and methods. Applied social research series,* Vol. 5. London: Sage.

Zopiatis, A., Pericleous, K., & Theofanous, Y. (2021). Covid-19 and hospitality and tourism research: An integrative review. *Journal of Hospitality and Tourism Management, 48,* 275–279.

Case 15 The growth of a family-run restaurant in Madrid through entrepreneurial innovation

Teresa Aguiar-Quintana and Jesús García Madariaga

Introduction and case selection

This case study examines the corporate entrepreneurship (CE) actions in a restaurant company that started its activity in 1934 in Madrid, Spain's Capital. According to Guth and Ginsberg (1990), CE refers to the process of organisational renewal related to innovation and venturing corporate activities. The main objective of this chapter is to study this restaurant's survival for almost a century through its CE actions.

First, we examine the antecedents of this company and its settings. We start this section by explaining the context of this organisation and the key elements that will be dealt with in this case. Secondly, we study the environment and create an overview of the region where the organisation carries out its activities. Thirdly, the origin and evolution of the key elements of the company's CE actions are described in detail, with the main learnings extracted from them.

For this study, two semi-structured interviews were conducted, one with Manuel Rodríguez and the other with his father, José Ramón Rodríguez. The interviews were performed between April 2022 and September 2022 following an interview guide.

Business profile and framework

When we studied the history of the organisation, we discovered that Restaurante Manolo's existence as a family business dates back to 1934, almost a century ago. In 1934, the founder (Manuel Rodríguez's great-grandfather) arrived in Madrid and worked at Café Varela. He opened his first bar in the Glorieta de Embajadores and, in 1942, moved to Princesa Street near Moncloa. In 1958, he bought the building where the restaurant was located (see Image 15.1). He had a grand vision of the future of the region as the area did not have many businesses at that time.

During the 1960s through until the 1980s, his grandfather (second generation) took over restaurant management. This part of the city centre was growing. Manuel's father, José Ramón Rodríguez (third generation of the family

DOI: 10.4324/9781003454465-16

Image 15.1 Restaurante Manolo in the 60s decade.

business), ran the Restaurante Manolo for 40 years, from the 1980s until 2020, in this location. His main role was to keep the business alive despite the changes in the area (new "intercambiador" and relocation of the university areas), leading to a new business model. During the pandemic, José Ramón had to stop working due to health issues, and the fourth generation of the company assumed responsibility for the business. José Ramón has three children. One of them, Manuel Rodríguez Fernández, the eldest, is the current manager of the restaurant. Manuel, born in 1985 (fourth generation of the family business), created a limited society called Manolo 1934 Bar Restaurante, S.L., together with his sister, Paloma, who studied hospitality, and his brother, Juan, who studied Economics. Currently only Manuel Rodríguez is member of the Society. Paloma and Juan are not working anymore in the Society. Their cousin Alberto is also part of the business, working in accounting.

Manuel Rodríguez Fernández, the current manager of the restaurant, studied History and Arts at the Complutense University of Madrid. He also earned a Master's degree in Hospitality Management. He created his first business training racehorses. At the end of this activity, he joined the family business and since he started working in the restaurant, he has focused on innovation and renewal of processes.

Before the pandemic, Manuel changed the organisational structure to four main business units: (1) the kitchen, with a chef named Manuel Besteiro from Lugo, who worked for 50 years, from 1970 to 2020, with five other people; (2) the bar, with a bartender named Ignacio Bara, who worked with five waiters; (3) the lounge, with José Antonio Urtado as lounge manager, working with four waiters; and (4) the administration department in charge of Alberto Rodríguez, his cousin, with an accountant and an administrative assistant. Manuel's father, José Ramón, was the owner and sole manager until the COVID-19 pandemic hit. Manuel Rodríguez's son focused on innovation and renovation. Since the lockdown, things have changed a lot. Manuel's father had to leave the company due to health problems, the chef retired after 50 years of working for the company, and the organisational structure changed. After the lockdown, these circumstances produced a change in the organisation chart. Thus, the new organisation chart has a board of directors (Manuel Rodríguez), the administration and finance department (Alberto), and three business units for the service departments (kitchen, morning-shift lounge, and afternoon-shift lounge). The kitchen has two chefs, and each lounge shift has two more managers.

Environment

From the 1980s to the mid-90s, the Moncloa area in Madrid started to be very commercial, not only with many other restaurants as competitors but also with many shops and distributors from many sectors. Likewise, there were some exclusive and high-quality hotels in the Moncloa area, such as EXE Moncloa, RIU Plaza, or Husa Princesa. Some colleges and universities such as CEU (Centro de Enseñanza Superior Luis Vives), the Nebrija University, or the Instituto Católico de Administración y Dirección de Empresas (Icade) were established in the vicinity of the restaurant. Some teachers and students used to have breakfast or lunch with a menu (although the average price per person was not low, around € 14,50). Business slowed down when the "exchanger" in Moncloa was created in 1995. Princesa Street was no longer an obligatory place of passage to get to the universities, as students could go directly by metro. This led to the closure of many restaurants, which were replaced by franchises and stores.

Related to the environment and the restaurant sector, this area has been gentrified since 1995, as many franchises and shops have occupied the premises on Princesa Street. This led to a decrease in the number of competitors for Restaurante Manolo. Although the recession of the global economic crisis (2008–2013) hit many families and local businesses in Madrid, the family could continue business because they didn't have a mortgage, as their property was already paid for. Nevertheless, they lost business and began considering a new business model.

In recent years, the environment has witnessed important opportunities affecting the restaurant sector, leading to benefits also for the Restaurante Manolo in Madrid. Some of them are mentioned in the report prepared by KPMG (2019) called Gastronomy in the Spanish economy in 2019. This report reveals the growth in the turnover of gastronomic tourism to more than € 15 million, 65.6% more than in 2018, as a consequence of the 16.7% increase in the arrival of gastronomic tourists. In addition, it represents 33% of the gross domestic product (GDP) and generates 20% of employment. The study highlights some aspects that make Spanish gastronomy a pillar of quality, such as the raw materials and the hospitality.

Such is the importance of gastronomy in the Spanish Strategic plans that in many of them, it is mentioned as one of the main characteristics of Spain in terms of quality. For instance, the Spanish Tourism Plan Horizon 2020 focused on promoting the development of Spanish tourism through better co-operation between public and private agents. This plan also includes gastronomy as an identifying factor for Spain to develop new tourist segments. It is associated with cultural tourism as an internationally recognised high-quality segment thanks to the Mediterranean diet. This tourist typology generates more benefits thanks to the higher spending per tourist. Consequently, in the last decade, Spain has gained an optimal situation in terms of quality and gastronomic offer, key factors for national tourism development. It translates into increased tourist movements motivated by high-quality, authentic cuisine and traditional gastronomy. This reputation conveys an identity to the national territory and positions Spain as one of the countries with solid gastronomic references in the European continent.

However, the COVID-19 pandemic was an external factor that impacted the tourism sector worldwide, and Spain also suffered a substantial economic impact. Before focusing on the impact on the gastronomic sector, we must first analyse some data on the pandemic's impact at a general level to estimate the tourism decline. The tourism data provided by the INE in its Border Tourist Movement Statistics reports (INE, 2020) shows an overwhelming reality for the sector. The decline was visible, especially in 2020 when the pandemic was at its peak. Control and closure measures were higher then, but at the end of 2021, there was a rebound in the number of visits to the country INE (2021a).

According to Pérez-Calle et al. (2021), Spain was one of the countries that suffered the greatest economic impact of the pandemic during the first months due to the high-level restrictions. Therefore, as these authors reported, it was one of the European countries with the worst forecast for the future. These hypotheses were supported by another report (the Spanish economy: impact of the pandemic and perspectives) published by the Bank of Spain in 2021 with the help of data provided by the National Institute of Statistics (INE, 2021b). This report also indicated that Spain was one of the economies most affected in the first half of 2020 compared to the impact of the pandemic in other international territories. The main reason was the large amount of small and medium-sized companies in the pre-pandemic situation. In addition, sectors requiring social relations, such as hotels, restaurants and leisure, suffered more than other industries, predicting innumerable losses and business closures.

The economic recovery began after the measures of social distancing and hygiene established by the Spanish government provided a safe climate in restaurants and bars, thereby increasing the volume of sales during 2021 and 2022. In addition, the recovery of this sector was possible through important measures such as acclimatisation and the use of outdoor spaces, creating steps to regenerate the social bond among participants.

Consequently, new opportunities and challenges arose for the e-commerce and the food delivery sector. These sectors experienced the most remarkable growth in pandemic and post-pandemic times due to the closure of tourism and mobility and the obligation to restructure establishments' strategies to adapt to the new situation. Thus, restaurants were forced to adjust their offer and change their marketing, improving the customer's experience. Therefore, investment in the restaurant business is usually high, especially when resorting to external companies for food delivery, such as Globo or Deliveroo, or to influencers who can promote food through social networks, increasing competition.

To contextualise gastronomic tourism and the impact of the coronavirus in the sector at a global and national level, we must consider the growth of gastronomic tourism in Spain and, specifically, in the country's capital, the city of Madrid. For this purpose, before developing the situation of gastronomic tourism in Madrid, we must comment on the importance of general tourism and its position in the capital of Spain compared to other regions of the nation. According to the data provided in the Tourist Expenditure Survey (Egatur) carried out by the National Institute of Statistics (INE, 2021), the Community of Madrid ranks above the rest in average daily expenditure per international tourist, which means that tourists are induced to spend more, reporting a greater benefit and positioning the region as one of the most important in the country in terms of tourism.

In addition, the capital of Spain, as a territory, bases its tourism promotion on the management of its tourism strengths to distinguish itself, and gastronomy is one of those points that generate attraction in the destination. Concerning this, the Director of Tourism of the Madrid City Council, Héctor Coronel, classified gastronomy as an important factor for the promotion of the city, highlighting its offer of restaurants with important awards such as Michelin stars and with a strong presence of international chains that are very attractive for tourists (data extracted from an interview for the Institute for the Digitalization for Tourism Vodafone Business CETT, 2021). The importance of gastronomy in the city is such that in 2020-21, Madrid was awarded the distinction of Ibero-American Capital of Gastronomic Culture, the seventh city in the world to achieve this distinction, converting and positioning Madrid as a territory of Ibero-American gastronomic development. This award helped to consolidate Madrid internationally and to promote and increase cultural and gastronomic tourism within the principal city of Spain.

Also, one thing that defines a region's gastronomic identity and positioning is the quantity and quality of its offer to visitors and the national population. Madrid manages large and varied gastronomic events that generate motivation to visit it. Feo Parrondo (2014) highlighted the exponential growth of the hospitality sector in Madrid thanks to the enormous variety of gastronomic offers, where visitors can enjoy both traditional and high-quality food. One of the central claims and core of gastronomic management in Madrid is the large number of gastronomic activities promoted by the Tourist Board of the Community of Madrid, with the development of fairs, markets, and workshops throughout the region. Among these activities, Madrid stands out for its international gastronomic fairs and congresses, led by Madrid Fusión Alimentos de España and Gastrofestival. Madrid Fusión is the most important culinary congress in the culinary world, held in person in 2021 after the pandemic. With a higher-than-expected presence of visitors (more than 15,000 people) and the participation of 183 companies, 400 people, and numerous international media, this congress is the main one in the sector for the promotion of high-quality cuisine and the development of new culinary trends (Madrid Fusión, 2021).

These characteristics are the main factors that position Madrid as a gastronomic benchmark and increase the management of this type of cultural tourism in the capital due to the proliferation of high-quality establishments. After the pandemic, the destination of Madrid made a strong effort to maintain the variety and quality for tourists, with different establishments providing image and identity, such as centenary establishments, gastronomic markets (there are sixteen in total), gourmet gastronomy spaces (e.g., San Ildefonso Market) and high-level modern restaurants, with the latest gastronomy and culinary trends. Some of these establishments are a symbol of the city and generate tourist attraction due to their distinctions or fame. Consequently, the role of Madrid in gastronomic tourism is clear. Manolo confessed that one of his future plans was to have two cooks in one of these important gastronomic markets to offer special and typical dishes from their cuisine.

Manolo was conscious of the importance of this gastronomic segment of tourism in Madrid and considered it one of the key elements of the business. In this regard, one of the main lessons he learned is to study not only his national competitors but also his international competitors. Manolo pointed out that his inspiration comes from different countries, especially on his trips to France, the UK, and Germany, where he picks up new ideas and trends. This trend in the gastronomic sector was called Fusion Kitchen. The competitors used to have the 5th Gama, which consists of pre-cooked food that is heated in the restaurant. However, Manolo knew he could innovate through what he calls 1st Gama. It is based on the supply of the entire menu prepared in the restaurant through skilled labour. 1st Gama means that none of the menus were pre-cooked; all food was cooked on the spot.

Manolo explained that the pandemic affected his decisions regarding organisation, pricing strategies, and business model. During this period, the number of employees was reduced, and customers demanded more service outside the restaurant, so much of his business came from terrace services. Likewise, during the years 2021 and 2022, other external factors, such as the war in Ukraine, caused changes in the price structure. The menu price is € 15.50, but prices are rising again due to the war crisis and the increase in the cost of raw materials (see Image 15.2). Thus, many competitors have closed due to the stagflation related to lower demand because of their customers' lower purchasing power and higher costs of commercial purchases.

Image 15.2 Restaurante Manolo in 2023 with terrace services.

Corporate entrepreneurship actions

The dynamism of the sector and the demand for new products and the need for a new business model forced Restaurante Manolo to develop new CE actions.

According to Guth and Ginsberg (1990), CE refers to the process of organisational renewal and is related to innovation and corporate venturing activities. Similarly, Phan et al. (2009) consider CE to include renewal activities that enhance a corporation's ability to take risks and compete with others, which may result in the addition of new businesses to the corporation. Some authors define this aspect of CE as *strategic entrepreneurship* (Kuratko & Audretsch, 2009) because it implies the identification and exploitation of opportunities while creating and maintaining a competitive advantage (Ireland et al., 2003). It is also related to strategic renewal, sustained regeneration, domain redefinition, organisational rejuvenation, and business model reconstruction (Covin & Miles, 1999).

Focusing on the issue related to innovation and the CE actions addressed by Restaurante Manolo, the most outstanding CE action carried out in recent years is the comprehensive renovation of the kitchen with an investment of € 200,000 in modern equipment. These CE actions in 2018 were mainly related to product differentiation through many initiatives carried out in the last five years. Some novelties in products and services offered to customers were a new lounge, gastronomic routes, new seasonal menus, and new services such as extended hours. In addition, new technologies were incorporated through a new property management system (PMS) with a point-of-sale terminal that helps the administrative processes because the system provides in real-time the family of products that were sold to the customer, time of sale and accurate and up-to-date inventory information.

Specifically, between 2017 and 2018, another innovative action introduced new dishes with more gastronomic design. For this purpose, they included fresh seasonal products and changed the menus, offering a standard "carta" and different seasonal menus. Regarding the menus, they incorporated some dishes for tourists with local food and typical and fresh Spanish soups. A children's menu was also incorporated. For this reason, its marketing strategies focus on differentiating the product with natural coffee, new bread from Lugo, new uniforms, new Wine tasting ("Catas"), a new fusion menu, and new changing rooms, among other initiatives. Likewise, within their marketing strategies, another innovative action was participating in gastronomic routes. Considering that Manolo's father is vice-president of Viña de Madrid (which includes the association of hoteliers in Madrid), Manolo explains the challenge of creating their own gastronomic routes. Manolo's father also belongs to the Madrid Chamber of Commerce, and this helped the business because he could disseminate new initiatives among the hotels and gather information about subsidies and credits with low-interest rates for businesses.

Another CE action was related to the Corporate Social Responsibility (CRS) strategy. Manolo and his family collaborate with non-profit organisations such as the Red Cross. Likewise, in recent years, they began to develop internal marketing, focusing on training their staff by offering free cooking courses. For instance, courses related to Mediterranean cuisine, or different styles of rice, or special training for elaborating homemade desserts. Other courses related to service quality were offered for waiters and lounge staff. These actions aligned with Manolo's leadership style based on inspirational motivation, intellectual stimulation, and individual consideration. His transformational leadership led to greater group and collaborative cohesion, with collective tips distributed among the team. Manolo incorporated new chefs, and 60% of the kitchen staff are new and have permanent contracts.

In addition, after the pandemic, Manolo started introducing longer opening hours, flexible shifts, and more days off for the staff to provide a better work-life balance and higher staff satisfaction. Employees work 40 hours for four days a week and have three days off.

Also, the organisation of the business changed after COVID-19, and Manuel Rodríguez focused on kitchen work despite being a board member. His sister is in charge of the lounge area and customer service, and his brother continues to carry out financial responsibilities and duties.

Thus, another CE action was related to digital marketing strategy through social networks to attract new customers, encourage them to repeat their experience and reinforce their loyalty by increasing regular communication with them by email or direct marketing. They received some funds for digitalisation. They are doing a lot of business with Glovo, which is like a virtual kitchen. For their deliveries, they work with Glovo, Just Eat, and their own delivery on their website.

The main supports to carry out these CE actions are the existence of alliances with other companies such as hotels and different associations, relationships with other agents such as the Chamber of Commerce, social agents, loyal customers, and the availability of technological, human, and financial resources. First of all, the technological resources are related to the company's digitalisation, which was possible thanks to a new software called Tspoonlab (developed by the famous Spanish chef, Ferrán Adriá) that controls the entire process of elaborating the dishes. It provides complete information on all the costs and the time needed to prepare menus. It is important for the company's future expansion plans to standardise the processes.

In addition, they have a new central reservation system called EVEVE and they receive all table reservations through this system. In the lounge, another action was optimising the space through different shifts. With this system, they avoid long waiting lists and can also increase their capacity by 20-30 persons per shift. They usually work with groups of retirees who have lunch at the same time every day of the week and with a reservation at their chosen time. The restaurant has a capacity of 70 people inside the restaurant. Before the pandemic, most of the business was done inside with a "menu a la carta", but after the pandemic, the business model changed completely, and the main business comes from the tables served on the restaurant's terraces.

The main barriers to the innovation processes were associated with the longevity of its employees, with a high percentage of people over 50 years of age and a high resistance to change. The owners overcame these difficulties by renewing the workforce and increasing human resource management policies with internal and external training for employees. Another barrier is the society of the three family members, who made decisions slowly after the pandemic.

Its main achievement is the increase in motivation among the employees. The shift to ten hours per day, four days a week, motivated the staff, as they had more flexibility in their lives and work-life balance was possible. In addition, the owners increased the wages with allowances for their employees, which was perceived as a reward for the goals achieved. Another achievement was a better delivery of services by increasing the point of sales, computerising sales, increasing the average daily rate, and using big data.

Other results derived from the CE actions undertaken are the renovation of the restrooms and the decision to improve the business model. The owners started a new project focused on the renewal of the entire business. For this purpose, they presented a special plan to the city council to change the licence of the first floor apartment (the top floor of the current restaurant) to a commercial category. This would allow an increase in the number of diners. The project has three phases. The first phase consisted of moving the warehouse, changing rooms and offices to the bottom floor. It took four months, from March 2022 to June 2022. The second phase will start when the special plan presented to the city council is approved. It consists of building stairs to connect the ground floor with the first floor. A chill-out area will be opened in the third phase to adapt the restaurant to the younger market segment.

Epilogue

Tourism has been gradually divided into various types with the development of different segments. One of these typologies arises because of the consumer's need to eat. The gastronomy of the place where the tourism takes place becomes attractive for a niche of tourists who want to get to know the place and taste both the local gastronomy and the signature gastronomy. From here, gastronomic tourism emerges as a form of cultural tourism. In the last decade, gastronomy has gradually been gaining space in the tourism sector, often representing a vital point to be managed by destinations to position themselves. This tourism segment shows an enormous capacity for connection with other types of tourism, such as rural tourism or heritage tourism, which makes it very attractive for the territory and generates the need for management and promotion to motivate the visit.

Likewise, the management and growth of gastronomic tourism brings benefits to the destination and, in this sense, a place's gastronomy could create an image and brand that differentiates it from other places, generating a perception of quality in the tourist and greater motivation to visit the place. Based on this image and gastronomic identity, we find that Spain is one of the best-positioned places, gastronomically speaking. Its capital, Madrid, is considered one of the most important European cities in terms of gastronomy due to the quality and high supply of its raw materials its price positioning, and its accessibility to consumers.

The restaurant Manolo in Madrid will celebrate its centenary in eleven years. One of the lessons learned from their entrepreneurial and innovative business activities is that they can provide customers with an authentic gastronomic experience and the possibility of satisfying their needs by visiting an establishment with almost one hundred years of history, with the 1st Gama production (e.g., preparing the entire process within the restaurant). They have survived for four generations thanks to the renewal of their business model, the company's digitalisation, and digital marketing and human resource management strategies to achieve high employee satisfaction.

References

de España, B. (2021). *La economía española: impacto de la pandemia y perspectivas.* Banco de España (BDE). Mayo. Retrieved on November 19, 2022 from https://www.bde.es/f/webbde/GAP/Secciones/SalaPrensa/IntervencionesPublicas/DirectoresGenerales/economia/Arc/Fic/arce260521.pdf

Covin, J., & Miles, M. (1999). Corporate entrepreneurship and the pursuit of competitive advantage. *Entrepreneurship Theory and Practice, 23*, 47–63.

Feo Parrondo, F. (2014). Working day gastronomic tourism in the Community of Madrid. *Cuadernos de Turismo, 33*, 31–58.

Guth, W., & Ginsberg, A. (1990). Guest editors' introduction: Corporate entrepreneurship. *Strategic Management Journal, 11*(1), 5–15.

Hosteltur Economía. (2017, 11 julio). *La gastronomía, tercer motivo más valorado para elegir un destino*. Hosteltur. Retrieved on December 21, 2021, from https://www.hosteltur.com/123032_gastronomia-tercer-motivo-valorado-elegir-destino.html

Hosteltur Economía. (2021). *Restaurantes centenarios, nuevo atractivo turístico para Madrid*. Hosteltur, 31 enero Retrieved on June 23, 2022, from https://www.hosteltur.com/141969_restaurantes-centenarios-nuevo-atractivo-turistico-para-madrid.html

INE (2020). *Movimientos turísticos en fronteras*. Instituto Nacional de Estadística. December, 13/14.

INE (2021a). *Encuesta de Gasto Turístico*. Instituto Nacional de Estadística, June

INE (2021b). *Movimientos turísticos en fronteras*. IInstituto Nacional de Estadística. October. 1/7.

Instituto Vodafone Business-CETT [Vodafone Empresas] (2021). *European Tourist Panel. Instituto Vodafone Business-CETT*. Observatorio Vodafone de la Empresa [Vídeo]. 11 junio YouTube. Retrieved on October 12, 2022 on https://www.youtube.com/watch?v=CVXRAeFJVwc

Ireland, R. D., Hitt, M. A., & Sirman, D. G. (2003). A model of strategic entrepreneurship: The construct and its dimensions. *Journal of Management*, 29(6), 963–989.

KPMG. (2019). *La gastronomía en la economía española: Impacto económico de los sectores asociados*. Enero, Retrieved on October 16, 2022 from https://assets.kpmg/content/dam/kpmg/es/pdf/2019/01/gastronomia-en-economia-espanola.pdf

Kuratko, D., & Audretsch, D. (2009). Strategic entrepreneurship: Exploring different perspectives of an emerging concept. *Entrepreneurship Theory and Practice*, 33, 1–17.

Madrid Fusión. (2021). *Madrid Fusión Alimentos de España 2022 28 al 30 de marzo, Recinto Ferial Ifema Madrid*. Retrieved on December 13, 2021 from https://www.madridfusion.net/es/magazine/post/mf-2022

Organización Mundial del Turismo (2021). Tourism Definitions. Recuperado December 2022, Retrieved on September 8, 2022 from https://www.e-unwto.org/

Phan, P., Wright, M., Ucbasaran, D., & Wee-Liang, T. (2009). Corporate entrepreneurship: Current research and future directions. *Journal of Business Venturing*, 24, 197–205.

Pérez-Calle, R., García-Casarejos, N., & García-Bernal, J. (2021). *La empresa española ante la COVID-19: Factores de adaptación al nuevo escenario*. *Retos*, 11(21), 5–24.

Case 16 Corporate entrepreneurship in Central American Tourism Agency (CATA)

Eduardo Parra-López,
Almudena Barrientos-Báez,
Leydy Cevallos Barberán
and Diego Guzmán Vera

Background: CATA in the Central American context

The Central American Tourism Agency (CATA) is a mixed public/private entity that defines itself as a technology organisation. Its purpose is to plan, coordinate, help, and stimulate the promotion of tourism in Central American countries. Its creation took place during the XXII Summit of Heads of State and Government of Central America through the Central American Tourism Council (CCT by its acronym in Spanish) and in coordination with the Federation of Central American Chambers of Tourism (FEDECATUR by its acronym in Spanish) in 2002. It has its permanent headquarters in Madrid (Spain). However, it has opened numerous branches and subsidiaries in other cities and countries around the world, with its sub-headquarters in El Salvador currently standing out. As has already been pointed out, its mission is to contribute to the promotion of tourism in these Central American countries, with marketing actions as a means of dissemination and international positioning: seeking to increase the general recognition of the geopolitical area and its components as a quality tourism product, highly competitive and innovative with the deployment of a diversified offer. CATA is the leading agency by size and focus, regarding the promotion and positioning of Central America as a multi-tourist destination at an international level.

Environment

Currently, the new trends in tourism promotion focus on young tourism, tourism intelligence (Moral-Moral, 2021), and/or the introduction of new destinations, highlighting those that are the strengths of Central America: nature tourism, adventure, ecotourism, archaeology, etc. The benefits for the region would be evident since publicising the beautiful landscapes it shares and promoting them is an unavoidable step for its economies to receive greater injections from international tourism. Therefore, the political interest in the matter is undeniable. Furthermore, for a government, a high rate of

DOI: 10.4324/9781003454465-17

tourism means that the rest of the world values its country or at least finds it interesting from a cultural, social, or economic point of view: as worth visiting, safe, rich in cultural or natural assets, etc. (Carbonell Curralo & Viñarás Abad, 2021; Fernández-Poyatos et al., 2019).

Similarly, the technological sector is very important in this search for a greater demand for tourist services at an international level. Mainly because, through technology and social networks, the promotion of city/region/country brands reaches more potential tourists (Barrientos-Báez et al., 2020; Caldevilla-Domínguez et al., 2021). Communication technologies have helped create promotional platforms that agencies like CATA can use and benefit from. They are used for purposes such as reaching the young sector of the audience (Conde del Río, 2021). These include traditional means of promotion, but facilitators of flights, hotels, stays, activities, products and services that make booking—. It also makes possible consumer discovery of trips or more flexible getaways more (Martínez-Sala et al., 2019). Regarding the sociocultural field, a greater influx of international tourism to Central American countries is essential for expanding Central American culture in the world and, therefore, improving the social and cultural well-being of the countries (Aguilar Valle, 2018).

The COVID-19 pandemic has made it easier to take steps forward in tourism and communication by forcefully accelerating the digitisation of multiple sectors of society. The tourism sector has to adapt to the social and technological progress established today. It is doing so at a speed that surprises many, facilitating the exchange of information in real time and increasing tourist loyalty, improving quality and increasing demand.

CATA implements new technological and digital resources as improvement tools in its field and, thus, actively and effectively collaborates in developing its objectives. Applying techniques that persuade and increase the interest of tourists is essential. For this reason, the importance of feelings in the human cognitive process and the emotions that arise from them are materialising (Barrientos-Báez et al., 2021).

The transmission of information—sometimes misleading—about tourist destinations causes distrust and restlessness in the target audience, a discouraging result for those responsible for CATA. This situation, added to the ease of diffusion through new technologies, forces us to redesign the approach to tourist packages. Tourism is devoted to a close understanding of ICT, a union that modern psychology must study in order to improve its imbrication. It is necessary to evaluate the new methods that promote attracting the attention, interest, and receptivity of the tourist.

In the last ten years, regional tourism has registered constant growth, only altered by the pandemic. According to data from the Central American Tourism Integration Secretariat (SITCA by its acronym in Spanish, 2018), in 2018, the region was visited by 24.2 million tourists and hikers.

Before the advent of COVID-19 (a situation to which the geopolitical area is no stranger, according to Parra-López et al., 2019; Vega Jiménez, 2021), tourism was already a significant economic and social tool for countries in the region, this industry being one of the main sources of work (Moreno-Gil et al., 2020). Around 1.3 million jobs emanate from direct links with tourism or its associated companies. In terms of employment demography, its contribution to the creation of opportunities for the populations of the destination countries can be measured in figures: approximately 90% of the suppliers in the sector are small and medium-sized businesses, 51% of which are owned or managed by women, and more than 60% of the work teams are also mainly female. In this sense, the CATA is currently immersed in the development of a strategy and roadmap to guide the transition between the relief, rescue, and reconstruction of the tourism sector phases in the markets of Central America and the Dominican Republic for the next three years. The deadline for this plan is 2023, and logically, it will be hampered by the unforeseeable factors that have characterised the post-pandemic, from the supply crisis and the war in Ukraine to the shortage of microchips (Barrientos-Báez et al., 2021).

Development

Participation of CATA in international fairs and tourism events

Corporate entrepreneurship and innovation actions in the creation of multi-destination products have been one of the most outstanding, if not the most outstanding, carried out in recent years by CATA. For example, in 2018, the agency received the, International Tourism Fair FITUR award for excellence in tourism (International Tourism Fair Madrid, Spain) for the first multi-destination tourism product Hackathon called *Juntos Sumamos*.

Collaborative work with agents, internationalisation, and regional integration, as well as the dissemination and learning of new tourism trends in the 2030 horizon, has led to the identification of micro-markets and decision-making following the principles of tourism intelligence, facilitating the application to the natural environments that Central America is lucky enough to have for later promotion.

Furthermore, CATA has participated in different activities to increase its exposure to the public and the industry as a whole. Among these, it is worth mentioning the participation in the Ibero-American Conference of Tourism Ministers and Entrepreneurs (CIMET) together with the heads of Tourism of 13 Ibero-American countries: Central American states.

Along with this, another of the most important events was the delivery of the CATA awards, where five businessmen from the sector and two specialised journalists were awarded for their continued and favourable work in recent years in promoting the multi-destination offer of Central America. The election of the winners fell on 40 Central American tour operators, who valued the work undertaken in promoting the offer and the gradual attraction of Spanish tourists to the region. Likewise, FITUR was chosen as the frame of reference in which to carry out the Transfer of the Pro Tempore Presidency of the Central American Tourism Council, which passed from Belize to the Republic of Guatemala at the stand of the latter. This joint action has had great results in terms of corporate entrepreneurship: understood as eclectic actions by their own vocation to respond to a wide range of circumstances and external and internal factors of the organisation to create value by promoting synergies with new business opportunities (Hornsby et al., 2013). CATA has participated in FITUR ever since, promoting the tourism resources of Central America and giving visibility to the importance that the sector has for these countries.

CATA is in the process of regeneration and updating. Furthermore, it is part of an unbeatable scenario and environment for generating synergies with the public, companies, institutions and markets that can create future opportunities in Central American countries. The agency has maintained its presence at various fairs and events during and after the pandemic as part of its planned efforts to rebuild, rescue, and advance the tourism sector in its member countries. The synergy with these meetings serves the purposes of CATA in terms of promoting tourism to Central America. These interactions serve as a corporate entrepreneurship catalysts, identifying opportunities that are as simple to conceive as they are powerful to carry out.

Some external triggers of the actions in corporate entrepreneurship for CATA are related to people in the region with action-oriented behaviours who represent a key factor in this process. The systems and processes of the business actions of the countries are another factor that has influenced this corporate entrepreneurship, especially the region as a factor that extends through the eight countries implementing joint and singular actions. The internal triggers are related to the entire set of small and medium-sized companies and their strong orientation towards entrepreneurship. It is about achieving differentiation with significant levels of innovation and growth in the region with commitment and development of capacities that accelerate the growth of new businesses.

However, CATA has found some barriers in the process of developing corporate entrepreneurship actions. The different barriers that have been encountered are: firstly, the stable and regular financing from the different organisations that support CATA (USAid Funds, Luxembourg Funds, Taiwan Funds or, more recently, German Cooperation Funds); secondly, another barrier has sometimes been the market conditions in the countries of the region, the commercial structure itself, or even the existing low-skilled labour force; and thirdly, another barrier identified is the lack of practical knowledge of entrepreneurship that has been solved with collaborative work.

Finally, the main achievements of CATA have been the creation of a strategic vision for the achievement of its established objectives through adequate strategic planning regarding its strategies with a long-term vision. For this, the leadership capacity, passion, and dedication of the Secretary-General has been an important factor.

Epilogue

The justification of CATA as a case study is due to the capacity it has as a regional organisation to coordinate entrepreneurial actions of eight countries due to its high dynamism in regional promotion, for contributing to the construction of collective efforts, and for their encouragement to regenerate the business fabric that gives life to the tourism value chain in Central America and the Dominican Republic.

The different actions this company has carried out have had a positive result for it and the tourism sector in general. The exposure of this sector of Central America in fairs, social networks and events is of vital importance so that the rest of the world can be aware of the virtues and cultural and natural strengths of these destinations, allowing them to grow and accumulate opportunities thanks to the arrival of international tourists and the residents themselves. These opportunities (sometimes economic) help socially drive countries beyond their borders and, of course, in terms of economic, sustainable, and cultural development.

Local administrations trust CATA as a point of creation of synergies with companies, population segments, markets, and global governments in events, congresses, and international fairs to promote this market interrelation. Its maintenance over time speaks of planning included in the specifications of CATA and of the need to maintain the actions in the face of the prospect of the increasingly deteriorated global situation in environmental, moral, religious, economic, and political terms.

One of the most important lessons learnt has been the ability to develop and innovate multi-destination products and services with a high value for the countries and focused on business actions. It has also achieved a systemic vision that supports and motivates organisations in the region.

Source consulted

For the elaboration of this case study, two persons were interviewed in April 2022:

Karina Canto is the secretary of CATA Tourism Agency.
karinacanto@catatourismagency.org
Carolina Briones is the General Secretary of CATA Tourism Agency.
cbriones@catatourismagency.org

References

Aguilar Valle, I. (2019). *Compendio de Estadísticas de Turismo 2019 de la Región del SICA*. Secretaría de Integración Turística Centroamericana. Available at: https://sitca.info/wp-content/uploads/2021/01/Compendio-Estadisticas_2018.pdf.

Barrientos-Báez, A., Caldevilla-Domínguez, D., Cáceres Vizcaíno, A., & Sueia Val, E. G. (2020). Sector turístico: Comunicación e innovación sostenible. *Revista de Comunicación de la SEECI*, *53*, 153–173. doi. 10.15198/seeci.2020.53.153-173

Barrientos-Báez, A., Martínez-Sala, A., Altamirano, V., & Caldevilla-Domínguez, D. (2021). Fake news: La pandemia de la COVID-19 y su cronología en el sector turístico. *Historia y Comunicación Social*, 26(Especial), 135–148. doi. 10.5209/hics.74248

Caldevilla-Domínguez, D., Barrientos-Báez, A., Pérez-García, Á, & Gallego-Jiménez, M. G. (2021). El uso de las redes sociales y su relación con la decisión de compra del turista. *Vivat Academia. Revista de Comunicación*, 154, 443–458. doi. 10.15178/va.2021.154.e1360

Carbonell Curralo, E. G., & Viñarás Abad, M. (2021). Museos y desarrollo sostenible. Gestión museística y comunicación digital para alcanzar los ODS. *Revista de Ciencias de la Comunicación e Información*, 26, 79–108. doi. 10.35742/rcci.2021.26.e143

Conde del Río, M. A. (2021). Estructura mediática de TikTok: Estudio de caso de la red social de los más jóvenes. *Revista de Ciencias de la Comunicación e Información*, 26, 59–77. doi. 10.35742/rcci.2021.26.e126

Fernández-Poyatos, M. D., Aguirregoitia-Martínez, A., & Bringas Rábago, N. L. (2019). La cocina de producto: Seña de identidad y recurso de comunicación en la alta restauración en España. *Revista Latina de Comunicación Social*, 74, 873–896. doi. 10.4185/RLCS-2019-1362

Hornsby, J., Peña-Legazkue, I., & Guerrero, M. (2013). The role of corporate entrepreneurship in the current organisational and economic landscape. *International Entrepreneurship and Management Journal*, 9(3), 295–305.

Martínez-Sala, A. M., Monserrat-Gauchi, J., & Segarra Saavedra, J. (2019). El influencer 2.0 turístico: De turista anónimo a líder de opinión. *Revista Latina de Comunicación Social*, 74, 1344–1365. doi. 10.4185/RLCS-2019-1388

Moral-Moral, M. (2021). La aplicación del neuromarketing al ámbito del turismo: Una revisión bibliográfica. *Vivat Academia. Revista de Comunicación*, 154, 429–442. doi. 10.15178/va.2021.154.e1359

Moreno-Gil, S., Parra-López, E., Picazo-Peral, P., & Díaz-Domínguez, C. (2020). The dissemination of tourism scientific research in Latin American journals. A bibliometric study. *Anatolia: An International Journal of Tourism and Hospitality Research*, 31(4), 549–564. doi. 10.1080/13032917.2020.1795892

Parra-López, F., Díaz-Padilla, V. T., & Martíncz González, J. A. (2019). Claves para el éxito de la relaciones público-privadas en la gestión turística: El caso de la relación INGUAT-CAMTUR en Guatemala. En *100 Soluciones a 50 Problemas para la Gestión Turística en Empresas en Iberoamérica. Manual de casos reales*. Editorial Síntesis.

Vega Jiménez, P. (2021). Costa Rica: Dos pandemias en un siglo. *Historia y Comunicación Social*, 26(Especial), 1–10. doi. 10.5209/hics.74236

Case 17 Viajes Insular

The internationalisation and entrepreneurial innovation of a travel agency in Spain

Silvia Sosa-Cabrera,
Teresa Aguiar-Quintana,
Ana Isabel Lemes-Hernández,
and José Manuel Sanabria-Díaz

Introduction

Viajes Insular is a tourism group specialising in distribution and intermediary services based in the Canary Islands (Spain), and with extensive professional experience of more than 50 years in a key international tourist destination. The Canaries is an archipelago of eight islands of volcanic origin, located off the coasts of Morocco and Western Sahara and enjoying a subtropical climate with great scenic and cultural wealth. It is one of the Spanish regions preferred by international tourists, having become a long-stay destination for European visitors, especially from Germany and the United Kingdom. In 2021, a year still marked by the repercussions of the COVID-19 pandemic, the Canary Islands received 6,697,166 tourists—far from the 15,975,509 visitors in 2017—who invested some € 7,200 million (Orús, 2022). Tourism is vital for the regional economy, generating more than 40% of employment and 35% of the Canary Islands' gross domestic product (GDP).

Travel agencies are the traditional distribution channel that operates in the sector, which has been influenced over time by the economic instability of destinations, the advent of the Internet and information and communication technologies (ICT), and the political situations of other destinations, among other factors. Thus, in recent years, there has been an increase in travel reservations via the Internet (for example, in Spain, only 9% of travel purchases are made through physical agencies) (Statistas Research Department, 2022), which generates uncertainty if the physical operators cannot anticipate and make strategic decisions that allow them to face the changes in this sector.

In the current business environment, characterised by globalisation and technological development, corporate entrepreneurship requires the search for new business opportunities that allow companies to renew and regenerate their competitive advantage, offering employees the possibility of developing their entrepreneurial spirit without assuming their own business risks, but

DOI: 10.4324/9781003454465-18

under the protection and security of their company (Smith et al., 2016). Likewise, in this search for new opportunities to translate into entrepreneurial intention, business alertness to changes in the environment seems essential (Lemes-Hernández, 2015).

To profoundly understand the process of continuous change and the generation of innovative initiatives in travel agencies, it is necessary to investigate the causes that drive decision-making, the way in which said actions are addressed and thus determine the keys to success in the travel agency and tour operator sector. That is why Viajes Insular S.A., which began its journey under the name Insular in 1961 (becoming Viajes Insular S.A. in 1963), constitutes an exemplary case that allows the process developed in its long history in the Canarian tourism market to be known in depth, allowing them to grow continuously, face critical situations, and continue in a competitive market threatened by digitisation.

In this way, following an inductive approach focused on the key agents of the innovation process, their interactions and their context, it is possible to inquire into the how and why of such decisions. Thus, the case study is the appropriate methodology for these ends (Sosa-Cabrera, 2003). In this case study, the company and its environment are presented first and later the case study itself is developed, detailing the intrinsic and extrinsic motivations of decision-making, as well as the actions undertaken and how they are developed, thereby determining the keys to Viajes Insular's entrepreneurial success. Their results apply only to this set of circumstances but constitute new elements that require further investigation to be transferable and generalisable (Smith et al., 2016; Sosa-Cabrera, 2003). The information in the case study was collected through a review of the literature, documentary analysis and semi-structured, qualitative interviews with the company's CEO, Mr Ignacio Poladura de Armas. These interviews were carried out between December 2021 and October 2022 in a guided manner, following a protocol that allows the generation of enriching data, monitoring of the conversation according to the interviewee's responses, and consistency with respect to the chosen areas of analysis.

Corporate entrepreneurship and innovation actions of Viajes Insular

The case under analysis, Viajes Insular, represents the corporate entrepreneurship (CE) and continuous innovation of a tourism group specialised in distribution and intermediary services. Guth and Ginsberg (1990) defined CE as related to two phenomena: (1) innovation and corporate venturing activities and (2) renewal activities related to a corporation's ability to compete and take risks. Hence, CE is the creation of new businesses, products, or services from inside an organisation to generate new revenue growth through entrepreneurial action. To delve into the entrepreneurial activity of Viajes Insular, it is necessary to know its context of activity, since many of the actions take place in response to changes in the environment.

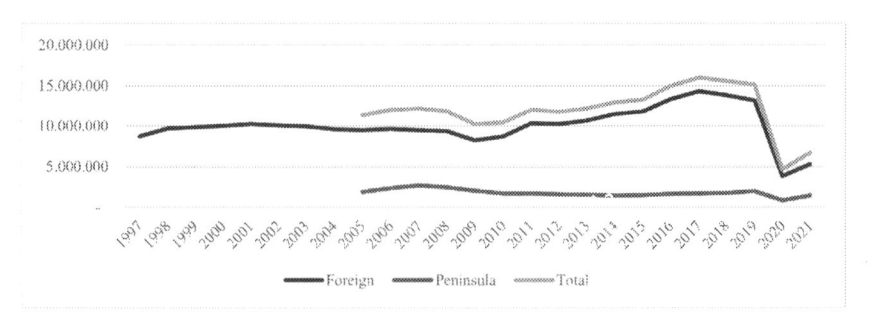

Figure 17.1 Evolution of the number of tourists arriving in the Canary Islands (1997–2021).

Source: Prepared by authors from Promotur. Canary Islands Tourism (2022).

With more than 50 years of history, its long journey has been subject to ups and downs in the Canarian economy and the tourism sector in general. Its founders detected from the outset the opportunity to help tourists and entities that had begun to see a potential mass-tourism destination in the Canary Islands in their mission to establish cooperation with the development of tourist activity in the Canary Islands.

The continuous increase in tourist activity in the Canary Islands up to 2019 has favoured the growth of the Canary Islands' economy above the national average since 2015, linked to the annual volume of tourists that the region receives, which exceeds 10 million—almost reaching the figure of 16 million visitors in 2017 (Figure 17.1). The tourist panorama suffered a huge setback with the COVID-19 health pandemic, which completely paralysed tourist activity and significantly affected the Islands and all tourism-related activities, including travel agencies. The Canarian economy was one of the worst affected in 2020 due to the high degree of tourism specialisation within the Canarian business fabric (Exceltur, 2021).

The activity of travel agencies and tour operators is fundamental to the Canarian economy, marked by their general vocation of service to tourists who visit the Islands. The Canary Islands, with only 7,447 km^2 in area, ranks as the eighth region in Spain in terms of population and has around 9% of the travel agencies in Spain, ranking fourth on the national scene both in number of establishments and in their turnover (Figure 17.2).

This tourism industry has also been affected by the adoption of digital technologies. Since the introduction of the first Global Distribution Systems (GDS), ICT have continuously affected the travel industry, with several waves of transformations; *digitisation*—also labelled by operators in this sector as "Tourism 4.0" or "smart tourism" (Pencarelli, 2020)—has generated a change in the entire travel ecosystem (Perelygina et al., 2022). In fact, digitisation has forced both small and large destinations to compete with each other in the global market (Montaudon-Tomas et al., 2020), which is a great challenge for travel agencies, traditional companies, and their distribution and intermediary activities.

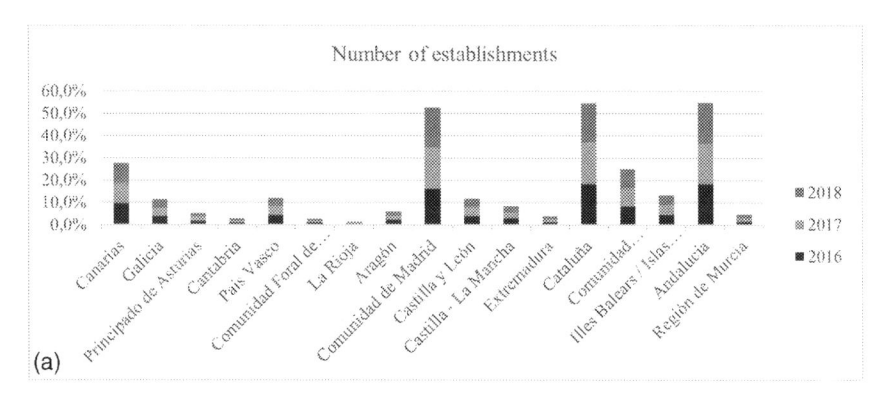

(a)

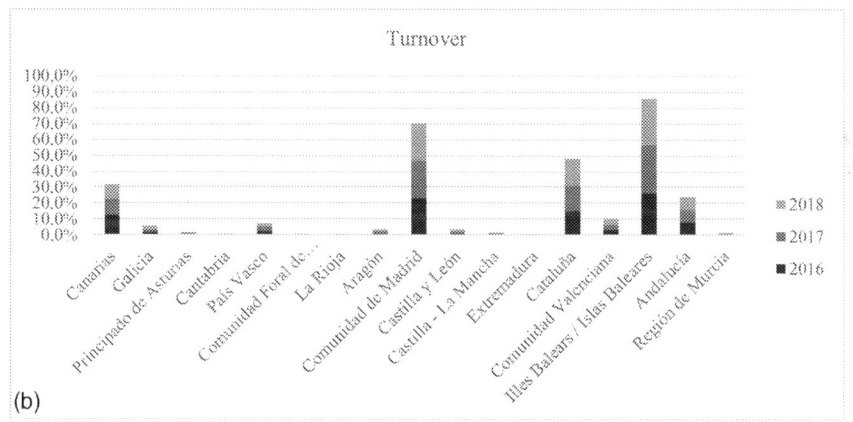

(b)

Figure 17.2 Relative positioning of the Canary Islands in Spain according to (a) the number of establishments and (b) turnover of travel agencies and tour operators.

Source: Prepared by authors based on the Canary Institute of Statistics -ISTAC (2021).

The incorporation of the Internet into daily activities and digitisation have led to the proliferation of online travel agencies (OTAs) and the continuous growth of their business figures. An example is the turnover of the company Booking.com (Figure 17.3), which has become the main benchmark in the online sector.

In this context of online and offline business coexistence, Viajes Insular competes mainly with Halcón Viajes (Globalia Group) and Viajes El Corte Inglés, the two main agency networks in Spain. The travel agency sector has generally opted for the *omnichannel strategy*, with both physical and online services. Thus, since 2017, Halcón Viajes began to close physical establishments, its offer via the web is in a constant process of improvement to be able to face the new business models (Salgado et al., 2021). Viajes El Corte Inglés has declared, among its main goals, its intention to become an 'omnichannel agency' and to be a benchmark in Spanish-speaking countries, making

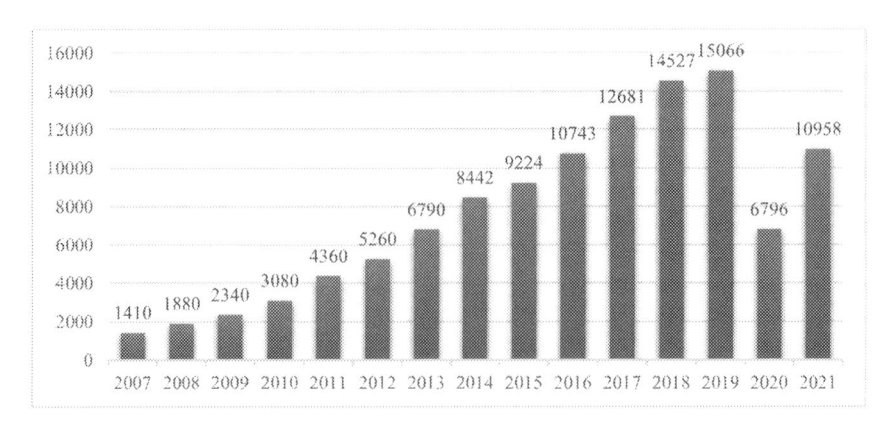

Figure 17.3 Evolution of Booking.com sales volume (in millions of USD).

Source: Statistas Research Department (2022).

significant investments in recent years towards creating a technological platform that allows its customers to make their reservations online easily and intuitively (Salgado et al., 2021).

The growth of business activity from its foundation in the 60s to the 80s allowed Viajes Insular to create a solid structure comprising a staff of about 200 people. In 1987 the company received the Gold Medal in Tourism granted by the Government of the Canary Islands and a special mention from the Ministry of Tourism and Industry of the Government of Spain. Currently, Viajes Insular is a company of recognised solvency in the tourism sector in the Canary Islands, with a team of 90 people, prepared to take on new challenges and consolidate its presence in the market.

Viajes Insular is involved in both inbound and outbound tourism, being both wholesalers and retailers and always specialising in the Canary Islands. This comprehensive vision of the intermediation business has generated a wide range of brands, all backed by the prestige and professionalism of Viajes Insular (Figure 17.4).

Viajes Insular is organisationally structured into business areas for the development of its activity. This includes area specialised in the inbound

Figure 17.4 Brands of Viajes Insular. Viajes Insular, S.A.

Source: Viajes Insular, S. A.

market, digital transformation, wholesale market, and new distribution channels. These are accompanied by an oversight of the islands' delegations and the management areas (administration, human resources and management assistance), all under the baton of general management.

Entrepreneurship and business innovation as signs of identity of Viajes Insular

Viajes Insular has been physically established, since its foundation, in the main tourist areas of the Canary Islands, with modern facilities and qualified professionals to offer its exclusive services for the inbound market to the most important tour operators in Europe, such as TUI and Thomas Cook. Their growth and relevance in the sector was such that they became the first company to contract a tour operation trip with Kuoni, the main long-distance tour operator in the United Kingdom, to bring British people to Gran Canaria, assuming all the risks that such an activity entails. This entrepreneurial initiative, which leads to the creation of a new product, is the result of the market vision of its founders, who realised the importance of tour operations and decided to venture, through cooperation, with a key outbound market for the Canary Islands. Thus, the main antecedents of this entrepreneurial action stand out both the dynamism and growth of the sector as well as the relationships with other agents to develop the new activity.

The collaboration with other travel agencies stands out continuously as being part of Viajes Insular's DNA. Proof of this is that, by the mid-seventies, they had already participated in the SUN SERVICE company, created as a promotional instrument for several national agencies—Cosmelli (Balearic Islands), Etusa (Costa Brava), Alhambra (Andalusia) and Costa Blanca (Levante)—to attend fairs with their own stand and carry out joint promotions.

In its eagerness to collaborate with the tourist development of the Canary Islands, it established a fleet of specialised transport vehicles in 1974, known as BUS Tour SA, for the transfer and excursions of its tourists in Gran Canaria, Tenerife and Fuerteventura. In addition, its vocation to help tourists and its concern for the promotion of tourism development in the region led Viajes Insular to schedule a wide catalogue of its own excursions, which, over time and together with other agencies, became a pool of air excursions between the capitals of the islands of Gran Canaria, Tenerife and El Aaiún, between 1966 and 1975. Years later, this initiative led to the creation of the company Tamaragua Tours SL, a small/medium-sized company involved in travel agency activity between 1984 and 2009.

As the Canary Islands grew as a tourist destination, the business structure of the sector underwent important changes, which led Viajes Insular to consider its strategy and positioning in the market. In the 1980s, the large tour operators created their own inbound agencies on the Islands, significantly increasing competition in the intermediary sector and causing Viajes Insular to lose customers it had previously served in the Canary Islands. It is precisely this increase in competition and the loss of customers that generated concern within the company. Thus, they expanded their own intermediary activities, entering the outbound market, both for individuals and companies, and also creating their own tour operators. These decisions were made due to the threat posed by competition in the sector, but they became business and growth opportunities after exhaustive analysis and surveillance of the sector. The detection of these new opportunities arises from the involvement of the company's management team and staff since Viajes Insular promotes the generation of initiatives, regardless of who is behind them. The company's staff is a true reflection of the corporate identity and is willing to train in new business areas.

Currently, outbound activity is one of the most important areas of focus for Viajes Insular, both in its retail and wholesale sections. As a retailer, it provides travel agency services to final customers, with 14 offices equipped with the latest technology and qualified professionals distributed throughout the archipelago (the only travel agency with this feature). At the same time, through the Business Travel Centre, the area of the company that deals with business trips, it offers comprehensive travel management for both SMEs (small and medium-sized enterprises) and large companies. Additionally, it has a "Groups" department that manages meetings, events, conferences, and seminars.

Furthermore, it has incorporated the wholesale function into the outbound business, creating Beway, a tour operator dedicated to island clients that provides access to various travel programmes with the professionalism of personalised advice offered by its expert agents. This wholesaler has also been able to take advantage of the direct connectivity between the Canary Islands and different national and international destinations offered by Binter Canarias, an airline based in the Canary Islands, and has demonstrated continuous growth both with inter-island flights and with direct connections to international destinations (Madeira, Lisbon, Czech Republic, Germany, etc.).

In addition, Beway follows the path of collaboration with other agents, which is why, in 2010, it began operating in the world of air consolidation, offering a personalised assistance service to all those travel agencies that do not belong to the International Air Transport Association (IATA), and who are looking for an air consolidator to provide them with the support they require. This decision was made in a growing tourism context, with an increase in the number of tourists arriving at the Islands and based on the company's original vision of collaborating with the tourism development of the Canary Islands. It is therefore a proactive initiative based on the continuous improvement of the business, the qualification of the company's personnel, and the business vision of its managers. All these are key elements in the development of CE.

In fact, these cooperation alliances with other competing travel agencies make it possible to strengthen Viajes Insular's business, always backed by the seriousness and guarantee of good work at all levels, and in 2017 they launched Travelagent.PRO as a platform that integrates flight consolidation, group management and billing control, aimed at these agencies. Once again, the consolidation of a business project based on quality, innovation and continuous improvement continues to prevail, even when the tourism

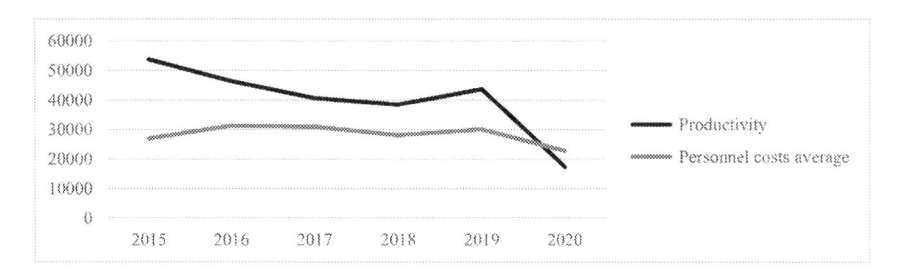

Figure 17.5 Evolution of productivity and personnel costs of travel agencies and tour operators in the Canary Islands.

Source: Prepared by authors based on the Canary Institute of Statistics -ISTAC (2021).

context—from time to time—invites a certain relaxation in decision-making: the number of tourists arriving in the Canary Islands continued to increase over the period 2010–2017.

However, beyond the arrival of tourists to the Islands, the specific environment of travel agencies and tour operators became somewhat turbulent in the Canary Islands. In fact, according to data provided by the Canary Islands Statistics Institute (ISTAC), the productivity of these operators—measured in euros per person—has suffered a continuous decline since 2015. Such is the case that a reduction of 23.61% was seen in just two years (2015 and 2017), while average personnel costs, over the same period, increased by 15% (Figure 17.5). The perspectives regarding these indicators do not show any signs of improvement, so it is necessary to analyse alternatives and make decisions in this regard. At the same time, the number of travel agent and tour operator establishments in the Canary Islands stood at 1,599 in 2017, having increased in a single year by 7.68%, while the staff employed by these operators represents an increase of 11.13%. Investment in tangible assets experienced a rise of more than 50% compared to 2016 (Figure 17.6).

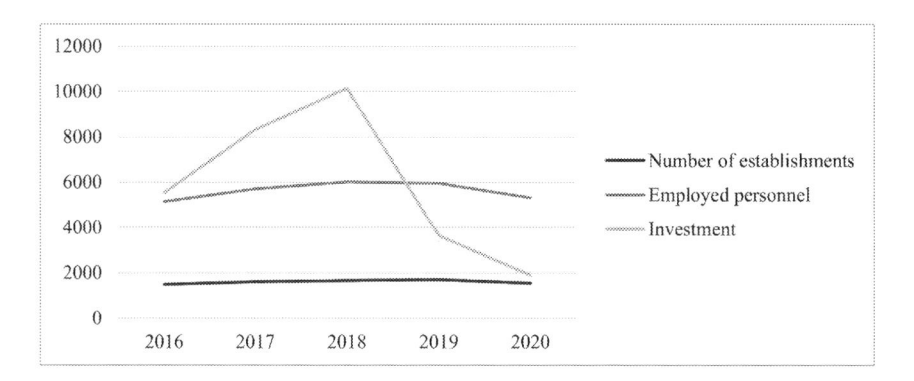

Figure 17.6 Evolution of the number of establishments, employed personnel and investment of travel agencies and tour operators in the Canary Islands.

Source: Prepared by authors based on the Canary Institute of Statistics -ISTAC (2021).

Thus, the general decline in productivity and the increase in the number of establishments, personnel costs and investment in tangible assets, has created a situation not previously experienced in the sector. It was time, then, to implement riskier actions that would allow Viajes Insular to continue differentiating itself by incorporating new products and services, adding digitisation to its business model. Thus, Viajes Insular takes advantage of digitisation to develop a new service, based on the availability of resources—technological, human and financial—and organisational support given to employees, capable of detecting new opportunities and generating new business ideas.

To that end, in 2018, Viajes Insular created Vimotions, betting on a perspective that goes beyond the conventional and makes the most of all the advantages offered by digitisation and online contracting. This new enterprise aims to offer customers—both visitors and residents—a wide range of tours and complementary activities that can be enjoyed in the Canary Islands. In this way, Viajes Insular entered a fairly significant market niche—that of the complementary offer—by providing experiences related to sport, nature, culture, gastronomy, entertainment, health and well-being, etc., and became an intermediary services provider and a viewing channel for local companies that do not have their product or service digitised. In fact, tours and activities constitute a field of the tourism sector that mass digitisation has not yet reached. Vimotions currently offers consumers more than 350 activities while making it easier for companies to sell their activities online, with the aim of providing 1,000 different tours and activities.

Vimotions represents a further advance in the business consolidation of Viajes Insular, faithful to its hallmark of facilitating the customer trip management process, offering a greater tourist offer with the collaboration of small companies in the sector that can provide their services through the platform—all of this always under the guarantee, service and support of Viajes Insular. To do this with Vimotions, the sales process is digitised, creating a single booking engine for the various websites of its service tour operators, such as Expedia, Viator and Atrápalo, among others, and also managing sales comprehensively. In fact, through this platform, the different Viajes Insular tour operators can sell their services online, saving time and money since Vimotions is in charge of the comprehensive organisation and charges them according to the sales actually made by the tour/activity provider. Therefore, Vimotions facilitates, through its tour operators, the sale of a variety of activities that can be carried out in the Canary Islands, an area in which Viajes Insular operates, at the same time that it publicises various existing activities taking place in the Islands that may be unknown even to residents.

In this way, Viajes Insular incorporates digitisation into intermediary activities and performs a fully integrated service with the providers of complementary activities, once again supporting, through collaboration, the development of the tourism sector and the Canarian economy. This initiative represents a great commitment on the part of Viajes Insular to the professional growth and leadership of a significant part of the tour operator sector.

However, for the development of this new proposal, Viajes Insular has not only had the participation of managers and employees of the company—as has been typical in its history—but they have also consulted and supported external professionals from the sector in order to assess feasibility and receive professional feedback in relation to the proposed strategy. Vimotions is the result of a year and a half of work to manage the digital transformation, subcontracting out the necessary technology in order to carry out the project. Thus, the incorporation of consultations with company personnel, the generation of dynamics with sector experts, and the continuous surveillance of the general and specific environments are just some examples of the internalisation of change processes within Viajes Insular, validated throughout its long history and during different stages of its life cycle.

Epilogue

Viajes Insular, a tourism distribution hub and intermediary service provider specialised in the Canary Islands, can be considered the embryo of the tourism birth in the Canary Islands, and its growth has developed in parallel to that of the region. Throughout its long business career, Viajes Insular has played a key role in the development of tourism in the Canary Islands, facing favourable and well-understood tourist situations, as well as unexpected and previously unexperienced ones. Its consolidation and recognition in the tourism context are undeniable.

The most relevant aspects of the CE actions of Viajes Insular are supported by the basic pillars of specialisation, continuous learning and training, the qualification and loyalty of its human resources, and innovation in its broadest sense, even taking into consideration the continuous reinvention of the intermediary business as its *leitmotiv*.

Since its inception, it has denoted the exclusivity of its services and personalisation as the main identifying elements of the company, being a *connoisseur* of the sector with extensive knowledge of travel agencies and tour operators, of the members of the distribution chain, and of the needs of customers—both individuals and groups. In fact, digital disruption in the tourism industry is characterised by customer orientation and a high degree of personalisation (Perelygina et al., 2022), clearly differential elements in the operations of Viajes Insular, as introduced by Rodríguez et al. (2015) when affirming that the coexistence of online and offline business is possible, and traditional agencies must add value to the supply chain and listen to the needs of the client.

The learning extracted from its strategic alliances, through cooperation and collaboration with other travel agents and members of the distribution chain, has been one of the strategies most used by Viajes Insular in launching innovative initiatives and generating new companies and supporting their decisions—both proactive and reactive. It has been fundamental in the integral management of the trip, customer satisfaction, and the personalised and qualified service offered by its staff. These decisions would not be possible without systematised sectoral surveillance, which has allowed it to transform, adapt and benefit, maintaining and strengthening its competitive advantage. The key factor is the specialised, loyal human team with a positive attitude towards continuous change, and with the impetus that comes from knowing they are valued. This human team has facilitated the design and implementation of the various entrepreneurial initiatives—being themselves participants in the generation of ideas, the commitment to quality, innovation and digital transformation, and the opening of new lines of business—led by a management team with a strategic vision of the business and with the clear objective of specialisation in the Canary Islands.

Thus, as pointed out by Smith et al. (2016), CE needs an organisation, a culture and a favourable environment in order to develop—characteristics that have been revealed by Viajes Insular throughout its history in its perpetual quest to change the organisational status quo and innovate from within the company. However, CE is not exempt from obstacles and barriers that must be managed. In the case under study, the company's managers demonstrate—in line with what was provided by Usman et al. (2021)—the need for creative profiles to exist within organisations, with different and divergent thoughts capable of visualising new business opportunities; with curiosity to capture changes in the market and the areas in which they occur. In this vein, Viajes Insular tried to align the interests of the company's different departments, seeking a level of synchronicity and coordination that benefits strategic activities. In addition, it has attempted to avoid information asymmetries between departments and workers in the face of a changing environment, promoting personal concern, risk-taking and business culture within a flexible organisational structure that does not hinder the discovery and promotion of new talent within the company. Thus, intrapreneurship is an intangible asset available to employees, providing the management team with the environment for innovation to flourish (Smith et al., 2016).

References

Exceltur. (2021). *IMPACTUR Canarias 2020. Estudio de Impacto Económico del Turismo sobre la Economía y el Empleo de las Islas Canarias.* Exceltur y Gobierno de Canarias.

Guth, W. D., & Ginsberg, A. (1990). Guest editors' introduction: Corporate entrepreneurship. *Strategic Management Journal, 11*, 5–15.

Instituto Canario de Estadística (ISTAC). (26 de 01 de 2021). *Principales magnitudes económicas de las unidades legales según actividad principal. España y comunidades autónomas desde 2016.*

Lemes-Hernández, A. I. (2015). *La intención emprendedora de los investigadores universitarios: el caso de las "spin-off" académicas.* Obtenido de http://hdl.handle.net/10553/17472

Montaudon-Tomas, C., Pinto-López, I., & Yáñez-Moneda, A. (2020). Tendencias de la digitalización en la hospitalidad y el turismo. *VinculaTégica Efan, 6*(2), 1169–1179.

Orús, A. (23 de 08 de 2022). *El turismo en Canarias - Datos estadísticos.* Obtenido de Statistas: https://es.statista.com/temas/4115/el-turismo-en-canarias/#topicHeader__wrapper

Pencarelli, T. (2020). The digital revolution in the travel and tourism industry. *Information Technology & Tourism*, 455–476. doi: 10.1007/s40558-019-00160-3

Perelygina, M., Kucukusta, D., & Law, R. (2022). Digital business model configurations in the travel industry. *Tourism Management*, 104408. doi: 10.1016/j.tourman.2021.104408

Promotur. Turismo de Islas Canarias. (2022). *Serie histórica de la llegada de turistas a Canarias e islas (FRONTUR). 1997 – 2021.* Obtenido de https://turismodeislascanarias.com/es/investigacion/serie-historica-de-la-llegada-de-turistas-canarias-e-islas-frontur-1997-2021/

Rodríguez, C., Juanety, O., & Álvarez, J. (2015). El impacto de las TICs en la gestión de las agencias de viajes. E. J. de Pablos, F. Campos-Freire, & J. Rúas-Araújo, *Las redes sociales digitales en el ecosistema mediático* (págs. 174–194). España: Sociedad Latina de Comunicación Social. doi. 10.4185/cac92

Salgado, E., Morejón, P., & Hernández, Y. (2021). Tendencias en la comercialización digital de las agencias de viajes en el escenario del COVID-19. *Revista Internacional de Turimos, Empresa y Territorio*, 5(2), 131–145.

Smith, L., Rees, P., & Murray, N. (2016). Turning entrepreneurs into intrapreneurs: Thomas Cook, a case-study. *Tourism Management*, 56, 191–204.

Sosa-Cabrera, S. (2003). *La génesis y el desarrollo del cambio estratégico: un enfoque dinámico basado en el "momentum" organizativo.* Obtenido de https://accedacris.ulpgc.es/handle/10553/20152

Statistas Research Departament. (13 de 11 de 2022). *Las agencias de viajes en España - Datos estadísticos.* Obtenido de Statistas: https://es.statista.com/temas/4005/las-agencias-de-viajes-en-espana/#topicHeader__wrapper

Statistas Research Department. (7 de 11 de 2022). *Booking Holdings. Ingresos anuales 2007-2021.* Obtenido de Statistas: https://es.statista.com/estadisticas/1009938/ingresos-anuales-del-grupo-turistico-booking-holdings/

Usman, M., Ali, M., Ogbonnaya, C., & Babalola, M. (2021). Fueling the intrapreneurial spirit: A closer look at how spiritual leadership. *Tourism Management*, 83, 104227.

Viajes Insular, S. A. (s.f.). https://www.viajesinsularcorporativo.es/index.php

Case 18 Innovation at Zuana Beach Resort and private investment with international standards of sustainability on the Beaches of Santa Marta, Colombia

María Luisa Galán Otero and Deiwi Jesús Zurbarán Arias

Introduction

Zuana Beach Resort Hotel: Historical and organisational overview

The Zuana Beach Resort Hotel is in the tourist sector of Bello Horizonte in the city of Santa Marta, Colombia. Its development was led by Constructora Bolívar, SA, part of the Bolívar Group, one of the country's most important companies, ensuring comprehensive support throughout the process. The first phase of the project was inaugurated in 1996, and the second phase in 2012. It is operated by CB Hoteles y Resorts, SA.

It has 331 rooms with a capacity for 1,240 guests, event rooms and common areas. It offers services with high-quality standards in accommodation, food and beverage, entertainment (bowling, spa, bar, and tourism), and events and conventions for timeshare partners and individuals. Its customer focus is aligned to provide memorable WOW experiences: it is authentic, inclusive, and permanently renewing and innovating in its services. Hotel Zuana Beach Resort[1] has the infrastructure, processes, technology, assets and, above all, a skilled human talent team, trained and aligned to the company's corporate values. These values are identified in Table 18.1 and form a fundamental part of its strategic outlook.

In terms of its organisational structure, Figure 18.1 shows the company's organisational chart up to the coordination level, then branches down to the most operational levels. At each level, committees are formed to deal with important issues related to the processes of each unit to control the operation and promote continuous improvement.

It is environmentally, socially, economically, and culturally responsible. It holds three certifications: Colombian Tourist Quality, complying for three consecutive years with the sustainability standards of the NTS TS 002-2 in its hotel plant and service; Colombian Environmental Seal, implementing the sustainability standards of the NTC 5133. At the international level, the *Blue Flag* ecolabel has allowed them to meet the sustainability criteria for beaches

DOI: 10.4324/9781003454465-19

Table 18.1 Strategic outlook hotel Zuana Beach Resort

Vision	In 2023, we will be recognised in the hotel sector as the top alternative for relaxation and fun for families in the Colombian Caribbean and as one of the best options for events in Santa Marta.
Mission	In the Zuana Family, our passion for hospitality drives us to generate memorable experiences for our clients and collaborators. We are committed to the environment, society and the continuous improvement of our processes.
Corporate values	(1) Discipline; (2) fairness; (3) honesty; (4) enthusiasm, joy, and good humour; and (5) respect.

Source: Zuana Beach Resort Hotel (2022).

since 2019. This allowed it to reinvent itself, transform itself and be part of this compilation of good practices of intrapreneurship (inclusive) that serves as an example for promoting sustainable management in hotel contexts.

External overview of Zuana Beach Resort: Regional and local viewpoint

The city of Santa Marta is the capital of the department of Magdalena, one of the most representative of the Colombian Caribbean region. It is comprised of a wide range of priceless natural beauty and mega biodiversity that emerges from the highest coastal mountain in the world near sea level (Sierra Nevada de Santa Marta) where four emblematic indigenous peoples of America— Koguis, Wiwas, Arhuacos and Kankuamos—reside, whose culture, traditions and ancestral knowledge constitute a valuable heritage for humanity (Situr Magdalena, 2020). In its foothills is the Tayrona National Natural Park. Santa Marta is not only nature, it is a cultural melting pot due to several historical events where Simón Bolívar, Colombia's liberator against the Spanish, is the protagonist. Its Historic Center, a national asset of cultural interest, stands out for its colonial architecture. Unfortunately,, it has been suffering from the inappropriate use of public space, mainly due to obstruction and commercial invasion. The capital is the cradle of hotel development and infrastructure at the national level, mainly concentrated in the beach sectors (Bello Horizonte, Rodadero, Buritaca, & Taganga).

In 2019, the department received mostly domestic tourists principally drawn to "vacation and recreation", with Santa Marta as the leading destination for overnight stays. By 2021, in full recovery from the COVID-19 pandemic, it received close to three million tourists, highlighting Bello Horizonte as one of the most popular places for visitors (Caracol, 2022; WRadio, 2022).

Tourism represents 11.39% of Magdalena's GDP (gross domestic product), and nearly 35,300 people are linked to tourism through direct, indirect and induced employment, contributing almost 10.8%. Hotels and restaurants employ 34.6% of the people employed in Magdalena (hotels and lodging, 48%). One out of every ten jobs in the world is in the tourism sector (Cotelco, 2020).

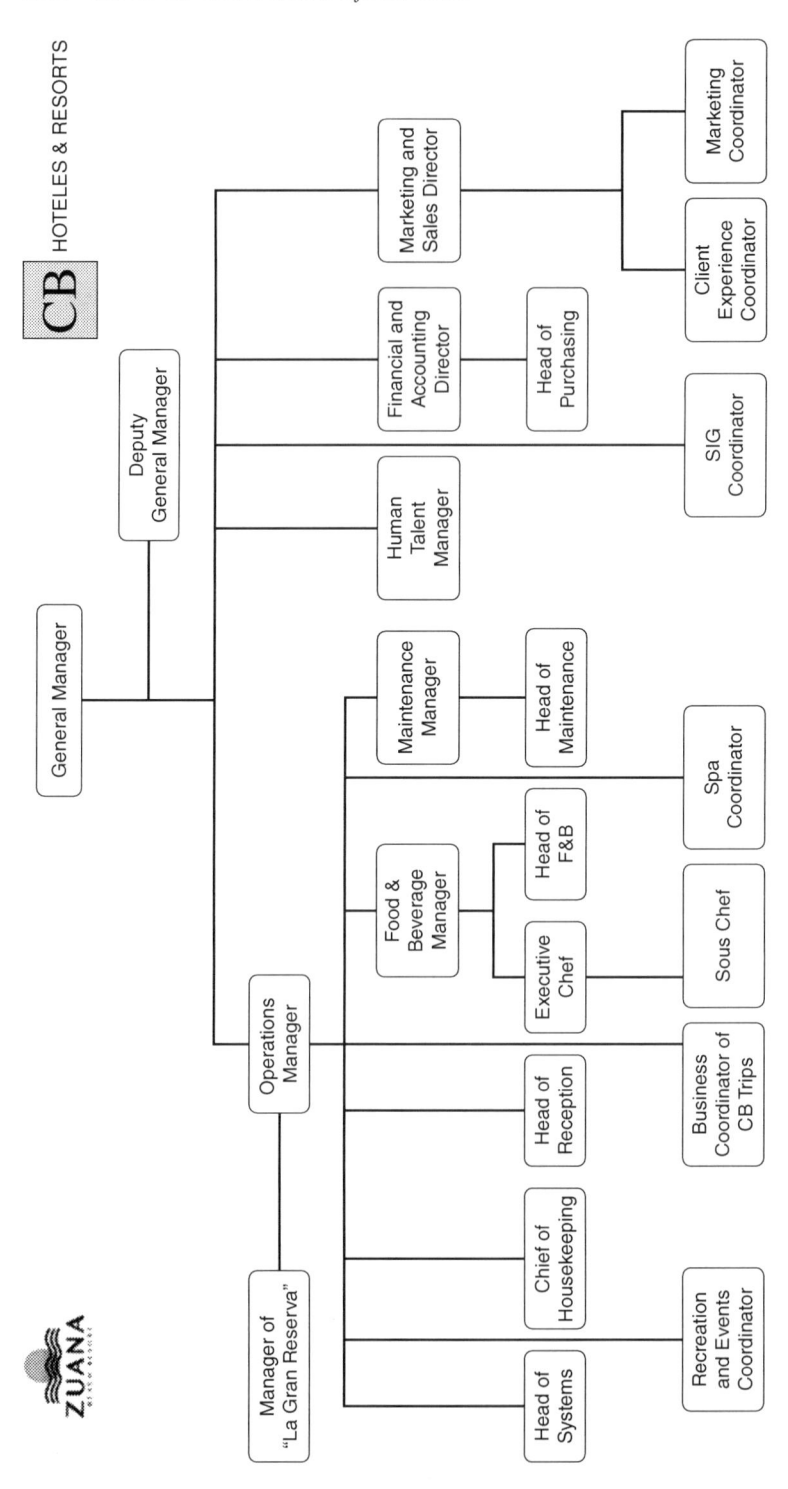

Figure 18.1 Organisational chart hotel Zuana Beach Resort.

Source: Zuana Beach Resort Hotel (2022).

Although declared a Tourist, Cultural and Historic District, the city faces several challenges:

- Expansion of the runway at the Simón Bolívar International Airport, with potential relocation to an area that guarantees a more modern infrastructure.
- Improvement of public services in the city.
- Modernisation of the Rodadero Sector.
- Revitalisation of the Historic Centre, not only in terms of infrastructure but also socially and culturally.
- Improvement of roads and sewage system in the Bello Horizonte sector.
- Public-private articulation, tourism competitiveness and reorganisation.
- Security in tourism sectors.

Origin and evolution of Zuana Beach Resort's key business elements

Data on the evolution of the key elements of the business under study are presented below. Two components are considered to present the analysis:

i Figures related to room sales, occupancy, number of guests and average rate, considering the last five years (2017–2021).
ii Qualitative analysis in relation to the sustainability of the hotel unit.

First, data related to room sales volume between 2017 and 2021 is presented. As evidenced in Figure 18.2, sales were on an upward trend until the COVID-19 pandemic struck, when they plummeted to −46.67%. Despite this, growth between 2019 and 2021 was still 32.7%.

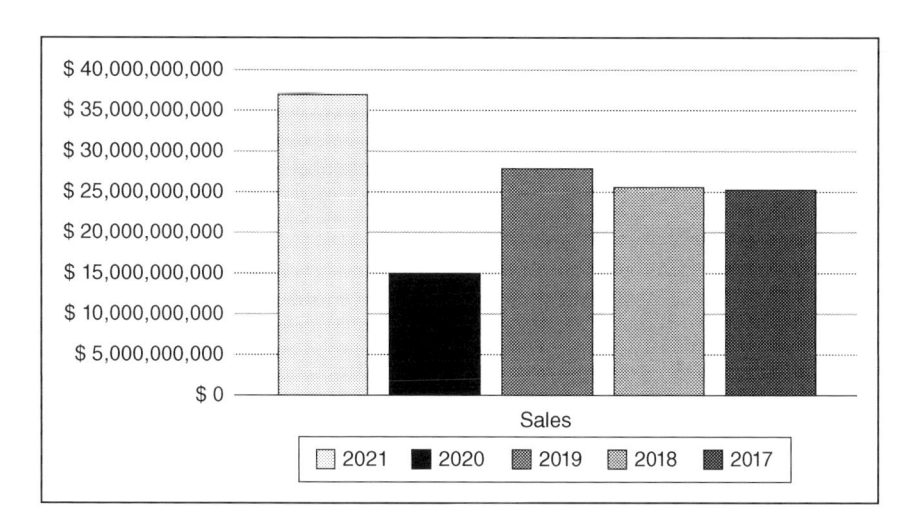

Figure 18.2 Evolution of sales per room (2017–2021).

Source: Zuana Beach Resort Hotel (2022).

Annual occupancy followed the same upward trend, except for 2020 and 2018, which decreased by -50.23% and 1.65%, respectively. However, between 2020 and 2021, it had a variation of 113.91%. Therefore, it stood out as one of the hotels with the highest occupancy rates at the national level in 2012. The average rate also increased over the years studied, from \$373.49 to \$461.197.

Although the object of analysis of the intra-entrepreneurship will be the international Blue Flag Certification (07 julio de 2022), Zuana Beach Resort has been performing positively in the compliance and implementation of sustainability requirements according to the national standard set by NTS TS 002 for lodging and accommodation establishments. It has shown a significant evolution in sustainability in recent years through the development and innovation of infrastructure, changes in its paradigms and the appropriation of a more efficient and environmentally responsible culture.

There are several orientations to the concept of intrapreneurship or corporate entrepreneurship (CE). For Seshadri and Tripathy (2006), corporate entrepreneurship and intrapreneurship are the same because they refer to the process through which an individual or a group of individuals, in association with an existing organisation, create a new organisation or instigate renewal or innovation within the organisation. However, Casson and Godley (2005) affirm that they are only comparable if they are developed under the integration and collaboration of entrepreneurs and their companies, which would allow the development of initiatives that generate economic capital and social welfare. For this article, the strategic position of Åmo and Kolvereid (2005) is taken because CE is conceived as a strategy to implement new ideas that allow the renewal and, therefore, the transformation of the organisation. According to Trujillo Dávila and Guzmán Vásquez (2008), "it is about seeking the best strategic fit of present needs with future visions" (p. 42) through CE actions that foster innovation. In turn, for this case, sustainability-oriented innovation (SOI) is relevant because it implies making intentional changes in an organisation's philosophy and values, as well as in its products, processes or practices, to fulfil the specific purpose of creating and realising social and environmental value in addition to economic benefits.

Some examples of CE actions at Zuana Beach Resort are the implementation of drinking water plants that ensure optimal quality of the resource for guests, its reuse through a wastewater treatment system that ensures proper destination and treatment (today, an average of 70–85 cubic metres per day are reused for irrigation activities in green areas, which represents 30% of total consumption); installation of a solar collector system for heating water for multiple uses, which saves 30% of natural gas used and 15% of electrical energy; replacement of two more efficient hydraulic pumps that reduce energy by 15% to 20%, in addition to reducing the emission of an average of 20 tonnes of CO_2 per year. Finally, in the middle of the pandemic, two major projects were initiated: 1) remodelling of the industrialised laundry area, which included changes in the entire system of washing, drying and ironing machinery; and 2) change and improvement of showers in all rooms. Finally, in 2021, the company opted for the LED lighting system, complying with international standards, which implies an execution rate of approximately 98% in this regard.

Development

Hotel Zuana Beach Resort has been characterised since its inception by directing its efforts to sustainable practices through developing social, environmental, and economic aspects of operations. Such actions focus their efforts on establishing solidarity and inclusive dynamics, where, in addition to sustainability, social innovation (SI) has become a new form of creation and management that is gaining importance. In the last five years, such actions have been framed in processes that have allowed them to obtain certifications and sustainability guarantee seals that contribute to the care and preservation of the environment and the local context. This, in turn, has resulted in attracting and consolidating not only national but also international tourism by promoting sustainable beaches according to the standards of Blue Flag[2]. The hotel's private beach, called Bello Horizonte, has this unique ecolabel in Santa Marta, which allows positioning the city nationally and internationally as a destination that aims to comply with international standards on sustainability issues. The Blue Flag management was a process, that began in 2018, was consolidated with the certification in 2019. This certification has been maintained for the last three years. The resort is currently working on improving its recertification indicators, which involve meeting the 33 criteria or standards in information and environmental education, water quality, environmental management, safety and services.

The initiative is the result of the determined management of the General Manager, the Operations Manager, and the group of leaders of the different functional areas. The Hotel Zuana Beach Resort was invited by Procolombia (7 de julio de 2022)[3] together with the government of the Dominican Republic to learn about the best practices in certified beaches, where it was possible to observe how the tourism service providers of this destination were organised in a coherent, collaborative, and articulated manner, allowing them to have certified beaches and real concrete sustainable practices. In this sense and articulated manner, from the perspective of the SI, strategies have been created to develop projects that provide solutions to structural problems, vulnerable groups and environmental issues. Focusing on climate change, Zuana Beach Resort has set challenges aligned with its philosophy, focusing on intra-entrepreneurship initiatives that articulate internal and external actors.

This framework also included current classic line knowledge and studies, which focus on innovative ideas that transform goods and services. Schumpeter (2004) defines innovation as a cause of development and the innovative entrepreneur as an enabler of innovation processes (Schumpeter, 1950). Social innovation is not exclusive to a particular sector of the economy but to the innovation in the creation of products and social results, regardless of where they are born. SI should cover all sectors and the relationships between them. Its capacity depends both on innovation in the structures, objectives and cross-border relationships of each of the four economic spheres, as well as on any specific role that each of the sectors has traditionally played (Andion et al., 2017). According to Murray et al. (2010), innovation can be considered in four stages: the generation of ideas by understanding needs; the identification of possible solutions; the development, prototyping and piloting of ideas; and the evaluation of the scale-up and diffusion of good ideas.

Thus, the challenge was to articulate different internal and external stakeholders to initiate the path towards obtaining the Blue Flag Certification. In fact, some of the requirements were already being implemented in the operation. The initiative was carried out with private capital investment provided by the hotel, and with the support of national and local government authorities, service providers on the beach, surrounding communities, local guilds, and all hotel staff during its implementation stage.

In Colombia only three beaches have been recognised with this certification: Bello Horizonte in Santa Marta; Playa Azul in La Boquilla, Cartagena; and Playa Jhony Cay in San Andrés; they will have the credential for the years 2021 and 2022. The beaches of Bello Horizonte, "Zuana sector" as it is called by the Hotel Zuana Beach Resort and the local population, are recognised for their organisation and the security provided to locals and visitors. In addition to being inclusive for people with reduced mobility or "physical disability", it has a walkway and an amphibious chair so that people with physical challenges can enjoy access to the sea. Some examples of intrapreneurship actions carried out by the company are identified in more detail below.

Intra-entrepreneurship actions led by Zuana Beach Resort in terms of environmental information and education, water quality, environmental management, and safety and services

Research on sustainability and environmental impact issues was conducted years ago, finding that obsolete equipment and other reasons generate a large amount of CO2. This prompted the search for new options involving a study in which Zuana Beach Resort (ZBR) identified how it was generating a negative impact on the environment, which, in turn, allowed it to generate strategies for the replacement, updating of equipment and implementation of renewable energy. In alliance with the Universidad Cooperativa de Colombia[4], ZBR developed the project to assemble a desalination plant with solar panels. The investment was provided by the European Union, which, in its call, was looking for large-scale companies that had already moved forward on advances in sustainable practices, but due to the appearance of the COVID-19 pandemic, the project was suspended. The replacement and updating of equipment and the implementation of renewable energies have resulted in a reduction of 115 tonnes of CO_2 per year.

Furthermore, in 2018, the hotel's main cold water pumping system was changed for a high-efficiency system, which reduced energy use by 15 to 20%, and a water heating system was acquired with solar collectors and heat exchangers. The latter take advantage of the heat generated by the air conditioning; with this, they can preheat the water, for example, in the jacuzzies. In addition, the heat from the condensation water from the laundry is used to heat the water, thus generating a reduction of about 30% in the use of gas. The project costs a total of $733,333.00 and was carried out between 2016-2017. With the new pumping system, $529,333.00 was saved with a reduction of 3,814,595 Kw, which is equivalent to 68% of the consumption according to the analysis, all of this up to October 2021, being one of the most remarkable actions in the last year. The hotel has a wastewater treatment plant that takes advantage of approximately 30% of the water, which is then used for gardening.

With the gas system, something similar happened, high-efficiency heaters were acquired that are attached to the collector system, and only one boiler was left to support the work in the laundry. Through this, $161,333.00 was saved with a reduction of 271,257 M3, which is equivalent to 44% of the gas compared to the old system. The two systems were put into operation in 2018. Additionally, the projects were paid off in a shorter period of time due to external conditions such as the increase in the price of energy.

Other important actions to highlight are those related to the generation of information and environmental education to ensure the well-being and health of internal and external stakeholders and compliance with environmental responsibilities. Thus, from 2017 to 2020, two initiatives were carried out: the Occupational Health and Safety Week and the Sustainability Week. For the year 2017, the "FASHION DAY ZUANA SUSTAINABLE" was carried out, which consisted of designing and building a wardrobe whose concept was recycling and had the participation of all functional areas of the hotel, training in hazardous waste management, ecological tour, beach cleaning, among others. In 2018, training was given in waste management and recycling, tourism safety and civility on the beaches, biodiversity and beach cleaning and the training involved 216 people. Subsequently, in 2019, the participation of employees increased to 265 participants. In 2020, training was conducted through digital media due to the contingency plan put in place for the pandemic. It included sustainability activities, socialisation of the emergency plan and a Santa Marta Tour, which were conducted in sessions of four groups per day, virtually.

In the year 2021, ZBR decided to carry out the first "Revitalmente Fest" in conjunction with Constructora Bolívar[5] in coordination with the area of Human Resources, Integrated Management Systems and suppliers or allied companies that, for a three-week period, sought to raise awareness about the importance of prevention, self-care, promotion of health and life, as well as the protection of the planet. During these weeks, activities, workshops and recreational, sports and artistic training, among others, are carried out virtually and in person.

An aspect of great importance is that the full payroll was maintained during the pandemic, and the number of employees increased, reaching more than 400. Likewise, ZBR accompanies and supports the professional growth of employees by creating the project of the "Zuana School", where the idea is to train people close to the environment in operational activities in bars, restaurants, rooms, reception areas and laundry units, among others. This model was later replicated in a shopping centre in Santa Marta, and today, Zuana aims to create a professional training centre.

Finally, in 2022, a "PLAYATÓN"[6] and the environmental walk were held on the beaches of the Bello Horizonte sector, as well as a theme linked to World Oceans Day, initiatives aligned with sustainable development policy and reiterating the responsibility with the Blue Flag Certification. The main objective was to encourage care for the environment and the marine area, promote responsible consumption of resources, mitigate the impact of solid waste on the marine environment, stimulate eco-environmental awareness through recreational and sports activities, and collect, classify, and weigh solid waste found on the beach.

The deployment of any initiative involves barriers. In this case, it's worth mentioning the lack of support from the public sector, even knowing that the area is now more visited due to the Blue Flag Certification. Another obstacle was water management: it was also a challenge for the communities to raise awareness and sensitise their inhabitants on proper water management; beyond the economic benefits for the hotel (savings), there are also environmental benefits.

Epilogue

Colombia's tourism and hotel sector is experiencing full tourism reactivation and operation, as well as climbing in the positive trend of domestic and international tourist arrivals. The environment is increasingly demanding, and competitive, and new sustainable challenges are appearing on the local and national scenes. The way in which organisations manage to develop differentiation strategies in their value proposition and the way they aim at achieving sustainability practices in their social, environmental, and economic dimensions, as well as the incorporation of innovation in their processes, will be a key factor into their consolidation and permanence in the market over the long term.

The Zuana Beach Resort Hotel is projected to continue positioning itself as one of the great hotels at the national and international level and as a pioneer in developing sustainability, environmental and inclusion projects. Its main achievements are evidenced in the impact on reducing energy consumption and CO_2 generation thanks to the replacement and updating of equipment and the implementation of renewable energy. Through the improvements in seaside services provided, beachgoers can enjoy a quiet and safe space. The community is involved in the management of environmental education activities and actively ensures that the water is suitable for the use and enjoyment of local and visiting beachgoers.

Although the initial reason to better position and differentiate ZBR in the sustainable lodging services market was to become certified, thanks to the development of entrepreneurship sustainable actions, the hotel generates a virtuous circle not only inside but in its environment and communities. As the main results obtained from the development of these actions, the following can be highlighted: horizontal internal relations (even though the resort's organisational structure is vertical); efficient management leadership, participatory and inclusive leadership; ongoing commitment to sustainability; innovative and intrapreneurial capacity along with the active involvement of the different stakeholders (community, employees, suppliers, investors); committed team eager to do a job that has a significant impact on their peers, their community and ultimately themselves, is part of the human talent philosophy; and, most importantly, that initiatives are undertaken and goals are set in the knowledge that it is possible and easy to maintain an environmentally sustainable business with an open and adaptable mindset to the challenges that may arise. Therefore, ZBR has created the ideal conditions to go one step further on the path of environmental intrapreneurship in the Colombian hospitality industry, not only as a pioneer in paving the way but also as creating a group of passionate collaborators who believed in the project in the change and made it possible through innovation-oriented to sustainability.

As for possible reflection issues, two are denoted. Even if the spark of intrapreneurship is still alive, how must ZBR consolidate their own intrapreneurial culture to continue betting on new ideas that will result in lower costs and environmental efficiency while maximising the guest experience? And how can the hotel go a step further in intrapreneurship by stimulating the creation of products and services from collaborators that benefit the hotel and, incidentally, become potential or new sources of income for the unit?

Notes

1 Over the last 8 years, it has been awarded the Traveller's Choice and best place to celebrate weddings, by the ZankYou platform in TripAdvisor. The MyHotel platform has rated the Yuluka Spa as best service in 2018 and 2022.
2 The iconic Blue Flag is one of the world's most recognised voluntary awards for beaches, marinas, and sustainable boating tourism operators. To qualify for the Blue Flag, a series of stringent environmental, educational, safety, and accessibility criteria must be met and maintained.
3 PROCOLOMBIA is the entity in charge of promoting tourism, foreign investment in Colombia, non-mining energy exports and the country's image. Through its national and international network of offices, it offers comprehensive support and advice to clients, through services or instruments aimed at facilitating the design and execution of their internationalisation strategy, which seeks the generation, development and closing of business opportunities.
4 Higher education institution located in Colombia: http://www.universidadcooperativa.com.co.
5 Constructora Bolivar is a company of the Bolivar Group, of which CB HOTELES Y RESORTS is also a member.
6 Playatón: event where various activities are held, including underwater and land beach cleanup, workshops, artistic and cultural events, contests, etc.

References

Åmo, B., & Kolvereid, L. (2005). Organisational strategy, individual personality, and innovation behavior. *Journal of Enterprising Culture, 13* (1), 7–19. doi. https://www.worldscientific.com/doi/10.1142/S0218495805000033

Andion, C., Lima Moraes, R., & Gonsalves, A. (2017). Civil society organisations and social in novation. How and to what extent are they influencing social and political change? *CIRIEC-España, Revista de Economía Pública, Social y Cooperativa, 90,* 5–34. Available at: https://www.redalyc.org/pdf/174/17452685001.pdf

Blue Flag (07 de julio 2022). Available at: https://www.blueflag.global

Caracol (2 de enero de 2022). *Cerca de 3 millones de turistas llegaron a Santa Marta durante el 2021.* Available at: https://caracol.com.co/emisora/2022/01/02/santa_marta/1641145133_368069.html

Casson, M., & Godley, A. (2005). Entrepreneurship and historical explanation. In Y. Cassis & I. P. Minoglou (eds.). *Entrepreneurship in theory and history* (pp. 25–60). Hampshire: Palgrave-Macmillan.

COTELCO (2020). *Informe de Indicadores hoteleros 2021.*

Murray, R., Caulier-Grice, J., & Mulgan, G. (2010). Social innovator series: ways to design, develop and grow social innovation. *The Open Book of Social Innovation.* Available at: www.socialinnovator.info

Schumpeter, J. (1950). *Capitalism, socialism, and democracy* (3rd ed). New York. Harper y Brothers.

Seshadri, D., & Tripathy, A. (2006). Innovation through intrapreneurship: The road less travelled. *Vikalpa: The Journal for Decision Makers, 31*(1),17–29. doi. 10.1177/0256090920060102

SITUR Magdalena (2020). *Conoce el Magdalena: Acerca del Departamento.* Available at: https://www.siturmagdalena.com/Departamento/AcercaDe

SITUR Magdalena, & COTELCO (2019). *Estadísticas de Turismo Receptor.* Available at: https://www.siturmagdalena.com/multimedia/informes/informe-54/archivo.pdf

Trujillo Dávila, M. A., & Guzmán Vásquez, A. (2008). Intraemprendimiento: Una revisión al constructo teórico, sus implicaciones y agenda de investigación futura. *Cuadernos de Administración, 21*(35), 37–63. Available at: http://www.scielo.org.co/scielo.php?script=sci_arttext&pid=S0120-35922008000100003&lng=en&tlng=es

WRadio (2 de enero de 2022). *¡Se batió el récord! Santa Marta recibió cerca de 3 millones de turistas durante 2021.* Available at: https://www.wradio.com.co/2022/01/01/se-batio-el-record-santa-marta-recibio-cerca-de-3-millones-de-turistas-durante-2021/

Case 19 HD Group

Business model based on innovation and diversification in shopping centres, supermarkets and hotels

Francisco Javier Gutiérrez-Pérez,
Francisca Rosa Álamo-Vera, and
Teresa Aguiar-Quintana

Introduction

The HD Group

Founded in 1947, the HD Group (Hermanos Domínguez) stands as one of the most representative conglomerates of companies in the economy of the Canary Islands (Spain). They currently employ 8,400 people and have an annual turnover exceeding € 1.065 billion (Canarias 7, 2020).

Since its inception, it has based its business activity on an organisational culture framed by solid *family values* and with the strategic vision of being a leading company in the main sectors of the Canary Islands' economy through an unwavering commitment to sustainability. In this way, the HD Group's objectives focus on three main strategic lines:

- *Sustainable growth*, which makes the Group stronger by seeking a balance between resources, people and the planet.
- A *drive for innovation*, so successes are transformed into new market opportunities.
- A *passion for service*, doing things authentically to make a mark on people's lives.
- *Strong and committed corporate culture*, focused on talent management and retention, continuous training and the personal and professional development of employees.

The HD Group has based its success on diversification, with a multi-sector business model developed through three business units:

- *Food distribution*. This was the company's first business, and it still represents a significant part of its activity. The group owns Dinosol Supermercados, SL, a leading retailer in the Canary Islands with 232 supermarkets and large retail outlets and 7,000 employees.

DOI: 10.4324/9781003454465-20

- *Real estate business*. The HD Group owns and manages two shopping centres—the Centro Comercial Las Arenas, on the island of Gran Canaria and the Centro Comercial El Campanario, in Fuerteventura—and also rents industrial warehouses, commercial premises and housing.
- *Tourism sector*. In 2004, the HD Hotels chain began its journey in the hotel industry when the company decided to adopt a strategy of diversifying its business portfolio around its traditional values: *customer orientation, family values* in leading the human team, and—perhaps most important—*passion, effort* and *perseverance* in all its actions.

Thus, the strategic orientation of HD Hotels is based on the following basic elements:

- *Purpose*: to be an actor in the industry that enhances customer satisfaction, integrating it with the local community and the destination.
- *Vision*: to be a reference in the tourism sector as a creator of experiences that enhance emotions with sustainable experiences between people, hotels and destinations.
- *Mission*: to offer a unique holiday concept ("New Luxury") by adapting experiences to each type of customer, creating "memorable moments" that make them feel special and integrated with the environment and the local community.

With this orientation, the HD Hotels chain positions itself in the tourist market of the Canary Islands with a hotel offer based on *customer orientation* and, more specifically, on the concept of *enjoyment*, *rest* and *fun* for clients visiting the Canary Islands archipelago.

As shown in Image 19.1, the chain currently has a portfolio of four hotels: HD Parque Cristóbal Gran Canaria and HD Acuario Lifestyle in Gran Canaria, HD Parque Cristóbal Tenerife, and HD Beach Resort & SPA in Lanzarote. In addition, the chain is continuing its expansion today, which will result in the repositioning of two new hotel establishments in the spring of 2024; one of them—HD Lobos Natura—is a new acquisition on the island of Fuerteventura (Image 19.1a–d).

In terms of its organisational structure, HD Hotels adheres to the following organisational hierarchy:

- *Board of Directors*. This is the highest decision-making and supervisory body within the chain. It consists of a group of executives and shareholders who establish the company's general strategies and policies.
- *General Management*. This is the chain's executive branch and is responsible for the daily management of the company. It is led by the General Director who is responsible for making strategic decisions and coordinating the various departments.

HD Parque Cristóbal Gran Canaria
(Playa del Inglés, Gran Canaria)

HD Acuario Lifestyle
(Las Palmas de Gran Canaria,
Gran Canaria)

HD Beach Resort & Spa
(Costa Teguise, Lanzarote)

HD Parque Cristóbal Tenerife
(Playa de Las Américas, Tenerife)

Image 19.1 (a)–(d) HD Hotel chain's portfolio, 2023.
Source: HD Hotels (2023).

- *Central departments*. Within HD Hotels, different departments are responsible for carrying out functions like commercial and marketing management, finance, human resources and operations, among others.
- *Hotels*. The chain currently comprises five hotels (including one soon to be opened) owned by the HD Group. Each hotel has a director responsible for its day-to-day management.
- *Personnel*. HD Hotels has a team of employees who work in different departments and hotels. Each of them has a specific function within the organisation and contributes to the company's success.

Environment

The tourism sector in the Canary Islands is one of the most important in Spain and one of the most dynamic in terms of innovation and growth. Economically speaking, in 2019—the last pre-COVID-19 year—it contributed 32.9% of the Gross Domestic Product (GDP). It generated 36.3%

of employment at the regional level (EXCELTUR and Government of the Canary Islands, 2022).

The Canary Islands has a great variety of tourist destinations that compete globally, especially with the Mediterranean and Caribbean regions. However, its competitive advantages are focused on unique and truly differentiating aspects, such as its warm climate, the attractiveness of its natural and cultural resources, and the wide diversity of its tourism and leisure offerings.

In this sense, although the beaches and coastal areas of the Canary Islands are among its biggest tourist attractions, the richness of its historical and cultural heritage, the uniqueness and picturesque beauty of its quaint villages, and the wide biodiversity of its natural landscapes allow it to offer diverse and high-quality tourist products (e.g., coastal tourism, wellness, 'active' and 'nature' tourism, cruises, cultural and gastronomic tourism, shopping tourism, sports tourism, etc.).

Regarding the source markets, the tourism sector of the Canary Islands attracts over 13 million tourists annually (ISTAC, 2023), mostly from Central and Northern Europe, with Germany, the United Kingdom, the Netherlands, the Nordic countries, Italy, and France being the main tourist markets.

Changes in the economic environment, consumer habits, and technology in the tourism sector have affected the hotel companies in the Canary Islands in various ways. According to several recent studies (Gössling et al., 2020), the main effects that these trends have had on tourism companies can be highlighted as follows:

1   *Impact on demand.* The global economic situation and the COVID-19 pandemic have negatively impacted tourism demand in the Canary Islands and the national and international tourism industry. This has directly affected the hotel companies, which have experienced a decrease in occupancy rates and income that has seemingly and gradually been recovering since the end of 2022.
2   *Changes in consumer habits.* Tourists are increasingly looking for *unique* and *personalised* experiences, which has affected hotel companies in terms of their business models. The more traditional modes of accommodation are no longer the only option for tourists, who, these days, tend to seek a wider variety of options for their stay in the Canary Islands. This has led to increased competition and has compelled hotel companies to be more creative and adaptable in order to meet the needs of their customers.
3   *Use of technology.* Technology has changed the way tourists search for and book accommodation, and this has had a real effect on hotel companies. Many companies have had to adapt to these trends through significant investments in digitisation and implementing technologies that allow them to reach a wider audience while offering a more personalised customer experience.
4   *Greater awareness* of the importance of sustainable development at tourist destinations. Sustainability has become an increasingly important topic in the tourism sector, and hotel companies have had to adapt to this trend

to remain competitive. More and more tourists are looking for sustainable and environmentally friendly accommodation, which has led to an increase in demand for companies that meet these criteria.

5 *Other important challenges* for the tourism industry in the Canary Islands such as increasing competition from emerging destinations and difficulties in ensuring talent retention.

In conclusion, to maintain its competitive position in the international tourism market and continue to grow, the tourism sector in the Canary Islands must continue to innovate, commit to sustainability in all its aspects (environmental, economic and social), train and empower its human resources, and adapt to new trends and the needs of tourists and the industry. In this scenario, the HD hotel group has found the necessary incentives to implement a differentiating strategy based on intrapreneurship.

There is a great variety of tourist destinations around the world competing with the Canary Islands, particularly in the Mediterranean and Caribbean regions. However, the Canaries' competitive advantages are focused on their unique and truly differentiating aspects, such as the year-round, warm climate, the beauty of their natural resources and attractiveness of their cultural activities, and the broad diversity of their tourism offer.

Development. Corporate entrepreneurship and innovation actions

HD Hotels adopted an intra-entrepreneurship strategy (Antoncic & Hisrich, 2003; Guven, 2020) during the COVID-19 pandemic to *reposition* its brand and *renovate* its hotels. Taking advantage of the general slowdown in tourist activity, the company's management team invested in a complete renovation of its hotel offerings, which would be available when the tourism sector returned to a state of normalcy or recovery. Ultimately, this strategy would allow HD Hotels to meet the new needs and likely demands of tourists after all the changes that had occurred.

To start with, HD Hotels' management team conducted an internal and external "Situation Analysis". This involved conducting a detailed market study and analysing the hotel chain's situation in relation to its competitors. They also formulated hypotheses about how demand would transform once post-pandemic normality resumed. The HD's 'intrapreneur team' identified the external and internal factors affecting its hotel business and established long-term objectives and goals for each hotel. They created a strategy that would allow them to reposition the hotel brand and renovate the hotels in the short term.

The strategy was focused on improving quality, adapting infrastructure, innovating, and differentiating the service offerings based on the customer experience. It also included room and channel mix strategies with new revenue and open pricing policies. They implemented a digital marketing strategy that would strengthen direct sales and customer knowledge once the product was repositioned and the 'new look' brand was established.

The pandemic and subsequent lockdowns were among the main antecedents of the environment that motivated HD Hotels' intrapreneurship actions. The hotel industry was one of the most harshly affected by the pandemic, and many companies were forced either to close or significantly reduce the scale of their operations. However, HD Hotels used this crisis as an opportunity to *rethink* its business model and *redesign* its commercial policies by leveraging its *internal talent* and embracing *innovative ideas* in order to develop new business lines.

Therefore, instead of just waiting for things to improve, HD Hotels chose to be *proactive* and take an innovative approach. 'Intra-entrepreneurship', or the promotion of innovation and entrepreneurship within the company, allowed HD Hotels to reinvent itself and improve its position in the market.

In this clear commitment to innovation, HD Hotels adopted solutions to improve processes, infrastructure, digital networks, and businesses. They also implemented actions to reposition products by implementing a customer-centric strategy, improving the customer experience, and increasing their operational efficiency. These solutions were conceived with a clear transversal focus on sustainability, allowing the company to improve its brand image and attract a more environmentally conscious clientele.

Additionally, the sales team took advantage of the demand for new tourism products in the Canary Islands, driven largely by the effects of the pandemic. Many holidaymakers who had previously travelled abroad opted for national and regional vacations at that time, making the Canary Islands a safe, popular and viable destination. HD Hotels quickly adapted to this trend by designing specific tourist packages for different types of travellers and promoting *sustainable* and *active* tourism offerings on Gran Canaria and the other islands.

Identifying the opportunity for intrapreneurship did not follow a clearly marked or well-defined process. The situation generated by the environment was pressing, and, in that turbulent time, the company fundamentally relied on leveraging its own talent in order to advance. However, the company also remained oriented towards meeting market needs and trends in the tourism sector by observing competitors, analysing internal data, promoting creativity and innovation, and establishing an 'idea management' system.

The execution of the intrapreneurship actions driven by HD Hotels *was* a structured and well-defined process to guarantee the success of the project. First, there was a need to *reposition the brand* and adapt it to a foreseeable scenario of returning to "the new normal" after the pandemic. Thus, these initial stages were followed:

1 *Design a marketing strategy* for the launch of an "umbrella" brand that would help implement the expansion of HD Hotels. This new brand would encompass different types of tourism products or concepts aimed at specific customer segments according to their travel motivations:

   • *Family & Joy*: aimed at reconnecting families through multiple activities where age does not matter (splash park, aquaspinning, yoga, sustainable adventure park, tended camps for children with outdoor cinema, eco-gardening workshops...)

- *Mind & Body*: through which HD Hotels also aims to be a reference for tourism activities and services related to health and well-being.
- *Friends & Lovers*: offer specifically oriented to adults who travel with friends or as a couple and seek fun or reconnection with their emotions.
- *Urban Life*: encompasses urban hotels and resorts aimed at tourists seeking authentic experiences during city travel.

2 *Creation of three transversal brands* in order to better understand the customer and offer a "New Luxury" experience, improved and adapted to their tastes:

- *We Connect*: a free loyalty programme that aims to reward the chain's most loyal guests with exclusive advantages and privileges.
- *Emblem*: a customisation and differentiation service aimed at offering additional benefits to the most discerning and demanding clients.
- *HD Sense Connect*: a value proposition to reinvent the traditional tourism model. With a clear focus on the guest ("customer-centric"), it proposes a system of innovation that redefines spaces and sustainable experiential services according to market demand, integrates the tourism offer with the destination, creates quality employment, and improves organisational efficiency through innovation, systems integration and data intelligence.

3 *Definition and establishment of milestones* for the different projects to be carried out in the different areas and, subsequently, the strategic objectives of the chain. In this way, during this phase, the objectives, scope, budget, and necessary resources were established to develop the project.

4 *Creation of a multidisciplinary team* composed of employees and some external firms that had resources or experience the company lacked (e.g., designers, architects, etc.). The team had the autonomy and support necessary to carry out the project, but always under the constant supervision of the Board of Directors.

5 *Development and implementation of detailed work plans* that established the deadlines, tasks, and responsibilities of each team member. With the help of agile techniques such as Scrum and OKRS (objectives and key results), these plans were adjusted according to the needs of each moment, promoting creativity and innovation within the team in order to generate new ideas and solutions. In addition, it was crucial to ensure that the project was aligned with the chain's strategic objectives and met market requirements in order to guarantee its continuity and sustainability. As we may recall, there was great uncertainty at the time, but this clear focus was essential in achieving the success of the brand repositioning process.

By having the resources and the support of the Board of Directors, the company was able to confidently address the minor difficulties that occasionally arose during the implementation of the intrapreneurship project. Consequently, no resistance to change was detected internally, as the responsible team was sufficiently qualified and motivated to tackle the brand repositioning and planned reforms.

However, a possible area for improvement that has been identified is related to effective communication. The flow of ideas and proposals is always a complex process, where the most creative components of the team often have to face the financial reality of the organisation and the tourism market, competing with other less risky—or more secure—proposals or simply with those representing different tastes.

Other challenges to be overcome in managing a project of this nature are related to the complexity of aligning *corporate objectives* with those of each business unit of the company, as well as the pressing need to be efficient in bringing new services to market as quickly as possible ("time to market") to facilitate adaptation to the new habits of the consumer.

In order to overcome these barriers or difficulties, it was crucial for the company to implement a "digital culture" based on the application of agile techniques to improve adaptability to change and the use of accelerating tools such as cloud storage services, which were very useful for sharing important information and documents, as well as keeping the human team updated. Among these measures, it is worth highlighting, in particular, the establishment of agile techniques based on SMART (Specific, Measurable, Achievable, Relevant and Time-Bound) goals and objective tracking tools linked to the tasks of each work team.

Another key aspect in overcoming these barriers was the identification of an important need that the organisation had in terms of improving its business analysis processes, which would allow for more efficient examination of the data and information from the environment and thus facilitate decision-making that would help reduce "time to market".

It was also critical to *develop* and *implement* a clear and detailed *communication plan* from the beginning of the project. This included defining what information was shared, identifying who was responsible for communication, and what channels would be used for knowledge exchange.

Finally, other fundamental yet intangible aspects important for achieving the objectives set with the intra-entrepreneurship actions were the *enthusiasm* and *corporate sense of belonging* of all personnel involved in this project. In this sense, constant feedback was key to good communication, and regular meetings ("stand-up meetings") were established to ensure that all team members were aligned within the project and able to quickly address any issues or concerns that may have arisen. All this allowed project follow-up meetings to be productive and efficient, addressing only the most important, or 'priority', topics in each one.

In summary, the main achievements or outcomes derived from the intrapreneurship actions undertaken by the HD hotel chain are:

1 *Renewal of the brand image*, making it more attractive and modern in order to represent the values of *innovation* and *quality* being promoted internally, resulting in an increase in its noteworthiness.
2 *Increase in the level of return on promotional campaigns* by establishing the client as the focus with personalised offers and promoting a change in mentality among all teams to improve the company's Net Promoter Score (NPS).
3 *Repositioning of the chain's hotels* with a crosscutting technological and sustainable approach in balance with the environment and community. In this way, a series of improvements were made to the facilities and services of all the hotel establishments in the chain, to offer a more comfortable and attractive, sustainable experience to customers. This included not only the modernisation of the rooms but also the "hyper-segmentation" of the rooms to adapt the products to different customer profiles and optimise "Total Revenue".
4 *Adaptation of the hotels' gastronomic offer* to suit new trends related to responsible, sustainable, and healthy consumption (e.g., km0, healthy food, etc.) as a new value proposition of the company.
5 *Strengthening the competitive positioning of the company* by introducing a fully experiential product in the activities offered under the HD Sense Connect brand.
6 *Increase in investment in training and staff development*, which contributed directly to improving the quality of the service.
7 *Increase in the financial profitability of the company*, as well as its market share. Customers responded positively to the changes implemented by the chain, resulting in an increase in occupancy rates and customer satisfaction.
8 *Introduction of new digital business models* with innovative systems that help adapt HD Hotels' product and service offerings to new market trends and consumer preferences.
9 *Improvement in levels of efficiency* in resource management and reduction in operating costs.
10 *Implementation of a renewed, innovative, and sustainable tourism business model*.

Epilogue

This part highlights the most relevant aspects of the corporate entrepreneurship actions described, such as the learning extracted from its development, raising possible reflection issues.

First, according to the management team of the HD hotel chain, the main lesson learned from the development of the brand repositioning strategy through an internal initiative is "undoubtedly, the importance of promoting a culture of intrapreneurship within the organisation and the active participation of employees in the identification of new opportunities and the implementation of new ideas and strategies". This process greatly helped in promoting key aspects critical for the company's survival in such a demanding and changing environment, such as *creativity*, *innovation*, and the *motivation* of the human team, which have significantly contributed to the success of the project.

Second, due to its intrapreneurship measures, HD Hotels have repositioned its renewed brand and significantly improve its profitability. Thus, the chain has increased its revenues and improved its reputation, which has allowed it to continue growing in a difficult and dynamic economic environment.

Finally, the management team of the HD chain is aware of the strategic importance and difficulties involved in promoting a culture of intrapreneurship in a privately held organisation. However, the capabilities developed during this process to promote the *active participation* of employees and to provide them with the necessary space and support to develop *new ideas* and *strategic actions* have resulted in significant benefits for the company. These results are not only reflected in economic and financial improvements but also in other strategic aspects crucial for the organisation, such as: 1) *increasing* and *strengthening* the company's competitiveness in the tourism market; 2) *identifying* and *creating* new business opportunities and models; 3) *improving* the customer experience; 4) *facilitating* higher levels of efficiency and productivity at the departmental and individual level; and 5) *ensuring* greater employee commitment to the company's goals and values, since they feel as though they are an integral part of it and its evolution.

References

Antoncic, B., & Hisrich, R. D. (2003). Clarifying the intrapreneurship concept. *Journal of Small Business and Enterprise Development*, 10(1), 7–24.

Canarias 7 (29/10/2020). *Grupo HD renueva su imagen y refuerza su presencia como uno de los principales grupos de Canarias*. Recuperado de: https://www.canarias7.es/economia/empresas/grupo-renueva-imagen-20201029145021-nt.html

EXCELTUR (Alianza para la Excelencia turística) y Gobierno de Canarias (2022). *Estudio de Impacto Económico del Turismo: IMPACTUR Canarias 2021*. Recuperado de: https://www.gobiernodecanarias.org/cmsgobcan/export/sites/turismo/downloads/Impactur/Impactur-Canarias-2021.pdf

García, A. M., García, M. G., & Gutiérrez, F. J. COVID-19 y turismo en España: impacto actual y disyuntivas futuras. *Economistas*, 172–173, 207–215.

Gössling, S., Scott, D., & Hall, M. (2020). Pandemics, tourism and global change: A rapid assessment of COVID-19. *Journal of Sustainable Tourism*, 22(3), 577–598.

Grupo, H. D. (28/01/2023). *Somos HD*. https://www.grupohd.com/somos-hd

Guven, B. (2020). The integration of strategic management and intrapreneurship: strategic intrapreneurship from theory to practice. *Business and Economics Research Journal, 11*(1), 229–245.

HD Hotels (15/02/2023). *Hoteles y destinos*. Recuperado de: https://www.hdhotels.com/es

Instituto Canario de Estadística (ISTAC, 2023). *Estadística de Movimientos Turísticos en Fronteras de Canarias: Series mensuales. Islas de Canarias. 2012–2023.*

Case 20 Innovation applied to online travel agencies

The case of Different Travel in Huesca, Spain

Silvia Abella-Garcés,
Ma José Barlés-Arizón,
Nuria Domeque-Claver,
Melania Mur-Sangrá,
Ana Monclús-Salamero, and
Ana Katarina Pessoa-de-Oliveira

Introduction

Different Travel SLU is a travel agency created in 2021. Its main business activity is developed on the internet, through centraldereservas.com, http://blog.centraldereservas.com/ and other associate websites. In 2002, the firm started to position itself in the online travel agency market, and it bought the domain through which it has operated since then.

In the following financial years, the company established commercial agreements with important operators in the sector, opened offices in other cities for customer assistance and developed new R&D&I projects. Throughout this process, the firm has maintained an innovative attitude which has led to several projects related to the development of technologies and original exploitation models which it has developed in collaboration with different public organisations (Centre for the Industrial Technologic Development, Secretaría de Estado de Turismo).

Currently, **Centraldereservas.com** is one of the leading booking portals for online accommodation, with more than 2 million accommodations all around the world in over 70,000 locations. In addition, it also commercialises all kinds of travel-related services, such as flights, activities, car rental, transfer, insurance, gifts, etc.

The headquarters of Different Travel is still located in Ainsa. Its origin in a rural environment and its corporate philosophy remain intact. However, the team, made up of around 150 people, is distributed over 20 different locations in Spain and the rest of the world (Ainsa, Zaragoza, Madrid, San Sebastián, Andorra, Italy, Ireland, USA, Australia, Cuba) with very different profiles (engineers, mathematicians, economists, tourism experts, programmers, etc.)

DOI: 10.4324/9781003454465-21

who complement each other and give the firm a wealth of experience based on a constant adaptation to the new contexts that arise.

Throughout these years, the firm and its general manager (Ricardo Buil) have received numerous awards. It has been recognised as online travel agency (OTA) with the highest sales volume in Spain (2004), Young Company Family Responsible Aragón (2011), Tourist Merit Medal of the Government of Aragón (2016), and Innovative SME by the Spanish Government (2019). In parallel, Ricardo Buil has received the Aragón Young Entrepreneur Award (2006), the National Young Entrepreneur Award (2008), the ADEA Entrepreneur Award (2013), and the Tourism Merit Medal of the Government of Aragón (2016).

The company is organised under its innovative structure of multidisciplinary teams working independently to achieve common objectives. It is a flat organisation without hierarchy or defined positions. Everyone can contribute ideas and work on them as they wish, avoiding routine and allowing job rotation, versatility, and professional growth.

This organisation model, called ***Beta Company***, is a model that allows for adapting to changes, modifying the structure of the firm at any time, and reorganising itself when something is not working correctly. The success of the model and its innovative philosophy have attracted so much interest that the model is beginning to be outsourced to other companies.

Environment

The online travel agency sector (OTAS) has grown exponentially, being the most successful sector of e-commerce (Comunicaweb, 2012). Currently, various sources claim that the sector is saturated and has some prominent brands (Zavarce, 2022), with Booking and Expedia dominating the market with different brands (Canalís, 2019). Booking Holdings includes brands such as Booking.com, Priceline.com, Agoda, and the metasearch engine Kayak, Booking.com, is the one that reports the highest volume travel organizations in the business. The Expedia Group includes Expedia, Hotels.com, HomeAway, Orbitz, Travelocity, e-bookers and the metasearch engine Trivago (Cajal, 2021).

Despite saturation, according to the Study Veepee-IESE (IESE, 2021) on the future of e-commerce in Spain, the sales of online travel will increase by 35% by 2025 (El Economista, 2021). In fact, in general lines, COVID-19 has accelerated the adoption of e-commerce by five years (Cajal, 2021). As for the profile of the online travel buyer, according to El Economista (2014), the study carried out by eDreams concludes these are middle- and upper-class urban women. Nonetheless, this profile is a dynamic one, as the incorporation of ICT (Information and Communication Technologies) into the tourism purchasing process offers two notable advantages: the reduction of uncertainty and, along with it, of the perceived risk in the purchase process (Duffus

Miranda & Briley, 2021). The reasons people make a reservation through OTAS, according to Statista, are three: price, speed-convenience, and product variety (STATISTA, 2019), but the digital tourist wants more: multichannel experience, 24-hour availability, immediate feedback, etc. The customer decides how and when they enjoy the service (Blas et al., 2014).

Since the creation of Different Travel in 2001 to the present day, the environment in which firms operate has changed considerably. The evolution of ICT has allowed profound changes in business models (Cano-Pita & García-Mendoza, 2018) and has facilitated companies internationalisation (Rodríguez, 2002), allowing them to develop their online commerce all around the planet without the need for direct foreign investment, as well as making it possible to hire human resources to work in places other than the physical location of the firm, thus allowing companies to make the best of their human capital. In the tourism sector, digitalisation has allowed consumers to search for information and select the option that best fits their requirements. Since COVID-19, online reservations of tourist products have increased, and forecasts, as we have mentioned, confirm their growth.

With the aim of getting information about the firm's economic-financial evolution in the last years (period 2010 to 2020), we have obtained information from the SABI database (Sistema de Análisis de Balances Ibéricos). We have selected absolute values, net turnover, the volume of assets, and the number of employees (Figures 20.1–20.3) as well as relative values (economic profitability ratios – ROA and ROE –, short-term – liquidity – and long-term – indebtedness – solvency ratios) (Figures 20.4 and 20.5).

The values of the different magnitudes analysed for Different Travel for the period 2019–2020 are conditioned by the worldwide health crisis caused by COVID-19, which had a significant impact on the companies operating in the tourism sector and also on the service firms engaged in the travel agency activity.

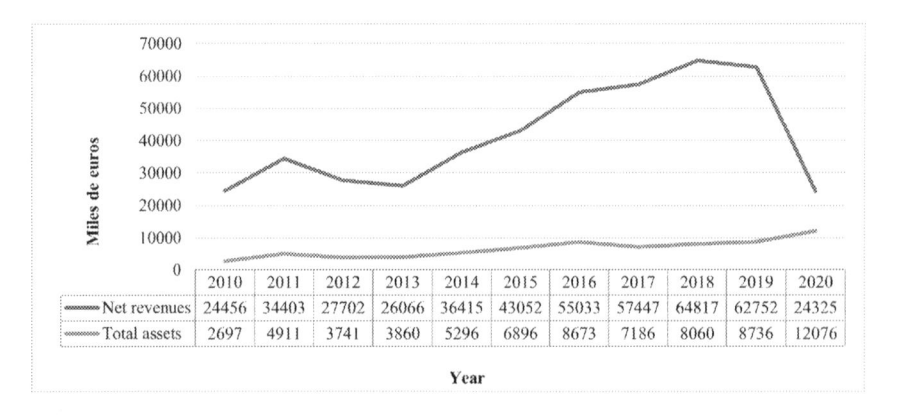

	2010	2011	2012	2013	2014	2015	2016	2017	2018	2019	2020
Net revenues	24456	34403	27702	26066	36415	43052	55033	57447	64817	62752	24325
Total assets	2697	4911	3741	3860	5296	6896	8673	7186	8060	8736	12076

Figure 20.1 Evolution of net revenues and total assets 2010–2020 (thousand euros).

Source: Prepared by authors based on SABI (2010–2020).

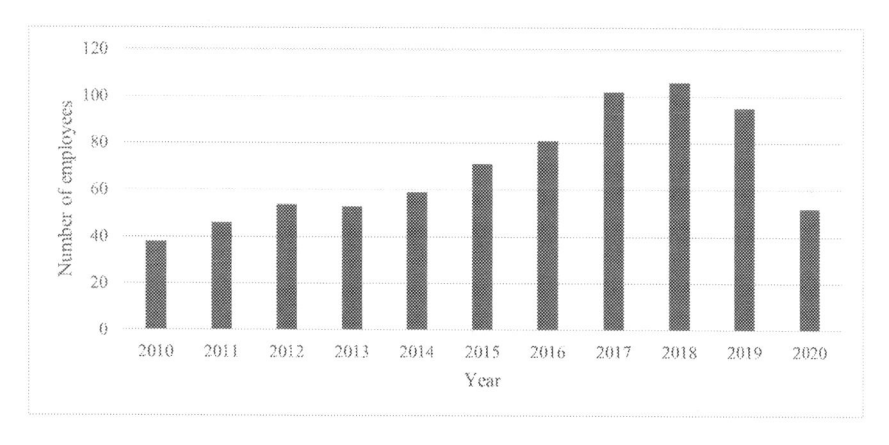

Figure 20.2 Number of employees (2010–2020).

Source: Prepared by authors based on SABI (2010–2020).

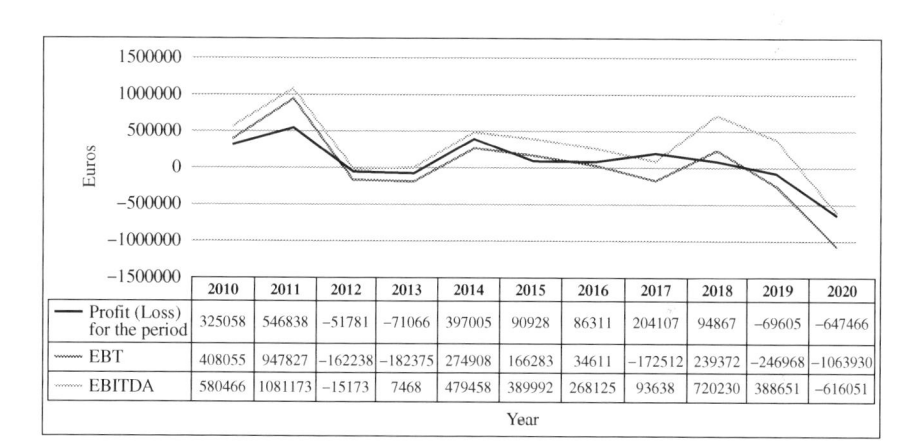

	2010	2011	2012	2013	2014	2015	2016	2017	2018	2019	2020
—— Profit (Loss) for the period	325058	546838	–51781	–71066	397005	90928	86311	204107	94867	–69605	–647466
······ EBT	408055	947827	–162238	–182375	274908	166283	34611	–172512	239372	–246968	–1063930
······ EBITDA	580466	1081173	–15173	7468	479458	389992	268125	93638	720230	388651	–616051

Year

Figure 20.3 Evolution of results, EBT and EBITDA (2010–2020) (Euros).

Source: Prepared by authors based on SABI (2010–2020).

In the case of Spain, the *Indicators of activity of the tourist sector* published by the National Institute of Statistics (INE) (www.ine.es) show generalised falls in different activity indicators (Figure 20.6), the annual variation of the Turnover Index for March 2020, experienced a decrease greater than 90%, which did not recover throughout the year (Figure 20.6).

Therefore, in the comments that follow, special mention will be made on the situation of the 2019–2020 fiscal year separately from the rest of the data series analysed in the document, in particular, in the performance indicators and ratios for whose calculation the net turnover is of relevance.

Firstly, in Figure 20.1, we show the evolution of both the net revenues obtained by the company and its assets during the period analysed both basic

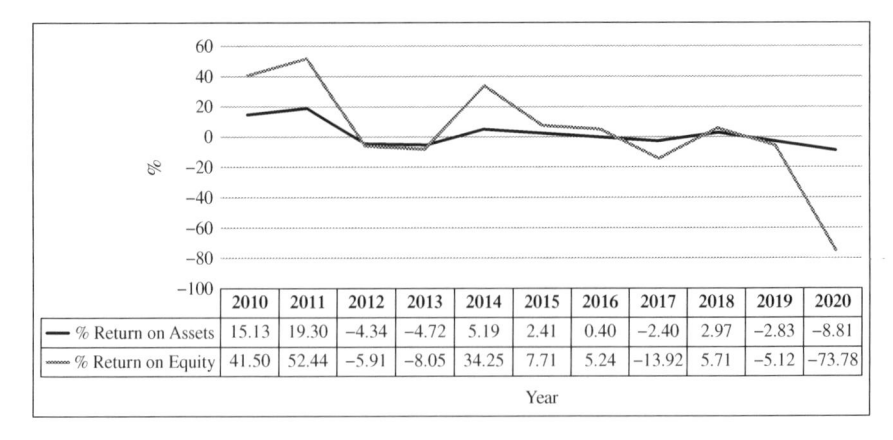

	2010	2011	2012	2013	2014	2015	2016	2017	2018	2019	2020
% Return on Assets	15.13	19.30	−4.34	−4.72	5.19	2.41	0.40	−2.40	2.97	−2.83	−8.81
% Return on Equity	41.50	52.44	−5.91	−8.05	34.25	7.71	5.24	−13.92	5.71	−5.12	−73.78

Figure 20.4 Evolution of ROA and ROE (2010–2020) (%).

Source: Prepared by authors based on SABI (2010–2020).

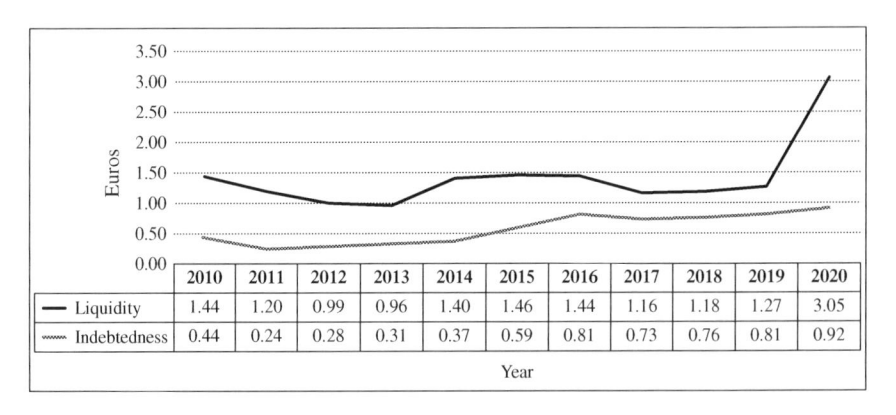

	2010	2011	2012	2013	2014	2015	2016	2017	2018	2019	2020
Liquidity	1.44	1.20	0.99	0.96	1.40	1.46	1.44	1.16	1.18	1.27	3.05
Indebtedness	0.44	0.24	0.28	0.31	0.37	0.59	0.81	0.73	0.76	0.81	0.92

Figure 20.5 Evolution of liquidity and indebtedness ratios (2010–2020) (euros).

Source: Prepared by authors based on SABI (2010–2020).

absolute values for the evaluation of the company over time. In both lines, a general upward trend can be seen for the period 2010–2019, although not without ups and downs in the case of turnover.

The company's revenues went up by 157% in the period from 2010 to 2019, with continuous growth, except for the period 2011–2013, when it registered a slight drop. However, if we analyse the entire period (2010–2020) represented in Figure 20.1, possibly due to the global health crisis caused by COVID-19, the level of turnover in 2020 is at a value similar to that reached in 2010.

The volume of assets of the company increased by 224% for the period 2010–2019, with a trend of continuous growth, except for periods 2011–2012 and 2016–2017, which experienced slight decreases.

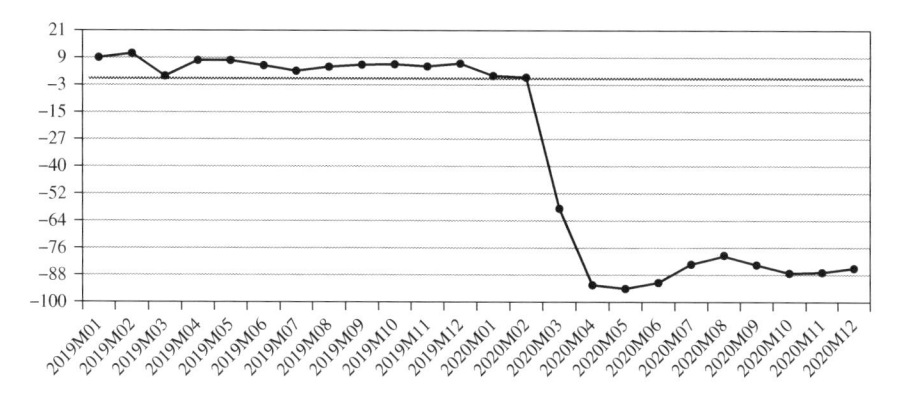

Figure 20.6 Annual variation in the Turnover Index of Travel Agencies and similar for the period 2019–2020.

Source: Prepared by authors based on the database www.ine.es.

When considering the analysed period 2010–2020 in its entirety, it seems that the evolution of the company's turnover has remained stagnant while the volume of its assets has gone up continuously. However, if the data relating to the 2020 financial year is removed from the analysis, it can be seen that both indicators (net turnover and volume of assets) have maintained an upward trend. This is due to the negative impact of the COVID-19 pandemic on the tourism sector. Anyway, throughout the period analysed, the percentage growth in the volume of assets has been higher than its turnover, an issue with an impact on the profit generated by the company.

Year after year, Different Travel has been increasing the number of workers, with 2018 showing the highest number of people collaborating in the company. However, as can be seen in Figure 20.2, there is a slight drop in the period 2012–2013 and a very sharp reduction of almost 50% in the period 2019–2020. So, from that, we infer that the pandemic crisis also affected the human resources of the company.

Throughout the period analysed, the results generated by the company: annual profit, EBITDA (Earnings before interests, taxes, depreciation and amortisation) and EBT (Earnings before taxes) presented in Figure 20.3 have followed an irregular and unstable trajectory: periods of significant growth in results (2010–2011, 2013–2014 and 2017–2018) have been followed by periods in which the trend is reversed, showing sharp declines (2011–2012 and 2018–2019) so that the levels of results achieved at the beginning of these periods disappear at the end of them. In 2019–2020, negative values are observed in all the result indicators analysed, even higher than the results achieved in 2012, when all these indicators also showed negative values.

Considering each result independently, the greatest stability is shown by the EBITDA generated, which is a good indicator of the management at Different Travel. The exception is found in periods 2012 and 2020, in which the gross operating profit was negative, reflecting a complicated financial situation that, at least with the available data, the company overcame in the first period.

With regard to EBT, we find several years (2012, 2013, 2017, 2019, and 2020) in which losses have been generated so that both the weight of amortisations and that of the interest on the company's debt have significantly reduced the gross operating results obtained in those years that, although not being very high, have ended up reversing their sign.

Logically, the third indicator shown in Figure 20.3, the Yearly Results, shows the management problems already reflected in EBITDA and EBT in the years; these two indicators already showed negative values. The exception is found in 2017, when the company achieves a notable profit despite starting from a negative EBT, probably derived from some tax benefit.

Related to what was discussed in Figure 20.3, the profitability ratios ROE (Return on Equity) and ROA (Return on Assets) achieved by the company reflect a high level of instability, as do its results figures, showing particularly worrying values in both indicators in 2012, 2013, 2017, 2019 and 2020—this last fiscal year, with an exceptionally inadequate value of the ROE (Figure 20.4).

Regarding the solvency of the company, both short-term (liquidity) and long-term (indebtedness) indicators have been considered. The liquidity index has generally experienced a positive trend in the period under analysis. The decreases in the level below one have not been relevant. A particular growth in liquidity was noted in 2020 (Figure 20.5), probably influenced by the increase in accounts receivable for the year and the special financial situation as a result of the COVID pandemic.

In contrast, the debt ratio has undergone a worrying increase; especially from 2016 onwards, the growth of the ratio has been continuous (with notable effects on the results generated, as shown in Figure 20.3) and almost reached 1 in 2020 (Figure 20.5).

Development: Corporate entrepreneurship and innovation actions

Different Travel is a very dynamic company that, since its inception, has been immersed in innovation processes. Also noteworthy are the actions carried out by the company that confirm its commitment to its employees. In this sense, Ricardo Buil affirms his belief in a flat structure, almost without hierarchy, with a great effort to motivate the staff working for the company, including programmes to improve food, sports, yoga, or even table football tournaments. The work environment creates an ideal business culture to carry out intrapreneurship actions.

Moreover, Different Travel is a highly innovative company with a long tradition of developing original technologies and operating models. Two of the main projects carried out by the company have been the development of an Integrated Multisectoral Management System for the Development of Business Interoperability in the Provision of Services and Resources for Online Transport and Accommodation (GESINTRAV) and an Intelligent Administrative Process Operator Assistance System (OASIS).

In the case of GESTINTRAV, the main trigger for the project arises from the need to interconnect tourism companies from different fields at a time, 2007, when the sector was very dynamic, and there was a significant growth in the demand for travel through the internet by users.

With regard to the OASIS project, the main external driver was the new technological opportunities in the market that, together with an increasingly dynamic sector, showed the need to develop a more efficient and personalised customer service system.

The main internal supports for entrepreneurship were: the existence of alliances and relationships with other companies, as well as relationships with social agents and customers, among others; the availability of human, technological and financial resources; support based on trust in employees to identify opportunities; providing procedures for managing new ideas; managerial support; facilitating the availability of time to search for and reflect on new ideas; having organisational goals on intrapreneurship; and having norms in the organisation on patterns of behaviour desirable for intrapreneurship.

One reason that led the company to develop GESTINTRAV was to solve the difficulties related to the variety of technologies used by different suppliers. In an attempt to solve the problem, the goal was to create a platform that would unify all these technologies and could show the end customer the information received from hundreds of suppliers clearly to be able to choose the best option. Making a single system capable of integrating all this required a lot of analysis and trial-and-error work that delayed the completion of the project by several months.

In the case of OASIS, its development was carried out due to the difficulties related to the different systems with which the assistant has to interact. The greatest complexity comes from the need to provide the system with flexibility, avoiding that it becomes an assistant with linear execution processes and of much less usefulness than if a dynamic process allows one process to start another and open up parallel actions.

GESINTRAV was a before and after in the development of the company. The system developed because of this project made available to the client a wide range of online accommodation and other travel-related services so reservations increased exponentially in a few months. This combination of technology and personal customer service made Centraldeservas.com position itself as one of the largest Spanish online agencies, and the company began to compete in the market with other major portals such as Booking, Destinia or Logitravel.

As for OASIS, the main achievement has been the efficiency and speed of response to customers, automating a large number of manual processes. The objective of the project has been achieved, which was to develop a digital assistance system for the telephone operator aimed at the automated management of administrative processes, which would guarantee the best provision of services, both from the point of view of the client and the company. The design paradigm of operator assistance software has been changed.

Epilogue

This work has reflected the commitment to intrapreneurship of Different Travel SLU, a travel agency created in 2001 in Ainsa (Huesca, Spain), whose main business activity is developed on the internet, through www.centraldereservas.com, http://blog.centraldereservas.com/, and other associated portals. Currently, centraldereservas.com is one of the leading online accommodation booking portals, with more than 750,000 references worldwide and has a team of almost 100 people distributed in different locations.

The actions carried out show the customer orientation of the company, seeking, on the one hand, a greater effectiveness in travel searches for the users that allows them to compete with the largest OTAS and, on the other hand, to make it easier for the telephone operator in carrying out their work that results in a better customer service. The actions show an interest in listening to both the customer and the employee as a result of valuing service satisfaction as a key and differentiating element.

It can also be inferred from this intrapreneurship action that the development of computer management software based on the experience of the company's staff allows the generation of solutions to specific problems that are difficult to address with standard packages. In the case of an OTA, this IT approach is an essential part as there is no personal interaction with the potential client, so the greater or lesser customer satisfaction necessarily depends on a friendly and functional interface.

References

Blas, S. S., Mafe, C. R., Pérez, I. P., & Ortega, B. H. (2014). Influencia de la cultura en el comportamiento de compra online de productos turísticos. El caso de España y México. *INNOVAR. Revista de Ciencias Administrativas y Sociales*, *24*, 153–163. Available at: http://www.redalyc.org/articulo.oa?id=81832222011

Cajal, M. (2021). OTAs: ¿Qué son y cómo funcionan las agencias de viajes online? (Ejemplos). In: *marketing turístico: Estrategias de marketing digital*. Available at: https://www.mabelcajal.com/2021/07/otas-agencias-viajes-online.html/

Canalís, X. (2019). Ranking de OTA y metabuscadores más usados por los hoteles. Hosteltur. Available at: https://www.hosteltur.com/133109_ranking-de-otas-y-metabuscadores-mas-usados-por-los-hoteles-de-cataluna.html.

Cano-Pita, G. E., & García-Mendoza, M. J. (2018). Las TICs en las empresas: Evolución de la tecnología y cambio estructural en las organizaciones. *Dominio de las Ciencias*, *4*(1), 499–510.

Comunicaweb (2012). Estudio Sectorial Agencias de Viajes. Madrid [etc]: Comunicaweb. Available at: https://comunica-web.com/pdf/Estudio_sectorial_agencias_de_viajes.pdf

Duffus Miranda, D., & Briley, D. (2021). Digital tourist: Variables that define your buying behavior. *Investigaciones Turísticas*, (21), 1–21.

El Economista (2014, 20 de agosto). Éste es el perfil de los comprador@s de viajes on line. *Noticias de elEconomista*. Available at: https://www.eleconomista.es/turismo-viajes/noticias/6020592/08/14/Este-es-el-perfil-de-los-compradors-on-line.html

El Economista (2021, 29 de diciembre). La venta de viajes a través de Internet crecerá un 35%. *Noticias de elEconomista*. Available at: https://www.eleconomista.es/transportes/noticias/11538520/12/21/La-venta-de-viajes-a-traves-de-Internet-crecera-un-35.html

IESE (2021). I Estudio Veepee IESE sobre el futuro del ecommerce en España. Madrid [etc]: IESE Business School. Available at: https://www.retaildigital.es/wp-content/uploads/2022/01/I-Estudio-Veepee-IESE-ecommerce-descargable.pdf

Rodríguez, A. R. (2002). La internacionalización de las empresas turísticas. *Economistas*, *20*(92), 31–45.

SABI Base de datos (2010–2020). Sistema de Análisis de Balances Ibéricos. Available at: https://sabi.bvdinfo.com/version-20221010/home.serv?product=SabiNeo&

STATISTA (2019). Principales razones para realizar compras a través de agencias de viajes online en España según una encuesta de 2019. Available at: https://es.statista.com/estadisticas/495315/motivos-para-hacer-reservas-a-traves-de-agencias-de-viajes-online-en-espana/

Zavarce, D. (2022). ¿Cuáles son las principales agencias de viaje online? *Agencias de Viaje Online, Canales, OTAs*. Available at: https://www.bebetterhotels.com/cuales-son-las-principales-agencias-de-viajes-online/

Case 21 Corporate entrepreneurship within a DMO

The case of Visit Greenland

Elizabeth Cooper

Introduction

Visit Greenland is Greenland's national DMO (Destination Management/ Marketing Organisation). It is funded by Greenland's Home Rule government, although it has the freedom to develop and market tourism in Greenland relatively independently and usually according to priorities set by the organisation's management. Visit Greenland is a small DMO, with just 11 permanent employees, nine in the office in Nuuk, Greenland, and two working remotely from Copenhagen, Denmark. The yearly budget allocated for the organisation is relatively stable but is nevertheless subject to the discretion of the government, in whose eyes the importance of tourism can fluctuate.

Organisational environment, and the evolution of tourism in Greenland

Tourism is relatively undeveloped in Greenland and when Visit Greenland was founded in 1992, the initial aim of the organisation was to develop a viable tourism industry in the nation. In these early years, he company even sold tourism products. Since 1997, however, Visit Greenland has been a non-commercial marketing and development agency. Visit Greenland is a relatively flat, project-based organisation, with a CEO, a middle management team of three, and seven other employees.

Tourism to Greenland is somewhat in its infancy, with pre-COVID tourist arrivals peaking at around 100,000 per year. The vast majority of tourists visit during the summer months (late June to early September), and particular destinations attract the bulk of tourists, while others remain relatively unvisited. Tourists to Greenland come primarily from wealthy, Western countries, with the top source markets being Denmark, Germany, France, the UK, the USA and Canada. Greenland's main competitors are generally considered other polar destinations which promise similarly remote and 'once in a lifetime' experiences, such as Iceland, Norway, Svalbard, Lapland and Antarctica.

Numerous contextual features of Greenland complicate the nation's tourism development, including its rugged landscape and harsh and unpredictable weather. The majority of Greenland's towns and settlements are not connected by road, meaning it is necessary to fly or sail between destinations,

DOI: 10.4324/9781003454465-22

which naturally adds time and expense onto any tourist itinerary. Greenland has a population of just 56,000 people dispersed over a landmass of over two million square kilometres, meaning that getting an education usually requires substantial mobility and financial investment, and human resources are, therefore, hard to come by.

On a political and social level, Greenland is decidedly post-colonial, as its economy still relies on a substantial annual block grant from its former coloniser, Denmark, and its external political affairs are still controlled by Denmark. Economic inequality and various social issues remain a major problem in some parts of the nation.

The COVID-19 pandemic had a dramatic effect on Greenland's tourism industry, as tourist arrivals fell by 85% in 2020. Greenland's tourism industry relies almost entirely on international arrivals, but since the nation also has very limited healthcare infrastructure, a large elderly population, and many remote communities, it was necessary to instigate strict border restrictions to protect the local community until most residents were vaccinated. Although efforts were made to attract domestic tourists during the COVID-19 pandemic, this is not a realistic option long-term, as economic inequality means that many local Greenlanders simply cannot afford to holiday in their own country.

After a brief explanation of the methods used, this chapter will analyse corporate entrepreneurship (CE) activities within Visit Greenland, according to an interview with Hjörtur Smárason, former CEO. The analysis is structured according to the three general levels on which Visit Greenland operates: the market, the industry and within the organisation itself. These levels of operation were identified as prominent themes during data analysis. The impact of the COVID-19 pandemic on CE activities in Visit Greenland will also be given attention since it has had consequences for the organisation on all three levels.

Methods

This case study is built around one interview with Hjörtur Smárason, the CEO of Visit Greenland from 1st April 2021 until 31st March 2022. The interview was conducted in January 2022, when Smárason was still CEO. The interview lasted 60 minutes and was audio recorded, transcribed and subsequently analysed to pick out themes. It should be emphasised that the perspectives discussed here are those of a single person and do not necessarily reflect the opinions of all employees at Visit Greenland. Nor do they necessarily reflect the opinions of Visit Greenland's current upper management, as each CEO brings their own priorities to the role.

Visit Greenland's role in relation to corporate entrepreneurship

Smárason spoke of Visit Greenland's role in CE both internally within the organisation and externally. Some existing literature conceptualises CE in a similar way, identifying internal (referring to the organisation) and external (referring to the organisation's operating environment) dimensions of the concept (Kwinje et al., 2020; Mamabolo & Ravjee, 2019). In Smárason's interview, however, he extended this conceptualisation to divide the external aspect into the market—i.e., (potential) tourists to Greenland—and the industry—i.e., the businesses and stakeholders that make up Greenland's tourism industry. The following section will be structured according to the three levels identified, to highlight the various challenges and opportunities associated with fostering CE as a national DMO.

Corporate entrepreneurship on the external level: The market

Smárason is clear about what he sees as the main purpose of Visit Greenland: "We are a marketing organisation. Our role is to sell Greenland, build up the brand of Greenland and market Greenland as a tourism destination" (Interview with Hjörtur Smárason). This comment feeds into the well-established debate on the role of a DMO: should a DMO focus on destination *marketing* or destination *management* (Ritchie & Crouch, 2003)? It seems that Smárason prioritises the former, although he does not see destination management as irrelevant. Rather, he sees it as an integral part of achieving successful marketing:

> We can do fantastic work in marketing and we could have one million tourists here next year. But if you would get one million people next year, we would have nine hundred and ninety thousand of them with a horrible experience because we wouldn't be ready to receive them and give them the experience we are selling.
>
> (Interview with Hjörtur Smárason)

It would appear that, for Smárason, the role of destination management from a DMO's perspective is primarily to lend authenticity to the marketing message and to enable the destination to follow through on this message. Smárason also points out that successful destination management is instrumental in ensuring that potential tourists actually choose Greenland, even after the marketing efforts have had their desired effect:

> If we focus on sustainability and space and nature and the Arctic, and it's Norway that delivers, then we are just marketing Norway, even though we put Greenland under it. Because people will very soon learn that, oh yes, this is a fantastic image that I'm seeing. This is something I really want to experience. And what I hear when I go on social media is that Norway's delivering it, and not Greenland.
>
> (Interview with Hjörtur Smárason)

Here, Smárason acknowledges that today, tourists receive marketing information not just from DMOs and tourism businesses but also from user-generated content and through word of mouth. From his perspective, this makes delivering on Greenland's marketing promise even more crucial through destination management.

In relation to CE Smárason sees the concept as essential to delivering on Greenland's brand promise: "It's not enough just to focus on the marketing and build that brand value. We really need to focus on how we can deliver that brand value, and that is where CE is extremely important" (Interview with Hjörtur Smárason). However, he simultaneously sees CE as difficult to conceptualise in the case of a DMO. As he explains, "We do not do product development because we don't sell any products. We sell the destination, and then we need to activate all the local operators and companies to do the product development and deliver on the promise that we are selling" (ibid.). When CE or innovation can no longer be understood in the relatively concrete context of product development, the question is raised of how the term is and should be manifested. If the bulk of the innovation in Greenland's tourism industry happens in businesses outside of Visit Greenland, then what is the role of Visit Greenland in relation to CE? A similar conundrum has been identified in the literature in the case of state-owned enterprises in China. Liu et al. (2002) argue that organisations owned by the state show a lower level of CE than privately owned organisations. However, the authors do single out state-owned enterprises in the services sector as demonstrating more CE than other types of public organisations (Liu et al., 2002). This is promising for Visit Greenland, which, although state-owned, has a service function and experiences a fair amount of management freedom.

Smárason continues: "This leaves us with the reality that maybe our biggest task is to support the industry in CE—in how they can develop themselves so that they can actually deliver on that [marketing] promise" (ibid.).

Corporate entrepreneurship on the external level: The industry

The previous section established that according to Visit Greenland's former CEO, Hjörtur Smárason, CE is essential to delivering Greenland's marketing promise. However, Smárason simultaneously points out that, although it is the publicly funded national DMO which is primarily responsible for delivering that message, private tourism operators are primarily responsible for realising that message in the form of delivering experiences to tourists. In this way, Smárason frames Visit Greenland as a supporting role for the industry, at least in terms of fostering CE. He describes Visit Greenland as "a small organisation with a big responsibility when it comes to CE" (Interview with Hjörtur Smárason).

Referring specifically to some of the contextual barriers to the development of Greenland's tourism industry, Smárason explains that the majority of Greenland's tourism operators are micro-sized enterprises with less than ten employees and argues that it is, therefore, unrealistic to expect them to find the resources required to undergo dramatic innovation processes alongside their everyday operations. Other authors have emphasised the importance of contextual factors for CE actions, mentioning available opportunities (Kakapour et al., 2016), and cultural factors (Lau et al., 2010). As a result of the small size of most of Greenland's tourism operators, Smárason sees it as Visit Greenland's role to enable CE processes: "When I think of our role as Visit Greenland, it is primarily inspiration ... Our biggest task is creating the right mindset. It's a mindset where you have that curiosity and that desire to be the best in a certain field" (Interview with Hjörtur Smárason). According to Smárason, this mindset is fostered partly by providing industry actors with tools:

> Our role for CE is primarily identifying these trends, identifying the opportunities, gathering data that the companies can use and then providing the inspiration and the tools for them to develop and innovate in a way that makes sense.
>
> (Interview with Hjörtur Smárason)

However, Smárason also acknowledges that, just as the majority of CE processes themselves occur outside the operations of Visit Greenland, they also primarily lie outside of Visit Greenland's control and are difficult to track and measure. He gives season expansion as an example of one of Visit Greenland's primary CE initiatives, which "is a challenge because of our limited control over it, but still one of our priority objectives ... Of course, you can't really measure our impact on it, but you can measure the development in the industry" (Interview with Hjörtur Smárason).

In the previous discussion about CE and the market, it was suggested that the industry has a responsibility towards Visit Greenland to deliver on the marketing message promised to tourists. When analysing Visit Greenland's role in CE on the industry level, it is clear that Smárason also perceives Visit Greenland to be responsible to the industry for enabling CE processes to occur within its businesses. For Smárason, Visit Greenland's main role on the industry level is to inspire and enable entrepreneurial and innovative initiatives in other organisations.

Smárason also spoke in detail about *how* Visit Greenland enables this process of innovation within the local tourism industry. He mentions the nation-branding process that Visit Greenland was undertaking at the time of the interview: "The key objective of that process is to get a consensus on some of our strengths and competitive advantages. Because if we do not agree on that, we start innovating in all sorts of different directions and focusing on different strengths, and it becomes diluted, and much less powerful" (Interview with Hjörtur Smárason). Solidarity in the direction and objectives of innovation can only be achieved, according to Smárason, through close collaboration and partnerships with the industry:

> This is not something that we decide on our own and then communicate to everyone else: our strengths and our competitive advantage

must be things that we identify with, not as an organisation, but as the entire destination, the entire country. And this can only be achieved through good collaboration. And that collaboration is executed through workshops and stakeholder involvement.

(Interview with Hjörtur Smárason)

Here, Smárason highlights the importance of partnerships with the industry to CE. This is perhaps a particular challenge in the context of Greenland because of the lack of infrastructure, and human and financial resources. Collaboration is a particular priority for Visit Greenland in terms of CE. However, declaring partnerships a priority does not mean that the organisation has overcome these challenges.

Corporate entrepreneurship on the internal level: The organisation

CE on the industry and market levels can of course not be achieved without attention being paid to CE within the organisation of Visit Greenland itself. Smárason sees "an innovative mindset within the corporation" as essential to support CE within the industry in general:

We need to be agile ourselves. We need to be experimental in what we're doing, in terms of the tools that we are using and the marketing methods that we're using … And we need to have the mindset of being willing to learn, to unlearn some of our old knowledge and to make mistakes.

(Interview with Hjörtur Smárason)

Although the small size of Visit Greenland as an organisation is often considered a hindrance in terms of its capabilities, Smárason sees it as an advantage when it comes to CE: "We're just a small team. We're lean, we're flexible, and there's good communication between all levels. So, in that sense, we have the agility of a small start-up company, with the security of funding, which is a luxury to some extent" (Interview with Hjörtur Smárason). In this way, it can be argued that there are both advantages and disadvantages to the organisational structure of Visit Greenland; while it lacks the financial and human resources that might enable more innovation, its "lean" structure can also allow for more freedom regarding potential CE actions.

Figure 21.1 Is an attempt to illustrate Visit Greenland's CE role as described by Smárason. The organisation's responsibilities, or actions, can be framed on three levels, and it uses CE differently in each capacity to different ends. However, each level of innovation feeds eventually into the main reason for innovating, which is to secure Greenland's share of the tourism market.

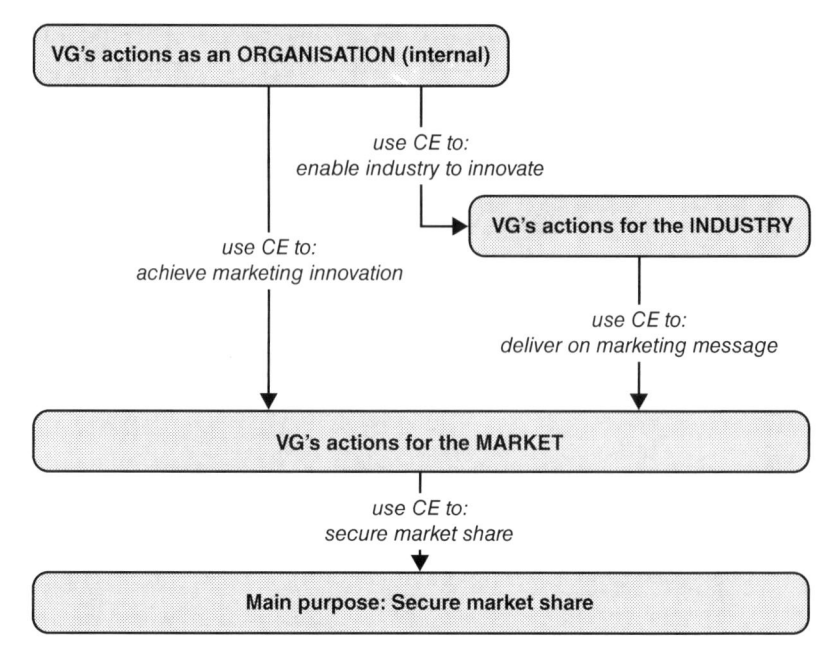

Figure 21.1 Visit Greenland's role in relation to CE.

Source: Prepared by author.

The impact of COVID-19 on corporate entrepreneurship in Visit Greenland

When asked about how the COVID-19 pandemic has impacted the CE actions and capabilities of Visit Greenland, Smárason had both positive and negative responses. On the market level, he argues that the pandemic has accelerated some trends, some of which can be beneficial, and some of which present challenges to the innovation of the sector. While he argues that post-pandemic tourists are seeking more remote and wilderness destinations (rendering Greenland more attractive), he also points out that the pandemic has potentially escalated the "flight shaming" trend: "[Before COVID], if you were choosing to fly, you were polluting the atmosphere. And now, on top of that, you are creating a disease risk when you're flying to a different destination" (Interview with Hjörtur Smárason). Smárason points out that this is an obstacle for tourism to Greenland in particular since tourists have no other option but to arrive by plane or cruise ship. Despite this, Smárason sees this challenge as an opportunity to innovate further, suggesting that Visit Greenland must now be creative with its B2C messaging in order to counter this trend.

On the industry level, Smárason argues that collaboration between Visit Greenland and other local tourism stakeholders has improved during the pandemic "because there's been a lot of communication and people know each other much better and what challenges they're facing" (Interview with Hjörtur

Smárason). He also mentions those tourism entrepreneurs who have continued operating during the pandemic have been forced to be innovative because they have had to adapt their products to the domestic market, "and all of that is going to benefit them when the tourists from abroad come again - they will have better products, they will have better price structures, and they will have learned a lot about how they can adapt and be more agile in their operations" (ibid.). Existing literature has identified CE as a survival technique for small and micro-sized tourism enterprises (SMTEs) in other contexts. Kwinje et al. (2020) argue that for SMTEs, CE is a form of resilience during harsh economic conditions. However, they also point out that it is particularly difficult for SMTEs to engage in CE because of their limited resources and expertise and their inability to influence external threats (Kwinje et al., 2020).

Finally, Smárason notes some impacts of the COVID-19 pandemic on CE on the organisational level: "The processes that we designed, we haven't really been able to execute because of COVID. So we are redesigning those processes so that we can do them digitally instead of in person" (Interview with Hjörtur Smárason). Visit Greenland's industry webinar series, which has continued even after the pandemic is over, is an example of a CE action provoked by the pandemic, but which has actually contributed towards improvement of a more permanent issue within Greenland's tourism industry, namely the difficulty of collaboration within an industry which has numerous contextual issues which seem to work against this.

Epilogue

It has been difficult to identify and discuss in detail concrete CE actions for the case of Visit Greenland, because of the complex roles and responsibilities of a DMO brought to light by this analysis. Since a DMO does not directly engage in any product development, its CE actions are rather abstract, and, as Smárason points out, many of them involve supporting other organisations to engage in CE actions. This potentially results in Visit Greenland and other DMOs feeling a lack of control over CE in their national tourism industry. Smárason does mention season expansion as an example of a relatively concrete CE action, but he admits that it is hard to measure Visit Greenland's specific impact on progress towards this goal.

This case study has presented lessons on theoretical, practical and social levels. On a theoretical level, a conceptual model was proposed (Figure 21.1) to outline the three main levels on which Visit Greenland employs CE. According to Smárason, Visit Greenland's innovation efforts are all channelled towards the same ultimate goal, which is to secure Greenland's market share by delivering on the experiences promised by marketing messages.

An important practical learning extracted from this case study relates to how a DMO might execute CE in practice. Visit Greenland's main responsibility in terms of CE in the industry is to support the businesses that make up Greenland's tourism industry in engaging in CE actions so they can deliver on marketing messages.

A social learning revealed by the analysis of this case surrounds context. Contextual issues of Greenland have been mentioned that hinder both CE within the micro-sized enterprises that constitute the nation's tourism industry and collaboration between Visit Greenland and these enterprises. Therefore, it appears that contextual issues relating to Greenland's environment, society, economy and politics are equally important actors in attempts to foster CE in Greenland's tourism.

The impact of the COVID-19 pandemic on CE within Visit Greenland was also discussed and was argued to have had both positive and negative effects. Indeed, Smárason noted that this crisis has even inspired innovations that have contributed to solving some long-term issues related to CE (such as Visit Greenland's difficulties collaborating with the industry).

Again, this chapter is not necessarily reflective of the perspectives of all current employees in Visit Greenland, but it still raises important issues surrounding CE both within a DMO and within a destination in which contextual constraints often have the final say. The COVID-19 pandemic has had a significant impact on CE actions and opportunities in Greenland's tourism industry, but this impact has perhaps not been entirely negative. This chapter has shown that the application of CE within a DMO is open to interpretation. Nevertheless, a model is presented here (Figure 21.1), in which CE is employed by a DMO in three main ways, this is the interpretation of one CEO of one DMO and is inevitably influenced by his own perspectives, his personal corporate strategies, and the context in which his organisation operates. It could be interesting to see further reflection on how CE is applied in other DMOs and to examine to what extent this model fits similar organisations in other destinations.

References

Kakapour, S., Morgan, T., Parsinejad, S., & Wieland, A. (2016). Antecedents of corporate entrepreneurship in Iran: The role of strategic orientation and opportunity recognition. *Journal of Small Business & Entrepreneurship*, 28(3), 251–266.

Kwinje, C., Mwando-Gukushu, M., & Zengeni, N. (2020). Corporate entrepreneurship strategy and the survival of small to medium tourism enterprises in Zimbabwe. *African Journal of Hospitality, Tourism, and Leisure*, 9(4), 732–746.

Lau, T., Chan, K. F., Tai, S. H., & Ng, D. K. (2010). Corporate entrepreneurship of IJVs in China. *Management Research Review*.

Liu, S. S., Luo, X., & Shi, Y. Z. (2002). Integrating customer orientation, corporate entrepreneurship, and learning orientation in organizations-in-transition: An empirical study. *International Journal of Research in Marketing*, 19(4), 367–382.

Mamabolo, M. A., & Ravjee, B. (2019). The impact of corporate entrepreneurship on service innovation: A case of a South African banking institution. *The Southern African Journal of Entrepreneurship and Small Business Management*, 11(1), 1–12.

Ritchie, J. R. B., & Crouch, G. I. (2003). *The competitive destination: A sustainable tourism perspective*. Wallingford: CABI Publishing.

Case 22 Innovative strategies applied in a mature destination before, during and after COVID-19

The case of *Turismo de Gran Canaria*

Antonia M. García-Cabrera,
M. Gracia García-Soto,
Pablo Llinares-de-Bethencourt,
and M. Carmen Cruz-Lecat

Introduction

The organisation: Turismo de Gran Canaria (Tourist board of Gran Canaria)

Tourism represents the fastest-growing activity sector in the economy (Vrontis et al., 2022), proving to be a solid option for wealth generation and progress towards achieving the goals of Agenda 2030, established by the United Nations in 2015 (Ferrer-Roca, Guia & Blasco, 2022). Thus, there is a growing competitive rivalry between the various tourist destinations, which compete on a global scale to attract travellers. To face this competition, destinations formulate and implement innovative strategies to increase their "attractiveness". On the island of Gran Canaria, the public body responsible for formulating and implementing these innovative strategies is the *Tourist Board of Gran Canaria*.

The Tourist Board of Gran Canaria was founded in 1975 by the Cabildo de Gran Canaria (Gran Canaria Insular Council) under the name "Patronato de Turismo de Gran Canaria"[1]. The mission of this public organisation is to protect the island's tourism interests, and it plans and develops policies in accordance with market changes (Turismo de Gran Canaria, 2022). Although, initially, the scope of its activity was provincial (including the islands of Gran Canaria, Fuerteventura and Lanzarote), in 1985, as a consequence of the rearrangement of control over tourism that took place after the ratification of the 1978 Constitution and the confirmation of the status of Spain's autonomous regions (Llinares de Béthencourt et al., 2019), it became insular.

The decision to create the Tourist Board of Gran Canaria was marked by the political and social conviction that the Canary Islands must not be left out of the decisions being made regarding tourism in Spain (Llinares

DOI: 10.4324/9781003454465-23

de Béthencourt et al., 2019). Once founded, this conviction led to the convergence around this organisation of an array of professionals, technicians and politicians who voluntarily contributed their knowledge and experience through their participation in work commissions (e.g., advertising, transportation, leisure diversification, etc.). The Tourist Board of Gran Canaria thus became a key entity in decision-making regarding the sector on the islands and a hub for the generation and accumulation of valuable knowledge on tourism management (Llinares de Béthencourt et al., 2019).

The Tourist Board of Gran Canaria has been characterised since its inception by its ability to adapt to the changes and challenges—sometimes unforeseen and complex—that the sector often faces (Llinares de Béthencourt et al., 2019) such as the economic recession associated with the 1973 oil crisis, the economic recession of 2008, the health crisis caused by COVID-19, etc., which have conditioned the growth of tourism on the islands. Adaptability and the ability to face challenges are part of the essence of this organisation; they are a sign of identity that reflects its past and present performances and guides its future actions.

The Tourist Board of Gran Canaria formulates and implements actions to manage and administrate the sector and ensure the island's positive image is present in the source markets. This task is carried out through three lines of work: (1) the promotion of Gran Canaria abroad, aimed at a multitude of markets with activities typical of a destination marketing organisation; (2) the constant improvement of the destination through the development of products and services and the implementation of tourism improvement projects; and (3) the public management of the insular tourism system, handling the processing of administrative records related to tourism establishments, which makes it possible to monitor the situation and learn about the changes brought about through the activity of the destination itself. All these lines of action are carried out by the Tourist Board of Gran Canaria in close collaboration with the island's business sector and with the insular, regional and national administrations, always with the understanding that public-private collaboration represents a significant way to guarantee the excellence of the destination and maintain the international positioning of Gran Canaria.

Regarding the successful work of the Tourist Board of Gran Canaria, the human team of highly qualified, motivated, proactive and effectively organised professionals that this organisation has been comprised of throughout its various stages has played an essential role (Llinares de Béthencourt et al., 2019). Currently, the organisation has a professionalised organisational structure in accordance with the challenges faced by a mature destination.

The environment in which the tourist board of Gran Canaria operates

In characterising the environment in which the Tourist Board of Gran Canaria operates, it is worth highlighting various factors of special interest as they affect the development of tourist destinations: international demand for tourism, new trends in tourism management, the existence of rival destinations, and the uniqueness of Gran Canaria itself. Therefore, these factors must be considered when designing the innovative strategies deployed by this organisation to fulfil its mission.

The international demand for tourism has been highly conditioned throughout history by global economic ups and downs—falling to record lows in 2020 as a direct result of the COVID-19 pandemic. This collapse in activity was due to the implementation of border closures and confinement periods, as well as the loss of *tourist confidence* due to fear of contagion (García-Cabrera et al., 2021). Currently (2023), however, forecasts are positive. In terms of international tourists, the World Tourism Organization says in the first quarter of 2023, the volume of tourists will reach 80% of pre-pandemic levels—a percentage that rises to 90% for Europe (UNWTO, 2023a). Despite this favourable forecast, according to estimates by the UNWTO Group of Experts, international tourism will not recover to the levels seen in 2019 (prior to the pandemic) until 2024 or later (UNWTO, 2023a). This is because new challenges currently affecting the global economy will act as obstacles.

As the UNWTO (2023b) reminds us, geopolitical tensions generate uncertainty and high inflation, and oil prices increase transport and accommodation costs. This may encourage tourists to focus more on nearby destinations and "value for money" in their choices.

Referring to the new trends in tourism management is aimed at responding to the need for a "rethink" in order to make the sector more sustainable, resilient and inclusive (UNWTO, 2023b), in line with the *Sustainable Development Goals* set out in the United Nation's *Agenda 2030* (UNWTO, 2023c, 2023d). With these objectives in mind, the UNWTO is setting out plans for the future of the sector to revolve around *education, innovation* and *sustainability* (e.g., employment of qualified workers; establishment of a degree in International Sustainable Tourism; reducing waste and increasing circularity in the sector; establishment of a global standard for measuring the sustainability of tourism, etc. (UNWTO, 2023b).

As for competitors, the main rival destinations for Gran Canaria are the islands of Fuerteventura, Lanzarote and Tenerife within the Canary archipelago itself; Benidorm, Costa del Sol and Mallorca in Spain more widely; and, internationally, Antalya, Hurgada and Santorini (Turismo de Gran Canaria, 2023b). Of these, the most relevant for Gran Canaria are Tenerife, the Balearic Islands and Antalya, which is why these three destinations have been chosen for a comparative analysis. As seen in Figure 22.1, although the global satisfaction of the tourist who visits Gran Canaria exceeds that registered in Tenerife, the main competitor within the archipelago, the index shows a score that is slightly lower than those achieved by the Balearic Islands and Antalya. In the longer term, it is worth being alert to the possible emergence of new rival destinations as a result of the efforts of the UNWTO and the governments of developing countries to turn tourism into the axis

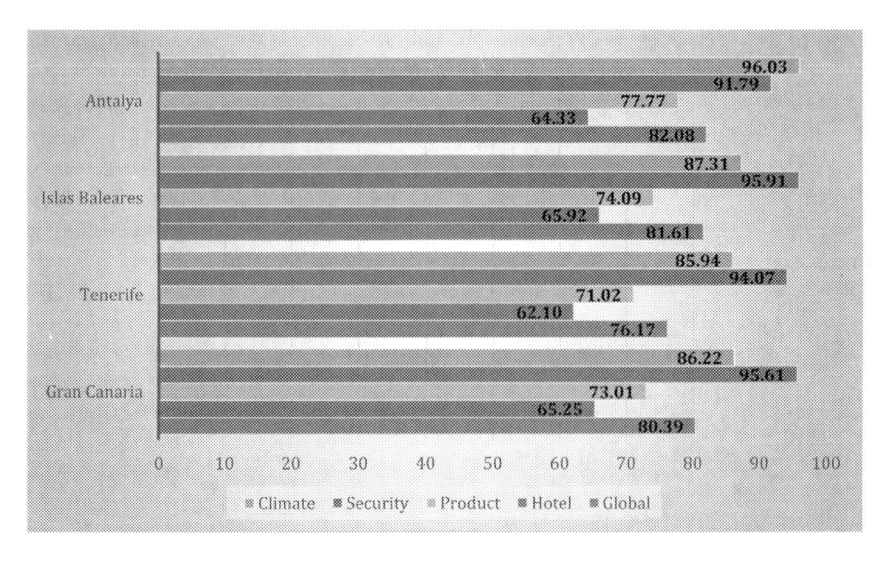

Figure 22.1 Gran Canaria's competitors as a tourist destination (**updated to May 2023**).

Note: Visitor satisfaction with the destination is measured through the tourist perception index on a scale from 0 to 100 points.

Source: Tourist Board of Gran Canaria (2023b)

of economic growth and generate opportunities in Africa and Latin America (Go & Kang, 2023; UNWTO, 2023b).

Finally, in this section on the environment, the uniqueness of the territory in which the Tourist Board of Gran Canaria carries out its activities—the island of Gran Canaria—is addressed. Geographically located 210 km from Africa and 1,250 km from Cádiz, Gran Canaria has an area of 1,560 km² and a coastline of 236 km. Due to its location, it has among the highest *average annual sunshine hours* in Europe, with temperatures ranging between 18°C and 25°C (Turismo de Gran Canaria, 2023a).

Furthermore, Gran Canaria has many high-value tourist attractions, causing it to stand out as a tourist destination in the Canary Islands (Turismo de Gran Canaria, 2023a). Among them, it is worth mentioning its natural heritage, represented in the singularity of its ecosystems, and, in particular, the fine sandy beaches, recognised with 12 awards from the Blue Flag programme, two awards for its marinas and two Blue Centre awards. Gran Canaria also has a rich archaeological, artistic (e.g., Flemish, Baroque, advanced autochthonous art) and ethnographic (e.g., agricultural landscapes, implements, hydraulic devices, milling, etc.) heritage. Added to this are its own cultural expressions, characterised by the lifestyle and open, cosmopolitan and multicultural character of its population. Its achievements regarding the high degree of conservation of its natural and cultural heritage are also recognised, such as being a UNESCO Biosphere Reserve, the inscription of 'Risco Caído' and the Sacred Mountains on the World Heritage List, and its consideration as a 'Starlight Tourist Destination', due to the quality of its night sky.

The island also has a range of first-rate health services, with modern public and private medical centres (Government of the Canary Islands, 2021). Regarding political stability and security, as a Spanish territory within the European Union, Gran Canaria offers a safe environment for foreigners and is favourable for foreign investment. In terms of infrastructure, Gran Canaria has a modern road and motorway network, as well as excellent connectivity, both by air (with airports in Spain, Europe and West Africa) and by sea (with Europe, Africa and America); the seaport allows not only the transport of goods but also plays a prominent role in the reception of tourist cruises (Turismo de Gran Canaria, 2023a). Finally, regarding investment in technology and telecommunications, the Island has a solid technological network that facilitates connectivity and Internet access (ACIISI, 2022). This has fuelled the growth of the digital sector, making Gran Canaria a desirable location for remote workers and digital nomads (Turismo de Gran Canaria, 2023a).

Results of the tourist board of Gran Canaria's activities

Since its creation, the Tourist Board of Gran Canaria has worked tirelessly for the tourism sector on the island of Gran Canaria, seeing it flourish. This has led to this sector becoming the main engine of the insular economy. On the Island, a fifth of employment is provided by the tourism sector, which also represents 30% of the island's GDP directly and 70% indirectly (Llinares de Béthencourt et al., 2019).

It should be noted that thanks to the Tourist Board of Gran Canaria, the island has managed to position itself—together with the other destinations in the Canary Islands—in the top 10 of the rankings of the main tourist destinations in Europe (European Best Destinations, 2021). In the field of domestic tourism, Gran Canaria polled in the top 3 "favourite places" for Spaniards in 2019 (if trips to seaside destinations are considered). Its capital, Las Palmas de Gran Canaria, appeared in the group of five "preferred Spanish cities" in 2020 (Hosteltur, 2020).

However, this favourable positioning has not prevented Gran Canaria—like other destinations—from suffering heavily from the consequences of the COVID-19 pandemic. Figure 22.2 shows the evolution of tourism during the two years prior to the pandemic (2018 and 2019), the pandemic year (2020) and the post-pandemic period of the slow return to normality (2021 and 2022). While with the arrival of the pandemic in 2020, tourist activity on the Island fell by approximately 70% (mirroring that experienced by the Canary Islands as a whole, falling lower than the national average), the recovery of tourist activity (figures of 2022 compared to 2019) has been somewhat slower in Gran Canaria (90.3%) than in the Canary Islands overall (96.7%), but faster than in

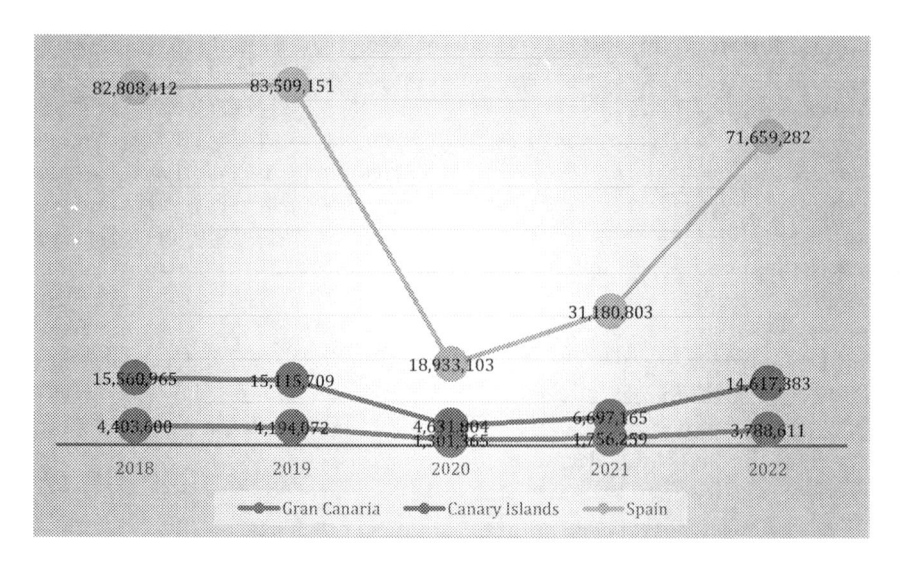

82,808,412 —— 83,509,151

71,659,282

31,180,803

18,933,103

15,560,965 —— 15,115,709

14,617,383

4,403,600 —— 4,194,072   4,631,904   6,697,165   3,788,611
1,301,365   1,756,259

2018   2019   2020   2021   2022

●—●Gran Canaria   ●—●Canary Islands   ●—●Spain

Figure 22.2 Evolution of tourism in Gran Canaria, the Canary Islands, and Spain.

Note: national tourists received, excluding residents of the Canary Islands holidaying in the Canary Islands and Gran Canaria. Foreign tourists received by Spain (all access routes).

Source: ISTAC (2023), INE (2023)

the national group (85.8%). In this regard, it should be noted that the efforts and initiatives of the Tourist Board of Gran Canaria to minimise the impact of COVID-19 on the island and contribute to the recovery of the sector have been extremely relevant. Along these lines, and with a view to the immediate future (May and June 2023), forecasts indicate that the recovery of the sector is continuing, with an estimated increase in tourist arrivals of 4.3% compared to the previous year (Turismo de Gran Canaria, 2023a).

In line with the international positioning achieved by Gran Canaria, most of its visitors in 2022 (3,788,611 tourists) came from abroad (85.8%)—Canarian residents were excluded from this registry (ISTAC, 2023). The proportion is not unusual, despite the unusual circumstances of 2022. Among the foreign tourists arriving in Gran Canaria in 2022, those from the United Kingdom (23.9%), the Nordic countries (22.2%) and Germany (21.7%) stand out, followed at a distance by those from the Netherlands, France and Italy (Turismo de Gran Canaria, 2023a)—this being an atypical year due to the slower recovery of Nordic and German tourism. It should be noted that tourists attracted to Gran Canaria contribute to the island that accounts for around 30% (29.1% in 2018 and 30.2% in 2020) of the *tourist expenditure* of the total number of visitors to the Canary Islands. This spending, although exceeding 16.8 billion in 2022 (the highest figure for the 2018-2022 period), represents a setback with respect to the proportion of spending by tourists in the Canary Islands, standing at 26.8% (ISTAC, 2023).

Innovative strategies developed by the tourist board of Gran Canaria before, during and after the COVID-19 pandemic

The Tourist Board of Gran Canaria, throughout its history, has successfully overcome many challenges that adversely affected the tourism sector, implementing numerous innovative strategies to do so. Given the significance of the health crisis caused by COVID-19 for the evolution of the sector, this is taken as a temporary reference to present the most outstanding innovations deployed by this organisation in the pre-pandemic periods (from its foundation until 2019), the pandemic year (2020) and the post-pandemic years (2021 and 2022).

Innovative strategies implemented prior to the COVID-19 pandemic

The innovative strategies implemented over this long period (1975–2019) have been very diverse and established the foundation for the sustained growth of the destination. Among them are:

- *Implementation of a new destination management process based on territorial decentralisation for decision-making*

  Since its foundation, the Tourist Board of Gran Canaria has made extensive efforts to introduce an alternative way of managing tourism in Spain, displaying intense activity to overcome centralisation in tourism planning and management. This innovation facilitated more effective promotion and marketing of the destination.
- *Development of a rapid response system aimed at deactivating negative external campaigns regarding the destination*

  This innovation has allowed the Tourist Board of Gran Canaria to quickly identify campaigns that question the quality or safety of the destination (e.g., boycott by Swedish agents due to the Euskadi Ta Askatasuna (ETA) trial in the 1970s, European publications on the threat of terrorist attacks in the Canary Islands, etc.), acting with haste to counter them. Implementing counter-propaganda to minimise the impact of these negative campaigns was decisive in maintaining the flow of tourists to Gran Canaria.
- *Opening strategy to new destination markets and reinforcement of market penetration*

  In its commitment to advancing the development of the tourism business and position of Gran Canaria as a preferred international destination, the Tourist Board of Gran Canaria was actively involved in attending trade fairs, professional conferences, meetings and presentations throughout Europe, at which it established contacts with tour operators, travel agencies and airlines. All this has allowed it to periodically show the sector the latest news regarding its tourist offer and improve air connectivity with new destinations and increase the frequency of existing routes (e.g., it went from connecting with 138 airports in 2015 to 151 in 2018, adding, among others, countries such as Hungary and The Gambia). The implementation of this strategy has also entailed supporting local companies in marketing their products.

- *Expansion of the tourist offer by highlighting intra-territorial singularities*
  With the tourism sector reaching the 'mature' stage, the traveller has improved access to information and is, thus, increasingly demanding. In response to this, the Tourist Board of Gran Canaria began to promote the attractions available on the island in its various municipalities to offer tourists a more varied and complete experience. It implemented a network of tourist information offices distributed throughout the island to support this strategy. This network has become a fundamental tool for guiding, advising and making the stay of tourists in Gran Canaria more valuable. As of 2023, the island has 30 offices and 45 tourist information centres after being forced to make some closures due to the drop in the tourism business during the pandemic year (2020).

- *Introduction of a comprehensive tourism planning and management system*
  Given the existence of an increasingly competitive market in which alternative tourist destinations are redoubling their efforts to attract tourists, the Tourist Board of Gran Canaria is committed to incorporating strategic planning into its management system, drawing up successive strategic plans aimed at increasing *spending, average stay duration and tourist satisfaction*, as well as improving the management of the island's natural resources and environmental awareness. The first plan was approved for the period 2011–2014, and this has been followed by others up to the present (2021–2025), which will be discussed later as part of the group of innovative strategies in the post-pandemic stage. The introduction of this comprehensive planning system has made it possible to align the management of the destination with the public policies deployed to support its development.

- *Development of strategic plans in tourism marketing operational plans*
  After the first experiences in the implementation of the Gran Canaria Strategic Tourism Plan, an innovation was introduced, consisting of the development of a strictly promotional operating plan in order to specify the pillars on which to base the marketing of the destination. The first Gran Canaria Tourism Marketing Plan 2017–2020 bases the marketing of the destination on four pillars: *connectivity, loyalty, branding and internal promotion.*

- *Introduction of a digital communication strategy*
  In response to the growing relevance of digitisation in all areas of the economy, the Tourist Board of Gran Canaria has made a firm commitment to digital communication since 2017. Through its website, social networks and other digital dissemination and information channels, it is at the forefront of interaction with potential visitors to Gran Canaria, becoming a pioneer in this area and an example for many other tourist destinations.

Innovative strategies implemented during the COVID-19 pandemic

2020 began with the declaration of an international public health emergency due to the COVID-19 coronavirus; By March 2020 this emergency acquired the category of global pandemic (e.g., García-Cabrera et al., 2021). Consequently, the world was plunged into an extensive quarantine and Gran Canaria entered a stage of "zero tourism". Given this, the Tourist Board of Gran Canaria had to respond quickly through actions to support the sector (e.g., orderly departure of tourists visiting the Island, the opening of a Virtual Tourist Information Office with 24-hour service in five languages, etc.). Soon, new strategic actions were designed and implemented to reopen the destination under the usual conditions of health security and trust. The innovative strategies that stood out in this pandemic year are presented below.

- *Innovative destination promotions based on taking advantage of the adverse situation*

    This strategy consisted of developing campaigns with various objectives. First, those aimed at raising awareness among residents and visitors about the importance of tourism for the development of the island and the need to reduce infection rates to levels that would allow activity to resume as soon as possible stand out. Additionally, campaigns were carried out to instil confidence in the destination while offering remote and free leisure activities to alleviate the hours of confinement (e.g., online visits to destination areas). All the campaigns carried out were based on optimistic content (e.g., Gran Canaria #muchoporvivir, Gran Canaria Inédita campaigns), adapted to different segments and offered through all types of devices and social networks. Likewise, images of emblematic areas of great beauty, totally deserted, were captured, which may never be repeated. This made it possible to renew the destination's audio-visual content catalogue, which is highly impactful in promotional terms.

- *Temporary modification of the priority market segments in the promotion of the destination*

    During the pandemic year, the Tourist Board of Gran Canaria intensified communication actions aimed at potential future tourists, acquiring special relevance to the local and national population, a segment to be prioritised in the face of intermittent border closures decreed by governments around the world.

- *Innovative campaigns aimed at generating confidence in the health security of the destination*

    The pandemic generated mistrust of the safety of travel in people who avoided carrying out tourist activities to prevent the spread of the coronavirus. In this context, the Tourist Board of Gran Canaria designed and implemented innovative marketing strategies to promote the image of Gran

Canaria as a safe tourist destination, maintain the positive reputation of the place and attract national and international tourists. Among them, the "Gran Canaria: a Great Summer!" campaign in collaboration with Grupo Atresmedia stands out, which included television and radio programmes with large audiences (e.g., Espejo Público, El Hormiguero) and the organisation of a visit by representatives of the UNWTO, national authorities, prescribers and journalists, in order to validate the health security of the destination. Gran Canaria obtained a positive assessment on this visit, generating numerous publications with favourable messages in both the national and international media.

- *Support Strategy for tourism companies in Gran Canaria regarding their access to official seals of excellence*

  In 2020, and within the framework of the SICTED initiative (Integral System of Tourist Quality in Destination), the Tourist Board of Gran Canaria collaborated with the Chamber of Commerce of Gran Canaria to offer training, assistance, advice and evaluation aimed at supporting the companies in their access to official seals of excellence. In 2020, the "COVID-19 Advanced Good Practices" seal was created to distinguish those companies that complied with preventive measures and demonstrated their adaptation to the new scenario caused by the pandemic. Access to a second distinction, "Commitment to Tourism Quality", although available since 2009, was also obtained in this pandemic year. The development of this strategy is due to the need to face the difficulties that the sector was going through because of the pandemic, and in which health security and quality have become essential elements for destinations.

Innovative strategies implemented after the COVID-19 pandemic

In this period (years 2021 and 2022), the recovery process of tourism began in the wake of the pandemic. Although the main activity of the Tourist Board of Gran Canaria was oriented towards restoring normality in the sector through, among other things, a commitment to sustainability, culture and digitisation, the year 2021 stood out for being one of the best in terms of progress in the internal management of this promotional body—e.g., updating of the Statutes, modification of the list of jobs, and updating of the organisational chart. Among the innovative strategies implemented in this period, the following are highlighted:

- *Implementation of innovations in the internal management of the Tourist Board of Gran Canaria*

  Among the innovative initiatives implemented in the period of return to normality, the renewal of the 1998 statutes is particularly noteworthy, with the update coming into force in 2021. The main elements of this renewal were represented by the name change of the promotional organisation, renamed '*Turismo de Gran Canaria*', as well as updating its purposes and powers; these modifications were intended to respond to the need to strengthen the Gran Canaria brand and to adapt the management structure to the island's tourism system (Turismo de Gran Canaria, s/f).

Other important changes implemented to improve the organisation's internal management include: (1) implementation of a Customer Relationship Management (CRM) to increase tourist loyalty and attract B2B participants; (2) creation of a system that strengthens the relationship of the promotion agency with the local tourism industry; (3) optimisation of organisational functioning, defining processes and procedures that allow it to improve its effectiveness and efficiency; and (4) implementation of an internal training programme that equips the human team with the necessary skills for the development of new processes and procedures and facilitates internal communication.

- *Commitment to sustainability and orientation to Agenda 2030 as distinctive values of the destination*

  The Tourist Board of Gran Canaria, taking into account the most recent trends in the sector and the 2030 Agenda, incorporated the commitment to economic, environmental and socio-cultural sustainability into its set of core management values, as transversal elements that support the growth of the destination (Turismo de Gran Canaria, 2023a). It promotes the adoption of good environmental practices for companies in Gran Canaria. For example, the Tourist Board of Gran Canaria has implemented awareness projects and facilitated sustainability management and the achievement of the corresponding certificate that accredits it through free access to the Biosphere Sustainable online platform. As a destination, the island as a whole seeks the commitment of Gran Canaria to the global Biosphere Destination Community. Additionally, tourism is intended to have a positive impact on society (e.g., quality employment, poverty reduction)and represent an engine of ecological transition.

- *Digitisation as a key element for the future of the sector*

  The development of Gran Canaria as a *Smart Tourist Destination* model (Turismo de Gran Canaria, s/f) has become a priority at this stage. To this end, the Tourist Board of Gran Canaria, among other actions, promotes the digital transformation of the tourism sector and supports the agents responsible for *Smart Destination initiatives* (Turismo de Gran Canaria, 2023a). For implementing this innovative strategy, the Tourist Board of Gran Canaria developed and provided to the sector an updated dashboard that has valuable reports and indicators for making the right decisions—i.e., *market intelligence* (Turismo de Gran Canaria, 2023a). For the success of this strategy, public-private collaboration and the development of joint initiatives by sectoral, regional, national and European entities is considered essential. One collaboration led to the implementation of SITGRAN, a system that integrates over 40 sources of information, available through interactive visualisations and open-use files, which offer data on tourist behaviour, the tourist offer, connectivity, resources and climate. (Turismo de Gran Canaria, 2023c; SPEGC, 2022).

- *Strategy for the development of tourism products at destination*

    Given that tourist spending in Gran Canaria in the post-pandemic period decreased, compared to that of the archipelago as a whole, along with the numbers of visitor arrivals to the island (which are yet to recover), the Tourist Board of Gran Canaria has developed new strategies to reverse this situation. These strategies are committed to: (1) an increase in tourist spending (e.g., promotions aimed at segments that seek well-being and health or that have greater purchasing power and stay longer on the island, such as those from the Nordic countries); (2) an increase in loyalty (e.g., promotions and events aimed at the various leisure segments (e.g., LGBTI friendly, etc.); (3) the diversification of markets that expand business opportunities (e.g., remote workers, 'pet friendly'); (4) connectivity through new routes and higher frequencies; (5) better distribution of tourist flows to the different municipalities of the Island (e.g., events to publicise the gastronomic, cultural, folkloric and artisanal legacy of each place); (6) the renovation and development of tourist infrastructures that contribute excellence to the destination; and—especially—(7) the rejuvenation of the destination (e.g., projecting a modern and familiar image of Gran Canaria).

Epilogue

The Tourist Board of Gran Canaria, throughout its years of experience, has successfully overcome numerous challenges and changes in the environment that have adversely affected the tourism sector in Gran Canaria. In order to face these challenges, this organisation has designed innovative strategies that have made it possible to convey the value of Gran Canaria as a top-tier tourist destination and reinforce its strengths. This has allowed the Tourist Board of Gran Canaria to acquire meritorious experience that currently represents a highly valuable resource in the face of new challenges that affect the sector on the island. In this sense, the innovative strategies successfully implemented in the pre-pandemic, pandemic and post-pandemic periods, which have been highlighted in this case study, reflect the adaptability of the Tourist Board of Gran Canaria and provide a valuable reference for other tourism promotion entities. Not surprisingly, thanks to its efforts, the island has become a mature, internationally recognised and valued destination.

Acknowledgements

A.M. García-Cabrera and M.G. García-Soto gratefully acknowledge the financial support received from Spain's Science and Innovation National Department (Project: PID2021-123274NB-I00).

References

ACIISI (2022). Informe Anual Banda Ancha en Canarias 2021. Retrieved from https://www.octsi.es/images/documentos/2023/informe_banda_ancha_canarias_2021_edicion_2022.pdf.

European Best Destinations (2021). European best destinations 2021. The best places to visit in Europe selected by travellers. Retrieved from https://www.europeanbest-destinations.com/european-best-destinations-2021/ [22.05.2023].

Ferrer-Roca, N., Guia, J., & Blasco, D. (2022). Partnerships and The SDGs in a cross-border destination: The case of The cerdanya valley. *Journal of Sustainable Tourism*, *30*(10), 2410–2427.

García-Cabrera, A. M., García-Soto, M. G., & Gutiérrez-Pérez, F. J. (2021). Covid-19 y turismo en españa: Impacto actual y disyuntivas futuras? *Economistas*, *172–173*, 207–2015. Available at: http://hdl.handle.net/10553/114659

Go, H., & Kang, M. (2023). Metaverse tourism for sustainable tourism development: Tourism agenda 2030. *Tourism Review*, *78*(2), 381–394.

Gobierno de Canarias (2021). Noticias. Retrieved from https://www3.gobiernodecanarias.org/noticias/online/ [22.05.23]. https://www3.gobiernodecanarias.org/sanidad/scs/organica.jsp?idCarpeta=aa98d8f0-ab2b-11dd-970d-d73a0633ac17

Hosteltur (2020). Datos de reservas en Atrápalo Ranking de destinos favoritos de los turistas españoles… y lo que cuestan. Retrieved from https://www.hosteltur.com/133810_ranking-de-destinos-favoritos-de-los-turistas-espanolesy-lo-que-cuestan.html [22.05.2023].

INE (2023). Movimientos turísticos en frontera. Retrieved from https://www.ine.es/jaxiT3/Datos.htm?t=13884 [fecha de consulta: 20.05.2023].

ISTAC (2023). Turismo en cifras. Retrieved from https://www3.gobiernodecanarias.org/istac/indicators-visualizations/indicatorsSystems/C00075B.html [20.05.2023].

Llinares de Béthencourt, P., Cruz Lecat, M. C., & Cantero Lleó, M. (2019). Patronato turismo gran canaria: 40 años de promoción turística del destino. In T. Aguiar-Quintana & R. M. Batista Canino (eds.). *100 soluciones a 20 problemas para la gestión turística en empresas de iberoamérica: Manual de casos reales* (pp. 163–174). Síntesis.

SPEGC (2022). Gran Canaria utiliza sistemas de inteligencia de datos para mejorar su competitividad turística. Retrieved from https://www.spegc.org/gran-canaria-presenta-un-sistema-de-inteligencia-turistica/ [23.05.23].

Turismo de Gran Canaria (2022). Información institucional. Retrieved from https://www.grancanaria.com/turismo/es/area-profesional/transparencia/informacion-institucional/ [19.05.2023].

Turismo de Gran Canaria (2023a). Dosier de prensa 2023. Turismo de Gran Canaria. Retrieved from https://www.grancanaria.com/turismo/fileadmin/arearestringida/GC_DossierPrensa.pdf [18.05.2023].

Turismo de Gran Canaria (2023b). Informes y estadísticas. Gran Canaria y sus competidores. Retrieved from https://www.grancanaria.com/turismo/es/area-profesional/informes-y-estadisticas-gran-canaria-y-sus-competidores/ [22.05.2023].

Turismo de Gran Canaria (2023c). Sistema de Inteligencia Turística de Gran Canaria. Retrieved from https://www.grancanaria.com/turismo/es/area-profesional/menu-superior/analisis/sitgran/ [23.05.23].

Turismo de Gran Canaria (s/f). Promoción Turística. Retrieved from https://www. grancanaria.com/turismo/es/area-profesional/promocion-turistica/plan-estrategico-y-de-marketing/ [23.05.23].

UNWTO (2023a). Barómetro. Retrieved from https://www.unwto.org/es/barometro-del-turismo-mundial-de-la-omt [22.05.2023].

UNWTO (2023b). El consejo ejecutivo de la OMT se reúne en punta cana. Retrieved from https://www.unwto.org/es/news/el-consejo-ejecutivo-de-la-omt-se-reune-en-punta-cana [22.05.2023].

UNWTO (2023c). Tourism 4 SDGs. *Join us on the 2030 Journey platform*. Retrieved from https://www.unwto.org/tourism4sdgs [08.05.2023].

UNWTO (2023d). El turismo en la agenda 2030. Retrieved from https://www.unwto. org/es/turismo-agenda-2030 [23.05.2023].

Vrontis, D., Christofi, M., Giacosa, E., & Serravalle, F. (2022). Sustainable development in tourism: A stakeholder analysis of the langhe region. *Journal of Hospitality & Tourism Research*, 46(5), 846–878.

Case 23 Innovation in the international educational experience for hospitality and luxury industry

Unleashing corporate entrepreneurship at Les Roches in Switzerland and Spain

Carlos Díez de la Lastra, Jon Loiti Perez de Labeaga, Raúl Castro-López, and Lidia Esther Hernández-López

Introduction

Les Roches Global Hospitality Education—a private, for-profit enterprise—is a renowned institution in hospitality education with a rich history dating back to 1954. Founded as L'École des Roches, an international boarding school by Messrs Clivaz, it evolved into Les Roches International School in 1979. It was the first hospitality school in Switzerland to offer all courses in English. The institution faced a significant setback in 1985 when its main campus was destroyed by fire, leading to a temporary relocation to hotels until the construction of new buildings in 1987. Later, in 1995, Les Roches Marbella, Spain, opened its doors.

In November 2000, Les Roches joined Laureate Education Inc., which also manages Glion Institute of Higher Education. A significant milestone was reached in 2006 when Les Roches received American accreditation from the New England Commission of Higher Education (NECHE), an AACSB and EuroCHRIE member and an affiliate member of the United Nations World Tourism Organization (UNWTO). In June 2016, Les Roches became part of the Eurazeo portfolio, one of the leading investment companies in Europe. It was rebranded as "Les Roches Global Hospitality Education".

In 2020, **Spark** was introduced to seek transformation based on Positioning-People-Premises. **Spark** is a physical innovation space on campus, an academic philosophy, and a means to incubate disruptive startups. Les Roches' goal with **Spark** is to expose its students to the latest technologies and innovative ideas driving next-generation hospitality. With industry and technology partners, **Spark** creates innovation-focused academic projects that are part of the curriculum for every programme taught at Les Roches. These projects allow its students to prepare for the future by working with early adopters of technological innovations that sit on the cusp of the mainstream. They are real-world projects with real-world potential.

DOI: 10.4324/9781003454465-24

In 2021, Les Roches achieved global recognition when the education company Quacquarelli Symonds (QS) ranked it among the top three institutions worldwide for its employer reputation in hospitality and leisure management. In QS Stars University Ratings, 2022, Les Roches achieved five Stars Overall Excellent. Additionally, in a ranking of 50 leading hospitality institutions, Les Roches was placed among the top three in Switzerland and the top five globally.

Les Roches primarily provides top-quality education and training in global hospitality. With a strong commitment to preparing students for successful careers in the industry, Les Roches offers comprehensive programmes that combine theoretical knowledge with practical experience. The institution attracts a diverse student body worldwide, with more than 1,500 students from 80 countries attending each semester. Additionally, Les Roches ensures strong industry connections through its advisory panel, consisting of representatives from major hotel chains.

The Les Roches Governing Board is the legally constituted body responsible for ensuring quality, integrity, and strategic direction. Comprising a fair representation of Les Roches' stakeholders and industry partners (see Table 23.1)—i.e., founder, hospitality experts, and higher education consultants—the board's composition aligns with the institution's vision and mission. They exercise authority and independence in supporting institutional strategic direction, approving policies, monitoring fiscal conditions, and endorsing major initiatives in consultation with internal and external constituents. To fulfil its fiduciary responsibility, the board conducts periodic assessments, including external audits, regulatory compliance, internal controls, and contingency management. Maintaining strong connections with the hotel and tourism industry, Les Roches benefits from an advisory panel comprising representatives from major hotel chains.

Table 23.1 Les Roches governing board

Dr Elmore Alexander	Chair, Dean Emeritus at the Ricciardi College of Business
Mr Francis Clivaz	Les Roches Founder
Mr Christian Karaoglanian	Consultant for Accorhotels, Member of the board of directors of various companies
Dr Stacy L. Sweeney	Higher Education Consultant
Mr Chad Thompson	Higher Education Consultant
Mr Benoît-Etienne Domenget	Chief Executive Officer Sommet Education
Dr Fabien Fresnel	Chief Operating Officer Sommet Education
Dr Valérie Truelle	Chief Financial Officer Sommet Education
Mr Jean-Jacques Gauer	Hospitality Expert
Ms Adela Martín	Spain Head of Private Banking and Asset Management at Banco Santander

In 2022, Mr Carlos Díez de la Lastra became the first Spaniard CEO of Les Roches and received the necessary authority and autonomy from the Governing Board to lead strategic initiatives and manage academic programmes and services on behalf of the institution.

Development: Corporate entrepreneurship and innovation actions

Guth and Ginsberg (1990) defined corporate entrepreneurship as applying entrepreneurial initiatives to large organisations. It implies that the essential ingredients of the corporate business function are that decisions are made, and actions are taken so they result in a new combination of resources that create value for the company's investors and customers.

According to these authors, corporate entrepreneurship is related to two types of phenomena: the birth of new businesses within existing organisations through internal innovation and the transformation of organisations through the renewal of the key ideas on which they are built. The corporate entrepreneur, whether as an individual or in a team, should carry out these functions in the business (Sharma & Chrisman, 1999).

Therefore, the role of the corporate entrepreneur will involve ensuring efficiency in using resources to achieve better results and continuously reconfiguring the company's business portfolio. In this sense, Les Roches has been looking for new opportunities for the company and has developed corporate entrepreneurship actions with a strong market orientation. With the aim to gain an advantageous position for the company in external markets, in October 2022, in Switzerland (Crans-Montana), the world's foremost hub for the luxury tourism industry, Les Roches signed an agreement with the University of Las Palmas de Gran Canaria, a leading university in tourism education in Spain[1] located in one of the most important tourist destinations in the world, Canary Islands[2]. This agreement created an alliance between these two higher education institutions to launch a new educational product: *International Program BACHELOR + MASTER of High Specialization in Hospitality and Luxury Tourism* to jointly train the talent for the world's future of the hospitality and luxury tourism industry.

The development and implementation of this innovation in the international educational experience would allow Les Roches and Universidad de Las Palmas de Gran Canaria to gain competitiveness in the hospitality and luxury industry. This collaboration promises to provide an exceptional learning experience, equipping individuals with the necessary skills and knowledge to excel in the dynamic world of hospitality and luxury tourism. The collective expertise and resources of both higher education institutions in tourism and hospitality will undoubtedly pave the way for a fruitful and rewarding educational journey for students and professionals.

Under the *International Program BACHELOR + MASTER of High Specialization in Hospitality and Luxury Tourism*, undergraduate students from the Faculty of Economics, Business and Tourism of the University of Las

Palmas de Gran Canaria (ULPGC) obtain, at the end of their undergraduate studies, the Bachelor honour's degree by the University of Las Palmas de Gran Canaria and Master by Les Roches.

The International Program is addressed to students at the Bachelor's level, in tourism and in administration and business management[3]. Students complete the first, second, and third years of their undergraduate degree at ULPGC. In their fourth year, the students are transferred to Les Roches, where they can study on any of its two campuses: Crans-Montana (Switzerland) or Marbella (Spain). At Les Roches, the student can take either Master programmes: Master in International Hotel Management or Master in Marketing and Management for Luxury Tourism.

In the Master in International Hotel Management, the student must complete its academic programme, which includes nine months of academic content in which the student learns the theory and strategy. One of the highlights of this programme is the state-of-the-art on-campus facilities—Les Roches virtual hotel—where students are immersed in a theoretical scenario that allows them to grasp the intricacies of hotel management. These facilities offer real hotel simulations, providing students with a hands-on experience that deepens their comprehension of every aspect of hotel operations. From top-level management to the nitty-gritty details, students gain valuable insights into how a hotel functions. Additionally, students participate in a business and networking trip, further enhancing their understanding of the industry where they have the privilege of meeting and being interviewed by CEOs, general managers or area directors from the industry, many of whom are Les Roches alums. Students also undertake an applied business capstone project to ensure a well-rounded education.

Following the academic phase, students embark on a six-month professional internship in one of the industry's most sought-after brands, which provides an opportunity to apply everything the students have learned during the academic programme in a real-world setting. The professional internship gives the student practical experience at industry-leading brands in Les Roches industry connections in international destinations such as Hong Kong, Qatar, Mexico and Dubai.

In the Master in Marketing and Management for Luxury Tourism, the nine-month academic programme focuses on the theory and practical know-how to excel in the fast-paced and competitive luxury industry. In addition, students participate in the Exclusive Brand Week, where their knowledge is enriched through presentations and seminars by top luxury brands. Each student must complete a capstone project that gives them valuable, hands-on experience in a real-world environment. A six-month professional internship follows the academic programme to apply what the student has learned in class in a top-end, real-world setting such as luxury hotels, restaurants or retail outlets.

The academic programme and professional internship of the master's degree are recognised as components of the undergraduate curriculum at ULPGC. The knowledge, skills, and competencies acquired through the academic content of the master's programme modules and the professional internship are aligned and, therefore, recognised with those developed in the curricula of the tourism, administration and business management programmes.

The student's successful completion of modules in the master's programme will be recognised and recorded in their academic record within their undergraduate programme at ULPGC. However, it is important to note that this academic recognition is contingent upon the satisfactory completion of the master's programme and compliance with the quality requirements established by ULPGC.

Upon the successful transfer of grades from the master's programme modules to the student's file at ULPGC, the student will have officially completed their degree programme at ULPGC. After successfully passing all the modules and meeting the academic requirements for a degree at ULPGC, the student becomes eligible to obtain a bachelor's degree. Upon meeting these requirements, the student will also be conferred the master's degree by Les Roches. Hence, when a student completes all modules in their undergraduate programme at ULPGC, making them eligible to receive the ULPGC degree, the Master's degree will be awarded by Les Roches.

Within four years, the student will obtain a Degree in Tourism or Administration and Business Management from ULPGC, alongside a master's degree from Les Roches. These two programmes provide students with comprehensive knowledge, skills, and competencies acquired in an international setting, combining high-level theoretical expertise with practical experience. This unique combination equips students with specialised hospitality and luxury tourism expertise.

The optimal timing for undertaking the academic mobility from ULPGC to Les Roches is the final year of the undergraduate degree. This timing lets students access Les Roches' employment exchange and job offers, providing them with exceptional opportunities to explore potential employment prospects. By adopting this strategic approach, students can effectively leverage the resources and support offered by Les Roches, further enhancing their chances of securing a promising career in their chosen field.

The *International Program BACHELOR + MASTER of High Specialization in Hospitality and Luxury Tourism* significantly enhances the employability and competitiveness of ULPGC students by offering them the opportunity to acquire two degrees (Bachelor and Master). Moreover, it facilitates the development of their professional skills within an international academic-practical framework, fostering high specialisation in the hospitality and luxury sectors. By engaging in this programme, students gain a distinct advantage in the job market, as they are equipped with a comprehensive academic background and practical experience that greatly contribute to their career growth and prospects.

With over 70 years of experience in hospitality and luxury education, this partnership marks a significant milestone for Les Roches, representing their first collaboration and agreement with a public university. This innovative project is pioneering for Les Roches, both within Spain and internationally. Before this collaboration, Les Roches had not entered into any partnership agreements with any other academic institution, making this venture a unique and groundbreaking endeavour for both higher education institutions.

The University of Las Palmas de Gran Canaria has demonstrated exceptional proficiency in international mobility programmes, specifically developing and implementing international agreements for double degree programmes with various European universities. The University of Las Palmas de Gran Canaria has implemented a comprehensive internationalisation strategy, positioning itself as a leading institution in global academic collaboration in Europe, Latin America, the USA and Africa. With over 500 international agreements and partnerships with prestigious universities worldwide, ULPGC offers an extensive range of student exchange programmes, research collaborations, and joint degree initiatives. One of the distinctive achievements of ULPGC is being the first public university in Spain to forge international agreements for double degree programmes. This innovative initiative dates back to the early 1990s when ULPGC collaborated with Kiel University of Applied Sciences in Germany to launch the pioneering Double Degree Program. This programme exemplifies ULPGC's commitment to providing students with exceptional educational experiences that combine academic excellence with a global perspective. This significant expertise played a vital role in facilitating the institutional coordination of the project. The success of this entrepreneurial endeavour hinged on finding a partner like ULPGC, capable of crafting an agreement that aligns seamlessly with the educational frameworks of both institutions and within the European Higher Education Area.

A significant factor contributing to the collaboration's success is the pre-existing working relationship among team members which brought mutual trust and expertise to the development of the collaborative action. The programme's technical team comprised individuals who had previously worked together for many years on projects related to international academic mobility at European higher education institutions in the field of tourism. The team had already drafted institutional agreements and managed more than 250 tourism students in a double degree programme. This collaboration was seen as a new opportunity for them to develop a project within their established organisations that would enable them to share their accumulated knowledge, experience and passion for helping students' employability in the tourism industry. Hence, mutual trust, expertise and passion for tourism students' competence development were key elements pushing forward to architecture an action that would genuinely benefit the students a project that would enhance the students' employability at the international level in the tourism industry. The team's collective expertise and shared vision were instrumental in developing a programme that maximised the students' potential and opened doors to global employment opportunities in tourism.

Another important element contributing to the corporate entrepreneurial actions was the common understanding and high value from both higher education institutions to the importance of the people behind this agreement. It would need a human team entrusted with resolving the challenges that may arise during the implementation process. So, before formalising the agreement, extensive meetings and visits took place to familiarise them with the institutions involved and the individuals spearheading the project. There was a common awareness that a successful execution would require a skilled team capable of problem-solving, effective collaboration, and upholding the cultural values of both higher education institutions. The flexibility and lightness displayed by the ULPGC, in contrast to the traditional perception of public universities as organisations with rigid muscle structures, were important in inspiring Les Roches to embark on this collaborative entrepreneurship initiative.

The awareness of this pivotal aspect would ensure that potential obstacles could be addressed proactively, minimising disruptions and maximising the likelihood of a seamless implementation. The success of any collaborative endeavour relies on the team members' collective expertise, dedication and harmonious collaboration. By establishing strong working relationships, mutual respect, and a shared understanding of each institution's cultural nuances, the team could navigate challenges and leverage their collective strengths to drive the project forward.

At the initial stage, it was not straightforward to identify the opportunity for Les Roches because the collaboration raised several questions: Why would the ULPGC send their undergraduate students to pursue a master's degree at Les Roches? Why would the ULPGC collaborate with Les Roches on a Master's level instead of engaging in direct competition? The answer was rather simple. The ULPGC acknowledged lacking the necessary resources and expertise to offer a master's degree programme in hospitality and luxury tourism. These particular areas of study do not fall within the ULPGC's competitive advantages. Consequently, partnering with Les Roches was seen as an optimal solution for their undergraduate tourism students to excel in these areas.

By collaborating with Les Roches on the master's level, the ULPGC could tap into their wealth of resources and extensive expertise in hospitality and luxury tourism education. This strategic alliance would allow ULPGC undergraduate students to access top-notch master's degree programmes offered by a renowned institution. The ULPGC recognised the importance of equipping its students with the highest quality education, even if it meant partnering with an external entity. The ULPGC's decision to collaborate with Les Roches on the master's level rather than competing was driven by a pragmatic understanding of its limitations regarding resources and expertise in hospitality and luxury tourism. By leveraging the strengths of Les Roches in top tourism education, the ULPGC could deliver enhanced educational opportunities for its students, ensuring their employability in a competitive professional landscape.

The strong endorsement from the governing bodies of both higher education institutions was instrumental in recognising this initiative as a significant opportunity for specialisation and international leadership in tourism, particularly for the Canary Islands and the ULPGC. This support underscored the shared vision of advancing the prominence of hospitality and luxury tourism in Spain for Les Roches. Moreover, it presented a valuable prospect to forge a collaborative framework with other esteemed educational institutions, fostering a competitive edge in hospitality and luxury tourism.

The language requirement was a significant challenge in initiating this collaboration. As the theoretical and practical training at Les Roches is delivered exclusively in English, students are required to have a high level of English proficiency to participate in the programme. This language requirement is a criterion for students to gain access to the programme, ensuring their ability to fully engage with the academic content and practical experiences provided at Les Roches.

Epilogue

Similar to the Batista-Canino and Medina-Brito case in Case 1, this agreement is a sign that cooperation is possible between a private, for-profit institution and a public, non-profit institution in tourism education. The ultimate goal of this agreement is to keep Les Roches and Universidad de Las Palmas de Gran Canaria competitive and to ensure their long-term survival as leading institutions in hospitality and luxury education by generating new value for tourism students and the hospitality and luxury industry.

The agreement strengthens the partnership of both institutions and serves as a catalyst for establishing new collaborative relationships with other higher education institutions. This corporate entrepreneurial action sets a precedent by highlighting the importance of recognising opportunities for collaboration with organisations operating in the same market, all in the best interest of their end users. In this instance, the collaboration aims to nurture and unleash the potential of talented individuals—ULPGC students—who will shape the future of the hospitality and luxury tourism industry on a global scale.

As Batista-Canino and Medina-Brito underline in the Introduction Chapter about the key elements of corporate entrepreneurs, an important learning from this partnership for both institutions is the importance that for this initiative to succeed, a key intangible was essential: an organisational culture open, permissive to change management, innovation and cooperation. Recognising the importance of a capable problem-solving team and conducting preliminary meetings to foster mutual understanding and respect set the foundation for a successful implementation. By valuing effective teamwork and respecting the unique cultures of each institution, collaborative efforts could overcome obstacles and pave the way for a fruitful and harmonious partnership.

Finally, a key element contributing to the growth and development of this initiative lies within its human capital: a team of employees bound by mutual trust, expertise and passion for elevating students' employability within the vibrant tourism industry. Their collective action would aid in putting leaders in the tourism industry.

Notes

1 In hospitality and tourism management, ULPGC ranked 1st in Spain, and 39th globally in 2021; in 2022 ULPGC ranked 2nd in Spain, and 39th globally 2022 by the Academic Ranking of World Universities (Shanghai Ranking).
2 Prior to the onset of the COVID-19 crisis in 2019, Canary Islands had recorded as the European regions with the highest number of nights spent in tourism accommodation by international tourists (83.9 million). In 2020, it recorded as the second European region with the highest numbers of nights spent in tourist accommodation (23.8 million) (EUROSTAT, 2022).
3 In Spain, undergraduate degrees have a duration of four academic years (240 credits of the European Credit Transfer System).

References

Guth, W. D., & Ginsberg, A. (1990). Guest editors' introduction: Corporate entrepreneurship. *Strategic Management Journal, 11*, 5–15. Available at: https://www.jstor.org/stable/2486666

Sharma, P., & Chrisman, J. J. (1999). Toward a Reconciliation of the definitional issues in the field of Corporate Entrepreneurship. *Entrepreneurship Theory and Practice, 23*(3), 11–28.

Case 24 Corporate entrepreneurship and intrapreneurship inside Accor as reflected in the innovation strategies of Novotel Hotel Paris Bercy

Christina Tschech and Philippe Frouté

Introduction and case selection

This case study analyses the corporate entrepreneurship strategies of Novotel Paris Centre Bercy as a franchise of the Accor group and its Novotel brand. While focusing specifically on the case of Novotel Paris Bercy, this study also tries to cross-reference the organisational structure of Accor with the notions of corporate entrepreneurship and intrapreneurship[1]. Let us first consider the historical background, business activity and organisational structure of Accor, the largest French company in hospitality and among the largest in the world, while providing a brief theoretical framework for corporate entrepreneurship.

Paul Dubrule and Gérard Pélisson opened their first Novotel in 1967. After several periods of growth and acquisitions, in 1983, the group re-emerged as Accor. Today, the company boasts 5,400 hotels, 802,000 rooms in 110 countries and 290,000 employees. Half of the hotels of the company are in Europe. Also, the group pursued a policy of international expansion, and nowadays, the group has more than 20 brands covering four segments: economy (IBIS, Hotel F1,.), mid-range (Mercury, Novotel…), premium (Pullman, Mövenpick…) and luxury (Sofitel, Fairmont…). The group is structured into two business lines: Hotel Services (around 71% of revenue) and Hotel Assets & Other (29% of revenue). In 2022, Accor was ranked sixth in the world in terms of the number of rooms available in hotels. Its main competitors in recent years have been American and Chinese hospitality companies.

Next, in Figure 24.1a,b we present the group sales and the hotel portfolio of the group's main competitors.

According to the recent Accor financial report, Accor's main internal strengths are its international ranking, the presence of the group in all market segments, from economy to luxury products. The main weaknesses are a relative lack of profitability for new segments (other than housing) the need to plan for heavy investments to launch new products and services. As to external threats, pandemic episodes that may jeopardise the profitability of ongoing transformation such as the digitalisation of housing activity remain a factor. Another threat concerns growing competition between the main

DOI: 10.4324/9781003454465-25

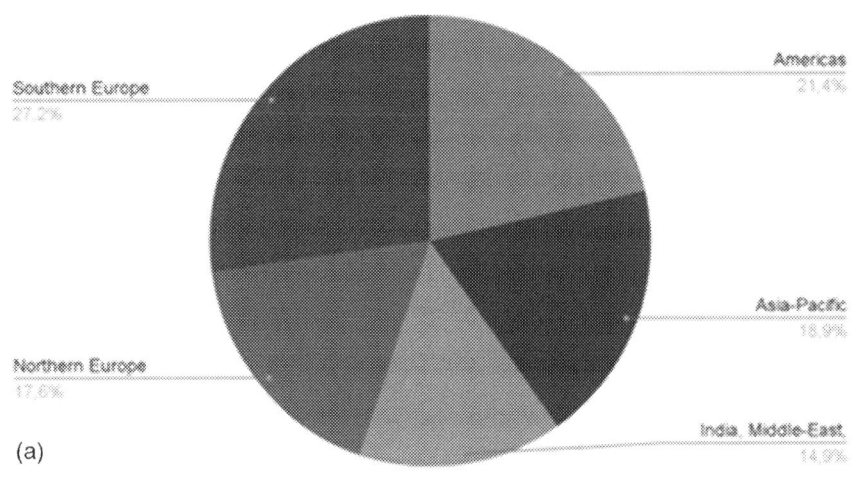

(a)

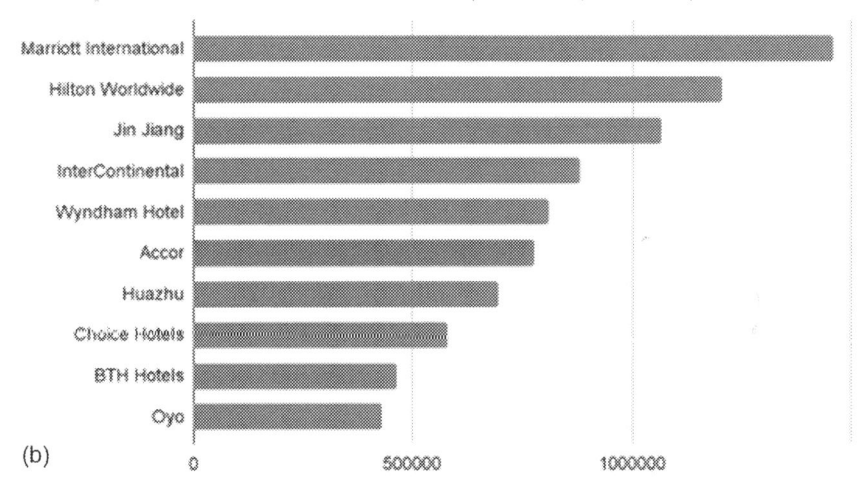

(b)

Figure 24.1 Accor group (a) sales and (b) hotel portfolio.

Source: MKG Consulting, comptes année 2022.

players in the industry. Finally, there are opportunities to be seized such as emerging trends with co-living and co-working experiences to which the tourism industry is now adapting.

An important action identified by Accor management in 2019 was implementing a new identity intended to "go beyond hotels[2]". That same year, Accor reinforced its partnership with AEG, the world leader in sports and live entertainment, and entered a strategic partnership with the American group

IMG (International Management Group), a global leader in marketing, events, sports management, fashion, and gastronomy, which in May 2019 drew crowds to the capital as it took the helm of Exhibitions International agency and the Tutankhamun exhibition at La Villette (Robert, 2019). In 2020, during the COVID-19 crisis, Accor joined forces with AXA insurances to offer unrivalled medical assistance in hotels around the world and then allocated € 70 million (€ 35.4 million allocated in December 2022) to launch the "ALL Heartist Fund", a fund to help the group's employees and individual partners affected by the global health crisis. This undertaking earned it the distinction of "Best initiative in social hospitality" (HospitalityOn, 2023).

Since its founding in 1983, the Accor hotel group has successfully managed several crises through effective restructuring. The latest of these has been underway since October 2022, with the aim of dividing the group into two distinct business lines by 2023: "Economy, Midscale & Premium" and "Luxury & Lifestyle". The objective is to strengthen the appeal and identity of the group's best brands by accelerating their development through franchising, modernising of brands, "industrialisation of operating methods" and targeting the best talent and the best locations (Bazin quoted by Vignon, 2022). After the impact of the last health crisis, which caused a considerable drop in sales in 2020 (1621 Mio.), the group slightly exceeded its 2019 sales (4049 Mio.) in 2022 (4224 Mio.). This is undoubtedly due to the open-mindedness and creativity of the group's managers, who since the 1990s have relied on a hybrid management approach that considers both the demands of their front-line employees and those of their customers. Forever looking for improvements and innovations, the managers seek the best service practices in the tourism sector, drawing not only on data from their own structure but also looking to the competition for inspiration. Recently, the group has made a name for itself in marketing through prestigious partnerships and naming, thus renaming the mythical "Palais Omnisports Paris Bercy" "Accor Arena", namely in anticipation of the upcoming 2024 Paris Olympic Games (Ville de Paris, 2022).

The company has gradually introduced a matrix organisation (Burton et al., 2021, 37–45). To begin, following the Gulf War crisis in the early 1990s, Philippe Brizon and Charles Pélisson, the new co-presidents, proposed a viable project outline for Novotel in 1992 by naming 18 members of the new top management team and shedding two superfluous layers of hierarchy, abolishing the quality control system. In 1994, "Progrès" Novotel is launched. The quality control system is abolished, the competencies of all employees are assessed, and progress groups and clubs are created, which are invited to make proposals that are implemented (Calori et al., 2020, 783). Then, with new CEO Denis Hennequin in 2011, there was a new impetus to strengthen the organisation's matrix dimension by grafting "brand management onto Accor's well-structured geographical organisation" (Palierse, 2011), a project applied solely to Europe and implemented from 2013, to "empower" the group's different brands. Hennequin saw this move as vital, given the group's rapid expansion through franchising and the growing importance of the internet in distribution (Palierse, 2011). This form of organisation, which is more flexible than the hierarchical organisation typical in France, is proving to be conducive to creativity, making administrative processes and decision-making easier and opening the way to corporate entrepreneurship and intrapreneurship. However, when he was reappointed two years later, time did not allow him to lead this project, though his initiatives are still relevant today. When Sébastien Bazin took over as head of Accor in 2013, he sought advancement and innovation, wanting to lead the group into the digital age. Competitors such as AirBnB were cause for alarm but also stimulated him to act, resulting in 2015, in the creation of a "shadow comex" (Cismaru & Lunius, 2020, 263), a team of young people aged 26–37, as a kind of decision-making council modelled on the group's executive committee. After the health crisis, Bazin stated in an interview that the group had transformed its business model and was in the process of rethinking its organisation to become more agile. To this end, his aim is to simplify operating methods, "to rediscover the spirit of conquest and initiative that characterises Accor" (Bazin quoted by Palierse, 2020), in other words, to continue pruning superfluous layers of hierarchy, since "the best decisions are taken as near to the ground as possible. We need a head office that surveys and delegates responsibility, but that also gives more room for manoeuvering and decision-making to those who are in daily contact with our customers and owners" (Bazin quoted by Palierse, 2020). Since 2020, after the emergency health crisis management, the Accor group has been undergoing constant restructuring, still flattening its structure, which is too complex and costly (Valentin, 2021, 118–125). In October 2022, this restructuring of the organisation to be more matrix-based continued. Well aware of the profound changes taking place in the hotel industry, the changing demands of customers and the recruitment crisis, the CEO believes that employees should be valued more: financially, in their career development and through empowerment (Lukinaitė & Sondaitė, 2017, 144–151). Thus, this company-specific strategy has effectively helped it through several crises, proving itself conducive to corporate entrepreneurship. On the basis of previous studies, in particular the major case study carried out by Roland Calori, Charles Baden-Fuller and Brian Hunt from 1994 to 2001 (Calori et al., 2020, 779–804), it is clear that the corporate entrepreneurship implemented by the Accor group at all levels, which generates continuous innovations involving not only management but also all staff and customers, probably stems from the change in management strategy which Accor adopted after the Gulf War crisis of the 1990s. This hybrid strategy, which already sought to simplify the structure and the communication and scope of action of managers at all levels, and which had propelled two managers to the head of the group, certainly also contributed greatly to reducing the collateral damage of the COVID-19 crisis and stabilising the group's financial situation.

The hotel chain's credo today is to stimulate its own talents, encouraging them to disrupt and innovate, and to do this, its managers are looking to corporate entrepreneurship and intrapreneurship. In this spirit of creative openness, Frédéric Fontaine, one of the group's managers, created the Accor Innovation Laboratory in 2016, which monitors, conceptualises, tests and pilots new intrapreneurship projects, an approach inspired by design thinking.

Corporate entrepreneurship is generally associated with innovation and considered as a "radical change mechanism" that promotes entrepreneurial behaviours within an organisation. It detects new potentials and opportunities, challenges bureaucracy, encourages, and stimulates innovation (McFadzean, O'Loughlin & Shaw, 2005, 351). Nevertheless, the understanding of corporate entrepreneurship, both from an empirical and a theoretical perspective is still an open issue (Kuratko et al., 2015, p. 247). McFadzean et al. (2005) pointed out the importance of the "entrepreneurial attitude", thus focusing on the personality of the entrepreneur, his flexibility, his ability to see what is missing, recognising opportunities, his talent to evaluate the environment, his ability to make changes and to generate opportunities. In this vision, innovation and success in corporate entrepreneurship depend above all on the character of the entrepreneur (McFadzean et al., 2005, 366).

While most studies do not distinguish corporate entrepreneurship from intrapreneurship, we concur with Stam (2013) and consider intrapreneurship as an initiative that comes directly from the employees, and as a tool of corporate entrepreneurship. In the case of Accor and its brand Novotel, of which Novotel Paris Bercy is a franchise, we consider the entrepreneurial actions carried out internally by the employee-led Accor laboratory as intrapreneurship, and those implemented by the general manager of the franchise Novotel Paris Centre Bercy as corporate entrepreneurship. However, if one of the projects is pursued in Novotel Paris Centre Bercy independently by one of the employees, it comes under the heading of intrapreneurship.

There is also a difference in the motivation for carrying out corporate entrepreneurship actions. While entrepreneurs can be driven by both financial and non-financial goals or by a negative context, for intrapreneurs, the need for achievement, new challenges and autonomy are more essential than the financial gain.

This spirit of originality and innovation, the company's participative strategy and its desire for disruption and agility led to developing corporate entrepreneurship actions and has become widespread across all the brands and all the sites. It seems that this form of management, which tends to involve and empower employees, has also enabled the Novotel Paris Bercy management team to get through the health crisis with no redundancies and to introduce several innovations in recent years. The Novotel brand, the predecessor and origin of the Accor group, reflects the group's strategy particularly well since 1983. Today Novotel is part of Accor's mid-range category, with 530 hotels and 105,162 rooms worldwide, representing 13% of the Accor group's hotel portfolio (Accor Key Indicators).

Novotel Bercy is a full-service hotel restaurant, including a hotel, restaurant, and seven meeting rooms. Currently 80 people work at the hotel, with general manager Richard Laine, who is supported by an eight-person management committee and several assistants and staff. According to the general manager, business at Bercy runs yearlong from 1 January to 31 December, with no peaks or troughs, as the company's "business" and "leisure" activities are consistently busy. The scope of the business includes the area around Gare de Lyon, one of Paris's major train stations, and the Bercy district (ZAC Bercy), a historic wine-growing area that has been transformed into a business and leisure district, much sought-after by Parisians. Bercy's proximity to the Ministry of the Economy and Finance, Quai de la Rapée, Parc de Bercy with its film library, Cour Saint Émilion and the Palais Omnisport Paris Bercy and the current Accor Arena make it a popular business and leisure district for Parisians, tourists and businesspeople alike. The Novotel Paris Bercy is located next to this sports and entertainment venue, which supplies yet other activities. According to Richard Laine, it is the hotel's central location and its formula combining "individual business" and "individual leisure", as well as its easy access to all the trade fairs, congresses and exhibitions held in Paris and from tourism in general in the capital that explains its success—see Figure 24.2.

Richard Laine identifies three areas of economic and political influence that support the property. The first is the local area in which the venue and the Accor Arena are found, which has a rich calendar of shows and sporting events. The second is the "Gare de Lyon" train station, a dynamic district with all the commercial and economic activities around it, such as the Ministry of Finance opposite the hotel, the headquarters of the RATP and the Locam company. In addition, an ambitious modernisation of the Seine side of the Gare de Lyon is under study, as it is currently an unattractive place

Figure 24.2 Novotel Paris Bercy.

Source: www.accor.com

Figure 24.3
Source: www.accor.com

with heavy traffic. The importance of Paris as a city of wide-ranging events and trade fairs has a direct impact on the hotel as well (see Figure 24.3).

The hotel is located in a highly competitive neighbourhood with more than 3,000 rooms within a radius of around 1.5 km. It is an area that today offers mostly 4-star hotels, as well as 2- and 3-star budget hotels, with chains accounting for around 1/3 of those and independents 2/3, according to Mr Laine. As for his competitors in the area, he particularly likes Courtyard, Citizen M and all the 4-star independent hotels.

As the capital city, Paris and the Ile-de-France suburbs have the largest accommodation capacity in Europe. With 1,601 hotels and 85,021 rooms, Paris alone accounts for 66% of the region's hotels, with 818 outside Paris. In the summer of 2022, tourist activity in the Ile-de-France region was close to its pre-COVID-19 level, with 45.5 million overnight stays for the 2022 summer season (a slight drop of 2.1% compared to 2019). However, in Paris, which accounts for more than half of all overnight stays in the region, tourist activity has exceeded its pre-crisis level. Since 2014, the number of 4-star hotels in Paris almost doubled, rising from 259 to 475. Thus, the Paris hotel industry has experienced several upheavals in recent years that have slowed tourism, such as the attacks in 2015 and 2016, the street riots linked to the yellow vests between 2018 and 2019, the frequent transport strikes in those same years, but the hotel occupancy rate had never fallen significantly (apart from in 2016). However, the health crisis in 2020–2021 caused occupancy to fall to such an extent that many hotels had to close their doors for several months. At present, the occupancy rate of beds in the capital has risen to 75%.

Regarding developments in terms of the company and employment, Richard Laine tells us that the management team at Novotel Paris Bercy was forced to make some choices during the health crisis. The main choice was to keep the 80 employees, which led to a salary review policy, which is usually revised internally every 4 to 5 years. According to its manager, the hotel encountered slightly fewer difficulties than the others, especially in terms of recruitment, because the hotel has always been lucky enough to be fully staffed. This fortunate situation is linked to a policy focused on pay, working conditions and well-being within the company. According to the manager, the hotel enjoys constant business throughout the year, which is not subject to seasonal fluctuations and is well managed, as the hotel has been open for over 33 years. The manager tells us they review their payment policy every 3 to 4 years, to make sure it is as close as possible to staff's expectations. To this end, in June 2021 he interviewed five recent employees who had been with the company for less than a year and five employees who had been with the company for more than 3 years to assess their expectations and to identify the trend. This approach proved both relevant and profitable, as he can now pride himself on having a full complement of staff, which is rare in this industry, where there is a constant shortage of personnel.

To retain high-quality teams, future talent must be trained from the outset. To achieve this, Richard Laine explains that he is working hard on developing apprentice programmes, taking on a significant number of apprentices: from the "Grandes écoles", BTS, bachelor's and master's degree programmes, who will provide him with a pool of employees in the long term. These apprentices are spread across all 14 hotel professions: reception, catering, across floors or in administration. Most will stay on after graduation for at least one or two years and are responsible for training new staff. Recruiting in this way has the advantage that the staff is trained to respond to the specificities of the establishment from the moment they are hired. Management has also entered partnerships with schools familiar with the company's expectations and send employees who meet them.

In addition, flexible managers are needed for a matrix-based structure to be efficient and allow intrapreneurship or corporate entrepreneurship. Thus, at the entire Accor group, particularly at Novotel Paris Bercy, the emphasis is on individuals thanks to what Richard Laine calls "a well-being policy" that relies on respect and clear, well-defined rules between staff. To keep up, we need to put in place forms of dynamics with challenges, because employees need to feel involved. To ensure staff well-being, the human resource (HR) department offers a range of activities, such as massages and talks by outside specialists, to encourage employees to discuss a range of issues. The most important task of the HR department, which is coached directly by Richard Laine, is to respond to all employee expectations and problems, whether personal or professional, and this works perfectly in this establishment, according to its director.

Corporate entrepreneurship and innovation actions

The concept of intrapreneurship, which emerged in the mid-1970s, is here to boost companies and help them meet the social and environmental expectations of today's society. It entails a unique experience of working for the common good in a comfortable setting, as an employee. As a result, project leaders feel more involved in projects that promote sustainability or have a social impact.

The Accor group has long understood that supporting original projects from its employees keeps creative minds and spreads positive energy throughout an organisation. Through its Innovation Lab, the group shows that innovation doesn't only belong to start-ups, but that a large company with a history of over 50 years, like Accor, is on an equal footing with its young rivals. In this sense, intrapreneurship has proved to be a business accelerator and an excellent way of developing an in-house culture of innovation.

Laurence Bordry, vice president of Accor's Innovation Laboratory, believes that intrapreneurship has a social impact "because we're looking after people, and the time spent with our entrepreneurs, helping them to develop, makes them think of others" (Bordry, 2020). Also, intrapreneurship often enables employees to reposition themselves within the company, make a name for themselves, and get the job of their dreams. Similarly, Frédéric Fontaine, (creator and former vice president of this laboratory), believes intrapreneurial initiatives have allowed projects to be implemented twice as fast as by calling on outside services. Frédéric Fontaine is behind the Accor Innovation Laboratory, which was set up in 2016. He was at the time the sales and marketing manager in the UK, and vice president of worldwide marketing for the Mercure, MGallery and IBIS brands at the group's headquarters in Paris. After designing the new "millennial lifestyle" brand, JO&JOE, and relaunching the WOJO co-working space (with a new identity and new services), he piloted the TECHSTARS partnership (start-up acceleration and corporate boot camps) and managed VIVATECHNOLOGY for 4 years.

Through these projects, he explored a wide range of issues in the transformation of hospitality, such as micro-hospitality, co-living, mobility, well-being, start-ups, and intrapreneurship. In an article published in May 2017, he deciphered the phenomenon of intrapreneurship and highlighted the importance of in-house employee-led projects. Frédéric Fontaine stresses the importance of defying conventional management structures and the importance of adopting a group posture. His strategy is to combine external talent with internal talent. He claims, "to coach these teams rather than manage them with benevolence, listening and respect" (Fontaine quoted by Roosen, 2018), to create a climate conducive to innovation. Regarding experts in sociology and design thinking, Fontaine believes every organisation needs to draw on this wealth of opportunities, talent and imagination to stimulate creativity and provoke its employees to take risks. Through his many successes, but also failures, he knows that it is the employees "who will fuel the dynamism of a group, affirm its innovation strategy and create value in the market" (Fontaine, 2017).

To demonstrate the importance attached to employees and the consideration given to each individual in all their diversity and creativity, at Accor, employees are not called "collaborators", but are considered talents and called "Heartists"—a contraction of "heart" and "artist"—because, as Nicolas Saint Marc, Vice President in charge of operations at Accor France, states: "our hotels are great stages where each person can express all their personality and know-how" (Saint Marc, 2022).

Richard Laine explains that the hotel is affiliated with a brand that it must respect. In the scenario of an introduction of a new technology, he depends on the Novotel brand and cannot implement a new product in the Accor scope because regarding matters of security, the group preserves itself. According to Laine, this means that anything that is deployed or that could be a new idea will be accepted, but if you want it to be connected to the hotel's computers, this is not necessarily validated by Accor. However, Accor is deploying a lot of products today, for example, in terms of digitisation, there is a small QR code in each room that gives guests all the information about the establishment and the city where the hotel is located. The option of ordering food and drink from the hotel room is also in line with the Accor brand.

One of the most remarkable projects undertaken by the hotel is the transformation of the old suites into flats. These suites had not been restored and had been offered for sale without success, even though the price per square metre in Bercy is quite high. Richard Laine then suggested to his teams that each suite should be converted into a bedroom, but before entrusting them with this project, he gave it some thought. In the end, the decision was made to convert the suites into flats, with a remarkable result, which, according to Richard Laine, is working perfectly today and has doubled the turnover of these rooms.

It was the Novotel Bercy team's own initiative and idea, implemented by a close-knit team based on creativity and innovation. The team's strategy is thinking, testing, and innovating like a think tank. According to Laine, it's a matter of "wringing out all the ideas that might be out there and then putting a fun side to things", because if you don't come up with innovations, if you don't have constant and lively activity, there's a risk that employees will get bored. These corporate entrepreneurship projects not only stimulate employees' creativity, but by involving them, giving them a voice and then responsibility for running the project, we also enable them to acquire new skills and greater flexibility.

Therefore, you must ask them directly, get them to make suggestions, enable them to implement them and then, above all, involve them in everything that is going to be done to bring about change in the hotel. As Richard Laine explains, the many renovations constantly taking place in the hotel involve all the staff in the department concerned. For example, in the sense of corporate entrepreneurship, the management gives them a budget and asks them to come up with projects in certain parts of the building. To the director, these front-line staff know the institution's needs best in terms of change, adaptation, or renovation, as they work there daily and are in constant contact with customers. All this contributes to the smooth running of the business ecosystem and allows the group to pursue a shared hospitality strategy.

One of the latest digital innovations at Novotel Paris Bercy is an innovative IT tool called 1 Check. This system provides a live vision of the staff on each floor and the technical teams so the receptionist can be informed in real-time of the condition of the rooms and the technicians of any malfunction. Richard Laine is against the excessive digitalisation of hotels. In his view, it is essential to preserve the human side of hospitality. Above all, he sees digitalisation as an entirely positive aspect in the administrative sphere.

Another innovative product, apart from digital, was the ladies' room, developed around ten years ago, to meet the expectations of female customers. To satisfy those specific needs, a survey of 50 female clients was conducted, and ten key points were identified, which led to the development of ladies' rooms. They are equipped with a full-length mirror and wellness products, including a range of herbal teas with a real porcelain mug, a "little" piece of chocolate and a glass vessel to hold all your make-up products. There are also a few shower-related products, such as a shower cap, exfoliating bath products and an emergency hygiene kit. In addition, three types of pillows are offered due to the different opinions on this type of product, which women consider especially important. As for the design of the rooms, the Novotel brand now offers four distinct types of rooms, with different colours and layouts. It is an interesting design option according to Richard Laine, because it allows the rooms to adapt to the environment of the establishment and to its clientele, business, or leisure, even if it is always standardised in some way.

To unite employees and motivate them to get actively involved in corporate entrepreneurship and to thank them for a low turnover, management implements small actions, such as a big general Kahoot! (a game-based learning platform) rewarded by an evening at the Accor Arena with dinner and a concert. Each hotel service gets its staff to either the Moulin Rouge or the Lido once a year, and other individual initiatives are taken. Employees who have worked hard and invested themselves well are financially rewarded every month with exceptional bonuses.

Regarding the management of entrepreneurial projects, Richard Laine explains that he does not manage the projects, although the initiative often comes from him. All ideas for innovation are submitted to the team and debated, and the implementation idea comes up in a group process. Then, once there is a project, it is entrusted to someone who will lead it. It will always be someone connected with the project.

One of the most recent projects involved major works to create 30 extra rooms, which resulted in a small terrace on the 3rd floor. A fruitful debate on innovative ideas for the space was launched. One interesting idea was the creation of a temporary outside meeting room, to be set up by the person in the sales department. She would oversee furnishing, decorating, and sales support, etc. Once her idea has come to a result, she has a date to file it with management, who will discuss it, promote it, and set the project in motion. This type of project is carried out within the framework of the franchise, independently of the Accor group.

As Richard Laine explains, the Novotel brand has its own set of rules laid down in a contract, which the Novotel Paris Bercy team respects while enhancing the value of the site. However, everything that is neither mentioned, nor forbidden in the contract, is authorised.

As part of their entrepreneurial activities, they also keep abreast of new trends. Once a year in July, Richard Laine goes on a trip for four days to visit all sorts of new hotels in Paris, taking with him four people from his management committee. Looking for inspiration, they make appointments with establishments that have just opened or that are completely different. For example, during the last inspirational getaway, they were surprised at the Citizen M hotel that the customer was totally involved. Since then, he has been thinking about possibly installing check-in and check-out kiosks or digitalising certain rooms to exploit the many possibilities of home automation. In terms of design, he states that he got inspired by the lifestyle decor with no constraints of the 25h-hotels chain, where bicycles with flowers instead of flowerpots, or even cars are displayed in the common spaces. Accor's Mama Shelter brand also uses this lifestyle decor.

He says he came up with the idea of an ephemeral meeting room after seeing an ephemeral room, a sort of bubble, in another establishment. This discovery would have made him think of something similar on the terrace of his hotel during the summer, powered by water and electricity[3]. As he points out, this kind of ephemeral room will probably be one of the next projects. According to Laine, he just needs to find a time slot and then think carefully about the marketing, offering it intelligently at the right time.

Another successful entrepreneurial project was the construction of large rooms in the hotel in a year and a half on a small piece of terrace. Richard Laine had consulted an architect for advice on exploiting this outdoor space, which had suggested the possibility of constructing a three-story building there. And yet, for 30 years, nobody had thought of using this place. Then there was a sort of stairwell with emergency landings inside. Richard Laine had consulted an architect for advice on exploiting this outdoor space, who suggested the possibility of constructing a three-storey building on the site. As a result, the hotel has been able to significantly increase its capacity and appeal, with two duplex rooms 30 metres high with a terrace and an incredible view over Paris- see Figure 24.4.

Finally, according to Richard Laine, who has been in practice for 40 years, corporate entrepreneurship means trying "to plan ahead, which means you first must know your business and how far you can go with your teams". You must know how to "get your staff on board", otherwise any attempt at entrepreneurship is doomed to failure.

Figure 24.4
Source: www.accor.com

Then, to Richard Laine, it's important to identify the business opportunity and to do so, you need not only to know the needs of your business but also to know how you can enhance it. One must keep an interest in what has not yet been discovered and be up to date on innovations in the hotel industry. All areas of the business need to be constantly evolving. Richard Laine sees the company's important vectors as a triptych, distinguishing between three categories: sales, marketing, and product, which crystallise around the HR department. The latter must ensure that staff feel at ease because they are responsible for the delivery of the service daily and, as Laine points out, without their satisfaction and cohesion, the establishment cannot function. According to the general manager, you need to be opportunistic, know how to stick to the trend and then seize the right moment and the opportunity to sell in terms of services. Indeed, it's often temporary, linked to a trend that will fade over time, like the brunch frenzy ten years ago, which Novotel Paris Bercy was able to take advantage of. It was the same with the concerts organised throughout the year by the hotel, then when the nightlife expanded to all the banks of the Seine near the hotel, Richard Laine and his team decided to reduce this service to four months of the year.

The director of Novotel Paris Bercy is convinced that it is necessary to keep moving, but also sometimes to challenge oneself, to avoid the risk of tiring employees by asking too much of them through creativity. In his eyes, managers need to relearn how to manage, motivate and involve their employees because mentalities are changing, and team managers are getting increasingly younger. Richard Laine didn't hesitate to take a 3-day training course with a coach, because he had difficulty understanding his young colleagues and thought it was up to him to adapt. After the Covid crisis, a complicated time for all hotel managers, he also needed a personal boost, a challenge he met thanks to six weeks of coaching. To look after others, manage a team, and motivate staff requires that you feel at ease yourself.

Epilogue

Within the Accor hospitality group, corporate entrepreneurship and intrapreneurship have generated a great deal of innovation in recent years. Intrapreneurship, as explored by Accor's Innovation Laboratory, but also by certain franchises such as Novotel Paris Bercy, is not only a driver of innovation through design thinking, but it is also a way of developing talents, "Heartists" as they are called at Accor. Employees who are given a project and a budget gain self-confidence and grow within the company. As this case study shows, not only training apprentices but also enabling employees to grow professionally through intrapreneurship, means building loyalty among staff who will stay for the medium to long term, which is a win-win situation in times of the current recruitment crisis in hospitality in France, following the COVID-19 pandemic.

At Accor, corporate entrepreneurship and intrapreneurship are enabled by the group's structured matrix organisation. Thanks to its flexibility, this form of management, which often relies on two leaders, enables teams to make rapid progress on projects since it ensures easy communication. However, if we want to achieve results through corporate entrepreneurship, human relationships must always come first. As Richard Laine says, and as Sébastien Bazin also mentions in most of his interviews, if you want to move ahead and innovate, you have to cherish your employees. Matrix organisations only work when the human dimension is placed first and when communication between managers and employees is facilitated. Removing superfluous layers from the hierarchy was already on the agenda in the 1990s, and a participative strategy and restructuring along these lines proved effective. The same objective is still guiding Sébastian Bazin's current restructuring. In his drive for innovation, he is supported not only by the Innovation Laboratory but also by chief digital officer Maud Bailly, an advocate of equality and diversity, who carefully selects the talents she then entrusts with important roles.

Sources and Acknowledgements

The following person has been interviewed to develop this case:

Mr. Richard Laine (General Director of Novotel Paris Centre Bercy)
Many thanks to Nathalie SENNÉ for editing and proofreading the English
language version of the text.

Notes

1 Urbano D. et al. (2022), "Corporate entrepreneurship: a systematic literature review and future research agenda", *Small Business Economics*, 59, 1541–1565.
2 Groupe Accor, « Notre Histoire », https://group.accor.com/fr-FR/group/who-we-are/our-history
3 In 2017, the Accor group developed an ephemeral container hotel concept with Lyon-based start-up Capsa.

References

Accor, Key Indicators, Parc hotelier. https://group.accor.com/fr-FR/finance/results-and-publications/key-indicators#anchor_1484046855344

Arnaud, J.-F. (2016). Quand Sébastien Bazin plonge Accor dans la nouvelle économie. *Challenges*, 14.02.2016. https://www.challenges.fr/entreprise/hotellerie/quand-sebastien-bazin-plonge-accor-dans-la-nouvelle-economie_39615

Bazin, S. (2022). Accor: Cette industrie peut mourir, si le service n'est pas là. Interview avec Vanguélys Panayotis, Hospitality, 28.10.22. https://hospitality-on.com/fr/ressources-humaines/sebastien-bazin-accor-cette-industrie-peut-mourir-si-le-service-nest-pas-la

Burton, R. M., Obel, B., & Haakonsson, D. (2021). How to get the matrix organization to work. *Journal of Organization Design*, 4(3), 37–45. Available at: https://ssrn.com/abstract=2088978

Calori, R., Baden-Fuller, C., & Hunt, B. (2020). Managing change at novotel: Back to the future. *Long Range Planning*, Published by Elsevier,12.2000, 33(6), 779–804. Available at: https://www.researchgate.net/publication/223682621_Managing_Change_at_Novotel_Back_to_the_Future

Cismaru, L., & Lunius, R. (2020). Bridging the generation gap in the hospitality industry: Reverse mentoring - an innovative talent management practice for present and future generations of employees. *Sustainability*, 12(1), 263. doi. 10.3390/su12010263

Druelle, S. (Insee) (2022). Été 2022 en Île de France: l'activité touristique est proche de son niveau d'avant crise. Institut national de la statistique et des études économiques, 30.11.2022.

Fontaine, F., « Pourquoi les meilleures innovations sont (aussi) à chercher à l'interne », 15.05.2017, LinkedIn. https://www.linkedin.com/pulse/pourquoi-les-meilleures-innovations-sont-aussi-%C3%A0-frederic-fontaine/?originalSubdomain=fr

Groupe Accor. Notre Histoire. https://group.accor.com/fr-FR/group/who-we-are/our-history

Groupe Accor. All Heartist Fund. https://group.accor.com/fr-FR/group/our-commitments/all-heartist-fund

Hospitality On (2020). Campaign - Discover the All Heartists Fund by Accor. *Hospitality On*, 09.11.23. https://hospitality-on.com/en/hospitality-awards/accor/discover-all-heartist-fund-accor

Kuratko, D. F., Hornsby, J. S., & Hayton, J. (2015), Corporate entrepreneurship: The innovative challenge for a new global economic reality. *Small Business Economics*, 45(2), 245–253. Available at: 10.1007/s11187-015-9630-8

Lukinaitė, E., & Sondaitė, J. (2017). Mindset of employees working in a matrix organisational structure. *Verslas: Teorija ir Praktika*, *1*, 144–151.

Palierse, C., Accor va mettre les marques au cœur de son organisation. 29.9.2011. https://www.lesechos.fr/2011/09/accor-va-mettre-les-marques-au-coeur-de-son-organisation-400346

Palierse, C., & Barroux, D. (2020). Interview avec Sébastien Bazin. *Les Echos*, le 4.8.2020. https://www.lesechos.fr/industrie-services/tourisme-transport/accor-se-reorganise-pour-devenir-plus-agile-1228479

Pouzadoux Bokobza, M. (2020). Retour d'expérience d'Orange, Accor, FDJ et de 2 expertes sur l'intrapreneuriat. 08.11.2020, *Make Sense*. https://france.makesense.org/media/retour-dexperience-dorange-accor-fdj-et-de-2-expertes-sur-lintrapreneuriat/

Robert, M. (2019). Le géant des Américains des évènements IMG fait le buzz à Paris. *Les Echos*, 09.05.2019. https://www.lesechos.fr/industrie-services/services-conseils/le-geant-americain-des-evenements-img-fait-le-buzz-a-paris-1017230

Saint Marc, N. (2021). Chez Accor, votre meilleur cv c'est votre Vice-Président en charge des opérations chez Accor France. *Pôle Emploi*, 2021. https://www.pole-emploi.org/accueil/actualites/2022/chez-accor-votre-meilleur-cv-cest-votre-personnalite.html?type=article

Stam, E. (2013). Knowledge and entrepreneurial employees: A country-level analysis. *Small Business Economics*, 41(4), 887–898. doi. 10.1007/s11187-013-9511-y

Urbano, D., Turro, A., Wright, M., et al. (2022). Corporate entrepreneurship: A systematic literature review and future research agenda. *Small Business Economics*, 1541–1565.

Valentin, S. (2021). Emergency measures, actions implemented, evolution of the offer: How Accor is managing the COVID-19 crisis and preparing for the aftermath. *Espaces, Tourisme & Loisirs*, 118–125.

Vignon, E. (2022). Accor: Sébastien Bazin en passe d'être renouvelé à la tête du groupe pour piloter sa réorganisation. 06.07.2022, *L'Écho touristique*, https://www.lechotouristique.com/article/accor-sebastien-bazin-en-passe-detre-renouvele-a-la-tete-du-groupe-pour-piloter-sa-reorganisation

Ville de Paris (2022). Pour Paris 2024, L'Accor Arena prend le rebond? 09.03.2022, https://www.paris.fr/pages/pour-paris-2024-l-accor-arena-prend-le-rebond-20428

Watkins, M. (2023). L'hôtellerie parisienne retrouve (enfin) des clients. *Coach Omnium*, https://coachomnium.com/bonus/hotellerie-parisienne/

Case 25 Barceló Hotel Group

The introduction of a Spanish company to the USA, LATAM, East Asia, Africa and Europe through horizontal and vertical growth strategies and innovation

Marta Jacob, Teresa Aguiar-Quintana, and Francisca Rosa Álamo-Vera

Introduction and case selection

The Barceló Group was founded almost a century ago by Simón Barceló in 1931 on the Balearic island of Mallorca (Spain). It is a family-owned firm that operates on every level of the tourism value chain and represents the first Spanish tourism group. Thus, it has been a vertically integrated tourism group since 2012, and its business model is made up of a hotel division, the Barceló Hotel Group, and a travel division, Ávoris. Both divisions are represented by their different hotel brands in the USA, Europe, East Asia and LATAM[1] and their travel division, including leisure travel agencies, general tour operators, regular airlines, and incoming services.

The hotel business group started with 37 establishments in 1995 and, in January 2023, had 277 hotels and more than 61,996 rooms across 25 countries and marketed under four brands: Royal Hideaway Luxury Hotels & Resorts, Barceló Hotels & Resorts, Occidental Hotels & Resorts and Allegro Hotels. In 2017, the Barceló Group acquired 60% of the capital of Crestline Hotels & Resorts, which, together with the 40% owned by Barceló previously, led them to become the sole owner of one of the most important independent hotel manager operators in the USA. The Barceló Hotel Group, the hotel division of Barceló Group, is the 2nd largest chain in Spain and the 31st in the world. In 2021 and 2019, it was awarded the prize for the world's leading hotel management company at the World Travel Awards. The travel division, Ávoris, has a network of 1,500 points of sales and more than 700 travel agencies operating in over 20 countries in five continents, with more than 25 travel brands and over 5.6 million travellers.

The Barceló Group has been owned by the Barceló family for three generations. With the passing of generations of family members in the Barceló Group, the company's governance structure has evolved towards a higher degree of managerial professionalism. In the past, apart from the board of

DOI: 10.4324/9781003454465-26

directors, there was a family board, which is currently inactive. The business corporation's current management structure reflects that professionalism, which has meant differentiating (family) ownership from company management, incorporating independent professionals from outside the family, establishing good corporate governance standards, and aligning family and business interests. The company's organisational structure is currently represented by: (1) co-chairmen: Simón Barceló Tous and Simón Pedro Barceló Vadell; (2) the Board of Directors: Simón Pedro Barceló Vadell, Simón Barceló Tous, Guillermo Barceló Tous, and Pedro Fernández-Martos Montero; (3) a controller of the Barceló group called Antonio Darder; (4) three CEOs: Raúl González (CEO EMEA of Barceló Hotel Group), James Carroll, CEO of Crestline Hotels & Resorts; and finally, Vicente Fenollar, CEO of Ávoris. There is an executive management composed of four people: (1) a Chief Financial Officer; (2) a managing director for Central and South America; (3) a managing director for Mexico; (4) a managing director for Caribe.

Business profile, framework, and environment

The business model of Barceló Group is the result of a strategy of decentralisation and geographic specialisation. In 1985, Barceló started its international operations by opening a hotel in the Dominican Republic, and from that date, Barceló has conducted an increasing internalisation process. This process has been carried out by adapting its profile based on the geographies where the company is present. The strategy covers all the stages in the value chain, from franchisors in Asian countries to full-cycle operators in Latin American and Caribbean countries, going through pure management in the USA and hotel operations in Europe, Middle East and Africa (EMEA) (Barceló Group, 2022). Presently, 44% of hotels are located in EMEA countries, 27% in LATAM countries and 29% in the USA. The hotel division has defined a multi-brand strategy to diversify, and each brand has been designed to ensure a complete customer experience and deliver results, as previously represented in Figure 25.1.

Barceló Hotel Group is the premier hotel company in Spain. The hotel division has different brands: Occidental, an upscale brand with functional hotels; Barceló, an upper upscale brand with innovative hotels adapted to the local culture; Allegro, an upper midscale brand with more casual hotels where the essence is energy, freedom and fun; and Royal Hideaway, an affordable luxury brand with luxury hotels recognised for their attention to detail, discretion and elegance. The Barceló brand represents 41% of supply, Occidental 22%, Royal Hideaway 3%, Allegro 3% and others in the USA 31%. The Barceló Group currently has only 4- and 5-star hotels, divided between leisure and urban hotels. The hotel portfolio is divided as follows: (1) all hotels in LATAM countries are owned and managed directly since they are the main source of revenues in the company, over 80% of total EBITDA[2] comes from this region; (2) in USA all hotels are under management contracts through Crestline; (3) in EMEA they are generally managed through the collaboration of investors; (4) in Africa some hotels are owned and managed by the group and some hotels with third-party partners; and finally, (5) only around 1% of hotels are franchises. This hotel portfolio is different from the one that we can find in Riu Hotels & Resorts where around 90% of hotels are owned and managed by the company.

In addition, to delve into the entrepreneurial activity of Barceló Group, it is necessary to know its context of activity since many of the actions take place in response to changes in the environment. Related to that, with almost a century of history, the company's long journey has been subject to ups and downs in the tourism sector in general. The founders of Barceló come from the Balearics and identified since the beginning the opportunity to contribute to the development of a tourist destination like the Balearics and the development of tourist activity in other parts of the world. Recently, the tourist panorama suffered a setback with the COVID-19 health pandemic, which completely paralysed tourist activity and significantly affected Spain, other destinations and all tourism-related activities. Barceló also suffered the consequences of this pandemic but has recovered very rapidly. In fact, in 2022, the Barceló Group repaid the € 320 million loan it had with the SEPI[3].

When focusing on the Balearic tourism industry, especially its multinational hotel chains, the industry and the hotel chains are well-known for their competitiveness maintained for decades (Aguiló et al., 2005). This is the result of intense innovation activity due to a high level of corporate entrepreneurship and internationalisation strategy (Jacob & Groizard, 2007; Jacob et al., 2003, 2010). In fact, Groizard and Jacob (2004) showed that in 2003, the hotel division was highly internationalised (78% of hotel supply), with 29.8% of hotels in LATAM countries, while in 2023, this percentage is 27%. Additionally, empirical evidence on innovation in the Balearic tourism sector shows first, the high innovation activity of Balearic tourism firms in general and of hostelry firms in particular (Jacob et al., 2003) and second, even more intense innovation activity when they internationalise in LATAM countries (Jacob & Groizard, 2007). Process innovations are the most common type of innovation and organisational innovations represent an important percentage of total innovation activity in the Balearics and in LATAM countries. Technological innovations are more frequent than non-technological innovations.

The development of corporate entrepreneurship and innovation

The case under analysis, Barceló Group, represents the corporate entrepreneurship (CE) and continuous innovation of a tourism group specialised in distribution and intermediary services. Guth and Ginsberg (1990) defined CE according to two activities: (1) innovation and corporate venturing activities, and (2) renewal activities or the corporations' ability to compete and take risks. CE is the creation of new businesses, products, or services from inside an organisation to generate new revenue growth through entrepreneurial action.

From a strategic perspective, corporate growth can take two directions: horizontal or vertical. Horizontal growth means the company develops new products, enters new geographical or customer markets, and diversifies by entering sectors that add businesses based on new products and markets to its portfolio. Vertical growth or vertical integration means that the company grows within its value chain; that is, it begins to carry out activities of its suppliers or its distributors/buyers, the first case being called backward vertical integration and the second, forward vertical integration. It is certainly a risky strategy, and its efficiency has been questioned since the company decides to conduct activities that are not related to its core business, such as manufacturing an input or raw material differs from assembling or producing an item, much less distributing it.

In the academic literature, it has been questioned whether companies can grow in both directions at the same time or if the fact of growing in one direction places them in a worse condition to grow in the other (García Soto et al., 2002). However, in the tourism industry, it is possible to find cases of corporate groups that show horizontal and vertical growth simultaneously. Thus, hotel chains integrate vertically forward by creating or acquiring their own tour operator and retail travel agency, or vertically backwards with their own catering company. As for horizontal development, the internationalisation of hotel chains or tour operators, the development of new services for hotel chains—such as trademarks in other customer segments—or the purchase of investment funds to diversify their tourism business show horizontal growth.

The Barceló Group is one example of both horizontal and vertical growth. It integrated vertically forward by acquiring its own retail travel agency and its own tour operator. The travel division, Ávoris, is a vertically integrated travel company gathering over 700 travel agencies on five continents, several tour operators and receptive operators, and even an airline. The hotel division is currently the result of a horizontal growth strategy due to its intense internationalisation strategy conducted since 1985 and its innovation activity over the years (Jacob & Groizard, 2007). At the close of 2021, the Barceló Group, which employs 27,617 employees (average active workforce), registered a turnover of € 2.822.2 million, an EBITDA (with IFRS 16[4]) of € 146 million and a Revenue Per Available Room (RevPAR) of € 39.4 per room. In 2022, Barceló Group reached an EBITDA (with IFRS 16) of € 422.6M and a RevPAR of € 65.6 per room.

Hence, the current business model of this business corporation, Barceló Group, is the result of a combination of vertical and horizontal growth strategies that lead the company to operate on every level of the tourism value chain and in many destinations worldwide.

Ávoris is devoted to serving all tourist segments: holidays, leisure, and business. They have five main areas: wholesale, retail, flights, incoming services, and gift boxes. First, the wholesale division can be subdivided into four specialised areas: (1) a Holiday Area, where the company works with B the travel brand through an extensive network of around 700 travel agencies in Spain and Portugal; (2) an Online Area, with two brands Iberojet and Mundoviajes.com, that operate as online travel agents; (3) a Corporate Area, with two brands: BCD Travel, a benchmark for business travel and corporate customers and BCD meetings & events, for event management services; and (4) a Conference Area, with a brand, BCO Congresos, for organising international conferences in Spain.

Second, the retail division is made up of 12 tour operators, of which six are generalist brands (Catai, Viva Tours, Quelónea & Jolidey, and Rhodasol & Bedtoyou, a bedbank open to all agencies with a network of over 100,000 hotels). The other six are specialised brands (Special Tours offers tour packages with a strong presence in Latin America, Le Plan, specialists in travel to Disneyland Paris, Le Ski Ski specialised on sport and adventure travels, Nortravel is a Portuguese tour operator specialised in tours around Europe and holidays and tours in Brazil, Azores and Madeira, Jade Travel which specialises particularly on road trips, and Le Musik, specialised on music and concert packages). Third, its incoming services division gathers the brand Turavia and the brand Colours. Fourth, the flight division is comprised of the airline company Evelop, which operates standard and charter flights to holiday destinations, especially to the Caribbean, the UK, and the Canary Islands. Finally, the gift boxes area where the company offers themed gift boxes at around 3,560 sale points in Spain.

However, unlike other sectors of the economy, the tourism value chain gives it a markedly cross-cutting and interdisciplinary nature. The tourism industry is a sector that depends on many inputs for its development and can generate knowledge and innovation for other sectors of the economy (through its value chain). It can also draw on knowledge and innovations from other sectors that provide technologies, supplies, or materials and from customers and other actors in a destination (Jacob, 2022).

Empirical evidence shows that the most frequent type of innovation in tourism is process innovation (e.g., Jacob et al., 2003, 2007; Orfila-Sintes et al., 2005), but organisational innovation is usually important (Ubierna & Pérez, 2016). Pikkemaat and Peters (2006) show that the most common innovation in the hospitality sector is process innovation and that product innovation is very rare. Camisón and Monfort-Mir (2012) indicate that a large part of the innovative efforts of tourism companies are focused on non-technological aspects.

When focusing on the hotel division, Barceló Hotel Group, the main corporate actions that have defined its current situation and its horizontal growth are: first, in 1995 they initiated a growth strategy in the urban segment with the lease of the Hotel Barceló Sants from Renfe and three hotels in the Basque Country, and by 2017 the urban hotel portfolio represented 52% of total supply, thanks to using leasing and management contracts (Roure & Segurado, 2019). Also, during this year, the corporation purchased three hotels in the Canary Islands, consolidating its position in the archipelago. In 1998, the company entered the capital of Globalia with 19.37% of shares. This year, the hotel division started a growth strategy through a joint venture agreement called Grubarges with Argentaria (now merged into BBVA) and Fomento de Construcciones y Contratas (FCC), a building company. That agreement allowed them to invest in purchasing hotels and construction of new ones in Mexico and the USA, as well as to be present in Cuba. The partnership dissolved in October 2003.

In 2001, the company started to operate in Cape Verd, Philippines, and Panama with management contracts, and one year later, they used the franchise formula to enter Malta operating a hotel. In 2003, the Barceló Group acquired Crestline Hotels & Resorts, a US hotel management company that allowed them to grow in the US market. The net investment made by the company to acquire it was $ 36 million, resulting in the creation of a new hotel company, Barceló Crestline Corporation. After the creation of Crestline and to keep growing in the US market, Barceló participated in designing and managing a real investment trust, Highland Hospitality Corporation. This trust went public in 2003 and attracted huge funds, allowing it to acquire hotels in the convention and congress segment, airport hotels, and resort hotels. Many of these hotels went to be managed by the Barceló Group (Roure & Segurado, 2019).

In 2015, the company became the sole owner of Occidental Hotels & Resorts and added 13 new hotels after the first purchase of 42.5% of the company and a later purchase of 57.5% from BBVA. This let them expand their presence in LATAM. In the last seven years, many CE actions have taken place in the company, with the repurchasing of 60% of Crestline, which was previously not controlled, incorporating 112 hotels in the USA. In 2017, the company acquired the first hotel in Mexico City called Barceló Mexico Reforma. Later, in 2020 and after the COVID-19 pandemic, Barceló sold the Formentor Hotel in Mallorca to Emin Capital for 165 million euros. Very recently, in 2022, the hotel division purchased and plans to refurbish the Barceló Carmen hotel, a 4-star establishment located at the heart of Granada. Following the growth strategy in the urban sector, Barceló has also bought the hotel Hilton Guadalajara, in Mexico.

When focusing on the travel division Ávoris is a vertically integrated travel company gathering travel agencies on five continents, several tour operators (Quelónea, Jolidey) and receptive operators, and an airline. Its current situation results from these main events, outlining the vertical growth strategy of the business corporation Barceló Group in the whole tourism value chain. The Barceló Group acquired the tour operator Turavia 43 years ago and became the representative of the tour operator, First Choice, in Spain by 1996. In 2000, the travel division entered the capital of First Choice (17%), and its participation increased to 21.2% by 2003. However, from 2004 until 2007, Barceló Group started to divest until it finally withdrew completely. In the last decade, there have been many CE actions. For example, in 2003, the tour operator Turavia was sold to Iberostar. In 2007, Barceló Business (the corporate travel division of Viajes Barceló) and American Express signed an agreement (joint venture) to merge their businesses and create American Express-Barceló Viajes. Later, in 2010, taking advantage of the fact that Viajes Marsans went bankrupt, the travel division of the Barceló business group acquired several of its travel agencies. In 2013, the Orizonia group was declared insolvent, and the company took the opportunity to buy the airline Orbest (currently called Evelop) and 157 agencies of the Vibo network. Two years later, the retail division brand changed from Barceló Viajes to B the Travel Brand (Roure & Segurado, 2019) to focus on providing an experiential relationship to the clients. Also, in 2015, the travel division purchased Ilunion Viajes, which previously belonged to the ONCE[5], specialised in providing travel services to disabled people and in the MICE (Meetings, Incentives, Conferences and Exhibitions) segment. During the same year, the travel division changed its name to the current Ávoris, and at the end of 2015, the company acquired the tour operator Special Tours, while six months later, it acquired another tour operator, Catai. In 2017, Barceló waived its share in American Express and sold it to American Express Business Travel. More recently, in 2020, the company launched Barceló Experiences, a digital platform that offers unique experiences at destinations. Very recently, in 2022, Barceló acquired from Globalia the 49.5% that Barceló did not control in Ávoris, taking over the entire management of a group with 1,500 points of sale and 6,000 employees. Now, 100% of Ávoris belongs to the Barceló Group.

Table 25.1 Key financial figures in M€. Barceló Group (2017, 2020, 2021, 2022) and information gathered through interviews with Barceló CEO

	2016	2017	2018	2019	2020	2021	2022
Turnover	3,081.9	4,313.4	4,383.4	4,779.3	1,483	2,822.2	5.729,8
Net financial debt	494.8	330.7	50.3	197.4	408.9	365.1	205.3
Total EBITDA (with IFRS 16)	338.6	495.6	348.0	474	80.4	146	422.6
PAT Profit or loss (net profit) (without IFRS 16)	125.4	243.3	180.3	142.0	-111.0	-23.4	184.5
RevPAR (euros)	54.4	57.9	57.2	59.7	24.8	30.4	65.6

All these actions and events outline the growth strategy of Barceló, resulting in the first tourism group in Spain. The main financial figures of Barceló Group are displayed in Table 25.1. The data in Table 25.1 indicates, first, that all financial figures followed a positive growth (negative in the case of net financial debt) till the COVID pandemic and started to recover gradually in 2021 and 2022, the business corporation turnover, EBITDA, profits and RevPAR exceeded the pre-pandemic figures, while net financial debt decreased substantially and reached a similar figure to 2019 (pre-pandemic situation).

Next, the information in Table 25.2 indicates that during the COVID-19 pandemic, the corporation reduced its workforce by more than 28%, and in the hotel division, hotel supply kept growing despite the pandemic. However, from 2021–2022, workforce figures exceeded pre-pandemic figures, while in the travel division, the supply of travel agency offices increased by 139% compared to 2020 figures.

Related to the innovative actions followed by the Barceló group, according to Jacob (2022), innovation is defined as any action that generates economic or social value for the business. With the new edition of the Oslo Manual (OECD/Eurostat, 2018), the definition of innovation used to measure innovation activity at the business/firm level has changed; now, it does not require

Table 25.2 Key figures of Barceló hotel and travel divisions. Barceló Group (2017, 2020, 2021, 2022) and information gathered through interviews with Barceló CEO

	2016	2017	2018	2019	2020	2021	2022
Hotels operated	229	234	246	250	265	271	277
Rooms	50.352	52,066	54,692	57,980	60,222	62,069	61,996
Travel Agency Offices	626	770	830	837	688	1,500	1,645
Employees (average active workforce)	25,127	31,768	33,378	33,708	23,617	27,617	34,458

to succeed in the market, but it must generate economic and social value. This new definition makes a clear difference between innovation itself and the activities made by the business to make its innovations possible and tangible. Consequently, business innovation is not only related to success but also the effort made to introduce innovations in the business.

Barceló Group is the first Spanish tourism group, and its hotel division, the Barceló Hotel Group, is the second largest hotel chain in Spain. Considering the above definition of innovation, Barceló must be an innovative company to survive in the market and to be the first Spanish tourism group. The actions conducted by the corporation over the years have led to the development of the actual tourism business portfolio (Figure 1). This business portfolio combines several business models, corporation strategies and joint ventures with other companies, mergers, and acquisitions (Roure & Segurado, 2019). Apart from the main key actions the Group took to grow horizontally and vertically described previously, the company has also carried out an intense innovation activity over the years. In fact, the results of Jacob and Groizard (2007) indicate that the innovation activity of multinational hotel chains of Balearic origin is high. Barceló Group has introduced processes and technological innovations, and organisational innovations leading to changes in governance structure and a higher decentralisation.

The entrepreneurial culture is part of the company, always looking for new opportunities. It was the first Spanish hotel chain to internationalise in 1985, opening its first hotel in the Caribbean, Barceló Bávaro Beach Resort in Punta Cana (Dominican Republic). Barceló was also the first Spanish hotel company to start operating in the USA. The company has also been innovative in introducing organisational changes for decentralisation in the company, a model different to the centralised one more common in the industry (Roure & Segurado, 2019).

In recent years, one lever of transformation driven by Barceló Group has been its digitalisation strategy, with the main goal to achieve a better knowledge of customers for a greater personalisation of their experience. Some of the latest innovative actions conducted by Barceló related to this digitalisation strategy are:

- **Barceló Stories.** A new platform where Barceló Group defines a new way of understanding and approaching the travelling experience, helping customers to find the destination that inspires them and that makes them feel something special using social media and the stories of experienced travellers, travel influencers and bloggers. The platform aims to be a Social Travel Content reference in Latin America. It combines the talent and style of 26 of the best travel bloggers from around the world to inspire its audience to enjoy unique experiences in the hotel chain's most exotic destinations.
- **Barceló Experiences**. The company has transferred all its extensive experience, expertise, and in-depth knowledge of the cities where its hotels are

located to develop a platform that enables travellers to become immersed at a destination, like locals, offering a unique experience at destinations. This is a new way of travelling by the hand of a destination's experts, a digital platform featuring the best guides on what to see and do at every destination. The traveller can discover the most complete tourist guide for their next trip. Guided tours, excursions and exclusive experiences that will make an adventure of his/her getaway.

- **Project Design Hub**. A digital platform for the complete management of hotel refurbishments, which is the first digital tool in the world to conduct hotel renovations, putting the customer at the centre of decision-making and is part of the technological transformation process being conducted by Barceló. Owners and hoteliers can manage the real impact of their investments. The tool reduces by up to six weeks the time of three to four months that is normally used to develop a refurbishment project, according to Raúl González, CEO of the EMEA area of Barceló Hotel Group. The platform allows all those involved to track active projects in the transformation phase and to consult the status of ongoing projects. This tool for the management of refurbishments makes it easier to optimise projects from the delivery of the briefing to the final implementation. It also makes it possible to predict the profitability of refurbishments by calculating the price increase of the refurbished rooms and their impact on demand.

- A **new hotel distribution digital platform and website** to boost direct sales, increase the use of cost-effective digital channels, improve customer intimacy, and support its new brand strategy. According to Accenture (2023), the main novelties that distinguish them from competitors are: (1) a responsive web design for ease of use across mobile devices, (2) a renewed and enhanced Microsoft Azure cloud-based technology platform to improve scalability, (3) improved integration with third-party digital channels, online travel agencies connected to the site through a single channel, (4) an updated central reserve system to improve the website's functionality and capabilities, (5) web design and content focused on the user experience, enabling customers to view rooms and hotel services and make bookings easily, (6) enhanced personalisation, multivariant testing and e-marketing capabilities to gain a better sense and knowledge of the customer, to improve marketing and offers, and (7) a call centre channel with Oracle RightNow customer relationship management software, back-office integration and customer chat capabilities. The new distribution platform is robust, scalable (access to all markets and segments, and available in eight languages), data-driven, and customer-centric, improving customer knowledge and optimising and personalising assets.

- **Barceló Campus.** An e-learning training platform for employees developed to guarantee online training, tailored to the learning speed of employees, visual and interactive, multi-language, and breaks down geographic barriers. Barceló selects its best content and combines it with external resources to create gamified, collaborative itineraries linked to career plans within the company. It won the bronze price as an award-winning innovative training tool in the Brandon Hall Group Technology Awards in 2021.

- **Artificial intelligence applications,** for example, the development of predictive models with customer cancellations to know if one is more likely to cancel than another, or in call centres, uses this technology to calculate the exact time of each call, as well as dead time without conversation.
- Development of **technologies to promote contactless** services and streamline processes in collaboration with the company STAY, with the objectives of providing the best guest experience, reducing waiting times, and being sustainable.

Epilogue

The most relevant aspects of these CE actions reveal that Barceló company is a leading global tourism group that has achieved its status through CE actions that are a combination of actions for vertical growth and actions for horizontal growth based on intense innovation activity and internationalisation process.

The primary information collected through several interviews with different general managers of the company has confirmed that the learning extracted from its development is that the group growth strategy has been relevant for the results of the group. Related to this, Barceló's entire growth strategy has been based on two premises: decentralisation and geographic specialisation. The current business portfolio combines several business models, corporation strategies and joint ventures with other companies, mergers, and acquisitions. Also, the success of this company is due to its innovation activity, which has been focused on process innovations, mainly in Information and Communication Technologies (ICT) and organisational innovations.

Sources

For the elaboration of this case study, the following CEOs of the company were interviewed:

- Raúl González, CEO EMEA of Barceló Hotel Group.
- Alfonso Girón (General Manager in Santa Catalina, a Royal Hideaway hotel).

Notes

1 LATAM – Latin America and Caribbean.
2 Earnings before interests, taxes, depreciations, and amortisations.
3 Sociedad Estatal de Participaciones Industriales.
4 International Financial Reporting Standard 16.
5 Organización Nacional de Ciegos Españoles - Spanish National Organization for the Blind.

References

Accenture (2023). Case study: Creating a five-star digital platform. Available at: https://www.accenture.com/hu-en/case-studies/travel/barcelo-hotels-five-star-digital-platform

Aguiló, E., Alegre, J., & Sard, M. (2005). The persistence of the sun and sand tourism model. *Tourism Management*, 26(2), 219–231.

Barceló Group (2017). 2016 Annual Report. Available at: https://www.barcelogrupo.com/en/publications/

Barceló Group (2020). 2019 Annual report. Available at: https://www.barcelogrupo.com/en/publications/

Barceló Group (2021). 2020 Annual report. Available at: https://www.barcelogrupo.com/en/publications/

Barceló Group (2022). 2021 Annual Report. Available at: https://www.barcelogrupo.com/en/publications/

Camisón, C., & Monfort-Mir, V. M. (2012). Measuring innovation in tourism from the Schumpeterian and the dynamic-capabilities perspectives. *Tourism Management*, 33(4), 776–789.

García Soto, M. G., Álamo Vera, F. R., & Suárez Ortega, S. M. (2002). Estrategias de crecimiento horizontal y vertical: ¿unas a expensas de las otras? *Investigaciones Europeas en Dirección y Economía de la Empresa*, 8(2), 181–198.

Groizard, J. L., & Jacob, M. (2004). Innovación, transferencia de tecnología y desarrollo de empresas hoteleras. Estudio de las contribuciones de las empresas de origen balear a las economías latinoamericanas. *Colección Premios y Ayudas de la FCI*, n° 5, Fundació Cátedra Iberoamericana. Palma.

Guth, W.D., & Ginsberg, A. (1990). Guest editors' introduction: Corporate entrepreneurship. *Strategic Management Journal* 11, 5–15.

Jacob, M. (2022). Innovación y Turismo. In *Informe técnico que permita conocer el concepto de innovación en turismo y su posible aplicación en la estrategia turística*. Document SEGITTUR, Ministerio de Industria y Turismo. Madrid.

Jacob, M., Florido, C., & Aguiló, E. (2010). Environmental innovation as a competitiveness factor in the Balearic Islands. *Tourism Economics*, 16(3), 755–764.

Jacob, M., & Groizard, J. L. (2007). Technology transfer and multinationals: The case of Balearic hotel chains investments in two developing countries. *Tourism Management*, 28(4), 976–992.

Jacob, M., Tintoré, J., Aguiló, E., Bravo, A., & Mulet, J. (2003). Innovation in the tourist sector: Results from a pilot study in the Balearic Islands. *Tourism Economics*, 9(3), 279–295.

OECD/Eurostat (2018). *Guidelines for collecting, reporting and using data on innovation* (4th ed). The Measurement of Scientific, Technological and Innovation Activities, Paris/Eurostat, Luxembourg: OECD Publishing.

Orfila-Sintes, F., Crespí-Cladera, R., & Martínez-Ros, E. (2005). Innovation activity in the hotel industry: Evidence from Balearic Islands. *Tourism Management*, 26(6), 851–865.

Pikkemaat, B., & Peters, M. (2006). Towards the measurement of innovation - a pilot study in the small and medium sized hotel industry. *Journal of Quality Assurance in Hospitality & Tourism*, 6, 89–112.

Roure, J., & Segurado, J. L. (2019). *The Barceló group: Entrepreneurial spirit and corporate governance*. IESE: E-206-E.

Ubierna, F., & Pérez, C. A. (2016). El desempeño innovador en las empresas turísticas españolas. *International Journal of Scientific Management and Tourism*, 2(1), 253–271.

Conclusion

Jonathon Day, Teresa Aguiar-Quintana and Francisca Rosa Alamo Vera

The chapters in this book showcase the extraordinary work of hospitality businesses worldwide. The organisations featured in these cases highlight the entrepreneurial spirit of the hospitality industry on five continents and the proven capacity of hospitality and tourism businesses to adapt and thrive in challenging times. While the COVID-19 pandemic may be fresh in our collective consciousness, it was not our industry's only challenge in recent decades. Through economic downturns, political uncertainty, natural disasters and health emergencies, hospitality companies have adapted and thrived.

In these cases, we recognise that corporate entrepreneurship is found in all types of tourism and hospitality organisations. At the book's heart is a set of hotel case studies where we explore various issues in corporate entrepreneurship and innovation in the lodging sector. Hotel companies, such as the Pestana Hotel Group, Seaside Hotels, Scandic Hotels, beCordial Hotels and Resorts, Cayuga Ecolodge Collection, Barceló Hotel Group and Lopesan Hotels and Resorts, provide valuable insights into resilience and the ability to navigate challenging times. In addition to hotel corporations, there are examples from restaurants, wineries, car rental companies, travel agencies and destination marketing organisations.

In the previous chapters, corporate entrepreneurship led to the growth of enduring companies that spread far from their origin destinations. There are examples of expansion across nations following entrepreneurial opportunities. While there are undoubtedly differences in how hospitality managers from different parts of the world implement corporate entrepreneurship, there are common themes across many examples. These themes include responsiveness to crises, an organisational focus on strategic and effective management, globalisation, the utilisation of technology to support corporate innovation and concern for sustainability.

It is said that "necessity is the mother of invention" and that has never been truer than in recent years. This book provides important examples of how companies have innovated during the difficult years of the pandemic. Several cases, including examining the Austrian hospitality industry, the Scandic hotel's case and the Cicar Cabrera Medina car rental case, as well as examining the immediate impact of the COVID-19 pandemic. Other cases

DOI: 10.4324/9781003454465-27

examine longer-term requirements for successful corporate entrepreneurship and growth. The importance of building effective management capabilities in small businesses like the family-owned businesses discussed in the Australian case or Restaurante Manolo, and larger organisations like the Italian state railways, beCordial hotels and Lopesan Hotel Group. The book shows that the entrepreneurial spirit in companies can be part of the DNA of organisations over decades.

This book documents small businesses that have grown into large corporations through a continuous focus on innovation and entrepreneurship. We recognise organisations that began with success in small communities and expanded internationally. In addition to lodging companies such as Pestana Hotel Group, Cordial, Barceló, Seaside and Lopesan Hotels, other types of companies such as Binter Airlines, El Grifo Winery and Viajes Insular have embarked on international expansion in search of entrepreneurial opportunities.

The utilisation of new technologies to support corporate entrepreneurship is evident across the cases in the volume. Cases addressing technology-driven companies like Different Travel and Viajes Insular and more traditional hospitality companies like Bamen, a worker cooperative, family-run Restaurante Manolo, or CATA, show the importance of adopting new technologies when innovating.

Sustainability is another theme that threads through many of the cases in the book. Applying corporate entrepreneurship to support sustainability goals is evident in cases such as El Grifo Winery, the Cayuga Ecolodge Collection, the case of Ferrovie dello Stato Italiane and the Zuana Beach resort, to name a few. The cases show the great range of entrepreneurial activities that hospitality businesses undertake. In several cases, corporate entrepreneurs have incorporated the unique character of their destination and cultural priorities to create memorable experiences. While entrepreneurs may be driven by growth and new profits, it is evident that many are also committed to ensuring the communities in which they operate and thrive. This is evident in several cases, including the South African, CATA and Visit Greenland cases.

The organisations in this book have shown their ability to implement corporate entrepreneurship. As noted by Batista-Canino and Medina-Brito in the introduction chapter, these companies have responded to the challenges of the environment and taken the initiative to ensure their competitive position. They have a strategic orientation to entrepreneurship. In addition, they have invested in human capital to ensure their teams are ready to pursue new opportunities. Entrepreneurship is part of the corporate culture of these organisations.

This book also presents extraordinary evidence of the innovative nature of hospitality companies. Throughout these pages are examples of hospitality companies utilising new production techniques, creating new products and seeking new markets. The commitment to innovation is evident in organisations as diverse as universities, workers' cooperatives, destination marketing organisations, state-owned transportation providers and lodging companies.

Our goal with this book was to create a resource to provide instructors, researchers and practitioners with examples of corporate entrepreneurship and innovation in hospitality and tourism. While these cases have been written in the aftermath of the COVID-19 pandemic and some address specific pandemic-related issues, the cases in this book have lessons for long-term resilience and strategic success. The cases explain strategies designed to stimulate corporate entrepreneurship used by tourism and hospitality organisations in different corners of the globe and show the results of those actions. These cases are both instructional and inspirational.

In presenting these cases, it was important to the editors to ensure that we included voices from around the world. We know that solutions to problems and exciting innovations are generated in all reaches of the globe, but too often, the stories of these solutions are not shared broadly. This book reflects the global nature of the hospitality industry and includes cases from Europe, the Americas, Africa, Asia and Australia. The book also recognises the breadth of the disciplines associated with tourism studies, and the case authors come from fields such as management, economics and tourism studies. Scholars and industry professionals wrote it. The result is the unique set of cases you are reading now.

In creating this book, we have been thrilled to learn more about the companies and their management. These companies are inspirational for academics and practitioners alike. We hope you have enjoyed learning about these thought-leaders, innovators and corporate entrepreneurs as much as we have in the collation of this book.

Index